Joint Ventures for Hospitals and Physicians

Legal Considerations

Ross E. Stromberg • Carol R. Boman
in cooperation with the Society for Hospital Planning and Marketing
of the American Hospital Association

AHA

American Hospital Publishing Inc.
a wholly owned subsidiary
of the American Hospital Association

Library of Congress Cataloging-in-Publication Data

Stromberg, Ross E., 1940-
   Joint ventures for hospitals and physicians.

   Includes index.
   1. Hospital-physician joint ventures—United States.
I. Boman, Carol R., 1940-   . II. Title. [DNLM:
1. Hospital Administration—United States—legislation.
WX 33 AA1 S89j]
KF3825.S77   1986   344.73'03211   86-17358
ISBN 0-939450-79-8   347.3043211

© 1986 by American Hospital Publishing, Inc.,
a wholly owned subsidiary
of the American Hospital Association

AHA is a service mark of American Hospital Association used under license
by American Hospital Publishing, Inc.
All rights reserved.
The reproduction or use of this work in any form or in any information storage
or retrieval system is forbidden without the express, written permission of the
publisher.
Printed in the U.S.A.
Text printed in Palatino

2.5M-9/86-0104

Sandra L. Weiss, Editor
Peggy DuMais, Production Coordinator
Brian W. Schenk, Editorial and Acquisitions Manager, Books
Dorothy Saxner, Vice-President, Books

Contents

Acknowledgments vii

Chapter 1. Economic Joint Ventures: An Introduction 1
What Are Economic Joint Ventures? 3
Why Economic Joint Ventures? 4
Objectives of Joint Ventures Participants 5
Overview of the Book 6

Chapter 2. Structure, Formation, and Operation 13
Basic Structures of Joint Ventures 15
Steps in the Formation of Joint Ventures 25
Operation of Joint Ventures 33

Chapter 3. Corporate, Securities, and Franchise Law 37
Corporate and Partnership Law 39
Securities Laws 43
Franchise Law 47

Chapter 4. Tax Considerations 55
Tax Relationship between Type of Project and Legal Structure 57
Acquiring Tax-Exempt Status for the Joint Venture 59
Taxability of Income 60
Tax Considerations for Tax-Exempt Participants 61
Legal Considerations for Taxable Venture Participants 65

Chapter 5. ERISA Issues 75
Introduction to ERISA Issues 78
Commonly Controlled Trades or Businesses 79
Affiliated Service Groups 80
Employee Leasing 91

Chapter 6. Regulatory Concerns 95
Health-Care-Oriented Regulations 97
Land Use and Environmental Impact Requirements 103

iii

Chapter 7. Reimbursement Concerns 111
Medicare Reimbursement 113
Reimbursement by Other Third-Party Payers 127

Chapter 8. Business Practices and Ethical Considerations 131
Corporate Practice of Medicine and Fee Splitting 133
State Laws on Self-Referrals 136
Medicare-Medicaid Antifraud and Abuse Statutes 138
Ethical Restrictions of American Medical Association 144

Chapter 9. Labor Law Issues 149
Collective Bargaining 151
State Employment Laws 162

Chapter 10. Antitrust Law 171
Per Se Rule and Rule of Reason 173
Problems Associated with Formation and Structure 174
Problems Associated with Operations 180

Chapter 11. Conclusion 187
Summary 189
Beyond Joint Ventures 190

Appendix A. Ambulatory Surgical Center Joint Venture 193

Appendix B. Magnetic Resonance Imaging Joint Venture 203

Appendix C. Occupational Medicine Center Joint Venture 211

Appendix D. Alternative Delivery System Joint Venture 217

Appendix E. Phased Joint Venture for a Reference Laboratory 225

Appendix F. Medical Pavilion Joint Venture 235

Glossary 243

Index 261

Figures

Figure 1. Example of Parent-Subsidiary Control in the Ownership of Medical Services, Inc., (MSI) and Health Care Corporation (HCC) 81
Figure 2. Parent-Subsidiary Control among Physicians and Memorial Hospital to Form MedClinic... 81
Figure 3. Ownership Interests in MedClinic; Medical Services, Inc., (MSI); and Health Care Corporation (HCC) 81
Figure 4. Organizational Structure of a Hypothetical Ambulatory Surgical Center Joint Venture 200
Figure 5. Organizational Structure of a Hypothetical Magnetic Resonance Imaging (MRI) Joint Venture 209
Figure 6. Organizational Structure of a Hypothetical Occupational Medicine Center Joint Venture 214
Figure 7. Organizational Structure of a Hypothetical Alternative Delivery System Joint Venture... 223
Figure 8. Organizational Structure for a Hypothetical Phased Joint Venture for a Reference Laboratory: First Evolution.............................. 228
Figure 9. Organizational Structure for a Hypothetical Phased Joint Venture for a Reference Laboratory: Second Evolution 230
Figure 10. Organizational Structure for a Hypothetical Phased Joint Venture for a Reference Laboratory: Final Evolution 232
Figure 11. Organizational Structure for a Hypothetical Medical Pavilion Joint Venture 238

About the Authors

Ross E. Stromberg is a partner in the national law firm of Epstein Becker Borsody Stromberg & Green and practices in its San Francisco office in the field of law governing health care and hospitals. He is the author of a number of publications on law and healthcare-related issues and is a frequent lecturer on hospital and health law matters.

Mr. Stromberg is a charter member and past president of the American Academy of Hospital Attorneys of the American Hospital Association. He is also a member of a wide range of related legal and professional societies, including the American Bar Association (Subsection on Law and Medicine), National Health Lawyers Association, Healthcare Financial Management Association, and California Society for Healthcare Attorneys. Mr. Stromberg holds a B.A. degree (summa cum laude) from Humboldt State University and a law degree from the University of California, Berkeley (Boalt Hall School of Law).

Carol R. Boman is a business attorney in the Law Offices of Darryl D. Ott in Oakland, California, and is a free-lance writer on related legal subjects. She received her law degree with high honors (Order of the Coif) from the University of California, Berkeley (Boalt Hall School of Law), where she was an associate editor of the *California Law Review*. She holds a B.A. degree (with highest honors) in English and French from Idaho State University, an M.A. degree in French from the University of Nevada, Reno, and a D.S.E.F. (with honors) in French from the University of Bordeaux, France. Ms. Boman has taught English and French at both the secondary and university levels.

Acknowledgments

The authors would like to thank the many people without whose help and encouragement this book would not have been possible. This book began while we were associated with the law firm of Hanson, Bridgett, Marcus, Vlahos & Rudy in San Francisco (then known as Hanson, Bridgett, Marcus, Vlahos & Stromberg), and the book was completed since joining Epstein Becker Borsody Stromberg & Green in San Francisco. Both law firms have been gracious and supportive of our efforts to develop this book, and many individuals within both firms have contributed immeasurably to the development of this work.

We would especially like to express our appreciation to the following persons at the Hanson firm: Joel S. Goldman, who offered significant guidance with respect to the organization and content of chapter 10 dealing with antitrust law and for his general encouragement; Craig J. Cannizzo for assistance on various reimbursement questions; Jerrold C. Schaefer, Bonnie Kathleen Gibson, and Douglas N. Freifeld, whose assistance in the area of collective bargaining agreements made possible chapter 9 on the effect of labor law on joint ventures; and Peter L. Dmytryk, whose help in assembling resources and initial research was invaluable.

We would also like to give our thanks to the following persons at the Epstein Becker firm: Mark T. Schieble and David Kempler, who offered extensive advice and guidance with respect to the organization and content of chapter 4 on tax issues; Robert J. Moses, who played a significant role in development of the chapter on reimbursement; and Diane W. Carter, Thomas C. Geiser, Gerald M. Hinkley, and Dena R. Belinkoff for their general support and guidance as this book developed.

In addition, we need to thank those support staff members at both law firms who aided our efforts immeasurably, especially Suzanne Cox (Epstein) and Laurie Jewkes (Hanson) for their sustained services.

Finally, we wish to acknowledge the staff of our publisher, the American Hospital Association, for their patience and guidance and our respective families for their forbearance, support, and understanding.

Chapter 1
Economic Joint Ventures: An Introduction

What Are Economic Joint Ventures?
Why Economic Joint Ventures?
Objectives of Joint Venture Participants
Overview of the Book
    Structure, Formation, and Operation
    Corporate, Securities, and Franchise Law
    Tax Considerations
    ERISA Issues
    Regulatory Concerns
    Reimbursement Concerns
    Business Practices and Ethical Considerations
    Labor Law Issues
    Antitrust Law
    Examples of Joint Venture Projects

Chapter 1. Economic Joint Ventures: An Introduction

The past decade has been a time of flux for many segments of the nation's economy, and for none more so than the health care industry. New advances in medical science and technology, the emergence of new delivery and payment modes, and the growth of new systems are all part of the changing pattern of health care delivery. Traditional entities such as the acute-care hospital that is staffed primarily for inpatient care and the small independent physician's office practice are being challenged by new organizational forms designed to respond to changes in economic conditions and health care philosophy. One phenomenon that has developed in response to these changing patterns is the economic joint venture between traditional and nontraditional health care providers. The form and structure of economic joint ventures, potential problems, and possible ways of avoiding such problems in order to form a successful venture are the topics of this book.

What Are Economic Joint Ventures?

An *economic joint venture* may be defined as the creation by two or more legally independent parties of a new enterprise that is jointly owned by such parties, who share the economic risks and rewards of the venture. The term *joint venture* is used in this book specifically to refer to ventures among health care providers.

Economic joint ventures are more tightly structured than are standard customer, or contractual, relationships, in which a health care provider, such as a hospital or a physician, buys services or products from another party or sells services or products to another party. An example of a contractual relationship is the typical relationship between a hospital and a hospital-based physician who, by contract, provides professional services, such as radiology. Although both parties in such a relationship may be seeking an economic benefit, there is no joint ownership of the enterprise.

On the other hand, economic joint ventures are more loosely structured than are more formal forms of affiliation, such as a merger between two health care providers. For instance, in a merger the parties are absorbed into one, and each party loses whatever independence from the other that it may have had previously: they become one entity.

In most joint ventures, the scope is limited to a particular project or a single purpose, and the participants mutually share the decision-making power and the right of control as to the specific activity to be undertaken by the venture. However, the authority that the participants may have over each other in a more closely knit enterprise is lacking in a joint venture. The participants retain their independent status for all activities outside of the venture.

In the health care industry, economic joint ventures may run the gamut from hospitals and physicians joining together to operate an alternative delivery system to several health care providers entering into an enterprise for non-health-related investment purposes. There are two basic types of economic joint ventures within the health care industry:

- *Special project joint venture,* in which, for example, two or more participants work together to purchase and operate medical equipment (such as a magnetic resonance imaging center or a lithotripter).
- *Alternative system joint venture,* in which hospitals and physicians form, for example, a health maintenance organization (HMO) or preferred provider organization (PPO).

A possible third form of joint venture is the *medical staff-hospital (MeSH) partnership*[1] or *integrated health care corporation* (IHCC). An IHCC is a joint venture between a hospital and members of its medical staff that is global in character: That is, the IHCC plans for and carries out a number of specific activities. This type of venture forms a bridge between conventional special project transactions and the alternative system enterprise. It is like the alternative system joint venture in that it establishes a structure that remains in place to provide various health care delivery services, such as utilization review, reimbursement analysis, and other hospital management services. At the same time, a MeSH or IHCC serves as a springboard to special project joint ventures, such as ventures for equipment acquisitions, or to the development of an outpatient care system.

Some ventures are achieved in phases and gain in complexity over time. For instance, a venture can commence with a relatively simple structure, such as when a hospital and several staff physicians participate in a partnership to form a clinical laboratory. This structure could gradually become more complex as outside investors acquire interests in the project and as the needs of the participants change. Thus, the venture may require restructuring from time to time to account for the new participants and evolving circumstances.

Some ventures require a complex structure from the outset. For example, a national investor-owned health care provider may be interested in forming a venture with a local provider for a series of projects in that local provider's region. The structure must account for the fact that multiple entities are participating. A general partnership or a similar simple structure by itself is probably not able to meet the needs of the parties. Moreover, legal problems usually seem to increase proportionately as the number of different types of participants in a venture increases. Such legal problems may require a complex structure.

Of course, joint venturing is but one of several alternative means for carrying out an enterprise, and it may not be the best way for a particular project. For instance, a hospital and physicians may be considering the development of a freestanding diagnostic imaging center to be located away from the hospital campus. The hospital could develop and operate the project by itself and merely contract with physicians for professional services. In that instance, the physicians would not have an ownership interest in the enterprise, and so the enterprise would not be a joint venture. Alternatively, several physicians could form an entity to develop the imaging center completely independent of the hospital. Either way of carrying out the imaging center enterprise is a traditional and acceptable alternative. Economic joint venturing is a third, middle-course alternative.

Why Economic Joint Ventures?

Economic joint ventures are clearly not a panacea for all of the present ills of the health care industry. However, at times there may be sound reasons for entering into an economic joint venture. This book describes those circumstances in which joint ventures might be considered as alternative means of pursuing an enterprise.

The reasons for the current trend in economic joint ventures are manifold. There are intense pressures working on the health care industry to force changes in the delivery of health care. Economic joint ventures may provide a means of making such changes without loss of economic independence. The forces influencing the way that health care is delivered, organized, and paid for include:

- *Altered third-party reimbursement,* as illustrated by the development of Medicare's prospective pricing system (PPS). This program has had a profound effect on hospital utilization patterns and on the way in which hospitals and physicians relate to one another. Although most hospitals seem to have fared well

economically under the first years of PPS, it is expected that any future benefits derived from the system will be gradually reduced, making it increasingly difficult for many hospitals to meet their capital needs from traditional inpatient revenue sources.
- *Development of other cost containment programs.* These developments are not limited to Medicare but include significant changes in Medicaid and private-sector programs.
- *Phenomenal growth of alternative delivery systems,* which are sponsored by both providers and payers and are responsive to the evolving trends of reimbursement and payment for health care services. With increasing frequency, hospitals and physicians are finding it necessary to negotiate key payer contracts in a *selective contracting* atmosphere, in which the existence of effective organizations of hospitals and physicians that can negotiate skillfully make the difference in securing vital contracts for significant numbers of patients. Developing such provider organizations has spurred a flurry of interest by hospitals and physicians alike in economic joint ventures.[2]
- *Proliferation of all kinds of ambulatory care and after-care programs,* many of which directly compete with more traditional inpatient and private physician services. In response to such developments, hospitals and physicians are busily exploring their options. Some providers are finding that economic joint ventures can be an effective means by which hospitals and physicians can enter these markets together.
- *Need for capital.* The hospital's need for capital increases as reimbursement tightens up, competition heats up, and technological advances continue. Unfortunately, under these conditions, access to capital becomes more difficult. As a result, many institutions have looked to emerging systems, both for-profit and not-for-profit, as a means of enhancing their access to capital. The sharing of economic risk, such as through capital pools and master indentures, by otherwise independent institutions is a form of economic joint venture. Moreover, interest in the development of desired projects through *off balance sheet financing* is increasing. In off balance sheet financing, the hospital's other venture partners provide the financing, and the expense of the project does not appear as a debit on the hospital's balance sheet. For example, physicians, through a limited partnership, may provide the financing for hospital-based projects, such as imaging centers.
- *Physician surplus and excess hospital capacity.* Given all the pressures described as well as excess institutional capacity and the physician surplus, it is no wonder that hospitals are seeking partnerships with physicians to fill empty beds and use underutilized services and that physicians are seeking linkages with hospitals and alternative delivery systems to secure patients, obtain a market niche, and achieve economic security.
- *Growth of competition.* Many states are allowing marketplace forces to replace regulations in the allocation of health care services and resources. As markets open up, those providers who are organized and who have entrepreneurial zeal as well as substantive resources will secure market shares at the expense of their competitors. In this new era for the health care field, economic joint venturing can be an important vehicle to bring physicians and hospitals together in a unified, integrated response to emerging market forces.

Objectives of Joint Venture Participants

Health care providers are conscious of the fact that they are in a "sink or swim" situation. Those providers who are not organized into systems or who do not seek to open new markets and find new sources of capital and revenues may not survive the present shakeout in the health care industry.

System building is the key. Hospitals and physicians who retain freestanding positions may have a sense of foreboding about emerging trends. However, they must realize that their fee-for-service, full-cost-reimbursed, regulated world is rapidly disappearing.[3] Those providers who are organized into systems stand a good chance of maintaining and even enhancing their market shares. The marketing of the products and services of these systems, particularly of alternative delivery systems, may generate an increased number of patients. These alternative systems will become revenue centers, while traditional hospitals will increasingly become cost centers. Thus, hospitals and physicians must consider ways to link together as a vertically integrated unit and, as such, to fully explore new approaches to capturing markets, developing alternative delivery systems and products, and otherwise diversifying.

Economic joint ventures are seen by many providers as a means of achieving a wide number of diverse goals while maintaining independence. The following are some common objectives cited by providers as reasons for undertaking an economic joint venture:

- Developing an effective working alliance between hospitals and physicians to carry out commonly agreed-upon strategies that are responsive to the pressures of reimbursement, competition, capital, capacity, and marketplace demands.
- Developing a means for the common sharing between hospitals and physicians in the economic success and risk of the venture, including participation in the venture's revenue stream, ownership, and governance.
- Developing compatible economic incentives between hospitals and physicians to at least minimize the impact of disparate incentives.
- Developing a base for enhancing physicians' loyalty to the hospital and the hospital's responsiveness to its physicians.
- Minimizing potentially unnecessary competition between hospitals and physicians and among physicians themselves.
- Spurring implementation of a diversification strategy designed to enhance market share and patient referrals or develop new sources of revenue or both.
- Responding to marketplace demands for cost containment and less costly alternatives to acute inpatient services.
- Enhancing access to capital, including equity capital and its leverage. The hospital's objective may be to develop projects with off balance sheet financing.
- Maximizing return to venture partners through a program of diversified investments and tax planning that requires analysis of cash flow, return on investment, and the potential for tax sheltering benefits.
- Matching the strengths of the parties to fill gaps that might otherwise exist and to borrow expertise from the various venture partners.

Overview of the Book

Most health care providers are aware that joint ventures are being formed, and many have thought of participating in a joint venture themselves. But joint venturing is an area that contains many traps and pitfalls for the inexperienced. The purpose of this book is to describe consequences, particularly legal ones, that may flow from decisions in structuring, financing, or operating an economic joint venture. Following is a brief summary of some of the issues raised by economic joint venturing. The remaining chapters of this book discuss these issues.

Before undertaking any actual project, the potential participants should consult with legal counsel who can give specific advice applicable to their particular situation. This book does not attempt to give any such legal advice. Comments regarding any applicable law or legal standards are of a generalized nature only. The sole intent is to indicate areas in which legal or other problems may arise and to point out possible solutions.

Structure, Formation, and Operation
Chapter 2

The choice of the structure of a joint venture is extremely important and must be carefully decided at the outset to prevent potential problems that might otherwise occur. The most common structures are contractual relationships; corporations, either for-profit or not-for-profit; partnerships, either general or limited; or some combination of these. Ventures can be fairly simple or extremely complicated with multiple entities. They can be formed for a single and limited purpose (for example, to purchase technological equipment) or for multiple purposes (for example, a MeSH venture).

The management and operation of the venture can also lead to problems. Planning is essential to the successful joint venture project. The management and control of the enterprise must be decided at the outset, and documentation should spell out clearly which joint venture participant has primary responsibility for such items as staffing and compensation. Financing, adequate business planning, and sharing of projected income or losses from the enterprise must be taken into account. Other decisions that must be made include what fees to charge for products and services, how to manage day-to-day operations, and how to market and advertise the venture.

Corporate, Securities, and Franchise Law
Chapter 3

State laws relating to corporations, partnerships, and other business entities and federal and state laws regulating securities can have an impact on joint ventures. The form of the venture and its participants may result in required registration of the venture as a security under the various securities laws, unless an exemption is available from both federal and state laws. In addition, disclosure requirements under these laws must also be taken into account. Failure to disclose any material fact may cause the promoters or sellers of the security to be liable for fraud. Furthermore, both federal and state laws require registration of any franchise and certain disclosures to potential franchisees. Because the wording of the laws is so broad, an agreement not intended to be a franchise can be designated as one if it contains a shared trademark and a centralized marketing plan.

Tax Considerations
Chapter 4

Tax planning generally is one of the most important aspects of carrying out a joint venture. Tax issues include the tax consequences for tax-exempt entities, such as not-for-profit hospitals, and the tax implications for nonexempt participants, such as physicians and other investors. In addition, the appropriate tax treatment of the venture entity itself should be taken into account.

For the participating not-for-profit hospital, appropriate planning should be undertaken to ensure that the hospital's tax-exempt status is not jeopardized through private inurement of charitable assets or through receipt of significant unrelated business income. Moreover, steps should be taken to determine the appropriate treatment of the hospital's proceeds from the venture in order to minimize taxation of unrelated business income.

Tax considerations are also important for nonexempt participants because tax benefits can reduce the initial expense of funding the project and can make it less expensive for participants to invest in the venture. For instance, investment tax credits and deductions for losses from the project in its early years may reduce the present taxes of participants. This present tax benefit can make up for additional taxes to investors on income received in later years of operation when the project is expected to make a profit.

Tax-planning options have become limited in recent years. These options will be even more limited if certain tax-reform measures under consideration in Congress in 1986 are eventually enacted and signed into law.[4] The proposed joint venture should be analyzed in light of the most recent regulations to be certain that tax benefits anticipated from the venture are still available despite the tax changes. The form of the structure may determine, for instance, whether investment tax credits (ITC) and an accelerated cost recovery system (ACRS) are available. If leasing is involved, particularly a sale or leaseback from or to a tax-exempt venturer, specific rules are brought into play that could nullify anticipated tax benefits from the venture.

ERISA Issues
Chapter 5

Care must be taken in structuring a venture in order to maintain the present tax-qualified status of the benefit plans of individual venture participants, such as physicians or a group of physicians. Benefit plans that presently qualify under the tax code may be inadvertently disqualified for tax purposes under the complex antidiscrimination provisions of the Employee Retirement Income Security Act (ERISA). Under these provisions, for example, two or more ostensibly separate entities may be grouped together as a single employer for purposes of determining whether their benefit plans discriminate against lower-echelon employees.

Regulatory Concerns
Chapter 6

Certain health-care-oriented regulations may affect the structuring of the joint venture. These laws govern certificate of need, licensure, and rate review. Whether or not these regulations are applicable depends on where the facility is located, who the venturers are, and what type of facility is planned. For example, a freestanding ambulatory surgical center probably needs a separate license in many states but may avoid this requirement in some states if it is operated as part of a physician's office practice.

Other regulations, which are often overlooked but which could have a significant impact on a venture project, are the various land use and environmental impact requirements. These regulations also depend on the particular state and local government laws.

Reimbursement Concerns
Chapter 7

The reimbursement that will be available for the contemplated facility or service is important in planning a venture. Under current Medicare regulations, hospitals are paid on the basis of diagnosis-related groups (DRGs), but specialty clinics and outpatient facilities continue to be reimbursed on a cost-based system. Freestanding ambulatory surgical centers receive facilities reimbursement (at 100 percent of a predetermined amount) separately from professional services reimbursement. Hospital-affiliated ambulatory surgical centers can choose to be reimbursed in this manner or as hospital outpatient departments (at 80 percent of reasonable costs). Other freestanding centers do not receive separate facilities reimbursement. Under new guidelines, HMOs may now be reimbursed on a capitation basis.

Business Practices and Ethical Considerations
Chapter 8

Certain states restrict the so-called corporate practice of medicine, in which an unlicensed entity holds itself out to the public as a medical practitioner. As a result, a joint venture may have problems if lay parties are included in the ownership of the enterprise. Some states prohibit fee splitting between licensed practitioners and lay persons, and a few states forbid the employment of physicians by lay entities. Certain business practices of the joint venture enterprise, such as payments for referrals, may run afoul of state medical practice laws prohibiting such payments or requiring disclosure of ownership interests, Medicare and Medicaid antifraud and abuse statutes, or ethical restraints of the American Medical Association.

Labor Law Issues
Chapter 9

Problems can arise for joint venturers when they make staffing decisions, particularly if their employees are governed by a collective bargaining agreement. In such an event, certain federal labor law principles apply:

- *Successor employers.* When a new entity replaces another but the work environment, services offered, and other aspects of employment do not substantially change, the new employer may be deemed the successor of the former and may be required to bargain with the existing union.
- *Decision-effects bargaining.* When a decision to change business operations is made, the employer may have a duty to bargain with the union, not only about the effect of that decision on union employees but also with respect to the decision itself.
- *Single-employer or joint-employer status.* Two employers may be deemed a single employer for collective bargaining purposes; or two employers, such as the venture entity and an employee leasing company, may be viewed as joint employers of the leased employees.
- *Accretion.* If a significant number of a venture participant's employees were sent to perform services at the new facility, the collective bargaining agreement between those employees and the venture participant would govern employment relationships at the new facility.

The relationship between employers and employees is also governed by other legal principles. For example, the federal government and some states have laws protecting employees, in certain instances, who report illegal activities of their employers. Even without statutory authority, a few states prohibit, on public policy grounds, retaliation against employees who report their employers or who refuse to perform illegal acts. Moreover, a number of states require employers to treat their employees in good faith with respect to termination and benefits and prevent employers from discharging employees without good cause, even in the course of a company reorganization. Any of these restrictions on employers' relationships with their employees can have an impact on economic joint ventures.

Antitrust Law
Chapter 10

Certain joint ventures may raise antitrust concerns. These concerns occur at the outset, when the venture is first formed, or later, when the venture is a functioning business. A joint venture will be scrutinized if it is:

- *Overinclusive,* thereby placing too great a restraint on competition
- *Underexclusive,* thereby excluding a competitor from an essential facility
- *Formed for an illegitimate purpose,* in which case a court will disregard the venture entity and scrutinize the activity, such as price fixing, in which the venture is engaged as if it is performed by two separate entities

Once a venture is in operation, it will be subject to all laws and regulations, including antitrust laws. Common problems that may occur are:

- *Exclusive dealing,* such as an exclusive agreement between a preferred provider organization (PPO) and a large employer in a community
- *Tying,* in which a person is coerced into buying a second product in order to obtain a first
- *Spillover collusion,* which occurs when legitimate ancillary restraints of the venture spill over into the venturers' separate businesses

Examples of Joint Venture Projects
Appendixes A-F

Six examples of joint venture projects are described in appendixes A through F. They illustrate different approaches to the structuring of a joint venture, various legal problems that can arise, and the way parties can work to resolve these problems by choosing one structure or type of venture over another. The six sample ventures are:

- Ambulatory surgical center joint venture (appendix A)
- Magnetic resonance imaging (MRI) facility joint venture (appendix B)
- Occupational medicine center joint venture (appendix C)
- Alternative delivery system joint venture (appendix D)
- Phased reference laboratory joint venture (appendix E)
- Medical pavilion (multifaceted) joint venture (appendix F)

The joint ventures in these case studies are hypothetical situations between fictional parties. Although an attempt has been made to create factual situations that resemble joint ventures that are typically undertaken, the facts presented are purely imaginary and are not based on any particular existing joint venture project. Moreover, readers should not rely solely on the suggestions described in the appendixes when structuring a joint venture.

Notes

1. *See* Ellwood, *When MDs Meet DRGs,* HOSPITALS, Dec. 16, 1983, at 62.

2. In a survey of health care providers participating in economic joint ventures, the development of alternative delivery systems ranked as the second most popular type of joint venture, after ambulatory care centers. *See* ERNST & WHINNEY, HEALTH CARE JOINT VENTURES: SURVEY RESULTS, at 66 (1985).

3. One commentator has predicted that by the year 1990, fee-for-service systems will represent only 5 percent of the private sector, down from 90 percent in 1980. *See* K. ABRAMOWITZ AND S. BERNSTEIN, THE FUTURE OF HEALTH CARE DELIVERY IN AMERICA (1985).

4. The tax reform proposals before Congress in 1986 significantly limit or reduce potential tax benefits, including limiting the deductibility of interest from limited partnership interests, lengthening depreciation periods, repealing the ITC, and extending the at-risk limitations applicable to interests in equipment leasing limited partnerships to real estate interests. *See Comparison of House-Passed Tax Reform Bill (H.R. 3838) and "Packwood Plan,"* DAILY TAX REP. 5-7 (BNA Mar. 14, 1986).

Chapter 2
Structure, Formation, and Operation

Basic Structures of Joint Ventures
    Legal Structures
        Contractual Form
        Corporate Form
            For-Profit Corporation
            Not-for-Profit Corporation
        Partnership Form
            General Partnership
            Limited Partnership
    Health Care Structures
        Health Maintenance Organizations
        Preferred Provider Organizations
        MeSH-Type Structures
    Combination Forms
Steps in the Formation of Joint Ventures
    Planning
    Financing
    Discussions with Legal Counsel
    Governmental and Internal Approvals
    Registration Requirements
    Interpretive Rulings
    Insurance
    Preparation of Legal Documents
    Closing
Operation of Joint Ventures
    Management
    Compensation
    Staffing
    Legal Compliance

This chapter discusses practical steps in forming a joint venture, from the first meeting of the potential participants through the operation of the venture. The chapter covers:

- Possible structures or forms that joint ventures may assume, reasons for selecting one form rather than another, and restrictions on the choice of form
- Formalization of the transaction, including legal documentation and other requirements for setting up joint ventures
- Operation of the joint venture

Basic Structures of Joint Ventures

Participants in a joint venture must decide what kind of structure is best for their particular needs. Before arriving at a decision, they should understand the legal and health care structures that can be used in a joint venture.

Legal Structures

A joint venture project can assume several legal entities or forms:[1]

- *Contractual relationship.* For example, a group of physicians leases from a hospital undeveloped land owned by the hospital to construct an ambulatory surgical facility and then leases space to a partnership of hospital staff members.
- *Creditor-borrower relationship.* For example, a life insurance company loans a for-profit corporation $30 million to construct a magnetic resonance imaging (MRI) center and takes as part of its security for the loan an equity interest in the new facility.
- *Corporation.* For example, two hospitals form a not-for-profit corporation to construct and operate a psychiatric facility.
- *Partnership.* For example, a hospital goes into partnership with several physicians to construct and operate an outpatient genetic testing and in vitro fertilization center.
- *Combination of any of these forms.*

Contractual Form

When potential joint venturers decide to do business by means of a contractual relationship, no new legal entity is formed. All of the terms of their agreement are set forth in a basic *contract.* There is no significant change in the legal status of the parties, except that they are bound to perform certain functions prescribed by the contract. Each participant in the venture continues to hold its assets in the same manner as it did before the agreement, although those assets may now be put to use in the service of the venture enterprise. Revenues from the project flow directly to the participants according to the contract terms. The contract also stipulates who will undertake management and operation of the enterprise and in what capacity.

The main advantage of this type of structure is that it is relatively simple to organize. Because no new entity is created, no significant paperwork is required to set up the transaction. Employees of the business generally retain as their employer whichever venturer hired them. This simplicity reduces the cost of doing business.

A contractual structure works best for short-term transactions requiring little formality, such as the acquisition of medical equipment that will soon be leased to another party. A contractual relationship also works well when the hospital and physician groups work together to plan activities that will actually be carried out by other entities.

However, for most joint ventures there are serious drawbacks to a contractual arrangement. One drawback is in the very simplicity of contractual relationships. The lack of any separate legal entity may represent a lack of commitment for the parties to the venture. This simplicity, this informality, may lead to unclear purposes, mixed signals, and eventually, failure through benign neglect. The contractual model may invite discord between the parties because there is no single management or operating entity. Another disadvantage is the fact that all of the participants are held liable for any loss or liability resulting from the operation of the venture, although the contractual terms may provide for the indemnification of one party by the other in the case of such losses. Moreover, the potential liability of contracting parties from the joint venture is not limited to their respective investments in it. Finally, as there is no new legal entity created, the venture provides no opportunity to capitalize on tax rules that allow certain types of legal entities to delay or reduce potential taxes on gains and losses from such a project.

Corporate Form

A *corporation* is a legal body created pursuant to and authorized by the laws of the particular state in which it is formed. Although constituted by one or more persons, a corporation is created to act as a single person, and it is endowed by law with the rights and liabilities of an individual. Once formed, a corporation is legally separate from the individuals who own it. Four basic characteristics distinguish a corporation from other business associations:

- *Continuity.* A corporation, unlike a person, does not die. It continues into perpetuity until dissolved by its current owner.
- *Centralized management.* Control and management of a corporation are vested in specific officers, through its board of directors, whose powers and authority are clearly specified in the articles of the corporation or its bylaws.
- *Limited liability.* The liability of the investors in a corporation for corporate losses and debts is limited to the amount of capital invested.
- *Free transferability of interests.* As a general rule, ownership interests in a corporation may be transferred without restriction from one owner to another.

There are two basic types of corporations: the for-profit corporation and the not-for-profit entity.

For-Profit Corporation

A *for-profit or business corporation* is formed for the basic purpose of making a profit. It is owned by shareholders, persons holding shares of stock in the company. Each share of stock represents a certain percentage of ownership in the business, depending on how many shares are outstanding. In privately held corporations, only a few owners collectively hold all the stock in the business. In publicly held companies, shares are held by many investors and are traded on an exchange. Privately held corporations may have the same amount of assets as a publicly held organization.

A significant difference between the privately and publicly held corporation is in how the shares are held and traded and the extent of government regulation. Both publicly and privately held companies must file necessary registration statements and other documents with the appropriate state authorities. In addition, because publicly held companies involve large numbers of investors, many of whom may be inexperienced with respect to sophisticated business transactions, such enterprises may have greater reporting requirements, including those imposed by federal regulations. Extensive disclosures to potential investors may also be required of publicly held corporations before additional shares of stock may be issued for sale.

A *share* in a corporation represents the right to receive dividends as they are declared by the board of directors and the right to receive a portion of the corporate assets if and when the corporation is liquidated. Ownership of a share does not entitle the holder to any specific asset of the corporation or any interest in its assets as a whole. The corporation owns the assets and cannot convey them to the shareholders.

Shares of one or more classes may be authorized in the articles of incorporation. All shares have equal rights unless otherwise stipulated in the articles. The more customary classes of shares, when there is more than one class, are common and preferred shares. Common stock is ordinary stock of the corporation, and it has no priority or preference over any other stock. Preferred stock has some sort of preference over other classes of stock as to dividends and rights to assets at liquidation. Holders of preferred stock have preference in receipt of dividends, whereas common shareholders have voting rights (the right to elect directors), that holders of preferred stock may not have. The possibility of offering several classes of stock, or of offering some preferred shares, is often considered in hospital-physician joint ventures.

The corporation is governed through a board of directors elected by the shareholders. The board is responsible for managing the business. Through its corporate officers, the board signs contracts, staffs the enterprise, arranges for necessary financing, acquires assets, and takes whatever other steps are appropriate in connection with the corporate business.

The for-profit corporate form has several distinct advantages. The for-profit corporation permits a great degree of flexibility in the business. This format allows a joint venture participant to spread the risks of the enterprise to more than one party and to reduce the amount of any one party's capital investment in the business. Despite reduced capital investment, that party may still retain the ability to establish policy and to make the major business decisions. The corporate form further allows the advantage of continuity. The departure of a significant number of shareholders from a corporation will not result in the dissolution of the business unless the shareholders take affirmative steps to dissolve the corporation. By contrast, a partnership does not endure once the partners within it choose to leave. Coupled with this advantage of continuity is that of a centralized management. By allocating management responsibilities to a board of directors, the investors are assured that attention is paid to the business of the joint venture.

The corporate format also has the advantage of *limited liability*, which means that because the corporation is a legal entity distinct from its shareholders, the liability of its investors for any losses or debts incurred by the corporation is limited to the amount of their respective investment in the corporation. In a partnership, by contrast, general partners are personally responsible to creditors for all debts and liabilities of the partnership. Limited liability may be desirable for any venture that carries significant economic risk.

However, in certain cases the shareholders may be held personally liable for the corporation's obligations, or occasionally, the corporation may be held liable for shareholders' obligations. This *piercing of the corporate veil* usually occurs for two reasons. First, the shareholders may have been using the corporate entity as their alter ego. The *alter ego theory* is applied if the shareholders use the corporation so that no separate company is really maintained. For instance, if shareholders use corporate assets as their own or if they fail to follow basic corporate formalities, such as maintaining corporate books and records or electing directors or officers, they may lose their limited liability. Second, the corporation may have been undercapitalized. This means that the corporation carried on business without sufficient capital to meet the obligations that reasonably could be expected to arise in that business.

A further advantage of the corporate format is that, as a general rule, ownership interests in the business are freely transferable, which means that the individual investor is not locked into an investment. Of course, even if the interest may be legally transferable, as a practical matter it may be difficult to sell or affix a value to the stock of a *close corporation*, which is a small corporation with only a few shareholders. Moreover, the parties may agree to impose restrictions on the transferability of the stock or to require mandatory buyouts, such as when a physician shareholder in an independent practitioner's association (IPA) terminates his or her professional services contract with the IPA.

The advantages of a for-profit corporation in a health care joint venture are counterbalanced by certain possible disadvantages. Corporations are required to fulfill all formal requirements of their state of incorporation, which means that there may be a greater amount of paperwork in setting up a corporation and in ensuring compliance with the statutory requirements for corporate operations than for a more informal business association. Corporations are required generally to keep corporate minutes, send required notices to shareholders, file tax returns, and fulfill certain reporting requirements that vary from state to state.

Another potential disadvantage in using a for-profit corporate form in a health care joint venture is the *double taxation* of corporate profits: the company's earnings are taxed first at the corporate level and then again when investors receive them in the form of dividend distributions. Double taxation is less of a disadvantage for a tax-exempt hospital shareholder because its dividends are tax free unless it borrowed money to acquire stock in the corporation (see the discussion of debt-financed tax rules in chapter 4). As a further disadvantage, taxable shareholders of the corporation cannot benefit from corporate losses or deductions to offset their individual incomes, as they would be able to do in a partnership structure.

Not-for-Profit Corporation

The laws relating to not-for-profit corporations vary from state to state. The assets of this type of entity are not held for the benefit of individual shareholders but rather are usually dedicated to charitable or public purposes. Many health care entities serve such public purposes and are thus organized as not-for-profit corporations. Because their purposes generally meet the requirements of the tax code, many not-for-profit health care providers are also tax-exempt. However, not all not-for-profit corporations are tax-exempt.

The not-for-profit corporation shares with the for-profit corporation the advantages of continuity and centralized management. However, the principal advantage of using the not-for-profit corporate form is the exemption from federal and state taxes that may accompany the not-for-profit status. Under Section 501(c)(3) of the Internal Revenue Code, an entity serving certain defined charitable purposes is entitled to an exemption from federal income taxes. This exemption can be a significant benefit for a health care enterprise that makes some income and would like to shelter that income from taxation. Further, an entity that is tax-exempt under Section 501(c)(3) may accept tax-deductible donations, which can be an important source of capital to the corporation.

One possible disadvantage to using the not-for-profit corporate form is the *charitable trust doctrine*. Some states provide that not-for-profit corporations hold their assets in a charitable trust for the benefit of the public. A clause to that effect may be contained in the articles of the corporation, particularly if the organization is exempt from federal taxation. The corporation must act within the confines of that trust. In certain instances, the actions of the not-for-profit corporation may be considered an abandonment of the charitable purposes announced in its articles of incorporation. The charitable trust doctrine reduces the flexibility of the not-for-profit corporation. For example, a not-for-profit corporation may be formed by two hospitals to operate a pathology laboratory that will provide services to their patients as well as do research. Under the charitable trust doctrine, this laboratory might not be allowed at a later time to change its direction to provide services principally to referring physicians in the area.[2]

The charitable trust doctrine can present additional problems if a not-for-profit corporation attempts to convert to for-profit status. In some states, a not-for-profit corporation cannot merely amend its articles of incorporation to state that it will no longer serve a public or charitable purpose. Because the corporation holds its assets in trust for public benefit, it cannot in such an instance convert its assets for private use. Such a conversion would violate its charitable trust. Most states only allow a conversion to for-profit status if the corporation promises to donate the present value of its assets to charitable use. Generally, the state's attorney general or the courts of that state will place a value on those assets for charitable trust purposes. This valuation procedure can be controversial and protracted because the amount of assets to be donated and the use to which they are to be put, such as a contribution to an existing charitable organization, must be negotiated with state authorities. Many not-for-profit corporations who wish to acquire for-profit status find the most practicable solution to be a corporate reorganization, in which a subsidiary or sister charitable foundation is formed to provide such functions as health care research and education. This new foundation can accept as a charitable contribution the value of the assets of the former not-for-profit entity.

Another possible disadvantage for not-for-profit corporations is their tax-exempt status. Under the tax law, profits from business activities deemed to be unrelated to the corporation's charitable or public purpose may be subject to income tax. In addition, more than an incidental benefit to private individuals from the corporation's efforts may result in the loss of the not-for-profit corporation's tax-exempt status (see chapter 4).

Partnership Form

Partnerships may be general or limited. Each type of partnership has its own advantages and disadvantages.

General Partnership

A *general partnership* is an association of two or more persons who agree to conduct certain business activities together. In a general partnership, all of the partners share the profits and bear the losses, debts, and liabilities from the association according to the percentage of their respective investments, which can be in the form of capital, equity, property, services, or anything else of value. The scope of the partners' responsibilities and benefits is defined in the partnership agreement. Unless the partnership agreement states otherwise, each partner is entitled to take part in the management and operation of the business and has an equal voice with respect to it.

The advantage of the general partnership form is that it is a way of avoiding the so-called *double taxation* of the corporation. The partnership itself is not a taxable entity. Consequently, tax benefits to the partnership in the form of depreciation allowances and various tax credits can be claimed by the partners on their individual tax returns. By taking advantage of such tax benefits, the partners may shelter income from other sources to a limited extent. A general partnership is therefore frequently the best choice of structure for capital intensive investments, such as real estate or equipment leasing.

General partnerships can also offer certain advantages to tax-exempt partners, particularly in a general partnership composed solely of tax-exempt partners (such as two or more hospitals). Although the law is not clear on this issue, income from a venture in which the partners are tax-exempt, such as the MRI joint venture described in appendix B, may not be subject to the unrelated business income tax (see chapter 4).

A disadvantage of the general partnership is that in a partnership of both taxable and tax-exempt partners, there may be some negative tax consequences to the exempt partner through unrelated business income or so-called *private inurement,* which occurs when private parties gain as a result of the substantial efforts of a corporation that is organized for a tax-exempt purpose. Private inurement can occur, for instance, when the other general partners have limited resources and creditors look primarily to the tax-exempt entity to advance money if the project fails. Because of this risk, a tax-exempt participant entering into a partnership with taxable parties should consider obtaining a *private letter ruling,* which is an opinion letter from the Internal Revenue Service (IRS) stating whether adverse tax consequences may result if the parties follow a certain proposed course of action (see chapter 4).

There are other drawbacks to the general partnership form. First, the individual partners are jointly and individually liable for all partnership debts. Second, an interest in a general partnership is usually not readily transferable. Finally, in some states, a general partnership might be considered a security in certain cases, and it would be required to register as such with federal and state authorities.[3]

Limited Partnership

A *limited partnership* is a partnership that has both general and limited partners. In a limited partnership, the general partners are responsible for the business operations of the partnership. The limited partners' interest in the enterprise is confined to the extent of their investment (as if they were inactive shareholders in a close corporation). The limited partnership has characteristics of both the corporate and general partnership form. It resembles a corporation in that limited partners, like corporate shareholders, are not liable for losses in excess of their capital investments. It resembles a general partnership in that it is "invisible" for tax purposes and thus can pass on tax-sheltering advantages to the partners.

Although a limited partnership might seem like a best-of-all-worlds structure, it has certain disadvantages. For example, a limited partnership might have to be registered as a security under federal or state securities laws.[4] This process can be costly and burdensome. Furthermore, when a limited partnership is involved, disclosures in all offering literature must be detailed, particularly with respect to goals and anticipated tax consequences. Moreover, limited partnership interests are generally not readily transferable.

However, the principal disadvantage of the limited partnership form is in the control and management of the enterprise. The roles of the limited partners with respect to the management and operation of the business are restricted. The general partner is exclusively responsible for managing the affairs of the enterprise. By law, the limited partners may not "take part in the control of the business."[5] Some states may permit a limited partner to offer advice, but general partners are under no obligation to accept it. If limited partners perform any management function or assume any role in the conduct of partnership business, they cease to enjoy the limited liability that makes the limited partnership form so desirable in the first place. For this reason, limited partners should confine their participation in a venture to investment only. Many participants in health care joint ventures may find this limited role unacceptable.

Although the general partners in a limited partnership may have control over the enterprise, they do not enjoy limited liability, whereas within the corporate structure, those same parties would enjoy limited liability no matter how much control they exercised over corporate activities. The issues of control and limited liability do not represent a major problem in many partnerships, however, because the parties can incorporate the general partner. If the corporation is adequately capitalized, its liability is limited to the extent of its assets; and its officers, directors, and shareholders are not liable for partnership losses or debts.

Health Care Structures

Besides considering the basic legal formats through which a joint venture may operate, the participants in a health care joint venture might also explore various structures or entities that are specifically health care oriented. Examples of these are health maintenance organizations (HMOs), preferred provider organizations (PPOs), and medical staff-hospital (MeSH) relationships as well as variations of these.

Health Maintenance Organizations

A *health maintenance organization* (HMO) is an organization that by contract furnishes or ensures the delivery of a variety of comprehensive health care services to a certain number of enrollees who have paid a fixed monthly or annual premium. An HMO is able to provide the services that it offers to enrollees through contracts with physicians, hospitals, and other providers, who are the sole providers that the HMO member may use within the scope of HMO coverage. In this respect, the HMO is a closed system. If an enrollee uses any other provider for health care services, the fee for such services is not paid by the HMO.

In the HMO arrangement, the HMO either reimburses individual physicians on a fee-for-service basis or pays participating physicians a fixed amount per member, that is, on a capitation basis. The fixed amount paid by the enrollee to the HMO, and by the HMO to contracting providers, does not vary with the frequency, extent, or type of health services actually furnished to HMO enrollees. The HMO assumes a certain risk of financial loss if the set fee is too low. It generally expects to be profitable because it exercises management controls designed to encourage efficient and economical use of the health services provided by the HMO, to avoid unnecessary procedures, and to exercise preventive care with the aim of avoiding greater future expenses.

Some HMOs are regulated pursuant to the Health Maintenance Organization Act of 1973 (the HMO Act)[6] as well as by various state laws. The HMO Act and the regulations for implementing it provide for the scope of services required to be offered to members, the manner in which premiums are structured, the procedures for review of quality assurance, the enrollment requirements, the relationship between the HMO and its health care providers, the licensing of the HMO, and the financial condition of the HMO.

Preferred Provider Organizations

A *preferred provider organization* (PPO) consists of a network of hospitals and physicians who have contracted with employers and insurance carriers to provide certain health services on a negotiated fee-for-service payment basis. Under this system, patients may use any physician or hospital they choose, but they are encouraged, by means of deductible rates, lower copayment requirements, and more extensive insurance benefits, to use those health care providers who have contracted for the specific pricing and utilization control requirements. A PPO does not assume actuarial risk, and therefore it may not be subject to licensure as is an HMO or insurance company.

The structure of a PPO is flexible. Its form is determined by the needs and objectives of the parties forming it. A PPO is a hybrid between a conventional indemnity-type insurance policy and an HMO. It is like the insurance policy in that the policyholder is free to choose his or her own personal physician, who is paid by the employer or insurance company on a fee-for-service basis. It may differ from the conventional policy because the conventional policy lacks one or more of the following, which are basic features of most PPOs:

- Panel of participating health care providers
- Previously negotiated fee schedule
- Some form of pricing or utilization controls
- Additional benefits or other financial incentives offered to those patients who choose a provider from the PPO panel
- Rapid payment of providers' claims

The PPO resembles an HMO by virtue of the preselected panel of providers and the use of utilization controls. However, a PPO differs from an HMO in several essential respects. First, the HMO is a complete entity that generally offers a full range of health care benefits and assumes actuarial risk. The PPO does not assume any actuarial risk.

Second, a PPO differs from an HMO in the freedom of choice of provider that a PPO offers to its subscribers. The HMO is a closed, locked-in system: its enrollees must use the services of providers who have contracted with the HMO to provide such services. The HMO does not reimburse the enrollee for any payment to a practitioner outside the HMO system if similar care could have been provided by an HMO practitioner. On the other hand, PPO subscribers may select any health care provider of their choosing and remain covered by the existing indemnity plan. If that provider is not part of the PPO panel, the enrollee may be obliged to pay the difference, if any, between the fee charged by the enrollee's physician and the negotiated fee for the same service charged by panel physicians. In addition, other financial incentives, such as a lower deductible, may be offered to the PPO enrollees in order to induce them to select providers from the PPO panel.

Third, perhaps the most significant difference between the HMO and the PPO is in the payment structure. The PPO contracts with providers and groups of providers in a community to provide services for a certain fee. Unlike the HMO-provider contract, the PPO does not prepay a capitation amount to providers. The PPO enters into a contract with its panel members for a set fee per service, which is usually negotiated at a discount over the usual and customary charge in the community for that particular service. As a result, unlike the situation in an HMO, no financial incentive is fixed into the payment structure to avoid unnecessary procedures. In a PPO, the more services the panel member provides, the greater the financial reward. Other control mechanisms, such as use of referral authorization, are necessary to control costs in a PPO.

The PPO format offers several advantages to its participants. Because of its flexibility, it can meet the precise needs of those forming it and using it. Some PPOs may be formed by providers such as hospitals or physicians to meet the competition of HMOs and other alternative delivery systems. Another PPO may have as its primary founder an employer anxious to reduce employee health care costs.

The PPO may offer distinct advantages for each participant. Hospitals see PPOs as a means of retaining patients in the face of competition from other alternative delivery systems. Physicians like PPOs because, even though they may be obliged to reduce their fees in order to participate, they see the PPO as a means of increasing their patient load. Additionally, the PPO format may offer physicians the advantage of rapid payment of claims. Employers hope that through PPOs they can reduce the cost of providing health care for their employees while still maintaining overall benefits. Employees like PPOs because they are ensured less out-of-pocket expenses for health care while still retaining the freedom of choice of providers.

However, PPOs are not without disadvantages. Because of the flexibility of the PPO, administrative problems can arise. How the panel of providers is selected and what restrictions may be placed on the practices of those providers can be particularly troublesome. Some PPOs limit the number of participants and also may attempt to restrict the right of their panel members to participate in other alternative delivery systems. Others may attempt to prescribe conservative medical procedures in an attempt to control costs. A number of PPOs may have a panel open to all practitioners in the community. A PPO that includes too many practitioners or too few or that imposes unreasonable restrictions on the ability of practitioners to freely practice may have negative legal consequences, such as liability for violations of the antitrust laws (see chapter 10).

Moreover, the comparatively loose structure of a PPO may hinder it in competing with HMOs in certain markets. The PPO may not be able to offer complete benefit packages and cannot guarantee a cap on health care premiums.

MeSH-Type Structures

The *MeSH-type structure,* now often called the *integrated health care corporation* (IHCC), is a recent development on the health care scene. It was developed as a means of creating incentives for cooperation between physicians and hospitals. Initially developed by Paul M. Ellwood, Jr., M.D., of Interstudy, this structure is designed to help hospitals and physicians create an integrated system out of which may come specific projects.[7]

A MeSH, or IHCC, is generally a corporation jointly owned by a hospital and members of its medical staff. The MeSH corporation has the capability of undertaking those tasks in which the economic interests of physicians and hospitals overlap. Examples of such tasks are utilization controls, mechanisms for negotiating with third parties, investment vehicles for participants, and joint marketing schemes.

By putting a MeSH, or IHCC, structure into place in a hospital, the venture participants can create an entity with a governing board that is fully capable of making business decisions regarding long-term strategies and development of new services. A MeSH structure is a means of providing management or capital for programs that neither the hospital nor physicians could effectively support alone. Consequently, mutually beneficial programs or ventures can be undertaken by a MeSH with less initial confusion and, it is hoped, expense than would otherwise be the case. For instance, through a MeSH, the participants can create a new alternative delivery system, such as an HMO or a PPO, or enter into contracts on behalf of the hospital and physicians to implement DRG requirements of Medicare and other third-party payers by means of utilization review systems, shared efficiency programs, and management information systems. A MeSH can facilitate the development of new investment and financing programs or health care services, such as off-campus laboratories, imaging centers, birthing centers, or rehabilitation institutes.

Certain legal issues are important to consider when becoming involved with a MeSH or similar structure. The more critical are ERISA problems (chapter 5); fee-splitting, corporate practice of medicine, and Medicare fraud and abuse issues (chapter 8); and antitrust problems (chapter 10).

Although a MeSH offers certain advantages to its participants, it is not without pitfalls. As a corporation, it is subject to regulation as such and must comply with all corporate and securities laws (see chapter 3). Also in practice, many MeSH-like organizations, especially those that have been formed with no specific activity in mind, have not been active or successful.

Combination Forms

As a practical matter, most joint ventures are not composed of one single structure but are usually a combination of several. A venture in which only a contractual or a creditor relationship is involved is rare. However, these two forms are frequently used in combination with the corporation and partnership forms.

Complex joint venture transactions may involve a combination of all of the legal structures described so far. For instance, a hospital might agree with a venture capital company to create a for-profit corporation that in turn will construct an MRI center and lease equipment from a general or limited partnership composed of physicians. The venture capital company may lend money to the new corporation, and the limited partner physicians might contract with the new corporation for various services.

Combining legal structures within a joint venture provides a myriad of possibilities for the participants. They can choose to operate the facility through a for-profit corporation that may be a subsidiary of a not-for-profit entity. This company may lease equipment from a general partnership or a limited partnership of physicians. In addition, some sort of franchise may be used (see chapter 3), or the whole transaction can be formed through an existing MeSH structure. The principal reason for choosing a combination of structures is that each legal entity has advantages and disadvantages and, by selecting a combined format, it is sometimes possible to maximize the advantages while minimizing the disadvantages.

In selecting a structure for a particular joint venture project, the participants must take into account several considerations, not the least of which is the primary goal of the venture. For instance, if the purpose of the project is to establish an outpatient center or to purchase expensive technological equipment to provide medical care mainly to tax-exempt hospitals, a partnership of those hospitals may be an acceptable structure for the venture (see chapter 4 for a discussion of the tax consequences for a partnership of tax-exempt hospitals). If, on the other hand, the primary goal is to maximize returns or referrals for taxable participants, a business corporation or a limited partnership may be a more appropriate structure, with the hospital's participation limited to a more passive role for tax purposes (see the discussion of inurement risks in chapter 4).

In deciding how to structure a joint venture, the parties must consider among other items:

- Which party or parties wish to participate in management and operations
- How risky the enterprise might be
- What tax benefits or negative consequences might result from the choice of form

Also to be considered in deciding on a legal structure for the venture are political or policy factors. Certain venture structures may be more acceptable to a community than others, and the degree of acceptability may determine whether governmental approvals that may be required before the parties can go forward with a project will be forthcoming. For example, depending on the political outlook of its leaders, a city may be more willing to modify its land use requirements to permit the establishment of an emergency clinic if the clinic were to be operated by a not-for-profit corporation whose primary purpose is to provide free or reduced-fee health care for the poor and indigent than if it were to be operated by a for-profit entity whose primary motive is to increase its private-pay market share (see discussion of land use regulations in chapter 6).

Finally, before adopting a particular structure, the participants, in conjunction with their legal counsel, must consider various legal issues. The most important of these issues, such as securities law, tax issues, and antitrust implications, are discussed in detail in chapters 3, 4, and 10, respectively, of this book. In addition to these legal problems, other restrictions could affect the participants' ability to participate in certain kinds of venture projects or in certain types of legal entities. For example, some religious denominations or orders may prohibit certain types of undertakings by their members. Some states may limit the ability of hospitals owned or operated by governmental subdivisions (such as cities, counties, hospital districts, and hospital authorities) to participate in some kinds of ventures, such as investing in for-profit corporations. The bylaws of some corporations and other contractual arrangements, including loan and security agreements and indentures, may limit the entity's ability to enter into new transactions or into certain types of agreements, such as a ground lease, as part of a joint venture transaction. These legal issues should be fully investigated before the parties commit themselves to participate in a venture. This form of fact-finding is often referred to as *due diligence.*

Steps in the Formation of Joint Ventures

Once health care providers have decided to form an economic joint venture and have selected its basic structure, they must next consider how they will actually form the joint venture enterprise. This section discusses the steps that participants may take, with the help of their legal counsel and other consultants, to bring the joint venture to fruition. Usually the steps to be followed, with some variation, are:

- Planning
- Financial decisions, including feasibility studies and negotiations with lenders
- Discussions with legal counsel to work out any legal issues that could arise to complicate the transaction
- Governmental approvals and any necessary internal approvals to enter into the arrangement
- Compliance with applicable federal or state registration and other requirements
- Interpretive rulings, such as tax rulings, from the appropriate governmental authorities
- Requirements of any insurers of the transaction
- Preparation of legal documents necessary to complete the transaction
- Closing of the transaction

Planning

The first step to establishing any joint venture, whether short term or long term, is planning. Planning is essential whether the venture is one of a passive, investment-oriented nature, such as constructing a medical office facility, or one requiring the active participation of the parties, such as an ambulatory surgical center. The participants must examine their generalized goals in entering into the venture and translate those goals into a structure that will meet them.

Planning has a business side and a financial side. On the business side, the parties must decide what products or services will be offered by the new enterprise, the scope of such products or services, and how the product or service will be provided and marketed. On the basis of these decisions, contracts are negotiated with outside parties, and prices or wages are set.

Financial planning should begin with a cost-benefit analysis and a feasibility study. Realistic projections must be made as to how many patients will use the new facility or program in its first years of operation; how those patients will pay for services, for instance, through Medicare or Medicaid, private insurance, employer payers, or other payers; how much the venture will cost in terms of equipment, staff, and other overhead expenses; and what return on investment is anticipated. Once these projections are made, the parties can determine how much capital is needed for start-up costs and how that capital is to be acquired.

Financing

Once the parties have determined their capital needs in implementing the venture, they can decide how best to acquire that capital. In a simple inexpensive venture, the participants generally provide whatever capital is necessary to finance the project. For instance, in order to finance the acquisition of a lithotripter as a joint venture among several hospitals and staff physicians, the hospitals could provide, as part of their equity contribution to the venture, the space and support services necessary to operate the new equipment as well as some capital, and the staff members could provide the cash to pay acquisition and start-up costs and initial salaries.

Many ventures use some form of debt to finance the enterprise. For instance, the hospital participants in the MRI facility described in appendix B lent the venture a certain amount of capital to pay construction and start-up costs. Another way to finance a venture is to have one hospital issue tax-exempt obligations. These bonds could be secured by a mortgage on the real estate and a security interest in the personal property. An outside lender, such as a bank or a life insurance company, might also loan money to the venture.

In a highly leveraged enterprise, that is, a business venture for which the parties have borrowed heavily to provide financing, a third-party lender may require that one or several venture participants guarantee loans to the venture. When the venture entity is a corporation, such guarantees can result in the personal liability of that guarantor for some venture losses for which the guarantor would not otherwise be liable. There is also a risk of an adverse tax impact if the guarantor is a tax-exempt entity. Depending on the nature of the guarantee, there is a risk of inurement, or benefit to the private parties involved in the venture (see discussion of inurement in chapter 4).

Other methods of financing are more complex and involve a variety of methods. Outside investors may take an equity interest in the venture in return for a capital investment. They may also loan additional money to the enterprise.

Another method of financing is leasing. For example, a hospital can lease land it owns to a partnership composed of itself and staff physicians for the construction of a medical facility. Part of its financial return from the venture would be in the form of rent from the partnership. Staff physicians could purchase medical equipment and lease it to a partnership that would operate it. However, unless the medical equipment qualifies as "high technology equipment" under the tax code,[8] the venture may lose the investment tax credit (ITC) if the lease is to a tax-exempt entity. To avoid this potential problem, the physicians can be the general partners in a partnership that leases and operates the equipment. The hospital's contribution to the venture can be to lease to the partnership a building in which the equipment would be located. Under tax reform proposals before Congress in 1986, the ITC, one important incentive for a physician to invest in an equipment leasing partnership, could be eliminated (see chapter 4).

One popular means of using leasing for financing purposes is the sale-leaseback. One party sells real estate or equipment to an outside investor and then leases it back from that investor. Proceeds from the sale are used to finance operations, and rental payments theoretically come from profits from the enterprise. A variation on the sale-leaseback arrangement is a sale of the equipment or real estate by one participant in the venture to an outside investor for cash. That outside investor then leases the property to a partnership of venture participants who actually operate the business.

Whenever leasing plays a role in the financing of a transaction, the parties should take care that the lease is characterized as a *true lease* rather than a *financing lease* for tax purposes. A true lease is one in which the lessor is the owner of the property, which will be reclaimed from the lessee at the end of the lease term and when reclaimed will have some useful life remaining. Rent payments constitute true market rent for the property. If the lessee has an option to purchase the property at the end of the lease term, the purchase price must represent the value of the property at the time of the expiration of the lease. A financing lease is not really a lease; it is a loan transaction disguised to look like a lease. In a financing lease, the lessee is the economic owner of the property for all intents and purposes. The lessor is in reality merely a secured lender who is treated as the owner of the property only if the borrower defaults. At the expiration of a financing lease, the property either has little or no remaining useful life, or the lessee has an unconditional right to buy the property for less than its appraised value.

If the Internal Revenue Service (IRS) determines that a transaction is a financing lease, the lessor is denied the investment tax credit for the purchase of new equipment normally allowed the owner of such property. To avoid this negative tax consequence, the IRS suggests several guidelines:[9]

- The lessor should have a minimum unconditional at-risk investment during the entire lease term of not less than 20 percent of the cost of the property being leased.
- The value of the property at the end of the lease term must be at least 10 percent of the property's cost. For these purposes, *lease term* means base term and any renewals if they are at predetermined rental rates.
- The lessee cannot have the right to acquire title to the property for a price less than fair market value at the time of the purchase. Moreover, the lessor may not require the lessee to purchase the property. Further, the lessee may not acquire an equity interest in the property during the lease term, that is, rent payments cannot be applied to the purchase price of the property. Also, the lessee may not lend funds to the lessor in connection with the lease.
- The lessor must reasonably expect to realize a profit from the transaction, exclusive of tax benefits.

For a discussion of legitimate methods to obtain the tax benefits discussed briefly in this section, see chapter 4.

There is an additional special caution in using the sale-leaseback when a tax-exempt entity is involved. A sale-leaseback from or to a tax-exempt hospital, for instance, could trigger the tax-exempt entity leasing rules of the 1984 Tax Reform Act, which could result in a loss of anticipated tax benefits for the parties (see chapter 4).

Discussions with Legal Counsel

At some point early in the negotiations, the participants should meet with their legal counsel to describe the type of project that they envision and discuss structure options. At this stage, legal counsel probably prepares a memorandum of potential legal complications and suggestions for structuring the venture to avoid them. Each venture varies in its terms, and hence the legal analysis also differs somewhat.

Each of the following chapters of this book provides a detailed analysis of the more common legal issues that need to be considered. In appendixes A to F, potential issues are discussed with respect to a specific joint venture project in a format similar to the memorandum that legal counsel might prepare.

Counsel also reviews all relevant corporate or partnership books and records as well as contracts, loan documents, and any other documents that could have an impact on the transaction. This review, which is usually done in great detail, is called *due diligence*. Counsel also requests from the appropriate state authorities copies of any financing statements on file with respect to any personal property (for example, medical equipment and office furniture) involved in the transaction as well as a title search for any real property involved.

Governmental and Internal Approvals

The parties to a venture should seek government approvals only after they have met with counsel and have determined that:

- They can undertake the project without violating any internal restrictions, such as those that might be in the corporate bylaws.
- There are no serious legal factors that may prohibit the project as proposed.
- The project is financially feasible.

Because the time frame for any one approval may take several months, participants should submit necessary applications early to avoid unnecessary delays. Among the approvals or certificates that may be necessary for the project are:

- Certificate of need
- License for a health care facility
- Land-use zoning approvals
- Environmental impact report or a negative-impact statement
- Building permits, which may be required for substantial renovation of an existing facility as well as construction of a new building

The specific requirements for any of the above certificates are discussed in detail in chapter 6.

The importance of these approvals should not be discounted. Failure to obtain a necessary approval may cause delays and ultimately could prevent the parties from going forward with the project. Legal counsel can advise the parties as to the necessity of an approval and can help them proceed with the application process.

In a timely fashion, the parties should also determine what, if any, internal approvals may be necessary before they can proceed with the proposed project. Obtaining internal approvals may be as simple as having the board of directors of a corporate participant approve resolutions authorizing the corporation to enter into the various agreements and financing arrangements. Sometimes, however, the parties may wish to undertake a project that is forbidden by language in either the corporate articles or bylaws. In such a case, this language will have to be amended, with shareholder or corporate membership approval in most instances. Any amended articles would have to be filed in the state in which the corporation is incorporated. If the proposed project is inconsistent with some restriction of a sponsoring entity, the parties may have to modify the project unless a waiver of that restriction is obtained.

Registration Requirements

As the closing date for the transaction draws near, the parties may have to prepare various registration and disclosure statements to comply with applicable laws. For example, if a security is to be purchased or sold, as in a corporate or limited partnership offering, the parties may have to register the securities, that is, file certain disclosure information with and obtain approvals from the federal Securities and Exchange Commission (SEC) and applicable state securities commissions, or apply for one of the limited exemptions available at both the federal and state level for certain offerings (see the discussion of securities law requirements in chapter 3). At any rate, certain disclosures have to be made to prospective investors, either in the form of a private offering statement or an official prospectus used in a public offering. Allowing sufficient time for registration is important because the preliminary offering statement must be prepared and approved in advance of the closing.

Additionally, if a public offering is envisioned as part of the transaction, the parties have to commence negotiations with the underwriters regarding the terms under which the underwriters will agree to purchase the securities for distribution to public investors. Generally, the underwriters will enter into a letter of intent as to these terms sometime in advance of the closing. Arrangements have to be made for printing the stock certificates as well as the official statement. If bonds are to be issued, arrangements have to be made for their printing. Furthermore, in such a case, the parties have to apply for a bond rating from one of the national indexes.

If a limited partnership format is to be used or if the joint venture enterprise falls within the definition of a tax shelter under the rules specified in the Internal Revenue Code, the parties have to register the transaction as such. Legal counsel can advise them as to the applicability of these rules (see the discussion of tax-shelter registration in chapter 4). Furthermore, if a new corporate entity is to be created, the parties should reserve a corporate name early in the transaction with the authorities of the state in which the corporation is to be incorporated.

As a final matter, in a joint venture in which a regional enterprise has decided to franchise one or more local entities, that franchise may have to be registered with the Federal Trade Commission (FTC) as well as with any appropriate state authorities (see the discussion of franchise law in chapter 3). Disclosures are similar to those required for a securities registration. Again, time is important for this type of transaction, and any such registration should be submitted early in the process to ensure that necessary approvals are obtained before the proposed closing date for the transaction.

Interpretive Rulings

The parties also discuss with legal counsel whether he or she is willing to provide an opinion letter at the closing. This opinion letter discusses certain potential legal consequences of the transaction and may indicate the probability or improbability of certain desired or adverse tax consequences. This letter is based on counsel's knowledge and understanding of the existing tax law as well as his or her interpretations of various tax court opinions and rulings of the IRS involving transactions similar to the one that the parties are proposing to undertake.

If the transaction involves a structure that presents an unusual set of facts or a novel situation, the parties may wish to obtain more than an opinion from legal counsel. Even if counsel is willing to give an opinion in such an instance, the opinion would probably contain so many qualifications if the law in that particular area is uncertain that the parties may not wish to rely on it alone. In that instance, they may also seek an interpretive ruling as to the legality of a proposed action. The most common of these rulings is a private letter ruling on the tax status of a proposed venture project as well as its impact on the exempt status of participants. If a private letter ruling is required, it should be obtained from the IRS at the outset of a venture. If the IRS responds negatively to a proposed structure, the structure should be changed before the parties are too far along in their negotiations. In addition to tax rulings, the parties may seek rulings and no-action letters on the legality of certain nontax aspects of the transaction from the SEC or from state corporate authorities.

The parties may also wish tax-exempt status for the new entity. If so, they should submit their application and supporting documentation to the IRS and to local and state taxing authorities well in advance to ensure that the application is acted on and final approvals given before the closing date.

Insurance

Some types of ventures may involve insurers who are guaranteeing certain aspects of the transaction. For example, when tax-exempt bonds are issued, the bonds may qualify for insurance from some state agencies that regulate health care. If an interest in real property is to be transferred or a lender takes such an interest as security for a loan, the parties may wish to obtain title insurance. These insurers may require additional certificates or other documentation that must be prepared in advance of the closing. For example, if title insurance is required, a title report or abstract of title should be examined for defects in title, such as the presence of an indenture from a prior bond issue that should have been released. These defects can often be removed, or for an additional fee, the insurance company may insure against them. The exact terms of the policy vary and are the subject of negotiation with title officers. The final form of the policy should be agreed upon prior to the closing.

Preparation of Legal Documents

As the closing date approaches, counsel prepares the necessary legal documents for the specific transaction. These documents are tailored to meet the specific terms agreed upon by the parties. Counsel will advise the parties as to the appropriate documents for their particular arrangement. Not all of the documents in the following list are required for any one transaction; and some documents that are not listed may also be required, depending on the needs of a particular venture:

- *Structure agreements*
  - *Joint venture agreement.* This document is the operative document for the joint venture. It contains a description of the specific purpose for which the venture is formed as well as all of the terms and conditions of the transaction, including the rights and obligations of each venturer with respect to the transaction, the allocation of control over the management and operation of the venture enterprise, and the financial aspects of the venture. Sometimes this agreement is called a memorandum of understanding or a preincorporation agreement. Often it is preceded by a less formal letter of intent.
  - *General partnership agreement.* This document is the governing document in a general partnership. It contains the names, rights, and obligations of the partners vis-a-vis one another and the partnership, the amount of capital contributions, distribution and allocation of income and losses, and restrictions on transfers of partnership interests as well as of partnership assets.
  - *Limited partnership agreement.* This document contains some provisions similar to those found in a general partnership agreement, but it also includes a statement of the purpose of the partnership; a designation of general and limited partners; capital contributions; allocation of costs and expenditures among the partners; rights, duties, and obligations of the general

partner(s); rights and obligations of limited partners; and the transferability of limited partnership interests.
- *Articles of incorporation.* This document is filed with the state in which the corporate entity is formed. It contains the name and general purpose of the corporation and its principal office and place of business. It may also list categories of stock or corporate membership; qualifications for corporate membership or shareholder status; a right of first refusal to purchase stock in the corporation; and the name(s) of the incorporator(s), that is, the person or persons forming the corporation, or of the initial directors, that is, those first directors of the corporation who are appointed by the incorporators at the time of incorporation.
- *Bylaws.* This document is the governing document for a corporation. It contains general provisions with respect to the operation and management of a corporation, including duties of officers, meetings, shareholders' rights, responsibilities of the board, voting procedures, notices, and stock transfers.
- *Shareholders' agreement.* This optional document gives existing shareholders of a business corporation control over the admission of additional shareholders in the corporation. It generally restricts the disposition of stock by providing for a right of refusal first in the corporation and second in the other shareholders who are party to the shareholders' agreement.

- *Financing documents*
    - *Indenture.* This document is used in the financing of a joint venture transaction in which debentures or bonds are issued. The indenture generally governs the terms of the financing, the rights of the holders of the debentures or bonds, and the right of the issuer to recall or redeem the debentures or bonds.
    - *Mortgage or deed of trust.* This financing document is used when real property is the security for a loan to the participants. The document describes the real property subject to the mortgage or deed of trust and lists the rights of the holder, including provisions requiring insurance, prohibiting waste, guaranteeing repayment of the underlying loan, and entitling the lender to foreclose in case of nonpayment.
    - *Security agreement.* This financing document is used to define the rights of the lender, who is taking, as part of the security for the loan, an interest in personal property, such as equipment. It contains provisions similar to those contained in real property security documents.
    - *Uniform Commercial Code (U.C.C.) financing statement.* This statement is filed with the appropriate state authorities to protect a lender's security interest in personal property.
    - *Personal guarantees* from one or more parties to the transaction.
    - *Assignment of leases* of real property interests held by the borrower.

- *Leasing documents*
    - *Facilities lease.* This document, or a similar *site lease* or *building lease*, is necessary in joint venture transactions in which one party is leasing real property, such as a floor of a building or a building itself, to another. This document contains the rights and obligations of the parties with respect to the property, including, besides the rental amount, who must maintain the property, who must provide for taxes and insurance, and who bears the risk of loss. This document may also contain a renewal option or a right to purchase the property. In addition to real property, a facilities lease may also provide for the leasing of equipment, or this may be provided for in a separate document.
    - *Equipment lease.* This document governs the rights and responsibilities of the parties with respect to equipment leased by one to another. It provides

for a lease term, a rental amount, and responsibilities for insuring and maintaining the property.
- *Ground lease.* Such a document is relevant if, as part of the transaction, one party leases from another the land on which a building will be placed. Its terms resemble those found in a facilities lease. However, there may be certain additions, such as a clause providing for the subordination of the ground lease to construction financing.
- *Purchase and related transfer documents*
  - *Purchase and sale agreement.* This document is necessary when parties intend, as part of a joint venture, to purchase either land or a building. This agreement covers the terms of the sale, including the purchase price, title to the property, and any financial arrangements between the parties.
  - *Bill of sale.* This document is necessary to convey title when equipment or other personal property is purchased as part of the transaction.
  - *Grant deed.* Also known as a *warranty deed* or a *statutory warranty deed* in some states; this document conveys title to real property.
- *Other documents*
  - *Licensing or royalty agreement.* This document governs the rights and responsibilities of parties to a transaction in which a regional center, such as a central laboratory, licenses local centers to provide services marketed by the regional center.
  - *Franchise agreement.* This document replaces the licensing agreement if the regional center chooses to have a greater amount of control over the local company's operations.
  - *Estoppel certificates.* These and other similar certificates assure the parties that certain facts are true and may be relied upon, such as that a lease to the property is in full force.
  - *Indemnity agreements.* Documents in which one party to the transaction promises to reimburse another for losses or damages in case of certain events happening or failing to happen.
  - *Service contracts.* In these agreements, one party uses equipment to provide services to another rather than leasing the equipment to that other party for its own use.
  - *Management contracts.* In these agreements, one party promises to provide management services for another.

In addition, certain types of ventures may require specific documents relating to that particular transaction. For example, a venture to establish a PPO probably requires a *physician participation agreement* or a *physician services agreement,* in which a physician or group of physicians agrees to supply services on behalf of the PPO, and a *hospital participation agreement* or a *hospital services agreement,* in which a hospital agrees to participate in the PPO and to provide services to patients subscribing to the PPO.

Closing

At the closing, the parties come together to sign, witness, and notarize the documents relevant to the transaction. Counsel makes certain that all documents are in place, that they are properly signed, and that all resolutions authorizing the signatures have been approved. Certain documents, such as the articles of any corporation formed and U.C.C. financing statements, must be filed with the appropriate state authorities. Other documents, such as mortgages or deeds of trust, assignments of leases, and a memorandum of each lease entered into, are recorded according to the laws of the particular state in which the real property is located. All necessary payments and distributions of money are made as provided in the various agreements. Copies of all documents, certificates, approvals, and disclosure statements are then distributed to the interested parties, and the transaction is closed.

Operation of Joint Ventures

Once the transaction is closed, the actual work of the parties begins. How the joint venture enterprise will operate is actually the most important aspect of the venture. As business managers, the participants know that the management and operation of a facility can make the difference between a successful enterprise and a failure. What they may not realize, however, is the extent to which legal issues can affect the operation of the facility and in some cases *determine* how a facility will be operated.

This section discusses general considerations that affect the operational decisions of a health care facility and describes briefly what impact legal factors have on those decisions. The major considerations that may involve legal issues include management considerations; compensation of participants and staff; and staffing decisions. Other considerations, such as fees for products or services and other aspects of day-to-day operations (including marketing and advertising decisions), are not discussed here. They may tangentially involve legal issues; when this is the case, the issues are discussed in the appropriate chapters, such as chapter 3 (regulation of franchises) with respect to marketing decisions and chapter 10 (antitrust) with respect to fees.

Management

In most joint ventures, the choice of which party controls the management of the enterprise is the most important decision made. In this sense, there may be a difference between major management directives and the day-to-day operation of the facility. For example, a hospital could participate with a group of physicians in the operation of an outpatient clinic. The hospital could construct the clinic facilities and lease them to a partnership composed of the physicians. This partnership might operate the facility and maintain control over its day-to-day operations, but major management decisions could be made by the hospital through the terms of its facilities lease. However, many hospitals want more direct control over the enterprise.

Conflicts may arise in a joint venture unless the parties have a clear idea of who has ultimate management authority. There are two specific areas in which control is important. The first of these is billing procedures. The joint venture agreement should clearly delineate which party does the billing for the enterprise or whether an independent management or service bureau is retained to perform this function. It is particularly important that billing practices comply with the various applicable requirements of third-party payers. The second area in which clarity with respect to management roles is crucial is staffing. Only one participant, or a committee of participants, can have control over the actual hiring and firing of employees.

The joint venture agreement should be specific in describing the rights of other participants in management decisions. There are two particular caveats to keep in mind. First, when limited partners are involved in a joint venture, they must be careful not to take part in the management of the partnership business, or they may lose their limited liability in case of a lawsuit (see the section on partnership in this chapter). Second, joint venture participants generally are not a homogeneous group. They cannot be expected to "speak with one mind." They are usually participating in the venture for a multitude of reasons, only one of which is potential profits. The joint venture documents should attempt at the outset to define the extent of involvement expected of various participants. It is better to resolve potential problems before they become problems.

Compensation

How participants are compensated and what other benefits they receive can raise various legal problems. For example, a compensation scheme based on the number of referrals that an owner makes to a facility may be illegal under Medicare laws and under some states' statutes and may also present ethical questions (see chapter 8). Salaries, fees, and distributions of profits to partners might pose inurement problems for a partnership composed of a tax-exempt entity and taxable individuals if these salaries are inflated or are otherwise deemed to be unreasonable (see chapter 4). Further, if a physician, or a group of physicians participating through their professional corporation, is characterized as an employer in the joint venture, the qualified status of their benefit plans could be jeopardized.[10] These and other issues related to compensation are discussed in chapter 5.

Staffing

How the joint venture is staffed is a vital issue that raises a host of questions. The participants must decide whether to hire new employees for the venture, to use employees of one or the other venture participant, or to lease staff from a personnel agency. Other problems may be encountered when one or more participants have collective bargaining agreements with their employees that may be applicable to employees of the joint venture. The effect of labor law on joint venture staffing decisions is the subject of chapter 9.

Legal Compliance

Finally, once the joint venture is in operation, it remains subject to all local, state, and federal laws, including antitrust laws. Business behavior by the venture that is anticompetitive will be scrutinized for possible antitrust violations (see chapter 10). To ensure that business practices are consistent with current laws and regulations, some system within the entity's management structure should be established to gauge and monitor compliance by the enterprise and its owners with all applicable laws.

Notes

1. In a recent survey of joint ventures, partnerships and contractual arrangements were found to be the most common legal structures used. Corporations were also commonly used but not quite so often. The most common joint venture arrangement was the limited partnership. *See* ERNST & WHINNEY, HEALTH CARE JOINT VENTURES: SURVEY RESULTS, at 5, 64 (1985).

2. *See* Queen of Angels v. Younger, 66 Cal. App. 3d 359, 136 Cal. Rptr. 36 (1977).

3. *See* PENNSYLVANIA SECURITIES COMMISSION BULLETIN, at 8 (Mar.-Apr. 1978): A general partnership interest might be an "investment contract" in which a general partner contributes capital but "otherwise performs no active functions with respect to the partnership."

4. *See, e.g.,* SEC v. Murphy, 626 F.2d 633 (9th Cir. 1980). This issue is also discussed in detail in chapter 3.

Notes

5. Cal. Corp. Code §§ 15507, 15632 (West).
6. Pub. L. No. 93-222, 42 U.S.C. §§ 300e *et. seq.*, as amended.
7. *See* Ellwood, *When MDs Meet DRGs*, Hospitals, Dec. 1983, at 62.
8. I.R.C. § 168(j)(5).
9. For these purposes, the leasing industry generally follows the guidelines specified in Rev. Proc. 75-21, 1975−18 I.R.B. 15 (May 5, 1975), and Rev. Proc. 75-28, 1975−21 I.R.B. 19 (May 27, 1975).
10. I.R.C. §§ 414(m), (n). *See also* chapter 5.

Chapter 3
Corporate, Securities, and Franchise Law

Corporate and Partnership Law
    Corporate Law
        For-Profit Corporations
        Professional Corporations
        Not-for-Profit Corporations
        Conversion to For-Profit Status
    Partnership Law
        General Partnership
        Limited Partnerships
Securities Laws
    Federal Securities Law
        Definition of a Security
        Registration Exemptions
            Intrastate Offering Exemptions
            Limited or Restricted Offering Exemptions
    State Blue Sky Laws
    Disclosure Requirements
Franchise Law
    Federal Franchise Law
    State Laws
    Elements of a Franchise
        Commercial Symbol
        Franchise Fee
        Centralized Plan or Community of Interest
    Effects of Franchise Law
        Medical Pavilion Lease or Licensing Arrangement
        Phased Laboratory Joint Venture
    Avoiding Franchise Law

Corporate and Partnership Law

Every state has statutes that regulate the lawful organization and form of corporations, general and limited partnerships, and other business associations such as cooperatives and business and investment trusts. Regulation by some states is more rigid than by others, but most have some requirements with respect to incorporation of for-profit entities, formation and governance of not-for-profit corporations, and organization of general and limited partnerships.

Corporate Law

Corporations are fictional entities that are endowed with a distinct legal existence if they are organized in compliance with the laws of the state in which the corporation is incorporated. These legal entities have certain powers, including the ability to contract with others, incur debt, own property, and sue and be sued. Because corporations are incorporated in one particular state, they are subject to that state's laws with respect to their governance. They may do business in other states but are usually required to register there as foreign corporations.

For-Profit Corporations

The major organizational and operative documents of the for-profit corporation are its *articles of incorporation* and its *bylaws*. The articles are executed and filed with the state at the time of incorporation. The corporate existence begins with the filing of the articles and generally continues perpetually, unless otherwise expressly provided in the articles or unless the corporation is dissolved at a later time by its shareholders. Upon incorporation, the new entity immediately acquires all of the rights and property of the association being incorporated and is subject to all of its debts and liabilities.

State corporate laws usually require that the articles set forth the following:

- Name of the corporation
- Purpose of the corporation, generally stated[1]
- Name and address of a person in the state who has the corporate authority to handle any problems or questions that arise as well as to respond to any lawsuits filed against the corporation in that state
- Statement with respect to the total number of shares to be issued and the rights, privileges, and restrictions placed on certain classes of shares

Other optional provisions, such as listing special qualifications required of shareholders or restricting the business in which the corporation may engage, are also generally permitted.

Bylaws, which are usually more extensive than the articles of incorporation, are adopted by the board of directors with the approval of the shareholders. The bylaws set forth provisions for the management of the business and the conduct of corporate affairs, including the number of directors, their term of office, the time and place of meetings, requirements with respect to proxies, the duties of corporate officers, and the rights of shareholders.

The bylaws cannot conflict with the articles or with any statutory requirement. Many provisions in the bylaws that relate to general housekeeping matters are also governed by statute, and so many bylaws echo the particular requirements of the law. These requirements include holding periodic meetings of shareholders and directors, preparing corporate minutes, electing directors and officers, and issuing stock certificates.

For-profit corporations are capitalized through the sale of stock to investors. Many corporations offer several classes of shares, the most usual being common and preferred stock. Common shareholders generally have voting rights. Preferred shareholders may or may not have the right to vote, depending on what restrictions, if any, have been placed on the stock; but they have preference over common shareholders in case of corporate distributions, such as dividends or the distribution of assets on the dissolution of the corporation.

In many transactions, the respective rights and obligations of shareholders are set forth in a *shareholders' agreement*, which covers, among other items, the sale of additional shares in the company and the ability of shareholders to sell existing shares before first offering them to the corporation or to the other shareholders. Shareholders' rights are also governed by statute. There are generally laws dealing with the issuance of shares, the types of shares that can be issued, restrictions that the corporation may place on the transfer or assignment of shares (particularly in a close, or family, corporation), and the surrender and cancellation of share certificates.[2] There are similar laws with respect to dividend distributions and redemption of shares.[3] The statutes are usually fairly clear with respect to shareholders' meetings and notice of those meetings as well as voting rights and proxies.[4] The laws also give shareholders certain rights of inspection of corporate books and records.[5]

The corporation acts through a board of directors elected by the shareholders pursuant to a procedure described in the bylaws and the shareholders' agreement. State laws generally provide for a minimum or maximum number of directors of a corporation and regulate the powers of the board. There are also provisions with respect to the removal of directors and filling vacancies on the board.[6] The board, or officers appointed by the board, sign contracts for the corporation, hire employees, arrange for financing, acquire real estate, and take any other actions necessary or desirable in connection with the operation of the business. These powers are also regulated by statute in many states.[7]

Professional Corporations

The laws in most states vary with respect to specific types of corporations, such as banking or insurance corporations. One such corporate entity that is specifically regulated by statute is the *professional corporation*. This entity is relevant to the health care industry because it permits one or several health care practitioners to incorporate their practice and thereby enjoy the advantages of being a corporation from the viewpoint of limited liability and tax planning.

Many states permit an individual or group of individuals engaged in the practice of a single profession, such as law or medicine, to incorporate under general corporation law (although in some statutes one professional corporation is not entitled to hold stock in another).[8] Some states permit certain professional corporations to consist of several allied professions. For instance, in California, up to 49 percent of the shares in a medical corporation may be held by other licensed persons, such as licensed podiatrists, registered nurses, or licensed clinical social workers.[9]

The general laws relating to corporations apply to professional corporations, with some variations. For instance, a professional corporation that has only one shareholder need have only one director, who is that shareholder and who also serves as the president and treasurer of the corporation. In such a situation, the state law might provide that other corporate officers need not be licensed persons.[10] In addition, the law might require that the articles of incorporation include a specific statement identifying the entity as a professional corporation.[11]

Only licensed persons may render professional services as employees of a professional corporation. Employees of the corporation who are not licensed may not render any professional services.[12]

Not-for-Profit Corporations

Different laws regulate not-for-profit corporations in most states. Not-for-profit corporations may be formed for a variety of purposes, such as rendering a charitable or public benefit, serving some religious purpose, or providing mutually beneficial services (such as those provided by a condominium owners' association).[13]

Not-for-profit corporations also have articles of incorporation and bylaws. The articles contain provisions similar to those of any for-profit corporation except that they are generally required by law to state that the entity is organized as a not-for-profit corporation and not for the private gain of any person. For purposes of obtaining a federal tax exemption, the articles of such a corporation generally include language relating to the charitable purpose of the entity. The bylaws contain administrative details similar to those contained in bylaws of for-profit corporations, except that not-for-profit entities are generally relieved of many corporate "housekeeping" requirements, such as minutes, reports to shareholders, and issuance of stock certificates.

Like their for-profit counterparts, not-for-profit corporations are governed by a board of directors. Directors are either elected by members or appointed by the incorporators. The board manages all corporate business through officers elected by it. The statutes generally provide for various contingencies with respect to directors, including replacement, standards of conduct, duties, and liabilities.[14]

Not-for-profit corporations do not have shareholders, although some may have members. In addition, there can be several separate classes of such members and defined *reserve powers*, that is, powers reserved by state statutes or corporate articles or bylaws to the members of the not-for-profit corporation.[15] For example, directors may have authority over most corporate decisions; but in not-for-profit corporations with reserve powers, the directors may be required by law to obtain approval of the membership for certain crucial corporate decisions, such as amendments to the articles or bylaws. Other reserve powers developed by the corporation as a matter of policy are, for example, the powers reserved to members to approve budgets. Where members are involved, the laws generally contain basic requirements with respect to meetings, notices to members, and requirements for a quorum. No distribution of dividends or corporate assets to members is allowed.[16]

Although not-for-profit corporations do not have all of the housekeeping duties of for-profit entities, they are not entirely free of administrative paperwork. Most states require that such corporations file certain forms, such as a report to the state attorney general,[17] and other forms applicable to exemptions from state and federal income taxes.

Conversion to For-Profit Status

As a general rule, a not-for-profit corporation may convert its status to that of a for-profit corporation by amending its articles of incorporation to replace the "not-for-profit" language with words to the effect that the entity is a "business" corporation. These amended articles are then filed with the appropriate state authorities.

Another way to change status is for the not-for-profit corporation to sell substantially all of its assets to a for-profit company. This for-profit company may be organized and capitalized by the same parties who governed the not-for-profit entity.

Some states do provide that not-for-profit corporations must donate to some charitable use the value of the assets that they hold in trust for the benefit of the public. This value is generally the subject of extensive negotiations between the state and the entity desiring to convert[18] (see the discussion of the charitable trust doctrine in the section on not-for-profit hospitals in chapter 2).

Partnership Law

State laws regulate general and limited partnerships.

General Partnerships

Many states have adopted the Uniform Partnership Act, which governs the organization and function of general partnerships.[19] Unlike corporations, which generally have many requirements as to their organizational structure, the Uniform Act contains few structural requirements. A *partnership* is defined under the law as an association between two or more persons to carry on as co-owners of a business for profit.[20]

In general, parties form a partnership by entering into a *partnership agreement.* They may also record a statement of partnership in the state in which they intend to do business. The partnership agreement is the critical document defining the rights and obligations of the participants. It contains provisions similar to those found in the corporate articles and bylaws and in the shareholders' agreement. More specifically, the partnership agreement describes the powers, duties, and obligations of the partners. It names the managing general partner, if there is one, and delineates the rights and obligations of the remaining partners. In the absence of such provisions in the agreement, the Uniform Act states that "every partner is an agent of the partnership for the purpose of its business" and that the actions of every partner, "including the execution in the partnership name of any instrument" for the carrying out of partnership business, bind the partnership, unless the party with whom the partner is dealing knows that that partner has no such authority.[21]

The partnership agreement also covers such items as contributions to the partnership, division of profits and losses, sales or other dispositions of partnership interests, sales and acquisition of partnership assets, and dissolution of the partnership. If the agreement does not cover these areas, the appropriate provisions of the Uniform Act apply. For example, the Uniform Act provides that real property can be acquired in the partnership name and, in such event, can be conveyed only in the partnership name. Property acquired with partnership funds is partnership property.[22] The act also contains provisions governing the relations of partners to one another, including a right of inspection of partnership books, a right to a formal accounting, and a duty of partners to disclose relevant facts to one another.[23]

Limited Partnerships

Many states have adopted the Uniform Limited Partnership Act or some similar statute governing limited partnerships. A *limited partnership* is distinguishable from a general partnership in that it inherently creates at least two classes of partners, with management responsibilities resting solely in the general partner or partners and not in the limited partners.

To form a limited partnership, the participants must substantially comply with the requirements of the act: They must sign and acknowledge a certificate of limited partnership stating:[24]

- Name of the partnership
- Character of the business
- Principal place of business
- Term for which the partnership is to exist
- Value of contributions by the limited partners
- Time when such contributions will be returned
- Share of the profits or other compensation that each limited partner will receive
- Right to admit additional limited partners
- Other rights of the limited partners with respect to their interest in the partnership

Each limited partnership must have at least one general partner. The general partner, unlike the limited partners, does not enjoy limited liability. In fact, general partners in a limited partnership have the same rights, powers, restrictions, and liabilities as they would have in a partnership without limited partners.

General partners are exclusively responsible for the management of the affairs of the limited partnership. However, limited partners have some right to ratify certain acts of the general partners that have a material effect on the partnership itself, such as accepting a judgment to be entered by a creditor of the partnership against the partnership, for a stipulated sum, without going through the litigation process; assigning the general partner's rights to partnership property; or admitting a new general or limited partner.[25]

The statute affords limited partners certain rights of disclosure and inspection of partnership books. Limited partners may also lend money to and transact other business with the partnership. However, any attempt on the part of a limited partner to control the business could cause the limited partner to become liable as a general partner unless the participation is limited to matters affecting the basic structure of the partnership, such as the termination of the partnership or the sale of substantially all of the partnership assets.[26]

Securities Laws

If a corporation or partnership is selected as the legal structure for the joint venture enterprise, an additional legal factor to be considered is the impact of federal and state securities laws and regulations. The purpose of these laws is to protect investors and potential investors who do not have sufficient business acumen to evaluate a transaction and its potential pitfalls. These laws and regulations require registration of any security sold or offered for sale unless some specific exemption applies. They also require disclosures to investors and potential investors.

Federal Securities Law

Definition of a Security

A *security* has been broadly defined as any instrument of ownership in which the following elements are present:[27]

- The investment is in a common enterprise.
- The investor is led to expect profits from it.
- Those profits are to be derived solely from the efforts of others.

A security can be stock in any corporation established to carry on joint venture operations or any option for such stock, or it can also be an interest in any limited partnership established as part of the joint venture transaction.[28] The name attached by the seller to the interest sold to the investor is of no significance in determining whether that interest is a security. If the interest is given in exchange for risk capital in the venture that is subject to the managerial or entrepreneurial efforts of others, it is a security. Consequently, an investment in third-party notes secured by a deed of trust has been held to be a security.[29] In certain limited instances, a security may also include an interest in a general partnership.

Although no one could deny that corporate stock or a limited partnership interest is a security, a more difficult question is whether the general partnership interest falls within the definition of an investment contract for securities law purposes. In most instances, this would not be the case.[30] Normally, it is assumed that the managerial powers vested in general partners give them the ability to protect themselves and that they therefore do not need the protection of the securities laws. This is usually so even if the general partner has only a minority interest. The issue is not actual control over partnership business but rather the *power* to exercise a role in crucial partnership decisions.[31] Even though general partners may not have an active role in the management of the venture, they usually possess voting rights, the right to attend partnership meetings, and the right of access to partnership books and records.[32]

However, the situation may be different when the actual control over the partnership by the managing partner precludes the involvement of other partners in partnership business.[33] A general partnership interest may in fact be an investment contract when a general partner contributes capital but otherwise performs no active functions with respect to the partnership. If the investor who purchased the interest was deemed to be too inexperienced to participate in the partnership's affairs and was forced to rely completely on the unique talents of the managing partners, then the partnership would most likely be considered an investment contract, or a security. In such an instance, the partner's absolute reliance on the other partners rendered him or her unable to meaningfully exercise his or her partnership powers.[34]

Under federal law, any offer or sale of a security must be registered with the Securities and Exchange Commission (SEC) unless an exemption applies.[35] The process of registering with the SEC is costly and time consuming because the preparation of considerable technical material by legal and financial advisors is required. Failure to comply with the registration requirements can lead to stringent penalties, including:

- Liability of the issuer to the purchasers to refund in full any money invested by such purchasers if the offer or sale violates registration requirements[36]
- Criminal sanctions, including fines or imprisonment, if the court decides that the failure to comply with any of the registration requirements was willful[37]

Registration Exemptions

Because of the burdens required by registration and the penalties for failure to comply with the Securities Act, a joint venture transaction should be carefully structured to avoid, whenever possible, the statute's registration requirements. The law affords certain registration exemptions that, in selected instances, may minimize the burdens associated with the securities laws: the intrastate offering exemption and the so-called limited or restricted offering exemptions. The requirements to qualify for these exemptions are not stringent, and many joint venture transactions contemplated by health care providers could qualify for one or the other. However, care should be taken in qualifying for the exemption. Because of possible sanctions, purchasers whose investment has gone down in value could recover their entire purchase price without having to show any fraud if the seller is unable to establish the necessary conditions on which it relied for the exemption from registration.[38]

Intrastate Offering Exemptions

Transactions taking place entirely within a single state are exempt from the federal registration requirements. Many joint venture transactions are on a small-enough scale so that it would not be difficult for them to qualify for this exemption. To be exempt, the following conditions must be met:[39]

- The issuer of the security must be a resident of the state in which the offering is to occur and be incorporated there.

- The issuer must do a substantial amount of its business in that state.
- All of the proceeds from the offering must be used within the state.
- All potential investors or purchasers must reside in the state.
- The actual securities must be in the hands of residents of the state when the transaction is completed.
- The entire issue of the securities must be offered and sold as part of the exempted transaction.

For example, a hospital and its staff members establish a joint venture for the purpose of setting up a clinical laboratory. A for-profit corporation, whose sole shareholders are the hospital and its staff members, is formed. The transaction would qualify for an intrastate offering exemption from registration requirements if the hospital is a not-for-profit corporation incorporated in and doing business in the state in which the laboratory is to be located and if no other participant is a resident of any other state.

Limited or Restricted Offering Exemptions

A joint venture transaction may qualify for a limited or restricted offering exemption in several ways.[40] First, a transaction not involving any public offering is by statute exempt from registration requirements.[41] There are no fixed rules for the applicability of this statute. Factors considered by the courts and the SEC in determining whether an offering qualifies are:[42]

- Potential investors are closely related to the issuer: They are personal friends, business associates, or other acquaintances who could be reached without relying on public forms of solicitation.
- In the reasonable belief of the issuer, potential investors are sufficiently experienced or sophisticated to evaluate the merits and risks of the investment or are able to bear the risk.
- Potential investors have the services of a representative who is knowledgeable about the nature of such transactions and has sufficient experience to make such an evaluation.
- Each potential investor must be supplied with information similar to that which is normally contained in an SEC registration statement.
- There can be no more than 35 purchasers, excluding those parties purchasing $150,000 or more of the securities.

The regulations promulgated under the statute provide three other conditions for obtaining a limited or restricted offering exemption:[43]

- Limited offerings in which the offering amount is less than $500,000. In this case there is no limit on the number of potential investors or purchasers, but advertising and solicitation are prohibited.
- Offerings in which the offering amounts are less than $5 million and in which there are no more than 35 investors. The regulation allows an additional unlimited number of *accredited investors*, such as institutional investors and tax-exempt organizations, as defined in the regulations.[44] Advertising and solicitation are prohibited.
- Private offerings with no monetary limit but a maximum of 35 "sophisticated" *nonaccredited investors*, who are investors who do not fall within the precise limits of the regulation but who have experience in financial matters. In other words, the issuer must believe that the investors have "such knowledge and experience in financial and business matters that [they] are capable of evaluating the merits and risks" of the investment.[45] An unlimited number of

accredited investors is also allowed in this instance, but here, too, advertising and solicitation are prohibited.[46]

If a joint venture has few investors, it can be structured to fit within the confines of these regulations. In addition, a participating tax-exempt organization, such as a hospital having assets in excess of $5 million, would be considered an accredited investor. By this means, it may be possible to escape the potentially onerous registration requirements of the Federal Securities Act. The major concern is that there be no public solicitation or advertising of the venture.

State Blue Sky Laws

Federal statutes are not the only securities laws having an impact on a joint venture project. Every state has some sort of registration requirement for a security. This requirement is usually similar to the federal law but is, in some instances, less burdensome than the federal law. These laws, commonly referred to as *Blue Sky laws*,[47] generally require disclosure of all material facts to potential investors and may also provide for some determination of the fairness of the investment before the securities can be offered or sold in that particular state.

State courts usually follow federal decisions in determining whether a security that is subject to the Blue Sky laws has been sold or offered for sale.[48] Some states have developed a definition even more liberal than the federal definition. For instance, in California, a security is involved if investors provide capital that is at risk in the venture.[49] The investment is considered a security even if investors participate in some respect in business affairs, provided that they do not take an *active* role in the management of the business.[50]

Like the federal law, the Blue Sky laws of most states offer some sort of exemption from registration for certain types of transactions. For example, virtually every state offers some sort of limited or restricted offering exemption that is similar to the federal exemption.

Some of the state exemptions are more restrictive than the federal ones, in that they permit fewer investors. For instance, some states exempt transactions having no more than 10 offerees.[51] Other states give exemptions for transactions involving *sales* to no more than a certain number of persons in the state.[52] A few states base their requirements on the *number of transactions* by a particular party in the state and grant exemptions to only a certain number in any given time frame.[53] Finally, some states give an exemption for *isolated transactions*,[54] that is, for a single transaction within a given time by a particular party. This requirement exempts the party who is not in the business of dealing in securities from burdensome registration requirements while still requiring registration for others who engage in a number of offerings in the course of a year, albeit to only a few investors at a time.

Most states require sellers who claim a particular exemption to file certain documents, forms, or applications with the state.[55] Massachusetts requires such a filing only if commissions are paid in connection with the transaction,[56] but most states require such a filing by sellers prior to making any offering in that state.[57]

Changes in state statutes in the area of exemptions are frequent. Although the trend is to add new limited offering exemptions rather than eliminate those that are already available, the parties should investigate applicable statutes and securities' regulations before embarking on a joint venture in any particular state to be certain that an exemption is available for the particular type of transaction envisioned.

Disclosure Requirements

Regardless of whether an exemption from registration is available under either federal or state laws, the participants in any joint venture transaction that includes the sale of a security are required by Federal Rule 10b-5 to make full and adequate disclosure of all material aspects of the transaction to potential investors.[58] There are serious penalties, including both criminal sanctions and civil damages, if some important item is not disclosed or if the disclosure is misleading or incomplete. Any seller or buyer of a security involved in the transaction can bring a private suit under Rule 10b-5.

Because of potential 10b-5 liability for failure to disclose material facts, participants in a joint venture in which a security is bought, sold, or otherwise transferred must be careful to reveal every fact that might be material to the decision to invest. This disclosure includes all relevant information about each major participant, including the hospital and other tax-exempt investors; any major outside investors; and any lender or other party contributing to the financing or operation of the joint venture. Relevant facts include:

- Names and functions of officers, directors, partners, and others involved in essential management decisions
- Financial data with respect to the venture and its major participants
- Rights of the shareholders or limited partners within the business
- Other relevant management matters that might affect the decision to invest, including tax consequences, as much as they can be predicted, and the assumptions upon which the potential consequences are based
- Potential and as yet uncertain consequences to the project as a result of various statutes and regulations, including Medicare reimbursement, the Employee Retirement Income Security Act (ERISA), and other regulations
- Any other information that might affect the viability of the project, including provisions in bylaws, contracts, or any other agreement of the participants with one another or any outside party
- Any laws, regulations, lawsuits, claims, or anything else that could have a serious impact on the venture

If fraud is found under Rule 10b-5, the penalties can be severe. Because of the disruptiveness of such suits on the operation of the joint venture and its financial viability, every effort should be made when structuring the venture to provide potential investors with scrupulous disclosures in order to avoid any potential 10b-5 liability.

Franchise Law

Many economic joint ventures are composed of a series of enterprises on a regional scale. For example, a central regional corporation might offer its services and expertise to enable local parties to establish individual ambulatory surgical centers or occupational medicine facilities, as described in appendixes A and C. Ventures between regional centers and local entities are fairly widespread because they enable participants to quickly develop a presence in new market areas while relying on the peculiar knowledge of established physicians and hospitals who are familiar with that particular locality.[59]

One legal problem that may arise from this sort of venture is the application of franchise laws to the relationship between the regional center and the local entities, even though the venturers themselves do not view their arrangement as a franchise. There are both federal and state laws affecting franchises. Because the definitions contained in these statutes are broad, many business relationships may fall within the scope of one or the other. Because franchises are subject to stringent regulation, the venture should be structured so that franchise regulations can be avoided whenever possible.

Federal Franchise Law

The Federal Trade Commission (FTC) has established rules that require elaborate disclosures from franchisors that are similar to the disclosure requirements of the federal securities laws.[60] Federal law requires that a business engaged in establishing franchises provide an extensive disclosure statement to the prospective franchisee. This statement must include certain prescribed information, such as the names of the franchisor's officers and directors, if it is a corporation, or the names of its principal owners. It must also give extensive financial information about the company, including any history of bankruptcies. The franchisee's rights and obligations, including financial contributions and use of required suppliers or distributors, must also be clearly described. Failure to comply with federal franchise disclosure rules constitutes an unfair or deceptive act or practice within the meaning of Section 5 of the Federal Trade Commission Act.[61]

State Laws

Almost every state regulates franchises in some way. However, states are constantly adding to or changing their franchise regulation legislation.[62]

Most state laws require registration of the franchise and a disclosure of the material terms and conditions of the franchise agreement as well as information about the franchisor. The state disclosure form is usually similar to the federal form.[63] Other states have their own franchise laws, which are often more stringent than the federal requirements. For instance, California's disclosure document requires profit-and-loss statements as well as an annual update.

Before the franchise can be registered, all disclosures are reviewed by appropriate authorities. This review can add some delay to a transaction, although most states apparently attempt to expedite the process.[64]

Elements of a Franchise

Because most statutes and regulations define a franchise quite broadly, business relationships, such as distributorships and licenses, that are not intended to be franchises by their participants can inadvertently fall within the scope of the law.[65] Many state statutes define a *franchise*, which must be registered as such, as an agreement containing the following elements:

- Substantial association between the franchisee's business and a trademark or commercial symbol that designates the franchisor
- Requirement that a franchisee pay a fee
- By the terms of the agreement, a centralized marketing plan prescribed by the franchisor[66] or a community of interest between the parties in the marketing of goods or services[67]

A brief description of each of these elements follows.

Commercial Symbol

One essential element of a franchise in most state statutes is the association between the business and the commercial symbol. Actually displaying this symbol is not required. Any use at all of such a symbol by the franchisee may be sufficient. Nor does the symbol have to be a specific trademark. It can be any distinctive sign that is in some way associated with the franchisor.[68]

Franchise Fee

The second element required is the franchise fee. Such a fee is, for example, "any fee or charge required to be paid or agreed to be paid for the right to enter into a business under a franchise agreement."[69] The fee may be in any form. It could be:[70]

- Payment for goods or services in excess of the fair market value of those goods or services
- Payment to the franchisor's advertising fund
- Payment to a creditor of the franchisor on behalf of the franchisor
- Any option payment to the franchisor for services suggested by the franchisor that will help in the successful operation of the business
- Payments for advertising of the facility if the franchisor has suggested to the franchisee the manner and content of the publicity

Centralized Plan or Community of Interest

The third essential element required by the statutes of most states is either a centralized marketing plan or a community of interest between the parties. To determine if a *community of interest* exists, the benefits that each party derives from the relationship are examined to verify whether the parties appear to have a joint or common interest in the operational and financial success of the franchisee's business.[71]

The giving of detailed recommendations or suggestions by the franchisor to the franchisee on how to market the product or services, even if these suggestions are not binding, is evidence that a centralized marketing plan exists. Other such evidence would be a suggested, but not necessarily mandatory, price list; management assistance; or operating techniques recommended by the franchisor.[72] This evidence is stronger when the franchisee actually follows the suggestions.[73]

Effects of Franchise Law

The following hypothetical situations demonstrate how franchise law can affect a health-care-oriented joint venture.

Medical Pavilion Lease or Licensing Arrangement

A nationally based health care services conglomerate, Health Care Management, Inc. (HCM), which provides varied health care management services on a national scale, wants to participate in a joint venture with Memorial Hospital to establish the medical pavilion described as a joint venture example in appendix F. The pavilion will be located in a state governed by franchise disclosure laws. A variety of health care practitioners will have satellite offices or ambulatory clinics in the medical pavilion. The pavilion will be called the HCM Total Health Care Center (the Center). A clinical laboratory (LabCo) will rent space in the pavilion, under a combined lease-licensing agreement.

LabCo will participate on a cooperative basis with HCM in advertising health-care-oriented services available in the Center. Under its lease, LabCo will pay HCM a fixed minimum rent plus a percentage of gross fees. LabCo will be required in the agreement to maintain certain levels of insurance, to obtain all necessary licenses, and to perform laboratory work consistent with the highest standards of the profession. LabCo's service forms, which will accompany all test results and other correspondence sent to referring physicians, will identify LabCo as operating in the Center under a license from HCM. The HCM name, followed with its logo, will appear on this notice.

The parties are concerned about whether their agreement will have to be registered as a franchise. If the Center is located in any state that identifies a franchise as having a centralized marketing plan, the relationship between LabCo and HCM might be classified as such because HCM has placed certain requirements on LabCo with respect to its business operations. LabCo has agreed to maintain insurance, conduct its business in conformity with the highest standards of the profession, and maintain certain licenses. This agreement might be viewed as a marketing plan prescribed by HCM. LabCo's business is associated with HCM's name through the joint advertising of services offered in the Center, by LabCo's presence in the pavilion, and by LabCo's notice to referring physicians that it is licensed by HCM. These actions might be interpreted as the use of HCM's commercial symbol or trademark. The percentage rent provision, as well as any sharing of advertising costs, might be viewed as a franchise fee.

To avoid regulation by the state as a franchise, the parties should eliminate from their relationship some of the joint cooperation that they have worked into it. The venture would more closely resemble a licensing agreement and look less like a franchise if LabCo did not attempt to associate itself with HCM's name or trademark. In addition, the lease between the parties should contain only those provisions commonly found in percentage leases, that is, leases that provide for a basic minimum rent and also entitle the landlord to a certain percentage, commonly between 3 and 7 percent, of the tenant's gross sales during the term of the lease. Aside from requiring the tenant to stay open for business a certain length of time each day and to do a certain minimal amount of advertising for its business, the percentage lease permits the tenant to conduct its business operations independently of the landlord. Through its lease with LabCo, HCM should not attempt to interfere with LabCo's marketing efforts.

For the venture to resemble a franchise, it should contain all the elements of one. By eliminating any one or all of the elements, the transaction will less likely be regulated as a franchise.

Phased Laboratory Joint Venture

The phased reference laboratory joint venture, described in appendix E, also raises possible franchising questions. In that example, the regional reference laboratory joint venture, Reference Lab, licenses local laboratories to provide laboratory services. To preserve its good reputation, Reference Lab maintains a certain quality control over services rendered by the local laboratories. It also reviews any advertising by the local laboratory in trade publications. Reference Lab encourages the licensees to exchange marketing ideas as well as results of research by staff members. As part of its licensing policy, Reference Lab offers local laboratories advice and information concerning new developments in the field. Typically, its licensees pay Reference Lab royalties and also a percentage of their fees for services. The purpose of this percentage is to pay for the development and marketing of new laboratory test procedures. In addition, the local laboratories contribute toward Reference Lab's national advertising program, which is administered by Reference Lab in cooperation with its licensees.

The venture described here is a typical licensing-royalty agreement. However, under both the central marketing plan and the community of interest requirements of the statutes in various states, it could be classified as a franchise and required to register as such. The continuing interest that both licensor and licensee have in maintaining the public image of Reference Lab and Reference Lab's interest in quality control could be evidence of a community of interest. The royalty can be seen as a franchise fee. Again, to escape regulation as a franchise, the parties should keep as much distance between themselves in their advertising and marketing efforts as possible and keep joint cooperation in the business to a minimum.

Avoiding Franchise Law

In most health care joint ventures, a licensing-royalty approach is preferable to an outright franchise agreement because of the desirability of avoiding burdensome registration requirements. However, as the examples described in the preceding section have illustrated, such a licensing agreement could be construed as a franchise agreement under various state statutes, especially if the licensor has established any controls over the licensee as to, for example, the quality of work performed, licenses to be obtained, or advertising policies.

Any licensing agreement entered into as part of a joint venture transaction should leave the licensee independent in marketing and developing the business. The parties should also probably avoid using a joint advertising program. Furthermore, the licensee should avoid using the licensor's logo for any purpose or otherwise associating itself with the licensor's commercial symbol. If care is taken in structuring the agreement, the transaction will probably not be subject to the various franchise disclosure laws.

Notes

1. *See, e.g.,* CAL. CORP. CODE § 202 (West). California allows the following prescribed statement with respect to the corporation's purpose: "The purpose of the corporation is to engage in any lawful act or activity for which a corporation may be organized under the General Corporation Law of California other than the banking business, the trust company business or the practice of a profession permitted to be incorporated by the California Corporations Code."

2. *See, e.g.,* CAL. CORP. CODE §§ 400 *et seq.* (West).

3. *See, e.g.,* CAL. CORP. CODE §§ 500 *et seq.* (West).

4. *See, e.g.,* CAL. CORP. CODE §§ 600 *et seq.,* §§ 700 *et seq.* (West).

5. *See, e.g.,* CAL. CORP. CODE §§ 1600 *et seq.* (West).

6. *See, e.g.,* CAL. CORP. CODE §§ 300 *et seq.* (West).

7. *See, e.g.,* CAL. CORP. CODE §§ 312 *et seq.* (West).

8. *See, e.g.,* CAL. CORP. CODE § 13401 (West).

9. CAL. CORP. CODE § 13401.5 (West).

10. *See, e.g.,* CAL. CORP. CODE § 13403 (West).

11. *See, e.g.,* CAL. CORP. CODE § 13404 (West).

12. CAL. CORP. CODE § 13405 (West).

13. *See, e.g.,* CAL. CORP. CODE §§ 5000 *et seq.* (West); NEV. REV. STAT. §§ 81.290 *et seq.*

14. *See, e.g.,* CAL. CORP. CODE §§ 5210 *et seq.* (West).

15. *See, e.g.,* CAL. CORP. CODE §§ 5310 *et seq.* (West).

16. CAL. CORP. CODE § 5410 (West).

17. *See* California Form CT-3. This periodic report to the California attorney general must be filed annually.

18. *See, e.g.,* CAL. CORP. CODE § 5913 (West) (requires that a not-for-profit corporation must give the state's attorney general 20 days' notice prior to dispersing substantially all of the corporation's assets).

19. *See, e.g.,* CAL. CORP. CODE §§ 15001-15045 (West).

20. *See, e.g.,* CAL. CORP. CODE § 15006 (West).

21. CAL. CORP. CODE § 15009 (West).

22. *See, e.g.,* CAL. CORP. CODE § 15008 (West).

23. *See, e.g.,* CAL. CORP. CODE §§ 15018 *et seq.* (West).

24. *See, e.g.,* CAL. CORP. CODE § 15502 (West).

25. CAL. CORP. CODE § 15509 (West).

26. CAL. CORP. CODE § 15507 (West).

27. SEC v. W. J. Howey Co., 328 U.S. 293, 300 (1946).

28. *See, e.g.,* SEC v. Murphy, 626 F.2d 633 (9th Cir. 1980).

29. Underhill v. Royal, 769 F.2d 1426 (9th Cir. 1985).

30. New York Stock Exch. v. Sloan, 394 F.Supp. 1303 (S.D.N.Y. 1975); Williamson v. Tucker, 645 F.2d 404 (5th Cir. 1981).

31. Odom v. Slavik, 703 F.2d 212 (6th Cir. 1983).

32. Goodwin v. Elkins & Co., 558 F.Supp. 1375 (E.D. Pa. 1983).

33. Wagner v. Bear, [1982-83] FED. SEC. L. REP. (CCH) ¶99,032 (N.D. Ill. 1982).

34. Morrison v. Pelican Land Dev., [1982] FED. SEC. L. REP. (CCH) ¶98,863 (N.D. Ill. 1982). *See* Williamson v. Tucker, 645 F.2d 404, 422 (5th Cir. 1981). There is an accord with this principle under California Securities Law. CAL. CORP. CODE § 25130 (West). Generally, the legal right of the general partner directly to exercise control over the operations of the partnership is considered to negate the existence of a security. Moulin v. Der Zakarian, 191 Cal. App. 2d 184, 12 Cal. Rptr. 572 (1961). However, if the persons who are given the legal status of general partners are nevertheless merely passive investors and the direction and control of the partnership is in the hands of only one or a few partners, the interests of the other partners may be securities under the statute. Goldberg v. Paramount Oil Co., 143 Cal. App. 2d 215, 300 P.2d 329 (1956).

35. Securities Act of 1933, 15 U.S.C. §§ 77a-77aa.

36. Section 12 of the Securities Act of 1933, 15 U.S.C. § 77l.

37. Section 24 of the Securities Act of 1933, 15 U.S.C. § 77l.

38. *See* Henderson v. Hayden Stone, 461 F.2d 1069 (5th Cir. 1972).

39. Section 3(a)(11) of the Securities Act, 15 U.S.C. § 77c(a)(11); SEC Rule 147, 17 C.F.R. § 230.147. The issuer must derive 80 percent of consolidated gross revenue from that state, have at least 80 percent of its consolidated assets there, and use at least 80 percent of the proceeds from the offering in that state.

40. *See* Securities Act of 1933, 15 U.S.C. §§ 77a *et seq.*; Regulation D, Rules 501-506.

41. Section 4(2) of the Securities Act of 1933, 15 U.S.C. § 77d(2).

42. SEC Rule 146, 17 C.F.R. § 230.146. *See* Doran v. Petroleum Management Corp., 545 F.2d 893 (5th Cir. 1977) (this rule is not the exclusive means of qualifying as a private offering). *See* SEC Release No. 4552 (Nov. 6, 1962); SEC v. Ralston Purina Co., 346 U.S. 119 (1953); Hill York Corp. v. American Int'l Franchises, 448 F.2d 680 (5th Cir. 1971); SEC v. Continental Tobacco Co., 463 F.2d 137 (5th Cir. 1972).

43. SEC Regulation D, 17 C.F.R. §§ 230.501-230.506.

44. These organizations are defined as exempt from federal taxation under I.R.C. § 501(c)(3) with assets of more than $5 million. Accredited investors can also be the issuer's directors, executive officers, and general partners. Rule 501(a), 17 C.F.R. § 230.504.

45. Rule 506(b)(2)(ii), 17 C.F.R. § 230.506(b)(2)(ii).

46. For purposes of Rules 405 and 506, corporations, partnerships, or other organizations may be counted as a single investor as long as the entity has not been organized for the specific purpose of acquiring the security. Rule 506, 17 C.F.R. § 230.506.

47. *See, e.g.,* CAL. CORP. CODE § 25130 (West) (necessity of qualification of security or exemption of security or transaction); Pennsylvania Securities Act § 201, 70 PA. CONS. STAT. ANN. § 1-201 (Purdon).

48. *See, e.g.,* People v. Graham, 163 Cal. App. 3d 1159, 210 Cal. Rptr. 318 (1975), *citing* the *Howey* decision, *supra* note 27.

49. Silver Hills Country Club v. Sabieski, 55 Cal. 2d 811, 13 Cal. Rptr. 186 (1961) (involving a limited partnership).

50. People v. Graham, 163 Cal. App. 3d 1159, 210 Cal. Rptr. 318 (1985). Goldberg v. Paramount Oil Co., 143 Cal. App. 2d 215, 300 P.2d 329 (1956), is in accord with this principle: A general partnership interest may be a security under state statute if those general partners are merely passive investors.

51. Alabama, Guam, Idaho, Montana, New Jersey, North Dakota, Oregon, Puerto Rico, West Virginia, and Wisconsin exempt transactions with 10 offerees or less in any 12-month period from securities registration. *See, e.g.,* WISC. STAT. ANN. § 551.23(11) (amended 1983, effective 1984); Rule 2.02(5), [1985] BLUE SKY L. REP. (CCH) ¶64,839.

52. Some states allow up to 35 purchasers: Examples are California, Florida, Georgia, Illinois, Iowa, Louisiana, Michigan, Mississippi, and Oklahoma. *See, e.g.,* CAL. CORP. CODE § 25102(f) (West), which has a limited offering exemption—not more than 35 persons; all purchasers have a preexisting relationship with the offeror, partners, or officers or could be reasonably assumed to have the capacity to protect their own interests in connection with the transaction; purchasers must be purchasing for their own accounts; and the offer and sale must not be accomplished by the publication of any advertisement.

53. *E.g.,* Missouri allows no more than 15 transactions during any 12-month period. MO. ANN. STAT. § 409.402(b)(10) (Vernon 1967, amended 1978).

54. Nebraska, New Hampshire, New Mexico, Oregon, Rhode Island, Utah, Vermont, and Washington. In New Mexico, this is the only exemption available for limited transactions. *See,* N.M. STAT. ANN. § 58-13-30(A) (1953, amended 1983) (refers to "any nonissuer isolated transaction").

55. The following states and territories do not have such a filing requirement: District of Columbia, Florida, Guam, Hawaii, Montana, Nevada, New Jersey, New Mexico, New York, Puerto Rico, Rhode Island, South Carolina, Tennessee, Virginia, West Virginia, and Wyoming.

56. *See generally,* MASS. GEN. LAWS ANN. ch.110A, § 402(b)(9).

57. Alabama, Alaska, Arizona, Arkansas, Connecticut, Georgia, Idaho, Kentucky, Louisiana, Maine, Michigan, Minnesota, Mississippi, New Hampshire, North Carolina, North Dakota, Oklahoma, Oregon, Pennsylvania, South Dakota, Texas, Vermont, and Washington have such a filing requirement. *See, e.g.,* ALASKA STAT. § 8-6-11(a)(9) (1959, amended 1979); ARK. STAT. ANN. § 67-1248(b)(9); MISS. CODE ANN. § 75-71-203(10) (1981).

58. *See* Section 10(b) of the Securities and Exchange Act of 1934 (15 U.S.C. § 78j) and Securities and Exchange Commission Rule 10b-5; 17 C.F.R. § 240.10b-5. Rule 10b-5 provides:
> It shall be unlawful for any person, directly or indirectly, by the use of any means or instrumentality of interstate commerce, or of the mails or of any facility of any national securities exchange,
> (a) To employ any device, scheme, or artifice to defraud,
> (b) To make any untrue statement of a material fact or to omit to state a material fact necessary in order to make the statements made, in the light of the circumstances under which they were made, not misleading, or
> (c) To engage in any act, practice, or course of business which operates or would operate as a fraud or deceit upon any person,
> in connection with the purchase or sale of any security.

59. *See Financing Woes Will Change Business,* MODERN HEALTHCARE, Jan. 4, 1985, at 112. In this article, one party who has studied ambulatory care centers from an investment point of view believes that the ambulatory health care industry will increasingly be regionalized with inroads by national for-profit health care conglomerates. "Small community providers probably won't have bargaining clout with major health care purchasers," he noted.

60. *See* 16 C.F.R. § 436.1, which requires franchisors to provide full disclosure of the terms of the franchise agreement, detailed financial statements of the franchisor, and business histories of the franchisor's owners and management.

61. *See* Federal Trade Commission Act, 15 U.S.C. §§ 41 *et seq.* 15 U.S.C. § 45 deals specifically with enforcement.

62. *See* Fern, *The Overbroad Scope of Franchise Regulation: A Definitional Dilemma,* 34 BUS. LAW. 1387, 1390 (1979).

63. *See generally* state franchise disclosure laws cited *infra* notes 66 & 67.

Chapter 3. Corporate, Securities, and Franchise Law

Notes

64. Apparently, in Michigan until 1985, it was extremely burdensome to register a franchise, sometimes requiring more than six months. See Carlson, *Michigan Seeks Better Image with a New Franchise Law,* Wall St. J., Mar. 26, 1985, at 39, col. 1.

65. *See* Fern, *supra* note 62.

66. *See, e.g.,* California Franchise Investment Act, Cal. Corp. Code §§ 31000 *et seq.;* § 31005 (West). *See also* Conn. Gen. Stat. §§ 42-133e *et seq.* (1977); Illinois Franchise Disclosure Act, Ill. Ann. Stat. ch. 121½ §§ 701 *et seq.* (Smith-Hurd 1974); Ind. Code Ann. §§ 23-2-2.5-1 *et seq.* (Burns 1975); Mich. Comp. Laws §§ 445.1501 *et seq.* (1977); N.D. Cent. Code §§ 51-19-01 *et seq.* (1975); Or. Rev. Stat. §§ 650.005 *et seq.* (1980); R.I. Gen. Laws §§ 19-28-1 *et seq.* (1973); Va. Code §§ 13.1-557 *et seq.* (1978); Wis. Stat. Ann. §§ 553.01 *et seq.* (1984).

67. *See, e.g.,* Minnesota Franchise Investment Law, Minn. Stat. Ann. § 80C.01 (1984); Haw. Rev. Stat. § 482E-2 (1983); N.J. Stat. Ann. § 56:10-3 (West 1964); S.D. Compiled Laws Ann. § 37-5A-1 (1977).

68. *See, e.g.,* Cal. Comm'r Corp. Op. No. 73/20F (1973).

69. *See, e.g.,* Cal. Corp. Code § 31011 (West 1970).

70. *See* Fern, *supra* note 62, at 1392, *citing* Cal. Dept. of Corp. Guidelines for Determining Whether an Agreement Constitutes a "Franchise." Del. No. 3-F (rev.) at 12 (Feb. 21, 1974).

71. *See, e.g.,* Shell Oil Company v. Marinello, 63 N.J. 402, 307 A.2d 598 (1973), *cert. denied* 415 U.S. 920 (1974). *See also* Wash. Rev. Code Ann. § 19.100.010 (2) (1976).

72. *See* Fern, *supra* note 62, at 1391. *See, e.g.,* Cal. Comm'r Corp. Op. No. 72/11F (1972); Cal. Comm'r Corp. Op. No. 73/5F (1973); Cal. Comm'r Corp. Op. No. 73/17F (1973), Cal. Comm'r Corp. Op. No. 73/25F (1973).

73. *See, e.g.,* Cal. Comm'r Corp. Op. No. 73/40F (1973).

Chapter 4 Tax Considerations

Tax Relationship between Type of Project and Legal Structure
    Tax Consequences of the Corporate Structure
    Tax Consequences of the Partnership Form
    Tax Consequences of the Limited Partnership Structure
Acquiring Tax-Exempt Status for the Joint Venture
Taxability of Income
Tax Considerations for Tax-Exempt Participants
    Loss of Tax-Exempt Status
        General Inurement Problems
        Inducements as an Inurement Problem
    Unrelated Business Income
Legal Considerations for Taxable Venture Participants
    Tax-Exempt Use Property Restrictions
        Equipment Acquisitions
        Real Estate Leasing
    Noncorporate Lessor Rules
    At-Risk Limits
        Deductions Limited to Amount at Risk
        Exclusion of Certain Nonrecourse Financing with Respect to ITC
    Pass-Through of ITC

No economic joint venture should be formed without considering the tax consequences for the individual participants as well as for the venture itself. Ventures undertaken without fully considering tax implications may have unanticipated consequences, especially in the aftermath of the tax reform proposals considered by Congress in 1985 and 1986. Whichever of these proposals, if any, is ultimately enacted and signed into law may substantially alter potential tax benefits described in this chapter. Before planning any joint venture, participants should consult with legal counsel about the current status of the tax law.[1]

Although the proposed tax changes will reduce planning opportunities, depending on when and the extent to which these changes are implemented, projects can still be structured to provide tax benefits to investors in appropriate cases. To realize potential tax benefits for the participants, those who select the structure of a joint venture should consider the following questions in terms of potential tax consequences:

- What type of project is proposed (for example, an acquisition of equipment or a real estate transaction or a service-oriented project)?
- What type of legal entity (corporation or partnership) provides the best format for the venture?
- Will the new entity be tax-exempt or taxable?
- What is the tax status of the participants? Will a tax-exempt entity, such as a not-for-profit hospital, be participating?
- What role will various participants play in the operation of the venture?

Tax Relationship between Type of Project and Legal Structure

There may be compelling tax reasons for structuring a transaction as a corporation or a partnership. For instance, a major consideration in choosing a legal structure is whether the enterprise is expected to be successful from the outset or whether it is expected to suffer losses in the first years of operation. If a capital-intensive project is envisioned, a partnership may be the appropriate entity because the availability of an investment tax credit (ITC) and a depreciation deduction may generate losses in the early years of operation to offset income that the partners receive from other sources.

On the other hand, certain ventures may expect to generate profits from the outset of operations. In such instances, other business considerations, such as control, limited liability, centralized management, and transferability of interests, may make the corporate form a more appropriate structure than a partnership. Such factors often recommend a corporate structure for a venture offering medical services, such as a clinical laboratory, a health maintenance organization (HMO), or an ambulatory surgical center.

Tax Consequences of the Corporate Structure

If the joint venture participants think that their project will be profitable within its early years of operation, they may want those profits taxed at what may be lower corporate rates. When considering the corporate form for a venture that expects early profits, however, participants should be aware that the income of business corporations is generally subject to double taxation. Thus, the business profits are taxed at the corporate level and then again when distributed as dividends to shareholders.[2] However, a not-for-profit shareholder, such as a hospital, is normally exempted from tax on dividend distributions from the venture enterprise, unless it borrowed money to purchase the stock.[3]

Tax Consequences of the Partnership Form

A partnership is usually a good structure for investment purposes, such as a real estate investment or an equipment acquisition, because the tax benefits associated with such transactions may then be passed through to the partners. For example, tax credits, such as a rehabilitation tax credit[4] or ITC, may be available.[5] Although tax credits are irrelevant to a tax-exempt partner, such as a hospital, they are of particular interest to taxable partners, such as physicians. Part of the tax credit available to the partnership may be allocated to taxable partners on the basis of their interest in the partnership. Tax credits such as these can provide an impetus to outside investors to enter into such joint ventures.

Another potential tax benefit available to partners in a partnership in some instances is the accelerated cost recovery system (ACRS), which allows deductions for accelerated depreciation. In a real estate transaction, for instance, an accelerated rate of depreciation is available over a period that is less than the actual useful life of the building.[6] Outside investors often find ACRS deductions attractive because they may exceed income from the project and can be used by the investors to offset income from other sources. Such a use of ACRS can therefore increase the after-tax yield from the investment.

A partnership may also be a useful structure in a venture in which all of the participants are tax-exempt entities, as was the case in the magnetic resonance imaging (MRI) facility joint venture discussed in appendix B. In such a partnership, the income from the enterprise that was passed through to the tax-exempt partners would probably be tax-free to them. The tax code provides that the tax status of an item of income realized by a partner is determined as if the partner had been conducting the business as an individual.[7] Income earned by a partnership of tax-exempt partners is therefore treated as if it were earned directly by those partners. If such income is substantially related to their tax-exempt purpose, it is tax-free. The IRS generally appears to take a lenient position toward the activities of tax-exempt hospitals as long as these activities further the purpose of providing health care in the community.[8] In a recent private letter ruling, the IRS determined that a venture between three tax-exempt hospitals to provide management services to an MRI joint venture was in furtherance of the tax-exempt purposes of the hospitals and that the income earned by those hospitals from the joint venture was not taxable.[9]

Tax Consequences of the Limited Partnership Structure

A limited partnership affords tax benefits to limited partners that are similar to those that are available to partners in a general partnership (see previous head). These benefits are in proportion to the limited partner's percentage equity investment in the business. In some instances, however, the tax law may require registration with the IRS of an interest in a medical joint venture that is structured as a limited partnership because the limited partnership falls within the statutory definition of a *tax shelter*.[10] The IRS defines a tax shelter as a business venture established principally for the purpose of generating losses and thereby allowing substantial tax write-offs for its members. A tax shelter must be registered if it contains the following elements:

- It represents an investment reasonably anticipated to have a ratio of tax benefits to investments of greater than 2 to 1 for any of its first five years.
- It is a substantial investment, which means that the total interests offered exceed $250,000 or that five or more investors are expected to be involved.
- It is required to be registered under or is sold under an exemption from federal or any state securities laws.

Because of the expansiveness of this definition, many joint venture enterprises that generate no losses, and hence are not generally considered tax shelters, are still required to register as such. Many health care joint ventures, such as an MRI facility, have at least five investors and a total investment of more than $250,000. In addition, an enterprise may have a tax benefit ratio greater than 2 to 1 in any of its first five years because of the way in which that ratio is calculated. In computing the amount of tax benefits (deductions and credits), the total amount of gross deductions (without allowing for income) for that year and all prior years, plus 200 percent of any credits potentially available, is divided by the cash investment in the enterprise.[11]

For example, if the MRI facility discussed in appendix B had been structured as a limited partnership, it would have had to register as a tax shelter given the following facts. Ten limited partners each contribute $50,000 to the partnership to cover the expense of equipment acquisition. In each of the first three years, the facility earns a gross income exceeding $2 million. Total deductible expenses, including rent and depreciation, amount to $1,500,000 after three years of operation. Each partner's share of those expenses is $150,000. Because the cash investment of any one partner was only $50,000, the tax shelter ratio is 3 to 1, and the enterprise must register with the IRS even though the enterprise earned a net profit in each of its first three years of operation.

Acquiring Tax-Exempt Status for the Joint Venture

In certain instances, the parties may want the venture enterprise to be tax-exempt for several valid reasons. The major one, of course, is that income earned by it in providing health care is exempt from federal and state income taxation. Other reasons include the ability to obtain charitable donations and to pay for projects by means of tax-exempt financing.

To qualify for a tax exemption, the joint venture entity must meet the requirements of the Internal Revenue Code (I.R.C.) Section 501(c)(3): the joint venture entity must be "organized and operated *exclusively* for religious, charitable, scientific...or educational purposes...no part of the net earnings of which inures to the benefit of any private shareholder or individual."[12] In determining whether the facility is entitled to a tax exemption, the IRS asks whether it is devoted exclusively to charitable or educational purposes. The IRS has developed several guidelines in this area. Generally, it considers the promotion of health to be a charitable purpose.[13]

However, the promotion of health alone may not be sufficient. For example, if the facility is intended largely to serve the private interests of a limited group, then it would probably not qualify for a tax exemption.[14] For instance, if the medical facility exclusively treats the private or insured patients of its physician owners, it could well be treated as a taxable entity. The IRS also denies an exemption if the entity offers virtually no emergency care to the community as a whole, if its medical staff is limited to a small group of practitioners, or if its owners receive substantial fees from the facility for a minimal number of services.[15]

Because of these restrictions, even health care enterprises may have difficulty in qualifying for a tax exemption. For example, based on these guidelines, the IRS has attempted to deny tax-exempt status to prepaid health plans, such as health maintenance organizations (HMOs), because they serve the private interests of their members.[16] To qualify for an exemption, the HMO must serve a sufficiently broad segment of the community. It should also have an open medical staff, which means it must offer medical privileges to a number of physicians in the community consistent with the size and nature of its facilities. It must also supply emergency services to the community, and its governing board must be dedicated to supporting public purposes.[17]

Other criteria used by the IRS in deciding whether a medical facility should be allowed a tax exemption include whether care of the indigent or emergency care is available, whether medical education and training are provided, or whether legitimate medical research activities are conducted at the facility.[18] If a substantial part of the facility's activities fall within these guidelines, the IRS will decide that these activities further the tax-exempt purpose of health care delivery and the facility will probably be allowed a tax exemption.[19]

Despite the advantages of acquiring tax-exempt status, including the ability to obtain charitable donations and to issue tax-exempt obligations, certain drawbacks to seeking tax-exempt status should not be discounted. The activities in which the entity may engage are limited to those that further its tax-exempt purposes. Aside from a few exceptions that are noted in the next section, any income from trade or business activities conducted by the tax-exempt entity that are unrelated to the tax-exempt purpose is taxed. In addition, as will be discussed in greater detail in a later section describing tax consequences of the activities of a tax-exempt joint venture participant, the tax-exempt entity must be careful that its activities provide no significant benefit to private parties.

A good illustration of the benefits and pitfalls attending the decision to obtain tax-exempt status for a joint venture is the example of the joint venture reference laboratory in appendix E. This laboratory was initially a part of the tax-exempt hospital's pathology department and as such was itself tax-exempt. After a corporate reorganization, the laboratory was entitled to tax-exempt status because it operated primarily as a laboratory-research center servicing patients of the hospital and also because it was a division of Outpatient Services Corporation (Outpatient Services), a not-for-profit, tax-exempt corporation that provided a variety of other tax-exempt outpatient health services, such as hospice, home care, wellness, and sports medicine. However, as the facility was used more and more to generate profits for its taxable owners, its charitable and research purposes became less important to the business. At that time, a substantial amount of income from the enterprise was treated as unrelated business income (see discussion in the next section). Because a large percentage of the facility's income was from sources unrelated to the entity's tax-exempt purposes, the entity feared the loss of its tax-exempt status. The participants therefore elected to make the reference laboratory a for-profit taxable enterprise. If they had attempted to continue operations in a tax-exempt form, the entire operation would have fallen under IRS scrutiny at the potential risk to the tax-exempt participants of the loss of their own tax exemption.[20]

Taxability of Income

The fact that an entity is awarded tax-exempt status does not automatically entitle it to a tax exemption for all of its income. The treatment that the IRS gives to income from a facility such as a joint venture reference laboratory or an MRI facility, whether or not it is tax-exempt, depends on the type of services offered and to whom such services are offered. The income of a tax-exempt entity is generally exempt from taxes unless that income is unrelated to the tax-exempt purposes of the entity. *Unrelated business taxable income* is the gross income earned by a tax-exempt entity from an unrelated trade or business activity regularly carried on by it. An activity is unrelated if it does not "contribute importantly" to the accomplishment of the organization's tax-exempt purpose.[21] The concept of unrelated business income is discussed more fully later in this chapter.[22]

If the joint venture is structured so that the enterprise is primarily owned or controlled by one or a partnership of several tax-exempt hospitals, with a hospital having primary control over day-to-day operations, the venture will probably not pay taxes on income earned from providing services to hospital patients.[23] In other words, the IRS would view income from fees charged by the facility to be derived in the furtherance of the tax-exempt parent's charitable purposes and treat it accordingly for tax purposes. The services performed by the facility, such as laboratory tests or diagnostic services, are deemed to be substantially related to the hospital's tax-exempt function of providing health care in the community.[24]

The situation is different when the joint venture is owned and controlled by both taxable and tax-exempt parents or when tax-exempt entities form a *subsidiary corporation*, as opposed to a partnership of solely tax-exempt partners, to operate the enterprise. Such a subsidiary corporation is only entitled to tax-exempt status if it qualifies under Section 501(c)(3), as discussed earlier in this chapter,[25] or if it meets the requirements of Section 501(e) by offering limited services, such as billing, laboratory, or purchasing services, solely to two or more tax-exempt hospitals.[26]

Whether or not the entity is a partnership of tax-exempt hospitals or a subsidiary corporation that is tax-exempt, income earned by it is taxable unless that income is derived from services performed for or on behalf of its inpatients or outpatients, is derived from persons receiving emergency or indigent care from it, or is otherwise derived from the provision of health care in the community. Income from commercial services rendered by the entity is probably taxable if it is received on a regular basis and if it is unrelated to the organization's tax-exempt purpose.[27]

This general rule has limited exceptions. If the nonpatients served by a tax-exempt facility are part of a limited group, such as hospital or facility employees or staff members, then under a so-called *convenience rule* the income from fees generated by these services may nevertheless be tax-exempt.[28] This rule allows a tax exemption for income earned for the convenience of a tax-exempt organization's "members," such as patients, students, staff, or any group of persons limited in size who are closely associated with the entity and are necessary to the achievement of the organization's purposes.[29]

A related exception is the so-called *casual sales exception*. The income from a business that is not regularly carried on by the tax-exempt entity is not taxable even if it is unrelated to the entity's charitable purpose. For instance, income derived from laboratory tests performed mainly for hospital patients and occasionally for a limited number of other persons can escape taxation if the service is rendered infrequently and to only a few nonpatients.[30] Under special circumstances, such as when the laboratory or MRI facility is the only one in the area that has the equipment and staff to perform certain services, the performance of those services by a tax-exempt facility for anyone in the area is considered related to the entity's charitable mission for tax purposes.[31]

Tax Considerations for Tax-Exempt Participants

Tax-exempt participants need to consider not only the potential tax consequences for the business enterprises that are created by means of the joint venture, but also the impact on their own tax status caused by their participation in the venture. In that respect, they should ask themselves two basic questions before entering into a joint venture transaction:

- Does the participant risk losing its tax-exempt status?
- Could any unrelated business income earned by the tax-exempt participant as a result of its participation in the joint venture be treated as taxable income?

Loss of Tax-Exempt Status

A hospital's activities in a joint venture may lead to the loss of its tax-exempt status if its joint venture business activities are not beneficial or necessary to the tax-exempt purposes of the hospital and if those activities constitute "more than an insubstantial part" of its total activities, that is, if the hospital becomes overly involved in those joint venture activities.[32] A tax-exempt entity may pursue a trade or business to further its tax-exempt purposes, such as providing health care, but that trade or business may not be its primary focus.

To avoid the risk of losing its tax-exempt status, a hospital taking part in a joint venture must be sure that, for the most part, its activities further its charitable purpose[33] and that the business-oriented activities of the venture remain an insignificant part of its total operations. In other words, those activities must remain incidental to the hospital's main purpose of providing health care. For instance, the hospital can probably offer management services to a health care provider in which it holds an interest without threatening its own tax-exempt status, because those services would be viewed as part of the hospital's overall purpose of providing diagnostic or other health care services to its patients.[34]

On the other hand, income from a hospital's activities as a service bureau, which offers advice and hospital management consulting services to various health care providers including for-profit hospitals and outpatient clinics in which the hospital holds no significant interest, may well be subject to taxation. If these activities become its main business, the hospital can lose its tax-exempt status.

A joint venture can be structured to minimize the risk to a hospital participant of the loss of its tax-exempt status. For instance, a hospital's tax-exempt status could be revoked if it provides hospital management and support services to nonrelated taxable entities and such services constitute a substantial part of its total activities. However, if these commercial activities were to be undertaken by a taxable *subsidiary* of the hospital, even a wholly owned taxable subsidiary, the risks to the hospital's tax-exempt status would be significantly reduced. In such an instance, the IRS asks whether the subsidiary has a bona fide distinct business function or whether it is merely an instrument of the parent and has no business function other than to act for the parent in the interests of the parent. In the latter case, the separate corporate structure is disregarded. However, if the separate entity performing the various nonexempt hospital management activities is sufficiently segregated from the hospital, if the hospital does not participate in its day-to-day operations, and if any transactions between it and the hospital are conducted on an arm's-length basis, the hospital's role with respect to the subsidiary would not jeopardize its own tax-exempt status.[35]

General Inurement Problems

A tax-exempt joint venture participant can also lose its tax-exempt status if its activities lead to *private inurement*, the conferring of significant benefits on private parties. In structuring the joint venture, the participants have to take into account the statutory mandate that the tax-exempt hospital's activities must serve a public rather than a private purpose and that "no part of [its] net earnings [can] inure to the benefit of any private shareholder or individual," that is, anyone "having a personal and private interest in the activities of the organization."[36] In all respects, the hospital should always receive equal value for whatever it puts into the enterprise. Problems arise particularly when outside investors appear to have received an additional benefit, such as a below-market interest loan from the hospital, a lease at below-market rental value, or inflated or otherwise unreasonable compensation.

Partnerships between tax-exempt entities and outside taxable investors can cause some concern because of the pass-through nature of the entity. In the past, the IRS was likely to closely scrutinize the role of a tax-exempt party as a general partner in a partnership with taxable partners for possible inurement problems because of the very fact of that partnership. The IRS and the tax courts have since tempered this approach.[37] Such arrangements are now approved on a case-by-case basis. Consequently, the parties may be generally uncertain whether a proposed joint venture composed of a partnership between tax-exempt and taxable partners has been structured to adequately ensure that individual participants do not benefit unduly from the venture in comparison with overall public benefit.

The main question to be asked is whether the tax-exempt general partner is adequately insulated from a potential conflict of interest between its tax-exempt purposes and its *fiduciary duty* to the private investors, that is, its duty to act always in the best interests of those investors and to maximize profits. Criteria that the IRS has applied to some proposed transactions include:[38]

- Whether the tax-exempt entity is the sole general partner
- What the tax-exempt entity contributes to partnership capital (the extent of the contribution)
- Whether the main goal of the venture is to provide a medical service or to make a profit for private investors
- Whether the venture would have been possible without private capital

To avoid potential inurement problems for the tax-exempt general partner, a proposed partnership agreement should be drafted with these criteria in mind. The agreement may include, among other things:[39]

- Providing for more than one general partner
- Having the provision of high-quality medical care as an expressed goal of the partnership
- Placing a ceiling on potential earnings to taxable partners, thereby avoiding an excess-compensation situation
- Avoiding special allocations of income and deductions to taxable partners

When the best structure for a joint venture is a partnership and there is a risk of inurement, a sound approach may be to insulate the hospital by creating a for-profit taxable subsidiary to act as general partner in place of the hospital. A wholly owned subsidiary of a tax-exempt hospital can act as general partner in a partnership whose purposes are unrelated to the hospital's charitable purpose without adverse consequences to the hospital's tax status if the subsidiary is independent of the hospital. The IRS will disregard the existence of the subsidiary only if that subsidiary is no more than "an arm, agent or integral part of the" hospital and the hospital's own role as general partner would have led to problems of inurement or unrelated business income.[40]

If a subsidiary is used, the parties should ensure that the hospital and the subsidiary are segregated into separate entities and that the hospital does not participate in the day-to-day management of the subsidiary or the partnership. The mere fact that private interests may benefit from an activity in which a tax-exempt organization is involved does not necessarily lead to inurement problems so long as the main activity of the tax-exempt organization furthers a charitable purpose and the private benefit is incidental, insubstantial, and not unreasonable in comparison with the public benefit that results from the activity.[41]

Inducements as an Inurement Problem

There is a special risk that inurement problems can occur when a tax-exempt participant in a joint venture that includes taxable participants offers some inducement to outside parties to participate in the venture or to a lender in order to obtain financing, such as a guarantee of repayment of a loan to the venture. The IRS examines these situations on a case-by-case basis to determine whether the arrangement allows for more than incidental benefits from the tax-exempt entity to taxable parties. In the case of the loan guarantee, for example, the IRS asks whether the lender is depending primarily on the tax-exempt party for repayment in case of default by the joint venture. If so, private inurement will result.

However, in limited circumstances, these incidental benefits have been allowed. For example, in one instance, the IRS approved the lease of land by a tax-exempt entity to an unrelated partnership and the *subordination* of that lease to the construction and take-out loans. If the borrower failed to pay back those loans, the construction and permanent lender would be entitled to take the land leased to the partnership. To avoid losing its land to pay the debts of the partnership, the hospital would have been obliged to pay back those loans. Nevertheless, the IRS decided in this instance that the loans were necessary to ensure the construction of a medical office building and only served private interests incidentally.[42] In another situation, the IRS approved a hospital's guarantee of financing for an MRI facility because that guarantee was only for a percentage of the amount borrowed for the project, and this percentage corresponded to the hospital's interest in the facility.[43]

If outside interests receive a benefit that is more than incidental and the public interests of the joint venture, and therefore the hospital, are not served by that private benefit, the benefit will not be allowed. For example, a hospital's offer to lease space to physicians for less than a fair market rental in order to lure them into a medical office building joint venture will be scrutinized for potential inurement problems.[44] To avoid these inurement problems and potential loss of tax-exempt status, the joint venture must be structured so that the private purposes of the taxable investors are not served at the expense of the hospital's public purposes. The joint venture should include the following elements:

- Profits and losses are shared by joint venture partners in relation to their investment.
- The joint venture pays no more than reasonable compensation to each partner.
- The facility's major goal is to generally provide services to or to treat patients of the tax-exempt hospital or to otherwise further the hospital's tax-exempt purposes.

If the major motive behind the hospital's involvement in the venture is the provision of medical care and not the profitability of the relationship to outsiders, no inurement problems should arise.[45]

Unrelated Business Income

In a previous section of this chapter, the question of taxability of income to the joint venture was discussed. Although a joint venture may be entitled to tax-exempt status, its income may nevertheless be subject to taxation if that income is unrelated to the tax-exempt purposes of the joint venture. Income of a tax-exempt joint venture participant may also be subject to taxation because of its participation in the venture.

Income from the activities of a tax-exempt joint venture participant must be substantially related to its public or charitable function, aside from its need for financial support, or the income will be taxed as unrelated business income. To avoid unrelated business income tax treatment of a tax-exempt joint venture participant, the parties should structure the joint venture so that the income to the tax-exempt participant from the joint venture falls within one of the following descriptions:

- It is derived from an activity that would achieve tax-exempt purposes if directly conducted by the tax-exempt entity.
- It is excluded from tax because it comes from an investment-type activity.

For instance, if a hospital participates in a taxable joint venture, such as a for-profit ambulatory surgical center, the transaction should be structured so that the hospital's return from the venture is in the form of such passive investment income as interest, dividends from a corporation in which the hospital is a shareholder,[46] or rent from real property rentals. However, if the payer of the rents or interest is controlled by the hospital, such income might be subject to taxation, unless the income earned by the controlled organization would not constitute unrelated business income if earned by the hospital.[47] Moreover, the rental income, or a part of it, would be taxable if the hospital were to lease equipment (personal property) as well as real property to the entity that is operating the center. Income from leases of personal property, unlike the rents from real property, is generally fully taxable unless the equipment and the real property are leased together under one lease and the portion of the rent payment attributable to the equipment does not exceed 50 percent of the total rent under the lease.[48]

Similarly, income could lose its tax-exempt character if so-called *debt-financed rules* apply. These rules require that the hospital include as an item of unrelated business income any income from debt-financed property, which is property that is acquired or improved by means of incurring indebtedness.[49] In other words, if the tax-exempt hospital borrows money to purchase the site for an ambulatory center that it will lease to the operating entity or to pay expenses in connection with renovating that facility, it may have to pay tax on a portion of the rental payments from the operating entity to the hospital.

The greatest risk of having unrelated business income occurs when a tax-exempt hospital participates in an actual business, such as an ambulatory surgical center or a referral laboratory, from which profits are passed to private individuals and over which it has decided to maintain control, either through a subsidiary corporation or as a general partner in a business partnership. In such an instance, the IRS may decide that the business activities are inherently commercial in nature and unrelated to the hospital's charitable purposes. Except for dividends received when there is no acquisition indebtedness, the income from this business activity would be subject to the unrelated business income tax.[50] *Acquisition indebtedness* refers to debt resulting from the borrowing of money to acquire the assets of the business.

Legal Considerations for Taxable Venture Participants

Participation in a joint venture can have tax consequences for taxable parties, especially when the venture has both taxable and tax-exempt owners. Certain joint ventures offer taxable participants, such as physicians, some opportunity to use certain deductions and credits generated by the venture, such as ITC and ACRS, to offset income from other sources.[51] Various tax amendments of recent years, including the tax reform proposals before Congress in 1985 and 1986, limit the use of these benefits, at least for the time being.[52] In addition to uncertainty with respect to future availability of ITC, joint venture participants should be aware of several other obstacles:

- Limits on ITC and ACRS when the property is owned by, leased to, or otherwise used by a tax-exempt entity
- Limitations when the lessor of the property is not a corporation
- Certain at-risk limits that could limit the availability of ITC and ACRS for joint venture participants

Tax-Exempt Use Property Restrictions

If property is owned by, leased to, or otherwise used by a tax-exempt entity, the tax law has placed certain limits on the availability of ITC and ACRS for the taxable participants in the venture. The rules vary depending on whether personal property, such as equipment, or real estate is involved.

Equipment Acquisitions

The tax law denies ITC for equipment owned by or leased to a tax-exempt organization, such as a hospital, unless the property is used predominantly in a taxable unrelated trade or business of the tax-exempt entity.[53] Moreover, any arrangement, including a partnership, that would be more properly characterized as a lease or that otherwise results in a tax-exempt organization obtaining the use of an asset is treated as a lease, thus denying ITC to the taxable investor. As an additional limitation, ITC must be recaptured (that is, the investor must repay the amount of any credit taken) if the equipment becomes tax-exempt use property after having been placed in service.[54] *Tax-exempt use property* is property owned by, leased to, or otherwise used by a tax-exempt entity. However, ITC will be allowed if the lease term, including all renewal options, is for less than six months.

The tax law also generally prevents investors from taking advantage of ACRS for tax-exempt use property.[55] There are, however, two special instances in which ACRS is allowed in the case of a lease of equipment to a tax-exempt organization. First, the depreciation allowance limitations do not apply to a lease of equipment to a tax-exempt organization when the lease term is less than one year, or 30 percent of the property's present class life (up to three years), taking into account all renewal options.[56] Second, there is an exception for leases of certain *high-technology equipment*, as this term is defined in the I.R.C.[57] When high-technology equipment, including high-technology medical equipment (which is deemed to be short-lived by the tax law), is leased to a tax-exempt entity for a term of five years or less, normal ACRS rules apply.[58] For other equipment not deemed to be short-lived, cost recovery can be significantly deferred when a lease to a tax-exempt organization is involved. These restrictions may make certain ventures, such as the purchase of laboratory equipment by physicians to be leased to a hospital, less interesting as investments.[59]

These tax-exempt use restrictions can affect many joint ventures between tax-exempt entities and taxable parties. For instance, these rules would have been triggered if the hospital had chosen to structure the ambulatory surgical center joint venture described in appendix A as a partnership that would operate the center and lease medical equipment from a separate equipment leasing partnership. If the hospital's participation in the operation of the ambulatory surgical center through a partnership with staff physicians constitutes an unrelated trade or business, then all income to the hospital from the operation of the facility is generally taxable,[60] but the partnership can avail itself of ITC or other tax benefits that may be available. However, if the income from the hospital's activities as a general partner in the partnership operating the center is not taxable, then a portion of any property owned by the operating partnership or leased to it would likely be designated as tax-exempt use property because of the tax-exempt use restrictions. Such a designation would result in the loss of ITC, as previously discussed, and would require that such property be depreciated over substantially longer periods than would otherwise be the case.

The tax-exempt use property designation can be avoided with respect to property *owned* by the operating partnership if the hospital is allocated the same share of each item of partnership income, gain, loss, deduction, credit, and basis; and this allocable share remains the same throughout the period of the partnership. If this test is not met, a percentage of all property *owned* by the operating partnership and, regardless of whether this test is met, a percentage of all property *leased* to the operating entity is considered tax-exempt use property. The percentage deemed to be tax-exempt use property is equal to the largest percentage of partnership income or gain that may be allocated to the hospital during the term of the partnership.[61]

One method that has been used extensively in the past to avoid restrictions on ITC and ACRS for equipment acquisitions is the so-called service agreement. In a *service agreement,* a for-profit corporation acquires the equipment, such as a lithotripter, and, instead of leasing this equipment to another party, keeps control of it and uses it to provide services. The corporation then sells these services to purchasers, such as a hospital. If this arrangement is properly structured, the corporation can obtain ITC and ACRS benefits as the owner of the equipment and pass some of the ensuing tax savings to the purchasers of services, including the tax-exempt hospital, in the form of reduced fees for the services provided. If the tax-exempt hospital is a shareholder in the for-profit corporation, it will also receive dividends from it on a tax-free basis. If the same transaction were structured so that the purchaser of the equipment were to lease it to the tax-exempt hospital, no ITC or ACRS would be allowed because of tax-exempt entity leasing rules.

However, the IRS may characterize such a service agreement as a lease to the tax-exempt organization if doing so more properly describes the real substance of the arrangement.[62] To keep an agreement from too closely resembling a lease, joint venture participants who are considering a service contract should take care that:[63]

- The tax-exempt entity is not in physical possession of the property and has no significant control over it.
- The service provider bears all risks of loss from nonperformance under the contract.
- The equipment is used to provide services concurrently to other parties unrelated to the tax-exempt entity.
- The total contract price does not exceed the rental value of the equipment and represents an accurate fee for the service.

If the arrangement is structured with care, it will be deemed a legitimate service contract, and tax benefits, such as ITC, will be allowed to the owner of the property.

Real Estate Leasing

Similar restrictions apply when real estate is owned by or leased to a tax-exempt organization. First, no rehabilitation tax credit is allowed for real estate that is tax-exempt use property.[64] Second, to the extent real estate is tax-exempt use property, it must be depreciated on a straight-line basis over the greater of 40 years or 125 percent of the lease term.[65] Tax-exempt use property in this instance refers to only that *portion* of the real estate that is leased to a tax-exempt entity under a disqualified lease.[66]

A *disqualified lease* is any lease of real estate to a tax-exempt organization if the portion of the property leased to it is more than 35 percent of the entire property, and any one of the following has occurred:[67]

- Part or all of the property is financed by tax-exempt bonds (and the tax-exempt entity participates in the financing).
- The lease has a fixed purchase option involving the tax-exempt entity.
- The lease term exceeds 20 years.
- The use occurs after the transfer by the tax-exempt entity, as in a sale-leaseback.

Leases for less than three years, taking into account all renewals except those at fair market rental at the time of renewal, are exempted from these restrictions. This tax-exempt-use taint is not permanent; if the disqualified use of a building falls below

35 percent, the entire building then qualifies for ACRS depreciation. In any event, only that part of the real estate actually used by the tax-exempt entity is so tainted; the remainder is not subject to these restrictions.

The following fact situation using the ambulatory surgical clinic described in appendix A is an example of how these rules apply. Memorial Hospital agrees to lease to a physician partnership the real estate on which the facility will be located. As part of the transaction, the hospital receives the right to purchase from the partnership at the end of the lease term the real estate and all other improvements then on the land. The hospital's outpatient surgery department is short of space, and so the hospital arranges, as part of the lease terms, to lease from the partnership for a five-year period one of the operating rooms located in the clinic as a site for use by the hospital outpatient surgery department. The leased area is in excess of 35 percent of the total space in the center. This arrangement constitutes a disqualified lease under the tax rules because the tax-exempt hospital has obtained in the lease a fixed purchase option and more than 35 percent of the property is leased to the hospital. The tax rules disallow ACRS for that portion of the property consisting of the operating room because of the hospital's purchase option. If, however, the hospital stops leasing the space in the building or reduces the amount leased to less than 35 percent, the tax-exempt taint would be removed. Moreover, if the hospital were to use the space in the building for some unrelated business, the income from which would be subject to income tax, then normal ACRS rules apply.

Attempts to circumvent these rules by creating a new taxable entity owned by the hospital that would enter into the lease would likely fail. The rules restricting the depreciation of tax-exempt use property are also applicable to property leased to a so-called *successor organization*. The tax law creates a five-year lookback rule which says that an organization may be treated as a tax-exempt organization with respect to any property leased to it if, at any time during the five-year period ending on the date the organization first leased the property, it was a tax-exempt organization.[68] The rule applies when the successor organization engages in activities that are substantially similar to those engaged in by a predecessor organization. Thus, a tax-exempt hospital cannot simply create a for-profit entity to perform activities in which it currently engages to avoid the tax-exempt use rules on depreciation.

For example, to establish the joint venture ambulatory surgical clinic, the tax-exempt hospital may reorganize to create a for-profit corporation that will enter into the lease with the partnership. This new corporation will either be a successor organization to the tax-exempt party or its wholly owned subsidiary. Even though the property is not leased to the tax-exempt entity as such, the property is deemed to be leased to the hospital for purposes of the tax-exempt leasing rules, because the property is leased to a successor entity or its wholly owned subsidiary. No rehabilitation tax credit, if applicable, or ACRS depreciation would be allowed. Outside investors may find such a transaction to be less attractive without these benefits.

Noncorporate Lessor Rules

A joint venture may be structured so that a partnership composed of a large number of physicians without regard to specialty is organized to purchase and own medical equipment. This leasing partnership then leases the equipment to a smaller operating company. This type of venture can be an attractive investment vehicle for physicians because of potential tax benefits ensuing from the equipment leases. Additionally, having the physicians acquire the equipment in such a venture can both reduce the hospital's share of risk in the project and increase the number of physicians who would be inclined to refer patients to the center. Of course, income to the physicians from the use of the equipment is taxable, but this income may be sheltered to a greater or lesser extent with regular depreciation deductions and ITC on all equipment acquired. Parties should be aware, however, that if a *partnership,* as opposed to a *corporation,* is used to acquire the equipment, the ability of the partners to obtain ITC will depend on compliance with so-called *noncorporate lessor rules.* These rules require that:[69]

- Deductible business expenses incurred with respect to each leased piece of equipment (other than expenses for depreciation, interest, or property taxes) must exceed 15 percent of the rent attributable to such an asset for the first 12 months of the lease.
- The lease term may not exceed 50 percent of the useful life of the leased equipment.

An equipment-leasing partnership may meet these tests without too much difficulty. However, if the owners of the leasing partnership and the operating entity are substantially identical (that is, if there is more than 50-percent common ownership), the lease between the two entities may not satisfy the noncorporate lessor rules because of a reasonable certainty that any and all equipment leases to the operating entity would be renewed indefinitely until the end of the leased asset's useful life. As a result, the leases would fail to meet the 50 percent of useful life test.[70]

If there is no lease, then the noncorporate lessor limitation does not apply. For instance, the equipment could be used by the physician partnership to provide services to the company pursuant to a legitimate service agreement.[71] The partnership would have no guaranteed return, like a rental, because payment would be on a use basis. Moreover, in a service contract, the owner retains the risk of loss or damage. A management contract with a third party may serve the same goals. The manager would be required by the contract to provide reports and arrange for use of the equipment.[72]

At-Risk Limits

The tax law imposes limitations on the ability of a taxpayer to claim ITC in excess of the amount to which such taxpayer is *at risk,* that is, the amount of the taxpayer's own money that the taxpayer has invested in the venture and that the investor risks losing if the venture is not a success. A partner may only take into account net losses to a partnership, or other pass-through entity, resulting from depreciation or deductions from equipment acquisitions on his or her respective tax return to the extent of his or her adjusted basis in the entity (how much he or she has invested in it). Taxpayers who are individuals or closely held corporations may only deduct the amount of such losses for which such individuals or corporations are at risk in the venture.[73] A *closely held corporation* is defined in the tax law as a corporation in which at least 50 percent of the value of its outstanding stock is owned by no more than five individuals.[74]

Deductions Limited to Amount at Risk

The tax law provides that if certain specified taxpayers are engaged in leasing depreciable property, they can deduct only such losses from that activity that equal the aggregate amount by which they are at risk, as such term is defined in the statute.[75] Those taxpayers to whom this law applies include individuals and closely held corporations. Amounts considered at risk in the statutory definition include the amount of money and the basis of property contributed by the taxpayer to the activity as well as amounts borrowed with respect to that activity, as long as the taxpayer is personally liable for the repayment of borrowed amounts or has pledged property (other than property used in such activity) as security for that borrowed amount. For the most part, borrowed amounts under this section are not considered to be at risk with respect to the venture if they were borrowed from another person having an interest in the activity or a related person.[76]

The law excludes from its restrictions equipment leasing by closely held corporations that earn 50 percent or more of their gross receipts in any taxable year by means of equipment leasing.[77] There is also an exception provided with respect to active businesses of a *qualified C corporation*, that is, any corporation to which subchapter C of the tax code applies other than a personal holding company or a personal service corporation. Each qualifying business carried on by the taxpayer is treated as a separate activity. A *qualifying business* is an active business that:[78]

- Has one full-time employee involved in the active management of the business
- Has at least three full-time nonowner employees
- Has deductions attributable to the business as employer contributions to employee deferred benefit plans
- Is not an excluded business (for example, equipment leasing)

Exclusion of Certain Nonrecourse Financing with Respect to ITC

The tax law also provides that the taxpayer's credit base in the property on which allowable ITC is founded must be reduced by the amount of nonqualified nonrecourse financing applicable to that property.[79] *Nonqualified nonrecourse financing* is any financing for which the borrower is not personally liable and that is not qualified commercial financing, for which there are exceptions. *Qualified commercial financing* is financing in which no related party is involved, the financing does not exceed 80 percent of the borrower's basis in the property, and the loan is from a party actively engaged in the business of lending money who has not received a fee with respect to the taxpayer's investment in the property.[80]

Taxpayers can encounter basis and at-risk problems with respect to assets that are highly leveraged. To be able to claim net losses from a venture as well as ITC, the taxpayer must have a sufficient basis and at-risk amount. In a highly leveraged transaction, basis and at-risk amounts are generally insufficient to permit the taxpayer to claim tax benefits that would otherwise be available. The solution is a joint venture that is less leveraged and in which individual participants in the joint venture have incurred some personal liability for at least a portion of the indebtedness necessary to acquire the assets of the enterprise.

When these at-risk rules are involved, it may be preferable to structure the joint venture so that the real estate activity is separate from equipment leasing, because losses from the holding of real property are not subject to these rules.[81] For example, there may be at-risk problems for a group of physician partners in an equipment leasing partnership that acquires MRI equipment and leases it to a corporation if the physicians had acquired the property in a highly leveraged transaction in which they incurred little or no personal liability. If the same physician partnership acquires both the medical equipment and also purchases a building to house the facility with nonrecourse financing and the facility incurs losses in its first years of operation, the partnership can deduct only the amounts actually at risk. Now, if the physician partnership acquires only the equipment for the facility and a separate entity acquires the real property and actually uses the equipment, the leasing partnership's ITC is reduced in relation to the amount of nonrecourse financing, but losses from the real estate aspect of the venture are not subject to the at-risk rules.

Pass-through of ITC

The tax code contains a provision whereby a lessor of new property for which ITC is available can elect to pass the available credit through to the lessee.[82] In the case of a short-term lease, the lessor can elect to treat the lessee as having acquired only a portion of the property for ITC purposes.[83] Under certain other tax provisions, a lessor not otherwise subject to the at-risk provisions discussed in the previous section of this chapter must satisfy them if ITC is passed through to the lessee. In addition, the percentage of the property by which the lessee must be at risk under these rules must equal or exceed the percentage required by the statute.[84]

Notes

1. As of mid-1986, two tax reform proposals were before Congress: the House-passed reform bill (H.R. 3838) and the so-called Packwood Plan, authored by Sen. Robert Packwood of the Senate Finance Committee. Both bills have an impact on physician-hospital joint ventures because the bills eliminate the investment tax credit (ITC), a major tax-sheltering benefit of many such ventures (see discussion of ITC later in this chapter). The effective date of the change in ITC benefits, if adopted, is still to be determined. It could be Jan. 1, 1986; Jan. 1, 1987; or any date in between. Many other critical changes are also under consideration, including significant changes in the areas of depreciation, other tax credits (such as rehabilitation tax credits), and rates of taxation. *See Comparison of House-Passed Tax Reform Bill (H.R. 3838) and "Packwood Plan,"* 50 DAILY TAX REP. 5-7 (BNA, Mar. 14, 1986) [hereinafter cited as *Tax Reform Comparison*]. Planners for joint ventures should take into account changes in the tax law as they evolve. Because at the time of publication of this book the tax reform bills had not been finalized and enacted into law, this chapter has been written without the benefit of knowing what tax changes, if any, will result from the 1986 legislative session.

2. The rules regarding taxation of dividends differ for the *subchapter S corporation*, a small business corporation with no more than 15 shareholders (all of whom are generally individuals) that is treated by the tax law similarly to a partnership: income earned by the subchapter S corporation is not subject to the corporate income tax. It is taxed to the individual shareholders. I.R.C. § 1366. The tax law imposes many requirements on subchapter S corporations, including a prohibition preventing another corporation from being a shareholder in a subchapter S corporation. For this reason, subchapter S corporations are not commonly used in health care joint ventures and are therefore not discussed in this chapter.

3. *See* I.R.C. § 514.

4. I.R.C. § 46(e)(4). As of mid-1986, this credit allowed 15 percent of qualified costs of rehabilitating a building 30 to 39 years old, 20 percent for a building 40 years or older, and 25 percent for a certified historic structure. Tax reform proposals in 1986 would reduce the percentages to 10 percent for nonhistoric structures; 20 percent for historic structures. *Tax Reform Comparison, supra* note 1.

5. Tax reform proposals considered by Congress in 1985 and 1986 would repeal the ITC. *Tax Reform Comparison, supra* note 1.

6. Until 1986, real estate could be depreciated over a 19-year period. Tax reform measures under consideration in Congress would create a new system ranging from 3 to 30 years. H.R. 3838. The Packwood Plan would retain current ACRS for certain types of equipment, but would put real estate in a 30-year class with straight-line depreciation. *Tax Reform Comparison, supra* note 1. The tax law limits ACRS when a tax-exempt user is involved. These limitations apply to the extent of "disqualified use" of the real property, if such use exceeds 35 percent of all uses. I.R.C. § 168(j)(3)(B). *See also* the discussion later in this chapter of the tax-exempt use property restrictions.

7. I.R.C. § 702(b).

8. *See, e.g.,* Rev. Rul. 69-463, 1969-2 C.B. 131 (approves the leasing of a medical office building and the furnishing of office services by a tax-exempt hospital to a group of physicians); Rev. Rul. 69-269, 1969-1 C.B. 160 (approves the operation of a profit-making parking lot for the use of hospital visitors and patients).

Chapter 4. Tax Considerations

Notes

9. Private Letter Ruling 8504060 (Oct. 30, 1984).

10. I.R.C. §§ 6111, 6112.

11. I.R.C. § 6111(c)(2).

12. I.R.C. § 501(c)(3) (emphasis added). The statute also prohibits propaganda or other attempts by the tax-exempt organization to influence legislation and participation in any political campaign on behalf of any candidate for public office.

13. Rev. Rul. 69-545, 1969-2 C.B. 117.

14. *Id.*

15. *See, e.g.,* Fort Scott Clinic & Hosp. Corp. v. Brodrick, 99 F.Supp. 515 (D. Kan. 1951); Sonora Community Hosp. v. Comm'r, 46 T.C. 519 (1966); The Lorain Avenue Clinic v. Comm'r, 31 T.C. 141 (1958).

16. *See* Sound Health Ass'n v. Comm'r, 71 T.C. 158 (1978).

17. *Id.*

18. Rev. Rul. 69-545, 1969-2 C.B. 117.

19. *See, e.g.,* Robert C. Olney v. Comm'r, 17 T.C.M. (CCH) 982 (1958); Anateus Lineal 1948, Inc. v. United States, 366 F. Supp. 118 (W.D. Ark. 1973); BHW Anesthesia Foundation, Inc. v. Comm'r, 72 T.C. 681 (1979); University of Mass. Medical School Group Practice v. Comm'r, 74 T.C. 1299 (1980).

20. *See* discussion below of tax considerations for tax-exempt joint venture participants.

21. I.R.C. § 513; Treas. Reg. § 1.513-1(d) (1985).

22. *See* discussion later in this chapter of unrelated business income in the section discussing tax considerations for tax-exempt joint venture participants.

23. *See* discussion earlier in this chapter of tax consequences of the partnership form.

24. *See* Private Letter Ruling 8504060 (Oct. 30, 1984).

25. *See* discussion earlier in this chapter with respect to the tax-exempt status of the joint venture.

26. *See* I.R.C. § 501(e).

27. *See* Carle Foundation v. United States, 611 F.2d 1192 (7th Cir. 1979) (a tax-exempt hospital pharmacy received unrelated business income from sales to a nonexempt medical clinic and to private patients).

28. I.R.C. § 513(a)(2).

29. St. Luke's Hosp. of Kansas City v. United States, 80-2 U.S.T.C. ¶9533 (W.D. Mo. 1980) (doctors on hospital staff are "members" for purposes of § 513(a)(2) and therefore income earned by the hospital in performing diagnostic tests for private patients of such doctors is not taxable). *See also,* regarding the convenience rule, Rev. Rul. 68-376, 1968-2 C.B. 246, which defines situations in which persons who purchase drugs from a hospital pharmacy are considered "patients" for purposes of the convenience rule exception to unrelated trade or business under I.R.C. § 513(a)(2).

30. Treas. Reg. § 1.513-1(c)(2)(iii) (1985); Rev. Rul. 68-374, 1968-2 C.B. 242 (the occasional sales of drugs to doctors maintaining offices in the hospital falls within the casual sales exception).

31. Hi-Plains Hosp. v. Comm'r, 670 F.2d 528 (5th Cir. 1982) (the availability of a hospital pharmacy for use by physicians' private patients was causally related to inducing physicians to practice in an isolated rural community).

32. Treas. Reg. § 1.501(c)(3)-1(c)(1) (1985).

33. As defined in I.R.C. § 501(c)(3).

34. Private Letter Ruling 8504060 (Oct. 30, 1984).

35. G.C.M. 39326 (Jan. 17, 1985).

36. I.R.C. § 501(c)(3); Treas. Reg. §§ 1.501(c)(3)-1(c), 1.501(a)-1(c) (1985).

37. G.C.M. 37852 (1979). *See* Plumstead Theatre Soc'y, Inc. v. Comm'r, 74 T.C. 1324 (1980), *aff'd,* 675 F.2d 244 (9th Cir. 1982) (the tax court rejected the IRS argument that the fiduciary duties of a general partner with regard to operating and maintenance practices

necessarily created a conflict of interest that was legally incompatible with the taxpayer's charitable purposes).

38. *See* Private Letter Rulings 8338127 (June 23, 1983) and 8344099 (Aug. 5, 1983).

39. *See* Private Letter Ruling 8325133 (Mar. 22, 1983).

40. G.C.M. 39326 (1985).

41. *See* Plumstead Theatre Soc'y, Inc. v. Comm'r, 74 T.C. 1324 (1980), *aff'd*, 675 F.2d 244 (9th Cir. 1982).

42. Private Letter Ruling 8232035 (May 11, 1982).

43. Private Letter Ruling 8504060 (Oct. 30, 1984).

44. *E.g.*, Harding Hosp. v. United States, 505 F.2d 1068, 1078 (6th Cir. 1974) (a hospital's tax-exempt status was revoked because it provided leases in a professional office building for less than fair market value). *See also* Rev. Rul. 69-545, 1969-2 C.B. 117.

45. See Private Letter Ruling 8206093 (Nov. 10, 1981) (involving the acquisition of a CAT scanner); Private Letter Ruling 8344099 (Aug. 5, 1983) (involving the purchase and operation of a full-body computerized tomography scanner by a limited partnership).

46. I.R.C. § 512(b)(1).

47. I.R.C. § 512(b)(13).

48. *See* I.R.C. §§ 512(b)(3)(A),(B). All rents received by a tax-exempt entity are excluded from unrelated business income tax except: (1) rents from personal property leased with real property if they exceed 10 percent of total rents (Treas. Reg. § 1.512(b)-1(c)(2)(ii)(*b*) (1985)); (2) rents from both real and personal property if more than 50 percent of total rents are attributable to personal property (Treas. Reg. § 1.512(b)-1(c)(2)(iii)(*a*) (1985)); (3) rents that are determined, in whole or in part, with respect to the income or profits derived from the leased property, other than rents based on a fixed percentage of gross receipts or sales (Treas. Reg. § 1.512(b)-1(c)(2)(iii)(*b*) (1985)); or (4) rents in which significant services are provided to the lessee under the rental agreement (Treas. Reg. § 1.512(b)-1(c)(5) (1985)).

49. I.R.C. § 514.

50. *See* I.R.C. § 512(c); Service Nut and Bolt Co. Profit Sharing Trust v. Comm'r, 78 T.C. 812 (1982), *aff'd*, 84-1 U.S.T.C. ¶9127 (6th Cir. 1983).

51. I.R.C. §§ 46, 168. According to tax rules in effect in early 1986, medical equipment is depreciated over five years, using accelerated or straight-line methods, and qualifies for a 10 percent ITC; certain other equipment is depreciated over three years and qualifies for a 6 percent ITC. Buildings are depreciated over 19 years and, except for rehabilitation costs of older buildings, do not qualify for any ITC.

52. Proposed tax law revisions would eliminate all ITC and extend the time frame for depreciation of buildings. *Tax Reform Comparison, supra* note 1. However, business groups will continue to exert pressure in Congress to retain ITC in some form.

53. I.R.C. §§ 48(a)(4),(5); Treas. Reg. § 1.48-1(j) (1985). *See* I.R.C. § 512(b)(1). *See also* discussion of unrelated business income in previous sections discussing the taxability of income of the venture enterprise and tax considerations for tax-exempt joint venture participants.

54. I.R.C. § 47(a)(1).

55. Depreciation of equipment is over the greater of the property's ADR midpoint life (or 12 years if no midpoint life) or 125 percent of the lease term, in the case of an equipment lease. I.R.C. § 168(j).

56. I.R.C. § 168(j)(3)(C).

57. I.R.C. § 168(j)(5)(E).

58. I.R.C. § 168(j)(5)(E).

59. If the full available ITC is claimed, I.R.C. § 48(q)(1) requires an adjustment to the basis of property on which the ACRS is claimed, unless the taxpayer elects to have I.R.C. § 48(q)(4) applied by reducing the amount of ITC that may be claimed from 10 percent to 8 percent. *Basis* is the price that was paid for the property by the taxpayer, increased by the amount of any capital expenditures made and decreased by the amount of any tax deductions claimed with respect to the property. When the property is sold, the basis that

Chapter 4. Tax Considerations

Notes

the taxpayer has in the property is subtracted from the amount received for it to determine capital gains tax.

60. I.R.C. §§ 48(a)(4),(5); Treas. Reg. § 1.48-1(j) (1985).

61. I.R.C. § 702.

62. I.R.C. § 7701(e)(1).

63. I.R.C. §§ 7701(e)(1)(A)-(F). Partnerships may also be recharacterized as leases under the tax law. I.R.C. § 7701(e)(2).

64. I.R.C. § 48(g)(2)(B)(vi).

65. I.R.C. § 168(j)(1).

66. I.R.C. § 168(j)(3)(B)(i).

67. I.R.C. § 168(j)(3)(B)(ii).

68. I.R.C. § 168(j)(4)(E).

69. I.R.C. § 46(e)(3). *But see Tax Reform Comparison, supra* note 1.

70. This result would be likely in the case of major medical equipment that is relatively immobile and not likely to be leased to another. *See* Peterson v. Comm'r, 44 T.C.M. (CCH) 674 (1982). *See also* Bloomberg v. Comm'r, 74 T.C. 1368 (1980). The noncorporate lessor rules can be avoided if the operating entity itself acquires the equipment to be used at the center. To accommodate passive investors, this entity can be organized as a limited partnership with those physicians who are actively engaged in the operation of the center as general partners. However, when operation and ownership functions are combined in one entity, such as a limited partnership, the return to the passive investors is based on profits from center operations rather than simply on the rental value of the leased equipment. Moreover, physicians who are making a purely passive investment in the business may find their qualified pension plans disqualified under relatively complex ERISA rules if they also use the facility to treat their patients. The application of these rules can generally be avoided with respect to passive investors if a separate equipment leasing partnership is used. See chapter 5 for a discussion of ERISA rules and their application.

71. *See* the discussion of service agreements and the IRS's ability to recharacterize these as leases in the preceding section on tax-exempt use property restrictions. *See also* I.R.C. §§ 7701(e)(1), (2).

72. *See* Meagher v. Comm'r, 36 T.C.M. (CCH) 1091 (1977) for a discussion of criteria for a valid management contract. *But see* I.R.C. § 7701(e), permitting recharacterization of contracts as leases for tax purposes in certain instances.

73. I.R.C. §§ 46(c)(8), 465, 704(d), 1366(d). *See Tax Reform Comparison, supra* note 1.

74. I.R.C. § 542(a)(2).

75. I.R.C. § 465(a).

76. I.R.C. § 465(b).

77. I.R.C. § 465(c)(4).

78. I.R.C. § 465(c)(7).

79. I.R.C. § 46(c)(8).

80. I.R.C. § 46(c)(8)(D)(ii).

81. I.R.C. § 465(c)(3)(1).

82. I.R.C. § 48(d).

83. I.R.C. § 48(d)(2).

84. I.R.C. §§ 48(d)(6); 48(d)(6)(B).

Chapter 5: ERISA Issues

Introduction to ERISA Issues
Commonly Controlled Trades or Businesses
Affiliated Service Groups
    Affiliated Service Group Defined
    A-Organization Affiliation
    B-Organization Affiliation
    Multiple Affiliated Service Groups
    Management Companies
    Application of Affiliated Service Group Rules
        Ambulatory Surgical Clinic
        Magnetic Resonance Imaging Center
        Occupational Medicine Center
        Alternative Health Care
        Reference Laboratory
        Medical Pavilion
    Avoidance of Affiliated Service Group Designation
Employee Leasing
    Safe-Harbor Pension Plan
    Common-Law Employees

Chapter 5. ERISA Issues

Participation in a joint venture by hospitals, physicians, and physician professional corporations can have a serious impact on the employee benefit plans of any or all of these groups. In certain instances, such participation may even cause the benefit plans to lose their federal tax qualification. This loss of qualification can lead to potential tax liability for both the employer and the employees.

Under the Employee Retirement Income Security Act (ERISA),[1] employee benefit plans, such as pension and profit-sharing plans, may qualify for or retain tax-qualified status only if they do not discriminate in favor of owner-employees or other highly compensated executives in comparison with rank-and-file employees.[2] For example, a plan that covers only an employer's highest-paid employees is almost always discriminatory and thus not permitted.

In the past, companies have attempted to avoid ERISA antidiscrimination laws by conducting business through interrelated businesses. For instance, the employer transferred all of the lower-echelon staff to a separate, but affiliated, organization that offered few, if any, retirement or other benefits. Then the business, which was now free of these low-paid employees, provided a favorable plan for its remaining high-paid executives. By using this strategy, the employer effectively avoided the ERISA restrictions. Congress responded to these attempts to avoid ERISA limitations with new laws that place restrictions on affiliated employers, either by treating them as a *commonly controlled business,* or by requiring them to be *aggregated,* that is, to be treated as a single employer in certain instances for purposes of testing compliance with the antidiscrimination and various other qualification rules.[3] Congress has also placed restrictions on employee leasing.

In the joint venture context, problems with ERISA can arise even though the participants did not enter into the venture with the intention of avoiding the antidiscrimination rules. For example, a number of physicians are investor-owners of a joint venture enterprise (such as an ambulatory surgical center) and also provide services to that business or to any third party through the organization. In such a case, all of the owner-participants in the venture are likely to be treated as a single employer for ERISA purposes and, as a result, will be required to meet all of the qualification requirements in the Internal Revenue Code (I.R.C.).

When a large number of plans are aggregated, such as in a joint venture with a large number of physician investors, compliance with ERISA rules can be extremely complex and uncertain. Consequently, whenever possible, it is best to avoid situations in which the ERISA rules apply. For example, any employees who already receive benefits pursuant to a collective bargaining agreement are disregarded in ERISA determinations.[4] Thus, if the employees of one owner of the venture are covered by a collective bargaining agreement, all employees of the venture could be covered under the same agreement, and the application of ERISA rules might be avoided.[5] Similar exceptions may apply for leased employees who are covered under plans provided by the leasing company if these plans meet current applicable rules of the Internal Revenue Service (IRS); see the discussion on leased employees later in this chapter.

Three basic topics must be discussed when considering ERISA issues and their application to joint ventures: *commonly controlled trades or businesses, affiliated service groups* (ASGs), and *leased employees.* The first part of this chapter introduces and defines these basic ERISA topics. For most readers, this introduction is sufficient to alert them to potential complex ERISA problems. Most readers will then want to refer their questions to their own tax counsel. For those desiring a more detailed description of ERISA problems, the remainder of this chapter provides an explanation of these topics and a brief discussion of their effect on several typical joint venture situations. Readers should be aware that ERISA rules are quite complex and can apply to many different situations, not all of which are considered in this discussion. Before embarking on any venture in which ERISA rules may have an impact, the participants should consult counsel knowledgeable in this area.

Introduction to ERISA Issues

The following discussion briefly describes the three areas in which Congress has placed restrictions on employee benefit plans. These areas are customarily referred to as:

- Commonly controlled trades or businesses
- Affiliated service groups (ASGs)
- Employee leasing

Businesses under common control are treated as a single employer for ERISA purposes. Under the ERISA rules, common control can be either:[6]

- *Parent-subsidiary control*, in which one organization owns at least 80 percent of one or more organizations
- *Brother-sister control*, in which five or fewer individuals, all together, own at least 80 percent or more of two or more organizations and the smallest interest held by each of such individuals in any of the organizations aggregates to more than 50 percent.

Even businesses that are not under common control are treated as a single employer under the ERISA rules if they fall within the definition of an affiliated service group.[7] *This definition is extremely complex, and before undertaking any venture that may fall within its purview, the participants should consult legal counsel to be certain that the contemplated enterprise meets the ERISA requirements.*

An ASG is a combination of certain organizations that are treated under the ERISA rules as a single employer if those organizations are considered to be one of the groups that fall within the following definitions:

- A *first service organization* (FSO) is an organization whose principal business is the performance of services as opposed to the generation of income through the use of capital, such as through inventory, machinery, or equipment.[8] Certain organizations engaged in providing health care and other enumerated services are automatically considered to be FSOs.[9] In order to be an ASG, a group of organizations must contain at least one FSO.
- An *A-organization* (A-ORG) is a service organization that:[10]
  - Is a shareholder or partner in an FSO
  - Regularly performs services for the FSO or is regularly associated with the FSO in performing services for third parties
- A *B-organization* (B-ORG) is any other organization, not necessarily a service organization, for which:[11]
  - A significant portion of its business is the performance of services for the FSO, A-ORGs, or both of a type historically performed by employees in the service field of the FSO or the A-ORGs
  - Ten percent or more of the interests in the organization are held by persons who are officers, highly compensated employees, or common owners of the FSO or of the A-ORGs

An ASG is composed of an FSO and either an A-ORG or B-ORG or any combination of A-ORGs and B-ORGs. Because an affiliation can be deemed by the IRS to be an ASG despite the intentions of the parties, participants in a joint venture should have the structure of their proposed transaction examined by knowledgeable counsel with the ASG rules in mind. The examples of several typical scenarios that are examined later in this chapter illustrate some potential problems.

A third area that may present ERISA problems is leased employees. The leasing of employees is a practice that is frequently used for legitimate business reasons, such as to reduce start-up costs. Nevertheless, unless the parties are careful, their benefit plans may be disqualified because of their failure to fully comply with ERISA rules.

Parties contemplating the leasing of employees as part of the venture plan should be aware that the ERISA rules afford a *safe harbor,* which is a set of guidelines to reassure the parties that their leasing scheme complies fully with the ERISA rules. This safe harbor allows an employer to exclude leased employees from its benefit plan if the leasing company maintains its own qualified pension plan that provides for immediate participation and total vesting of all pension rights and interests. The leasing company must contribute an amount equal to at least 7.5 percent of each employee's gross annual earnings, in addition to any social security contributions.[12]

Any employee not entitled to participate in the leasing company's benefit plan must be included as an employee of the health care employer for ERISA purposes. Additionally, if the employee is the so-called *common-law employee* of the health care employer, that employee must be covered by the health care employer's benefit plans. An employee is deemed to be the common-law employee of an employer if that employer has real responsibility for that employee and controls the employment conditions of that employee, such as supervision, payroll records, recruitment, job assignments, compensation, and employee discipline.

These general areas are the ones that can be affected by ERISA rules. The remainder of this chapter contains a more detailed discussion of these general principles as well as examples of their application for those persons interested in more specific information about the relationship between the ERISA rules and joint ventures. The discussion in this chapter is not intended to replace the guidance of counsel with respect to any particular joint venture.

Commonly Controlled Trades or Businesses

Businesses that are under common control must be viewed as a single employer for ERISA compliance purposes. Under the tax law, a *trade or business,* for purposes of the ERISA rules, can be any business entity, including a corporation, a partnership, or a sole proprietorship. There are basically two types of control relationships: *parent-subsidiary control* and *brother-sister control.*

Parent-subsidiary control exists when one organization owns at least 80 percent of one or more other organizations.[13] *Brother-sister control* exists when five or fewer individuals own, in the aggregate, at least 80 percent or more of two or more organizations and the smallest interest held by each of such individuals in any of the organizations aggregates to more than 50 percent.

For example, Dr. Smith owns 80 percent and Dr. Jones owns 20 percent of Medical Services, Inc. (MSI), a professional service corporation. Dr. Jones also owns 80 percent and Dr. Smith owns 20 percent of Health Care Corporation (HCC), another professional service corporation (see figure 1, page 81). Under the I.R.C., MSI and HCC will not be deemed commonly controlled trades or businesses. First, there is no parent-subsidiary control because neither organization owns 80 percent of the other and no one person owns 80 percent of *both* organizations. Second, there is no brother-sister control because, although five or fewer individuals together own at least 80 percent of each organization, the smallest interest that each owner holds in either organization (that is, 20 percent) aggregates to only 40 percent, not the 50 percent required by the I.R.C.

However, the situation changes if these two physicians decide to join Memorial Hospital, a local hospital, in a venture to establish MedClinic, an outpatient clinic.

Dr. Smith and Dr. Jones each acquire a 40 percent interest in MedClinic, and Memorial Hospital acquires the remaining 20 percent (see figure 2, next page). Both MedClinic and MSI and MedClinic and HCC are viewed as brother-sister commonly controlled trades or businesses under the I.R.C. This result occurs because both Dr. Smith and Dr. Jones together hold at least 80 percent of MedClinic and of MSI, and the smallest interest each holds in either MedClinic or MSI aggregates to 60 percent (that is, Dr. Smith has a 40 percent interest in MedClinic, the smallest interest held by either Dr. Smith or Dr. Jones in MedClinic; and Dr. Jones holds a 20 percent interest in MSI, the smallest interest held by either Dr. Smith or Dr. Jones in MSI) (see figure 3, next page). The analysis is identical for the relationship between MedClinic and HCC. Therefore, MedClinic and MSI are viewed as one employer for ERISA purposes, and MedClinic and HCC are viewed as one employer. As a result, MSI and HCC are also viewed together as a single employer. For ERISA compliance purposes, the pension and other benefit plans of Dr. Smith and her employees are grouped together with the plans of Dr. Jones and his employees, as well as with any benefit plans provided to employees of the joint venture.

Affiliated Service Groups

The rules for affiliated service groups[14] were enacted to respond to partnerships of professional service corporations in which only the corporations maintained employee benefit plans and to corporations that employed only rank-and-file employees and offered no benefit plans and then contracted to provide services to persons who actually owned the corporations and who provided generous benefit plans to themselves. Although the rules for ASGs effectively prevent such abuses, they unfortunately include within their broad sweep arrangements that have no potential for abuse. The ASG rules require that any employer who enters into certain defined relationships with another is deemed affiliated for ERISA purposes, that is, all employees of the various employers are treated as having a single employer.[15] As a consequence, the nondiscrimination rules apply. The most liberal plans are disqualified if they discriminate against lower-paid employees.

To provide guidelines for applying the ASG rules contained in the I.R.C., the IRS has proposed certain treasury regulations, referred to in this chapter as the proposed regulations. The final form of these proposed regulations is not expected to be substantially different. Consequently, joint venture participants should strive to comply with these proposed regulations.

Under the proposed regulations, an ASG contains a *first service organization*, which is defined as an organization whose principal business is the performance of services.[16] An FSO can be a sole proprietorship, partnership, corporation, or any other type of entity, regardless of its ownership format.[17] The ASG rules automatically apply to certain organizations engaged in the provision of health care and to organizations providing legal, accounting, and other enumerated services.[18]

Other organizations may also be considered to be FSOs unless capital is a material income-producing factor for them. An organization is not considered an FSO when a substantial portion of its gross income is attributable to the employment of capital in the business, such as when the business has made large investments in inventory, plant, machinery, or equipment and when most of the income from the business relates to these investments and is not derived from fees, commissions, or compensation for personal services performed by individuals.[19]

The proposed regulations also state that no corporation, other than a *professional service corporation*, shall be treated as an FSO for purposes of ASG rules.[20] Such a professional service corporation is one that is organized for the purpose of rendering

Chapter 5. ERISA Issues

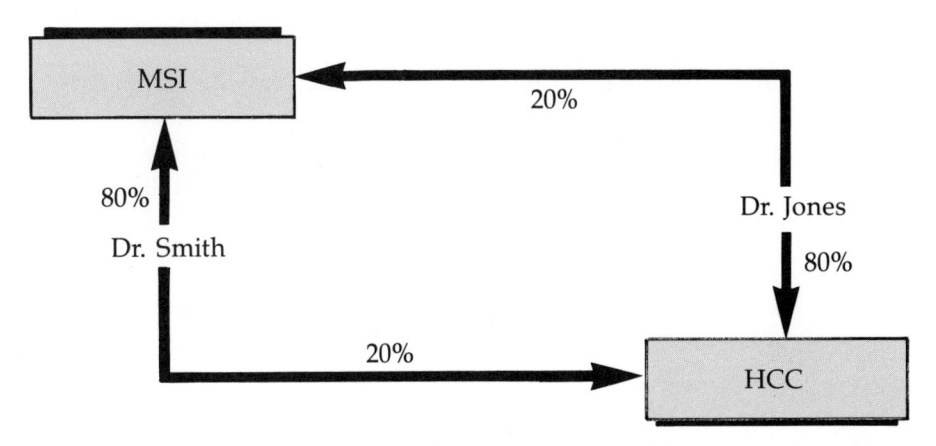

Figure 1. Example of Parent-Subsidiary Control in the Ownership of Medical Services, Inc., (MSI) and Health Care Corporation (HCC)

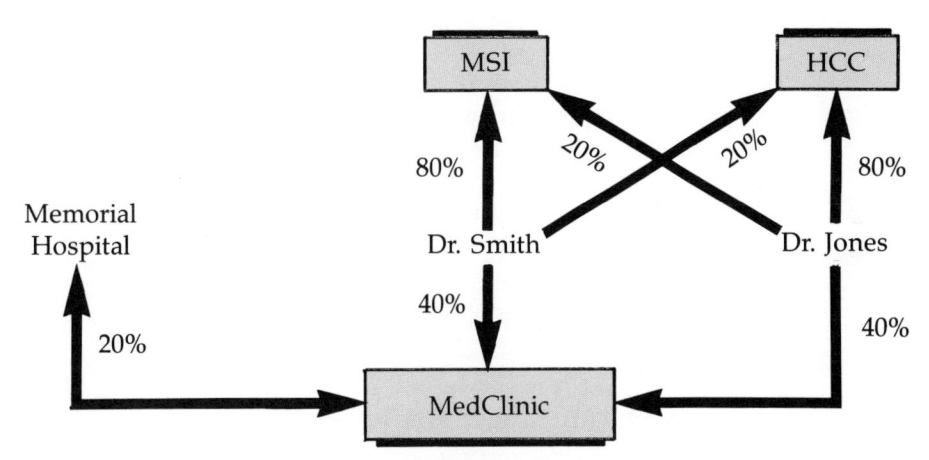

Figure 2. Parent-Subsidiary Control among Physicians and Memorial Hospital to Form MedClinic

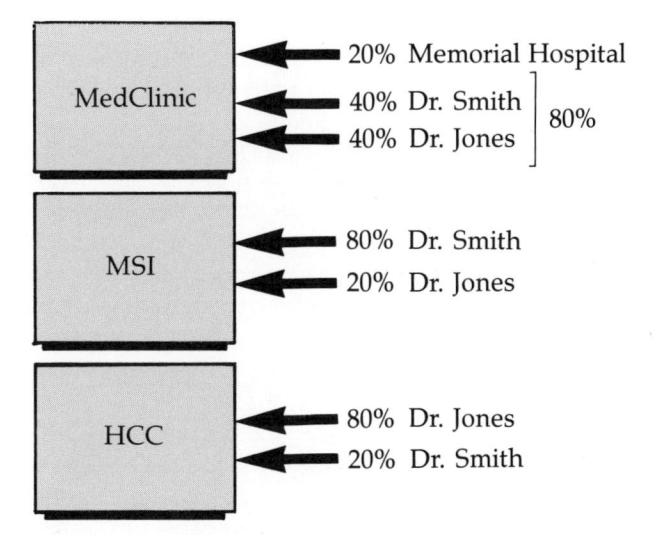

Figure 3. Ownership Interests in MedClinic; Medical Services, Inc., (MSI); and Health Care Corporation (HCC)

81

professional services and that has at least one shareholder who is licensed under state law or is otherwise legally authorized to provide the type of services for which the corporation is organized.[21] A doctor's office practice group that is organized under state law as a professional corporation is an example of a professional service corporation for ERISA purposes. On the other hand, the fact that corporations other than a professional service corporation, such as for-profit business corporations, are not generally deemed to be FSOs is an important exception in the proposed regulations that is readily adaptable to many joint ventures.

Affiliated Service Group Defined

An affiliated service group is the combination of a first service organization and one or more of the following:[22]

- Another service organization called an A-organization, if it is a shareholder or partner in the FSO and if it regularly performs services for the FSO or if it is regularly associated with the FSO in performing services for third parties
- Any other organization (not necessarily a service organization) called a B-organization, if the following two conditions are met:
  - A significant portion of the business of the potential B-ORG is the performance of services for the FSO, for A-ORGs, or both of a type historically performed by employees in the service field of the FSO or the A-ORGs
  - Ten percent or more of the interests in the organization are held by persons who are officers, highly compensated employees, or common owners of the FSO or of the A-ORGs.

A-Organization Affiliation

Two key issues must be examined when determining whether a service organization is an A-organization. The first of these is the question of ownership. The regulations define an A-ORG as an organization. Therefore, it would seem that one way to avoid aggregation would be for the physician rather than the professional corporation in which he or she is a shareholder to own an interest in the joint venture entity. As an individual, the physician is not considered an organization and therefore could not be an A-ORG performing services for third parties through the first service organization.

However, the tax code has anticipated this possibility, and *attribution rules* are applied in conjunction with ERISA rules. These rules regard the interest held in the name of one party as being held by another party, if the result more honestly reflects the reality of the situation. Under the attribution rules, if a physician owns more than 50 percent of the stock in a professional corporation that provides services to the joint venture organization and if the physician is a shareholder or partner in the joint venture, then the professional corporation is treated as the owner of the joint venture entity because the tax rules attribute the physician's ownership of the entity to the professional corporation for ERISA purposes.[23]

The second key issue is whether the purported A-ORG "regularly performs services for" or is "regularly associated with" the FSO.[24] The IRS looks at all of the facts and circumstances within the relationship between the two organizations to determine whether this test has been met. One aspect to be considered is the amount of earned income that the organization derives from performing services for the FSO or from performing services for third persons in association with the FSO.[25] Clearly, if a physician performs services for the joint venture organization on a full-time basis, such services would be considered *regular* for the purposes of A-ORG affiliation. The more important question is whether a physician's part-time services (for example, one afternoon per week) are deemed to be regular. The proposed regulations are unclear on this matter.[26]

An example of the aggregation of an FSO and an A-ORG under this definition is a professional service corporation whose sole shareholder is a medical doctor aggregated with a group practice partnership in which the professional service corporation is a partner. This type of situation arises frequently in the health care context because so many physicians have incorporated themselves and are investing in joint ventures and in other organizations that provide health care, such as health maintenance organizations (HMOs) and preferred provider organizations (PPOs), either through their professional corporations or as individuals.

B-Organization Affiliation

When analyzing a relationship between organizations to determine if the affiliated service group rules apply or whether one or several of the organizations is considered a B-organization, three major issues must be examined:

- *Whether the services provided represent a significant portion of the total business of the company.* The determination of whether the services provided by an organization for a first service organization, for one or more A-organizations, or for both constitutes a significant portion of the business of the organization for aggregation purposes is based on individual facts and circumstances. When business is minimal, however, the proposed regulations do set out a *safe harbor*, which is a set of guidelines that, if met, protects the organization from undesirable consequences. The IRS does not consider the performance of services for the FSO or A-ORG or both to be significant if such performance constitutes less than 5 percent of the organization's service receipts. This calculation is based on the so-called *service receipts percentage* (SRP), which is the ratio of the receipts derived from services for the FSO, the A-ORG, or both to the organization's total gross receipts that are derived from performing services.[27]

    When business is more than minimal, the proposed regulations suggest a threshold of 10 percent of the *total receipts percentage* (TRP), which is calculated in the same manner as the SRP except that gross receipts are used in the ratio without regard to whether or not they were derived from performing services.[28] If the amount of services provided to the FSO or A-ORG exceeds this threshold limit, then the IRS will consider those services to be a significant amount of the organization's business for aggregation purposes.
- *Whether the services are those historically performed by employees in that service field.* Services are considered of a type historically performed by employees in a particular service field if the performance of such services was not unusual for those employees on December 31, 1980.[29] Examples of such services are secretarial services, nursing services, and services by medical technicians and by other health care support staff. Nontraditional services, such as technical services using a lithotripter (which were not available in 1980), would not fall within the definition, and the organization performing them would not necessarily be a B-ORG.
- *Whether 10 percent or more of the interests in the organization are held, in the aggregate, by persons who are officers, highly compensated employees, or common owners of the FSO or A-ORG.* For the purpose of determining whether 10 percent or more of the interests in the potential B-ORG are held by officers, highly compensated employees, or common owners of the FSO or A-ORG, owners of the

FSO or A-ORG who are not also officers or highly compensated employees of the FSO or A-ORG are deemed common owners only if their interests constitute, in the aggregate, 3 percent or more of the total interests in the FSO.[30] The situation of Health Care Clinic (HCC), a service organization, illustrates this common-ownership principle. Nursing Services Corp. (NSC) is a corporation whose sole function is to provide nursing services to HCC. Dr. Jones owns all of the stock in NSC and has a 2 percent interest in HCC. Dr. Jones is not an officer or a highly compensated employee of HCC. According to the definitions, HCC may be an FSO but NSC will not be considered a B-ORG because 10 percent or more of NSC is not owned by any officer, highly compensated employee, or common owner of the FSO. Because Dr. Jones owns less than 3 percent of HCC, he is not considered a common owner of the organization, as required by the proposed regulations.

The following hypothetical example shows when a business in the health care industry is deemed a B-ORG. Health Care Services (HCS) is a medical group practice that has 11 partners. Each partner in HCS owns 1 percent of the stock in Nursing Services Corp. (NSC), a corporation that provides the partnership with the services of nurses. A significant portion of the business of NSC consists of supplying services to HCS. If the group practice is considered to be an FSO, then NSC is a B-ORG because a significant portion of the business of the corporation is the performance of services for the group practice of a type historically performed by employees in the service field of the partnership (health care services) and a greater than 10 percent interest in NSC is held, in the aggregate, by the 11 common owners of HCS. Accordingly, NSC and HCS constitute an ASG.

Multiple Affiliated Service Groups

Several affiliated service groups may at times be aggregated into one larger one. Special aggregation rules apply with respect to such multiple ASGs.

Not all ASGs are aggregated into one larger group merely because they share a common organization, such as a first service organization, A-organization, or B-organization. The formation of a multiple ASG requires a common FSO. Sharing a common A-ORG or B-ORG does not suffice.[31] If an organization is an FSO with respect to two or more A-ORGs, or two or more B-ORGS, or a combination of A-ORGs and B-ORGs, all of the organizations will be aggregated into a single ASG.[32] The hazards associated with such a designation are obvious: each employer who has been thus affiliated must examine not only the benefits provided to its own employees, but it must also consider the benefits provided to the employees of all of the other affiliated employers to determine whether its employee benefit plan is qualified. Whenever the benefits provided to some of the employees of the affiliated employers are not comparable to those provided by the other affiliated employers, the employee benefit plans of *all* of the affiliated employers will lose their qualified status.[33]

An example of a multiple ASG is the following: Dr. Smith is incorporated as a professional corporation, Medical Services Corp. (MSC), which is considered a professional service corporation under ERISA regulations. All of Dr. Smith's secretarial services are provided by Temps Agency (TA), and all of his nursing services are provided by Nursing Services Corp. (NSC). The professional service corporation, MSC, owns 20 percent of TA and 25 percent of NSC. Assuming that the tests for a B-ORG are met, MSC would be an FSO, and both TA and NSC would be B-ORGs. Dr. Smith is the common owner of MSC and TA and of MSC and NSC. Thus, each group is an ASG and, pursuant to the proposed regulations, will be aggregated into one multiple ASG.

However, the situation is different in the following example: in the medical pavilion joint venture example described in appendix F, a corporation, Secretarial Services Inc. (SSI), offers secretarial services to the physicians renting space in the pavilion. The physicians otherwise have no relationship with one another. Dr. Smith owns 20 percent of SSI and accounts for 20 percent of its gross receipts. Dr. Jones owns 25 percent of SSI and accounts for 25 percent of its gross receipts. Dr. Smith is an FSO, and SSI is a B-ORG because 20 percent of the gross receipts of the company are derived from performing services for Dr. Smith of a type historically performed by employees of physicians. Dr. Smith also owns more than 10 percent (20 percent) of SSI. Thus, Dr. Smith and SSI are an ASG. The same analysis applies to Dr. Jones' relationship with SSI: for the same reasons discussed with respect to Dr. Smith, Dr. Jones and SSI constitute an ASG. However, Dr. Smith is not affiliated with Dr. Jones merely because SSI is a B-ORG with respect to both physicians. The ASG of Dr. Smith and the ASG of Dr. Jones are two separate groups and will not be aggregated.[34]

Management Companies

For taxable years beginning after 1982, the I.R.S. deems the following organizations as an affiliated service group:[35]

- An organization whose principal business is performing management functions on a regular and continuing basis for another organization (or related organizations as determined in accordance with the regulations[36])
- The organization, or related organizations, for which such management functions are performed

If such an ASG is found to exist, then all employees within it are treated as working for a single employer for purposes of applying the employment benefit requirements.

These rules were designed to prevent employers from creating separate management companies composed of former management and executive-level employees in order to provide disparate benefits. In such a scenario, instead of creating a separate service company composed of former lowly paid employees and providing few or no benefits to them, the company spins off its highly paid employees. The separate management company would then provide generous benefits to the executive-level employees, while the original company provides few benefits to the remaining lower-echelon employees.

The ASG rules governing management companies have a broad-enough application to create potential problems for many health care joint ventures. For example, if an ambulatory surgical center joint venture, such as that described in appendix A, decides to form a separate service bureau entity to provide management-type services to the center on a regular and continuing basis, the center and the service bureau will be aggregated by the terms of the special management company rules. Aggregation is especially likely if the sole or principal client of the service bureau is the surgery center.

Application of Affiliated Service Group Rules

The rules for affiliated service groups can affect various joint ventures unbeknownst to the participants. Each situation is different and must be separately analyzed by counsel knowledgeable in this field. Studying the joint venture examples described in the appendixes illustrates some of the potential problems.

Ambulatory Surgical Clinic

In the example of an ambulatory surgical clinic joint venture, described in appendix A, Memorial Hospital participates in a joint venture with staff physicians to establish and operate an ambulatory surgical clinic. Under this arrangement, the hospital and the physicians each own an interest in the venture. For purposes of this example, the hospital employees are not covered by a collective bargaining agreement. If both parties provide services to the enterprise, as is likely the case in certain fact situations, they may be affiliated.

If the joint venture entity is organized as a partnership rather than a business corporation, it would be deemed a first service organization under the proposed regulations. Each of the physicians, whether organized as a sole proprietorship, partnership, or professional corporation, and possibly the hospital would altogether as service organizations be A-organizations with respect to the FSO because they are owners of the FSO and either regularly perform services for the FSO or are regularly associated with the FSO in performing services for third parties. As a result, the employees of all of the joint venture participants will be grouped to determine if their benefit plans still meet the requirements for federal tax qualification. This determination can only be accomplished by means of an actuarial study. However, if this joint venture entity is organized as a business corporation instead of a partnership it may escape aggregation under the ASG rules because the proposed regulations, as they are presently drafted, appear to exclude a corporation other than a professional service corporation from treatment as an FSO.[37]

Magnetic Resonance Imaging Center

In the example of a magnetic resonance imaging center joint venture, described in appendix B, Memorial Hospital and Community Hospital decide to create a magnetic resonance imaging (MRI) center. If one or both hospitals have collective bargaining agreements with their employees, as is likely the case, it is probable that the employees of the new venture facility will be covered by one or the other of those agreements and will receive whatever benefits those agreements provide. In that event, the affiliated service group rules are not applicable.

However, if no collective bargaining agreement exists, this joint venture could technically be affected by ERISA rules. In this situation, both hospitals would each own an interest in the new facility. They, or their owned subsidiaries, would also provide the new facility with services, such as hospital management services, billing services, or utilization review. If the ERISA rules are applied literally, the hospitals could be affiliated according to the provisions of the proposed regulations. Both Memorial Hospital and Community Hospital would be A-organizations to the joint venture entity, which is a first service organization, because both hospitals own an interest in the venture and either regularly perform services for the new facility or are regularly associated with the new facility in performing services for third parties. As a result, they would be required to group all of their employees to determine whether their benefit plans meet the requirements for federal tax qualification. However, under the proposed regulations as they are presently drafted, if the joint venture entity were a business or a not-for-profit corporation, it would not be an FSO, and there might not be an ERISA problem.[38]

The application of the ASG rules to two hospital participants in a joint venture is simply theoretical; as a practical matter, the IRS is not likely to attempt to aggregate the parties to this particular type of joint venture. The rationale behind the ASG rules is to prevent abuse of the antidiscrimination provisions of ERISA by *professionals*, not hospitals. In the face of any audit by the IRS, two *hospitals* participating in a venture without the complicating presence of any individual professional participants would have a strong argument that Congress never intended the ASG rules to apply to them when the law was enacted.[39]

Moreover, even though two hospitals may technically be members of one ASG because they jointly own the joint venture entity, aggregation may not have an adverse impact on their pension plans. The ERISA rules prohibit discrimination in favor of certain highly paid employees, shareholders, and officers.[40] However, ERISA permits employers to maintain different pension plans for different classes of employees if there are legitimate reasons for such classes and if there is no resultant discrimination of the type envisioned by the statute.[41] If challenged, two hospitals should have no problem showing the reasonableness of their schemes.

Occupational Medicine Center

In the example of an occupational medicine center joint venture, described in appendix C, Memorial Hospital decides to participate in a joint venture with a medical equipment supplier to establish and equip two regional occupational medicine centers. These regional centers will in turn equip local occupational medicine clinics, which will have local physicians participating.

The participants decide to structure the individual centers in the form of a partnership, with the regional facility and local physician participants as general partners. This partnership acquires all real and personal property to be used by the local clinic and leases it to a separate operating company, which is a professional corporation composed only of participating physicians. If one or more of the participating physicians acquires an ownership interest in the operating company and then regularly provides occupational medicine services to patients of the center, such physicians and the operating company would probably be affiliated. The operating company, a professional service corporation, would be a first service organization, and the physicians would be A-organizations. Unless the plans of such affiliated service group members did not violate other ERISA rules with respect to the employees of all ASG members, such plans may be subject to disqualification. However, if the participating physicians become investors in the partnership that *leases* equipment to the operating company, they may avoid the ASG rules because leasing equipment does not constitute a *service* under the proposed regulations.

Alternative Health Care

In the example of an alternative health care joint venture, described in appendix D, various relationships can trigger an application of the rules for affiliated service groups. In this example, a new preferred provider organization (PPO) will be formed by means of a joint venture between the parent of a health maintenance organization (HMO), two hospitals, and a physician practice group consisting of individual physicians or their professional service corporations. The impact of ERISA rules on this venture probably depends on the nature of the physician practice group. If it is an integrated entity under one qualified pension plan and the hospitals and the HMO are all governed by collective bargaining agreements with their employees, then participation in the venture will probably not create problems for them.

Potential problems arise if several practice groups or individual physicians participate in the venture. If care is not taken in structuring the venture, this relationship could possibly result in the health care entity and the physician practice groups becoming an ASG, with the PPO as a first service organization and the physician groups as A-organizations. However, the PPO could make a strong argument that the kinds of services it performs, such as utilization review, are not the kinds of regularly performed services that would trigger application of the ASG rules because they were not performed by hospital employees in 1980. Similar problems can arise in the formation of a medical staff-hospital (MeSH) organization, depending on the services provided to the venture by the physician staff members.

However, although the ASG rules are arguably not applicable to PPOs, they are more likely to be applicable, at least in a technical sense, to an *individual practice association* (IPA), which is an association of individual physicians organized to contract with HMOs and other alternative delivery systems. If a physician is an owner of an IPA and treats patients assigned to the IPA, that physician may be aggregated with all the other physician owners of that IPA, which could have more than 100 members, into one ASG. All the physician-owners would therefore be treated as a single employer for ERISA purposes. Aggregation may result even if the IPAs were created to serve the legitimate purpose of implementing alternative delivery of health care and were never intended to provide a vehicle for physicians to discriminate against their lower-echelon employees.

Despite the potential risk of the application of ASG rules to the IPA, many IPAs are formed without ever being scrutinized. The participants of such IPAs may not be aware of the rules or may be convinced that, if audited, they could convince the IRS that the IPA situation is not among the abuses that the ASG rules were designed to correct. Rather than take the risk of an audit, other physicians are designing a particular model IPA that seemingly avoids the ASG threat. This IPA has only one shareholder-physician, who then contracts with other physicians to provide health care services through the IPA.

Another way of avoiding the application of the ASG rules may be to form the IPA as a for-profit business corporation or a not-for-profit corporation in which the individual physicians are *members* instead of owners. However, if the IRS decides to make IPAs subject to the ASG rules, it may not accept this distinction as having any real substance.[42] The proposed regulations exempt corporations, other than professional service corporations, from the application of the ASG rules.[43] Therefore, the IPA can argue that the corporation, particularly if it has nonphysician owners as well as physician owners, does not fall within the scope of the ERISA rules because it is not a so-called professional service corporation. However, if the IPA is organized as a corporation other than a professional service corporation and has only professional (physician) owners, its structure may be viewed by the IRS as form over substance, and the IRS may apply ASG rules just as it would if the organization had been structured as a professional corporation or as a partnership.[44]

Reference Laboratory

In the example of a reference laboratory joint venture, described in appendix E, Memorial Hospital, after restructuring its pathology department, participates with several senior staff physicians in the establishment of a reference laboratory, which will service patients of the hospital. Memorial Hospital has no collective bargaining agreement with its employees.

The participants can choose to organize the laboratory as either a partnership or a for-profit corporation. For reasons unrelated to the ERISA rules, they may decide that a partnership is the most appropriate legal structure for the venture. Each physician owns a 5 percent interest in the laboratory. The hospital provides services to the business in the form of billing and specimen review. Physicians provide supervisory and other related services. All secretarial and bookkeeping services for the laboratory are performed by an outside agency. Although this agency supplies staff to several health care providers in the area, a significant part of its services (more than 10 percent) is rendered to the joint venture reference laboratory. Each physician investor in the joint venture project also owns 15 percent of the agency.

Because the venture participants have elected to structure the joint venture reference laboratory as a partnership instead of a corporation, the ASG rules may apply.

According to the proposed regulations, a business corporation, that is, a corporation other than a professional service corporation, is not viewed as a first service organization.[45] However, a partnership may be treated as an FSO. The hospital and physician investors, who provide services to the laboratory, would then be A-organizations, because they own the laboratory and regularly perform services for it (billing and supervisory services) and regularly associate with the laboratory in performing services for third parties (analysis of specimens and laboratory work for hospital patients). The agency would be a B-organization because it does a significant amount of its business for the joint venture reference laboratory (the FSO), and provides services that are historically performed by employees of reference laboratories. More than 10 percent of the agency is held by common owners and highly compensated employees of the reference laboratory.

In this situation, a multiple ASG might be deemed to exist. The laboratory is an FSO with respect to an A-ORG (the hospital) and a B-ORG (the staffing agency). The reference laboratory and the hospital are one ASG, the reference laboratory and each physician investor would also be an ASG, and the reference laboratory and the staffing agency would be another ASG. Under the proposed regulations, the joint venture laboratory, the hospital, the physicians, and the staffing agency could well be aggregated into one larger multiple ASG, which means that, for tax purposes, plans of the various entities must be assessed to see if they remain qualified.

These problems could be avoided by structuring the laboratory as a business corporation instead of a partnership, because under proposed regulations, such a corporation will not be deemed to be an FSO for ASG purposes. Without the single FSO, none of the other organizations would be aggregated into a single ASG.

Medical Pavilion

In the example of a medical pavilion joint venture, described in appendix F, the participants, Medical Building Associates (Associates) and Memorial Hospital, together set up a joint venture to create a medical care pavilion in a downtown office complex. The two parties form a partnership that leases space in the building and subleases that space to various enterprises, who provide such medical services as a pharmacy, doctors' satellite offices, and an ambulatory clinic.

This joint venture may experience some ERISA problems if, for example, in addition to merely offering management services within the center, the participants also form a separate company to offer various services to pavilion tenants. That new company may be viewed as a B-organization if its employees provide physicians and others leasing space in the building with services that constitute a significant part of the company's business and that are of a type historically performed by employees in the service of physicians. An affiliated service group may be formed between the service bureau (the B-ORG) and any physician group or other health care entity located in the pavilion (the first service organization) that uses the services of the service bureau and that also owns 10 percent or more of the company, if the holders of that 10 percent interest are also officers, highly compensated employees, or common owners of the FSO.

Avoidance of Affiliated Service Group Designation

Because of the complexities of the rules for affiliated service groups and the numerous forms that a joint venture in the health care field can assume, there are no simple or generally applicable solutions to avoid being classified as an ASG. Every situation must be analyzed on its own facts. Joint venture participants must be careful in organizing the enterprise and in staffing it to avoid potential problems and should seek advice from legal counsel, whenever they consider entering into a new relationship with another organization.

Sometimes choosing the corporate form over a partnership is an easy way to avoid such classification. The proposed regulations provide that a corporation, other than a professional service corporation, will not be viewed as a first service organization.[46] If the joint venture entity can be organized as such a nonprofessional corporation, which might be the case if a hospital or other nonprofessional investor owns an interest in the joint venture enterprise, it is unlikely that the joint venture would be considered an FSO. However, the ramifications of such a decision should be explored with someone knowledgeable in the field before that decision is made. Often, for reasons other than ERISA considerations, organizing the joint venture as a corporation may not be feasible. For example, structuring the enterprise as a for-profit corporation, with a lay investor rather than physician investors, could lead to a corporate practice problem that is as undesirable as application of ASG rules (see the discussion of corporate practice issues in chapter 8).

Another way to structure a joint venture to avoid the undesirable application of the ASG rules may be through the use of *equipment leases.* An equipment lease does not call for a *service* to be provided and therefore does not fall within the definition of an organization subject to aggregation. In creating a joint venture entity, such as an ambulatory surgical center, the participants can provide for investment by physicians by means of a limited partnership that purchases the equipment and facilities needed by the center and leases these to the owner of the center, which is some party other than physicians. Structuring the joint venture in this fashion enables the individual physician investors to participate in the venture without the risk of aggregation that may otherwise result if a different structure for the venture was selected.

The present tax law contains one other apparent loophole. Affiliation may be avoided even when a professional service corporation is involved if the professional service corporation provides professional services to the FSO but the physician's ownership interest in the FSO is held by the physician *himself* and not by the professional service corporation. Under attribution rules contained in the tax code, the physician's ownership interest in the FSO would be attributed to the professional service corporation, thereby leading to A-organization status for the professional service corporation and ASG treatment.[47] However, this result can be avoided if the physician owned less than 50 percent of the stock in the professional service corporation.[48] A professional service corporation composed of several physician members would not be an A-ORG if it had no ownership interest in the FSO, even if individual physician owners of the professional service corporation, each holding less than 50 percent of the stock in that professional service corporation, also held ownership interests in the FSO.[49] This apparent loophole may not be applicable in all cases, however. Before relying on it when forming a venture, legal counsel should be sought. Further, the tax law is always subject to change. Relying on an apparent discrepancy is risky when forming a venture.

At times, even though ERISA rules result in the aggregation of the organization, the result may not be so egregious. With the aid of counsel, the parties should study the affected pension plans of the various joint venture participants actuarially to determine how similar or dissimilar they are. Modification of the plans to conform to the ASG requirements is an appropriate course of action in some instances, especially where a small number of plans are involved and the study shows minimal disparity.

Because the ERISA rules are in a state of flux and because new regulations issued may retroactively affect business arrangements, joint venture participants should seek private letter rulings from the IRS as to the applicability of the various rules to a specific set of facts. Moreover, because the tax legislation gives the Treasury Department the authority to prescribe additional regulations to prevent the avoidance of employee benefit requirements whenever possible, venturers should request that these private letter rulings assure them that the IRS will not at a future date construe a proposed business transaction that is presently legitimate as one resulting in the creation of an ASG.

Employee Leasing

The leasing of employees, such as nurses and technicians, from other organizations is a prevalent business practice in the health care industry because it can significantly reduce start-up costs or other burdens in joint venture enterprises. In addition, the use of leased employees can at times permit employers to avoid the ERISA antidiscrimination rules. This situation was especially true in past years. Prior to the passage of the Tax Equity and Fiscal Responsibility Act of 1982 (TEFRA), some employers were able to maintain otherwise discriminatory plans by directly employing only professional personnel. All other employees were leased by means of a contract with a personnel service agency. Because the leased employees were not counted as employees of that employer for purposes of measuring whether the pension plans of that employer qualified under tax rules, plans that were extremely generous to the professional upper-echelon employees did not lose their tax qualification.

The enactment of TEFRA significantly modified the employers' ability to avoid the discrimination rules through the vehicle of employee leasing. Under present tax law, an employer who has not leased employees in the past and who maintains a qualified pension plan must count as its own employees for pension qualification purposes all of the leased employees who have provided services of a type historically performed in the business field of the employer and who have performed these services on a substantially full-time basis for at least one year.[50] Leased employees who are attributed to the employer under the leasing rules are considered to be that organization's employees for purposes of, among other requirements, nondiscrimination and benefit coverage, minimum participation and vesting standards, and maximum limitations on contributions and benefits.

Safe-Harbor Pension Plan

The tax law provides a *safe harbor*, which is a set of guidelines that, if followed, enable an employer who maintains a bona fide leasing arrangement to exclude leased employees from its pension plan. For an employer to qualify for such safe-harbor treatment, the leasing company must maintain its own qualified money-purchase pension plan that provides for immediate participation and total vesting of all pension rights and interests. A *money purchase pension plan* is one in which contributions are predetermined but are not dependent on the employer's profit. Pension contributions made by the leasing agency under this plan must equal at least 7.5 percent of each employee's gross annual earnings, in addition to any social security contributions.[51] Also, each leased employee must be a full participant in the leasing organization's plan for the full plan year, which must correspond to that of the employer's pension plan. Any employee not entitled to all of these benefits under the leasing agency's plan must be counted as an employee of the health care employer for purposes of the tax qualification of its plan.

Common-Law Employees

Despite the safe-habor provision, the IRS only allows employees to qualify as safe-harbor leased employees if they are not viewed as employees of the lessee under common-law principles.[52] In other words, the leasing agency must be the real employer of the leased employees. Employees who nominally work for a leasing agency but who provide all of their services to one employer and who are treated by that employer as its own employees in everything except its pension plan and other benefits are deemed by the IRS to be the common-law employees of that employer. To arrive at this determination, the IRS considers all of the circumstances surrounding the suspect employment and decides who has the real responsibility for the employees.

Several key factors that can be relevant in determining whether a leased employee is a common-law employee of an employer are:

- Whether the leasing agency has direct and daily supervision over the leased employees or whether the employing company supervises the employee
- Whether time and payroll records are recorded and maintained by the leasing company or the employing company
- Whether the leasing agency has total responsibility for the recruitment of employees and for job assignments and discipline
- Whether the leasing organization or the employer sets employee compensation levels and determines what, if any, benefits are available for that employee

The risks associated with the status of common-law employer are substantial. Such an employer remains liable for withholding income tax, and all of its common-law employees must be counted for purposes of determining benefit plan qualification. In this event, such leased employees would be entitled to participate in the common-law employer's pension plan even though the leasing agency has already provided them with pension benefits that fully satisfy all present safe-harbor rules.

The ERISA rules with respect to employee leasing are complex even for the tax practitioner. They are relevant, however, to any consideration of a joint venture project that might use some sort of leasing arrangement. If the leasing agency that provides the leased employees to the joint venture enterprise does not maintain its own safe-harbor pension plan, the participants might want to consider other staffing possibilities because, without such a plan, the joint venture is required to provide for pension plan participation for its leased employees on the same terms as are made available to other joint venture employees.

Notes

1. I.R.C. §§ 401 et seq.
2. I.R.C. § 401(a)(4).
3. ERISA rules that may have an impact on employee plans include:
    - Employee participation and eligibility, discrimination, and vesting requirements and the employee benefit and contribution limitation rules that are imposed on qualified pension, profit-sharing, and stock bonus plans (I.R.C. §§ 401(a)(3), (4), (7), (16); §§ 410, 411, 415)
    - Funding requirements and employer deduction rules in the case of multiemployer pension plans (I.R.C. §§ 412, 413, 414(f))
    - Antidiscrimination rules imposed on self-insured medical expense reimbursement plans (I.R.C. § 105(h))
    - Rules that are applicable to cafeteria plans (I.R.C. § 125)
    - Rules that are applicable in the case of qualified employee pension plans (I.R.C. § 408(k))
4. See I.R.C. § 410(b)(3). This is most often the case when hospital employees are involved.

Chapter 5. ERISA Issues

Notes

5. An existing collective bargaining agreement may have as part of its terms the requirement that employees of new joint ventures in which the employer participates be covered under the existing collective bargaining agreement. *See* the discussion of collective bargaining agreements in Chapter 9.

6. I.R.C. § 414(c); Treas. Reg. § 1.414(c)-2 (1984).

7. I.R.C. § 414(m); Proposed Treas. Reg. §§ 1.414(m)-1 *et seq.* (1984).

8. I.R.C. § 414(m)(3); Proposed Treas. Reg. § 1.414(m)-2(f)(1) (1984).

9. Proposed Treas. Reg. § 1.414(m)-2(f)(2)(i) (1984).

10. I.R.C. § 414(m)(2).

11. *Id.*

12. I.R.C. § 414(n)(5).

13. I.R.C. § 414(c); Treas. Reg. § 1.414(c)-2 (1984).

14. I.R.C. § 414(m); Proposed Treas. Reg. §§ 1.414(m)-1 *et seq.*(1984).

15. *See* Proposed Treas. Reg. § 1.414(m)-1(b) (1984).

16. I.R.C. § 414(m)(3).

17. Proposed Treas. Reg. § 1.414(m)-2(e) (1984).

18. Proposed Treas. Reg. § 1.414(m)-2(f)(2)(i) (1984).

19. Proposed Treas. Reg. § 1.414(m)-2(f)(1) (1984).

20. Proposed Treas. Reg. § 1.414(m)-1(c) (1984).

21. Proposed Treas. Reg. § 1.414(m)-1(c) (1984).

22. I.R.C. § 414(m)(2).

23. *See* I.R.C. § 318(a).

24. I.R.C. § 414(m)(2).

25. Proposed Treas. Reg. § 1.414(m)-2(b)(2) (1984).

26. Proposed Treas. Reg. § 1.414(m)-2(b)(2) (1984). This section provides that the amount of the earned income derived from performing services for the FSO or from performing services for third persons in association with the FSO could be determinative of whether that organization *regularly* provides such services. But the "Supplementary Information" provided in the Notice of Proposed Rulemaking first containing the proposed regulations seems to contradict it by stating that "aggregation will be required . . . regardless of how small the interest is that the A Organization holds in the First Service Organization, . . . *even if the services performed for the First Service Organization only constitute an insignificant portion of the business of the A Organization*" (emphasis added) [1983] Fed. Tax Coordinator (CCH) ¶8966. Final regulations on this problem containing some definition of the term *regularly* as it is used in the statute may be issued in 1986.

27. Proposed Treas. Reg. §§ 1.414(m)-2(c)(2)(i), (iii) (1984). This ratio is the greater of the ratio for the year for which the determination is being made or the ratio for the three-year period including that year and the two preceding years or the period of the organization's existence, if less. Proposed Treas. Reg. § 1.414(m)-2(c)(2)(iv) (1984).

28. Proposed Treas. Reg. § 1.414(m)-2(c)(2)(v) (1984).

29. Proposed Treas. Reg. § 1.414(m)-2(c)(3) (1984).

30. Proposed Treas. Reg. §§ 1.414(m)-2(c)(4), (6) (1984).

31. Proposed Treas. Reg. § 1.414(m)-2(g)(1) (1984).

32. Prop. Treas. Reg. § 1.414(m)-2(g)(2) (1984).

33. In testing for plan discrimination in favor of one group over another, all of the compensation paid to each employee must be considered, not just the percentage of compensation paid by one ASG member maintaining the plan. For example, common-law employees of B-ORGs will have FSO plan benefits measured against B-ORG compensation to see whether FSO plan benefits discriminate in favor of the prohibited group.

34. This example is derived from Proposed Treas. Reg. § 1.414(m)-2(g) (1984).

35. I.R.C. § 414(m)(5).

36. As determined in accordance with the rules for determining *related persons* under I.R.C. § 103(b)(6)(C).

Notes

37. Proposed Treas. Reg. § 1.414(m)-1(c) (1984).

38. Proposed Treas. Reg. § 1.414(m)-1(c) (1984).

39. In enacting the ASG rules, Congress specifically stated that it was acting for the express purpose of overruling results that it deemed to be unfavorable in two cases. In the *Kiddie* case (69 T.C. 1055 (1978)) and in the *Garland* case (73 T.C. 5 (1979)), the tax court held that the plans established by the professional corporations involved in those cases were not subject to the antidiscrimination rules and therefore did not have to provide coverage for rank-and-file employees. Congress determined that the use of separate entities should not enable individual professionals to avoid employee benefit requirements. *See* Committee Report on Pub. L. No. 96-605 in [1985] STAND. FED. TAX REP. (CCH) ¶33,342.

40. I.R.C. § 401(a)(4).

41. I.R.C. § 410(b)(1)(B); Treas. Reg. § 1.410(b)-1(b)(2) (1985). For a discussion of the application of this provision to different fact situations, *see* [1986] FED. TAX COORDINATOR 2d (RIA) ¶H-6512-13.

42. Geiser and Belinkoff, *Trends in Physician Organizations*, CALIFORNIA HEALTH LAW NEWS (to be published in 1986).

43. Proposed Treas. Reg. § 1.414(m)-1(c)(1984).

44. As at least one tax commentator has noted, the commissioner of the IRS may determine that, in practice, the exception in the temporary proposed regulations for corporations other than professional service corporations has resulted in the avoidance of the purpose of the ASG rules, thereby circumventing Congressional intent. If the IRS finds that this exception is used too often to avoid the application of the ASG rules, this exception may be removed from the final regulations. [1986] FED. TAX COORDINATOR 2d (RIA) ¶150,825.

45. Proposed Treas. Reg. § 1.414(m)-1(c)(1984).

46. *See* Proposed Treas. Reg. § 1.414(m)-1(c)(1984).

47. I.R.C. § 318(a).

48. *Id.*

49. *See* Peters, *Participation in Joint Ventures, PPOs and IPAs May Threaten Pension Plans*, HEALTHCARE FINANCIAL MANAGEMENT, Oct. 1984, at 69.

50. I.R.C. §§ 414(n)(1), (2).

51. I.R.C. § 414(n)(5).

52. Rev. Rul. 69-144, 1969-1 C.B. 115.

Chapter 6: Regulatory Concerns

  Health-Care-Oriented Regulations
     Certificate-of-Need Laws
     Licensure
     Rate Review
     Regulation by Type of Facility
        Hospital Outpatient Facilities
        Outpatient Centers Operated by Licensed Professionals
        Laboratories
        Equipment Acquisitions
        Alternate Delivery Systems
           Health Maintenance Organizations
           Preferred Provider Organizations
  Land Use and Environmental Impact Requirements
     Environmental Impact Statement
     Zoning
     Example

Chapter 6. Regulatory Concerns

Health-Care-Oriented Regulations
Certificate-of-Need Laws

Federal and state statutes and regulations have an impact on the type and legal structure of joint ventures that a health care provider may ultimately undertake. These regulatory concerns are of two basic types: regulations specific to the health care industry and general regulations that affect any industry, including health care. The principal health care regulations other than reimbursement regulations, which are discussed in chapter 7, are certificate-of-need (CON) requirements, licensing requirements, and rate review. The most important general regulatory concerns are those relating to land use and the environmental impact of the new facility.

Health-Care-Oriented Regulations

State statutes regulate health care activities in three major ways:

- They limit the amount of capital outlays that a particular health care facility may make by issuing or denying a CON.
- They mandate or regulate the budgets for health care facilities or the fees that the health care provider may charge.
- They control the licensure of the facility or of its operators.

Each state has different approaches to licensing and regulating health care facilities. Moreover, the state statutes are constantly undergoing review and revision. Before commencing a joint venture project, the participants must know and understand the regulatory approach of the state in which the project is to be located and must be prepared to structure the venture to comply with that state's requirements.

Certificate-of-Need Laws

A federal statute mandates CONs for various health care facilities and certain equipment within them and also mandates their form and substance.[1] These certificates, which show that the facility or equipment is necessary, must be issued before a new health care facility can be constructed or, in some cases, before its ownership can be transferred or capital outlays for expensive medical equipment can be made.

Because the federal statute is implemented in states at their option,[2] many states do not precisely comply with it.[3] There is therefore considerable variation in CON requirements from state to state. Local circumstances are largely determinative of whether capital expenditures are restricted in certain cases and to what extent. Some states are less restrictive than the federal government in fixing maximum threshold levels above which a CON will be required.[4] Others do not have any specific CON legislation, although in those states there is generally some form of review over capital expenditures by health care providers.[5] Several states, such as Utah, prefer to permit market forces to control expenditures and have allowed or are allowing existing CON legislation to expire.[6] In a number of states, however, there is presently some control over capital expenditures for certain types of health care facilities that must be taken into account when planning joint ventures. Depending on the way the joint venture is structured, a CON may be required.

Not all health care facilities or equipment purchases require a CON. Various factors can trigger a CON review:

- A CON review is applicable to capital expenditures for a covered health care facility if those expenditures exceed a certain threshold amount or if the facility changes bed capacity or substantially changes the services it offers.

97

- A CON is also applicable to acquisitions of major medical equipment above a certain dollar threshold if the equipment is owned by or located in a covered health care facility or is used for inpatient care. Undertakings of such defined magnitude *by or on behalf of* covered health care providers, such as hospitals and skilled nursing facilities, usually require a CON.
- Certain other new facilities, such as specialty hospitals and ambulatory surgical centers in some states, may be subject to review.
- Even though a hospital or other provider whose actions generally require CON review does not itself operate the facility, a CON review may be necessary in either of the following instances if:[7]
  - The provider is significantly involved with others in a project (such as owning 50 percent or more of the facility), that would have required CON review if that provider had undertaken the project alone.
  - The facility will be used to provide health care services to the covered provider's patients, even if the facility is not owned by or located within the covered provider's facility. A substantial ownership interest may not even be necessary. An example of such involvement may be a guarantee by the covered provider of capital to a group of physicians to enable them to acquire an ambulatory surgical clinic or magnetic resonance imaging (MRI) equipment that those physicians will operate. The important element is the capital expenditure *by or on behalf of* the covered facility.

In those states that require a CON before a project can be undertaken, the application process can be slow, expensive, and generally frustrating for the parties. The parties must file a notice with the designated planning agency before making the capital expenditure. Then, within a period specified in the statutes the agency recommends approval or disapproval. A hearing may be held during the agency review. Once the agency has issued its final determination, further review under the federal Section 1122 program may be necessary. Review of any particular project is under the law of the state in which it is to be located.[8] After such a review, the Secretary of Health and Human Services makes a final decision. If the decision is unfavorable, the parties can request reconsideration within the time specified by the agency, depending on the nature of the application.

If the parties do not receive a notice of final determination from the agency, the capital expenditure can be made under federal law. However, without the CON, Medicare and Medicaid reimbursement will be denied for expenses related to the expenditure. This burdensome regulatory process may be reduced somewhat once changes in the program made in 1985 have been fully implemented.[9]

Before granting a CON, state authorities take into account various factors, all of which must be adequately documented. In most states, the party requesting the CON must show that it is needed.[10] The proposed impact of the new health care facility on existing facilities is frequently a major consideration to CON approval. For instance, an existing inpatient facility could oppose a CON application by claiming that it can provide the same services to be offered by the new enterprise; comparative expense is not taken into consideration. This argument could tempt health care planners who seek to ensure full utilization of existing facilities before approving new ones.

A project that requires CON review and for which the application has been denied cannot be undertaken without risk of sanctions. The penalties for failure to comply with the law vary, depending on the state, but they can include loss or denial of government funds and reimbursement; loss or denial of licensure for the facility; civil or criminal penalties, such as fines; and even a court-ordered closing of facility operations.[11] Consequently, when determining how to structure a joint venture, the parties should take these laws seriously and act to either obtain the requisite CON or avoid the application of the law.

Because a CON may be denied, particularly if it is contested by a competitor, and because considerable delays and expense may be involved, participants in a joint venture may want to avoid the CON process whenever possible.[12] A CON review can be avoided in several ways:

- The participants can choose a party other than the hospital to operate the joint venture facility. For example, a hospital might participate with outside investors in a joint venture to establish an ambulatory facility that will offer emergency services. In some states, such a facility is covered by CON requirements if the facility is established as a new department of the hospital or if it is organized as a freestanding center operated by or on behalf of the hospital, but the facility will escape review if it is operated solely by a group of physicians as a physician office practice. In this instance, the hospital may indirectly participate by acting as a *service bureau* and by providing services directly to the physician operating group. Of course, the hospital receives compensation for all services that it provides.
- Sometimes the type of facility determines whether a CON review is required. For instance, an ambulatory surgical center that is physician owned and controlled may nevertheless require CON approval in one state, while an emergency clinic might escape review, even though the basic appearance of and the equipment in the two centers are similar.[13] One state exempts from CON review capital expenditures by health maintenance organizations (HMOs) that meet the statutory definition for an HMO as well as expenditures by any facility providing services to an HMO or to persons served by the HMO.[14] That same state requires CON review not only for hospitals but also for hospices, nursing homes, rehabilitation facilities, and home care agencies.[15]
- Another means by which a hospital may avoid the CON process is through a holding company. The hospital could reorganize to create a parent holding company with several subsidiaries. One of the subsidiaries is the hospital, and another is an outpatient service corporation that is separate and distinct from the hospital. Either the parent holding company or the new outpatient service subsidiary could participate in the joint venture and thereby minimize the risk that state authorities would deem the expenditures for it to be *by or on behalf of* a covered health care facility.

Licensure

As with CON, licensure requirements vary significantly from state to state, and there are no set rules that apply to all projects in all states. When organizing a joint venture, the participants must ascertain whether the enterprise requires a distinct license or certification before deciding on the actual legal structure of the venture.

Some states require licenses for new hospital facilities but exempt many types of ambulatory care clinics. For example, an ambulatory surgical center in California or Texas that is operated as a distinct entity consisting solely of physicians can function under the physicians' existing licenses (as a physician office practice) and can permit other legally authorized health care professionals who are not members of the entity to perform surgical procedures at the center without having to obtain a special license.[16] On the other hand, many states require licensure of freestanding ambulatory surgical centers.[17] Pennsylvania, for example, requires a license for ambulatory surgical facilities that include distinct outpatient treatment on a regular and organized basis even if the facilities are organized as physician office practices.[18]

Some types of facilities can only be reimbursed by Medicare if they are licensed by the state in which they are located.[19] In those instances, if the participants find that Medicare reimbursement is important to the financial feasibility of the joint venture, then it may be worthwhile to obtain a license despite the expense and delay.[20]

Other licensure questions must also be considered by economic joint venture participants. One question that must be answered when planning a health care facility such as an ambulatory surgical center is whether the requirements for obtaining hospital licensing are applicable. Many states have extensive regulations with respect to building safety requirements, staffing, and other aspects of the hospital facility that must be met before the joint venture facility can obtain a license.[21] Meeting these requirements can be prohibitive for a new facility, and yet, such licensure may be a precondition to third-party reimbursement. Another question is whether a proposed transfer of activities or assets from a licensed health care facility to the joint venture organization requires licensing approval. Finally, when a joint venture facility is served by licensed health care professionals, the issue of the so-called corporate practice of medicine must be considered (see chapter 8).

Rate Review

Many states have no form of rate review, but in those states that do, joint venturers must take into account the impact that mandatory rate setting or budget review can have on the revenues of the joint venture. Generalized statements about how states regulate the rates that facilities may charge are impossible to make. Each state statute is different.

For example, a number of states have statutes establishing programs for the regulation of inpatient hospital rates.[22] Some of these programs, such as that in Maine, are applicable to the rates of facilities providing outpatient services if hospitals have a significant degree of involvement (for example, more than 50 percent) in the operation of those facilities.[23] In some of these states, such as Washington, although participation in rate review may be mandatory, actual compliance with the suggestions of the reviewing board appears to be on a voluntary basis.[24] Other statutes are more stringent. West Virginia's statute provides that no rates may be approved unless costs are reasonably related to the services provided and rates are reasonably related to those costs.[25] Connecticut provides for public notification (by means of a newspaper notice) of any hospital rates that it deems to be excessive.[26] Other jurisdictions have related provisions. Several states, for instance, have rate disclosure laws that provide for public disclosure of hospital rates and services as well as other information with respect to hospital budget review.[27] At times, rate review is interrelated with the CON application process and, in fact, at least one state has placed CON and rate review under the control of a single board.[28]

Regulation by Type of Facility

How these various health care regulations affect a joint venture depends on what type of facility is projected. Various health care enterprises that may receive differing treatment under CON, licensure, or rate review statutes are hospitals and outpatient facilities operated by hospitals; outpatient centers run by other licensed professionals, such as physicians; laboratories; equipment acquisitions, such as MRI units or lithotripters; and alternative delivery systems, such as HMOs or preferred provider organizations (PPOs).

Hospital Outpatient Facilities

In any state requiring CON approval, the construction or renovation of a new health care facility covered by the CON law (such as a hospital or skilled nursing facility) or an addition to such a facility, an increase in beds, or a significant change in services triggers a CON review if expenditures for constructing or improving the facility or for the changes to it exceed the threshold amounts required by the law of the particular state in which the facility is located.[29] Similar rules apply to the construction of a new specialty facility or outpatient department by or on behalf of such a covered facility. A CON is required by any state that reviews such capital expenditures. In addition, states require that hospitals meet minimum requirements for licensure, which vary from state to state but which usually include some provision with respect to building safety requirements, staffing, and inspections.[30]

Outpatient Centers Operated by Licensed Professionals

The treatment of health care facilities operated as physicians' offices varies from state to state for CON and licensing purposes.[31] As a general rule, no CON is required for clinics, such as ambulatory surgical centers or emergency treatment clinics, that are operated by licensed professionals other than hospitals. Neither do these facilities have to seek a separate license. They can be operated as physicians' offices under the health care professional's existing license.

Some states are more exacting with respect to such ambulatory care centers. A number of states now require CON approval for freestanding ambulatory surgical centers regardless of ownership.[32] Pennsylvania's statute requires a CON for all health care facilities, including ambulatory surgical centers, except for offices used *exclusively* for a physician's private practice.[33]

A few states require ambulatory surgical centers to be licensed separately.[34] These states usually license surgicenters separately but include facilities that are part of a hospital within the scope of the hospital's license.[35] Other states license freestanding centers but exclude from such licensure surgical suites located within or adjacent to physicians' offices. Such suites are operated under the physicians' existing professional license.[36]

At least one state requires that any ambulatory health care facility, whether freestanding or operated in connection with a hospital, be licensed.[37] Only the legally authorized practice of surgery within a physician's private office is excepted.

In most states, other types of facilities, such as occupational medicine centers and other clinics, escape CON review and licensure if they are located in or operated as part of a physician's office practice. There are some exceptions. A number of states require licensure of home health care agencies.[38] Several states license hospices[39] and birthing centers.[40] Finally, in a few states, such facilities must obtain a CON before a license is issued.[41]

Laboratories

The CON requirements of most states do not apply to medical facilities other than primary care facilities and certain freestanding clinics. A freestanding clinical laboratory would generally not be subject to CON review. The CON statutes in a few states specifically exclude the acquisition of major medical equipment acquired by or on behalf of a clinical laboratory independent of both physicians' offices or a hospital.[42]

Licensure and rate review also depend on specific state laws. Most states provide for the licensure of laboratories or require that such facilities be operated under the supervision of a licensed medical professional.[43]

Many states may have other, more specific, requirements. For example, Florida sets minimum standards with respect to the acceptance of results of diagnostic x-ray and laboratory test results as part of its licensure process.[44]

Equipment Acquisitions

In the past, acquisition of medical equipment by parties other than hospitals was outside the CON process. This situation has changed as many states attempt to review projects that are not specifically sponsored by hospitals.

So far, only a few states require some sort of review of capital expenditures for diagnostic equipment, including MRI units, regardless of the purchaser.[45] In those states, a joint venture for an MRI center in which physicians purchase the MRI unit and operate it separately from the hospital requires CON review.

In the future, more states will probably limit capital expenditures by all parties acquiring expensive diagnostic and other equipment. Eventually, purchases of MRI units will likely be limited to ownership by facilities or to centralized ownership of a restricted number of units within a given geographical area. In such a regulatory environment, a hospital may not escape CON review for such an acquisition by having its staff members own and operate the equipment while it participates only indirectly in the joint venture by means of a facilities lease or a management contract.

Alternative Delivery Systems

Federal and state regulations affect the formation and operation of alternative delivery care systems: health maintenance organizations (HMOs) and preferred provider organizations (PPOs).

Health Maintenance Organizations

Although several HMOs, such as the Kaiser Foundation Health Plan, have been operational for several decades, the popularity of HMOs has increased dramatically in the past several years. Commensurate with the general growth of HMOs has been the interest by hospitals and physicians in developing HMOs and other alternative delivery systems on a joint venture basis. In so doing, joint venture participants should take into account applicable regulations at both the federal and state levels.

The HMO can seek federal qualification under the Health Maintenance Organization Act of 1973 (the HMO Act).[46] Federally qualified HMOs are required to set their premiums according to a *community rating* as established by federal statutes and regulations. This rating system requires that an HMO's premium rates may not vary from group to group on the basis of individual group health service utilization experience. Conventional health insurers, on the other hand, use an *experience rating* procedure, in which the premium rates charged to a particular employer group are based on that group's own utilization experience.

Other areas regulated under the federal statute and also by state law are the scope of benefits available to members, the manner in which premiums are structured, procedures for review of quality assurance, enrollment requirements, the relationship between the HMO and its health care providers, licensing, and financial condition. For example, HMOs must file periodic reports with, and are subject to periodic review by, the federal and state licensing authorities that regulate the HMO.[47]

The HMO must provide members with certain basic services, including primary care physician services, specialist physician services, inpatient hospital care, outpatient surgical and medical care, emergency department services, and various diagnostic services. These services are usually offered on a fixed, prepaid fee basis. The HMO is further required to have a policy-making body, one third of which must be members of the HMO unrelated to the management or owners of the HMO, and it is also required to have quality assurance and educational programs for all the health care professionals used by the HMO and HMO members. Only HMOs that continue to meet federal criteria for sound fiscal operation may retain their qualified status.

The federal HMO Act takes precedence over any state law purporting to regulate HMOs. Any HMO qualified under the federal act is exempt from state laws that require medical society approval or physician governance, subject the HMO to state insurance laws requiring certain capitalization of reserves, or prevent HMOs from soliciting members through advertising.

Nevertheless, HMOs must comply with provisions of state HMO, health, and insurance laws that are not in conflict with federal laws, and these laws can vary extensively.[48] Most states license HMOs and regulate their financial condition as well as the structure of their premiums. In addition, there are often restrictions on the ability of HMOs to cancel enrollees and to reduce or eliminate benefits provided to members. The premium rates of HMOs may also be subject to approval by the insurance commissioner of the state in which the company is located. In a number of states, HMOs are specifically subject to local CON laws,[49] although at least one state exempts from its CON requirements capital expenditures by or on behalf of HMOs or for services to be used by HMOs.[50]

Preferred Provider Organizations

Basically, PPOs are arrangements whereby a group purchaser contracts with a number of providers to render various health care services to a specific group of people at a negotiated rate. The providers are paid on a fee-for-service basis. A few states have enacted statutes specifically dealing with PPOs.[51] Other states may eventually consider similar legislation.[52]

By the end of 1985, only two states directly regulated PPOs to any extent.[53] However, other states may regulate insurer-sponsored PPOs to a limited extent through the provisions of their insurance laws.[54] A PPO may be regulated as an insurance company if it meets the definitional characteristics of such an entity under that particular state's insurance code. For example, if a PPO is structured so that it assumes the economic risk of any subscriber's illness, it may fall within the scope of laws regulating insurers or HMOs.[55] Most states regulate the business of insurance quite extensively.

The various PPO statutes vary in their terms. Some statutes regulate only a form of PPO called an *exclusive provider organization* (EPO). An EPO differs from a PPO in that the EPO obliges the enrollee to select a provider from a defined group of contracting providers, whereas the PPO affords the enrollee the option, on a case-by-case basis, of using a contracting provider or a noncontracting provider. For instance, California's legislation authorizes and, by means of regulations promulgated under this legislation, prescribes minimum benefit standards and standards for availability and accessibility of preferred providers.[56] The Virginia statute, on the other hand, expressly forbids such EPOs. It merely allows insurers to negotiate and enter into contracts for alternative rates with licensed health care providers.[57] Indiana's statute authorizes PPO agreements and authorizes its insurance commissioner to issue regulations prescribing reasonable standards with respect to the accessibility and availability of health care services.[58] Minnesota's law imposes annual reporting requirements for insurers offering PPOs.[59]

In addition, PPOs are regulated by all other federal and state laws and regulations that apply to any business association. These laws and regulations include those specific to the health care industry, such as rate review statutes, and other general business statutes, such as state corporation statutes, state and federal tax laws, and antitrust laws.

Land Use and Environmental Impact Requirements

Although not uniquely applicable to health care joint ventures, the requirements of a particular locality with respect to land use and environmental impact must be considered in determining whether a joint venture is feasible on a particular site and how it should be constructed so as to comply with the various regulations. In this area, as in the areas of health care regulation and licensing, no specific rule is applicable everywhere.

Local land use requirements can affect a proposed joint venture project in two major ways. First, before a project that will have a significant impact on the environment can be constructed, many states require a report on the resulting environmental impact. Second, most localities have some sort of land use requirements that regulate the location of a project and its physical components.

Environmental Impact Statement

Many states require that environmental impact statements be submitted for every major project having an impact on the environment.[60] The purpose of the environmental impact statement is to provide public agencies and the public in general with detailed information about the effect that a proposed project is likely to have on the existing environment. The report also lists ways to minimize those effects and suggests alternatives to the project.[61]

After the local planning agency carefully considers all relevant areas of environmental concern, it can waive the required environmental impact statements. In that event, the project's sponsor can substitute for the environmental impact report a finding that the effect of the proposed project will not be significant or potentially adverse. This finding is called a *negative impact report*.[62] Because the process of preparing and processing an environmental impact statement is time consuming and expensive, it is best to structure any project proposal so that the statement will not be required and a negative impact report will suffice.

Zoning

The zoning requirements of a particular locality can also have a serious impact on a joint venture project. These requirements are peculiar to each locality, and a project that might be accepted in one area could be denied a permit in another. For example, in the case of the medical pavilion proposed as a hypothetical joint venture in appendix F, whether the project is feasible may depend on the zoning at the site selected for the clinic. If the pavilion is to be located in an industrial zone, for example, in a high-technology computer complex, it would probably be approved in most localities because many zoning ordinances allow for higher uses but not lower uses in any zoning category. Industrial use is usually the lowest use, and therefore any higher use, such as the health care clinic, would be permitted. If, on the other hand, the proposed site is in a commercial office building zoned for residential or light commercial use, the project might not be feasible if such health care centers are classed in a lower category.

Most states require that local governments have some sort of master plan.[63] Zoning ordinances must comply with the requirements of this plan. Even when a project proposal is in perfect compliance with the plan and with all local ordinances, the approval process can be lengthy and costly in many localities.

Problems can arise when the project represents a deviation from the city plan. Then a *variance* may be required to permit the project to be built.[64] When a proposed use of land requires a deviation from established zoning practices, notice of the proposed variance must be sent to all affected landowners, and a hearing on the proposal is held. At the hearing, interested parties may voice their approval or disapproval of the proposed project. The applicant must usually show some hardship or other legitimate reason for requesting a variance.[65] In most cases, that means that the hardship must arise from the zoning ordinance, not the actions of the applicant.[66]

The hearing process can be lengthy and at times costly, and there is always a risk that the request will be denied. Even if it is granted, disgruntled landowners may continue to fight the proposed project in court.

Example

The following example shows how land use problems can frustrate a project.

A hospital decides to participate in a joint venture with local physicians to construct a freestanding ambulatory surgical center on a site that had been originally acquired by the hospital for administrative offices. The site is in geographical proximity to the hospital. On the site is a large old home that has been converted into several apartments. Although the area is zoned for residential use, city officials have expressed a willingness to rezone the property or at least grant a variance in order to permit construction of the ambulatory surgery clinic, because they recognize the changing needs of the neighborhood. Notice is sent to all property owners in the neighborhood of the proposed city action, and a hearing is held.

After the variance is granted, several parties protest the proposed use and threaten legal action. The legal owner of the property adjacent to the proposed site, who did not receive notice of the hearing because she had only recently acquired the property and her name had not yet appeared on city lists of property owners, is protesting the validity of the hearing-notice procedures of the city. She also claims that the negative impact report filed with the city by the project's sponsors is unjustified because increased traffic flow in the neighborhood and parking congestion caused by the new facility will have a significant adverse impact on the environment. She is demanding that an environmental impact statement be prepared.

Also protesting are the tenants in the apartments that are to be destroyed when the new building is constructed. They are claiming that the proposed construction is a violation of local rent control laws, which forbid taking rental housing off the market. Finally, a neighborhood group is charging that the house that the hospital intends to demolish is a historic landmark and is entitled to classification and preservation as such.[67]

Even if the claims of these disgruntled parties have little merit, any lawsuit on their complaints would be costly and could cause delays that might even kill the project.[68] For that reason, the parties to a joint venture project should, in the early planning stages of a project, review all local planning laws and ordinances, including those relating to environmental impact, land use, rent control, and historic preservation, to determine whether or not the proposed project will comply. In addition, they should assess the political impact of their proposal. In this example, the parties were suing because they were unhappy with the idea of having an ambulatory surgery clinic in their neighborhood. If the joint venture proponents had considered the attitudes of potential opponents of the project and had taken these into account when planning it, they might not have encountered such vehement opposition.

Notes

1. Social Security Act § 1122, as added by Pub. L. No. 93-641 § 221(a), codified at 42 U.S.C. § 1320a-1.

2. It will be required of all states by Oct. 1, 1986, if capital expenditures are not built into the Medicare prospective pricing system by that time.

3. Congress has indicated a desire to allow variation in state and local programs by prohibiting the imposition of statutory sanctions against noncomplying states. Hill-Chinn, *State Legal Initiatives Status Report: Health Planning and Capital Expenditure Regulation*, 7 HEALTH LAW VIGIL, Dec. 7, 1984, Supplement 1 [hereinafter cited as Hill-Chinn].

4. Nine states (Alaska, Arizona, California, Colorado, Montana, Utah, Washington, and Wisconsin) had one or more CON thresholds above maximum federal levels in 1984. *Id.* Connecticut's new CON law requires a CON for capital expenditures exceeding $600,000 or acquisitions of major medical equipment exceeding $400,000. CONN. GEN. STAT. ANN. § 19a-155 (1985 Special Pamphlet). Washington only requires a CON for capital expenditures or for the acquisition of major medical equipment for which payments exceed $1 million. WASH. REV. CODE ANN. § 70.38.025.

5. Louisiana does not have a CON law. Laws in Idaho, Minnesota, and New Mexico have expired. *See, e.g.,* N.M. STAT. ANN. §§ 24-3A-1 *et seq.* (effective until July 1, 1983; repealed 1981 N.M. Laws ch. 300, § 9). However, all four states review capital expenditures under Section 1122 of the Social Security Act, 42 U.S.C. ch. 7. *See, e.g.,* IDAHO CODE §§ 39-1401 *et seq.;* MINN. STAT. ANN. § 144.072 (West). *See generally* Hill-Chinn, *supra* note 3.

6. In Utah, the CON law expired on Dec. 31, 1984. That state has not agreed to perform capital expenditure reviews under Section 1122 of the Social Security Act. *See Utah First State to Deregulate Health Care Capital Spending,* HOSPITAL WEEK, Jan. 11, 1985, at 2. The CON laws in Kansas and Arizona were scheduled to sunset in the summer of 1984. The Kansas statute was extended to July 1, 1985. In Arizona, the CON law was extended to Mar. 1, 1985, and a rate freeze and moratorium on new beds and new hospital construction was imposed. Minnesota's CON law expired on June 1, 1984, but a three-year moratorium on new facility construction was imposed. Hill-Chinn, *supra* note 3. The CON program also expired in 1985 in Indiana. IND. CODE ANN. § 16-1-3.3-16 (West Supp. 1986). Legislation passed in California in 1984 suspends the CON program in that state as of Jan. 1, 1987. CAL. HEALTH & SAFETY CODE § 439.7 (Deering Supp. 1986). Washington's CON law provides specifically that it will sunset on June 30, 1990. WASH. REV. CODE ANN. § 70.39.110.

7. *See, e.g.,* 35 PA. CONS. STAT. ANN. § 448.701-(a)(5) (Purdon).

8. *See, e.g.,* FLA. STAT. ANN. § 395.007 (West 1982).

9. *See* 50 Fed. Reg. 2008 *et seq.* (Jan. 14, 1985) (listing certain 1985 changes in the program).

10. *See, e.g.,* 35 PA. CONS. STAT. ANN. § 448.101 (Purdon).

11. *See, e.g.,* KAN. STAT. ANN. § 65-128 (an application for a health facility license must be accompanied by a CON). In Connecticut, the superior court may enforce any CON requirement, and failure to comply could result in a contempt of court citation. CONN. GEN. STAT. ANN. § 19a-159 (West Special Pamphlet 1985). In Washington, there is a $100 fine for each day the CON has not been obtained. WASH. REV. CODE ANN. § 70.38.125.

12. When considering an application for a CON that is being contested by a competing facility, courts have held that, following the *Ashbacker* rule, the party contesting a CON that would conflict with its own project must be given a hearing. *See* Ashbacker Radio Corp. v. FCC, 326 U.S. 327 (1945).

13. *See, e.g.,* WASH. REV. CODE ANN. § 70.38.105; ME. REV. STAT. ANN. tit. 22, §§ 303 *et seq.*

14. *See* WASH. REV. CODE ANN. § 70.38.111.

15. WASH. REV. CODE ANN. § 70.38.025(7).

16. CAL. HEALTH & SAFETY CODE § 1206 (West) (except for surgical clinics, any place owned, leased, or operated as a clinic or office by a licensed health care professional and used as an office is exempt from licensing requirements). *See also* TEX. HEALTH & SAFETY CODE ANN. tit. 71, art. 4437f-2, § 4(b)(1) (Vernon).

17. *E.g.,* Texas. TEX. HEALTH & SAFETY CODE ANN. tit. 71, art. 4437f-2, § 4(a) (Vernon).

18. 35 PA. CONS. STAT. ANN. § 448.802a (Purdon). Vermont authorities will also not consider a facility a physician's office for licensure purposes if it offers services above and beyond those of a normal physician's office. Hill-Chinn, *supra* note 3.

19. *See* 42 C.F.R. § 416.10.

Chapter 6. Regulatory Concerns

Notes

20. In some states, obtaining a license can be optional, as in California, for example, for clinics operated as physicians' offices. *See* CAL. HEALTH & SAFETY CODE § 1206 (West).

21. *See, e.g.,* CAL. HEALTH & SAFETY CODE §§ 1200 *et seq.* (West); FLA. STAT. ANN. § 395.005(a)(d) (West).

22. *See, e.g.,* Connecticut (CONN. GEN. STAT. ANN. § 19a-156 (West 1984)); Florida (FLA. STAT. ANN. §§ 395.502 *et seq.* (West 1982)); Maine (ME. REV. STAT. ANN. tit. 22, §§ 381 *et seq.* (1983)); Maryland (MD. PUB. HEALTH CODE ANN. §§ 19-201 *et seq.* (1984)); Massachusetts (MASS. GEN. LAWS ANN. ch. 6A, §§ 31 *et seq.* (West 1983)); New Jersey (N.J. STAT. ANN. §§ 26: 2H-4.1 *et seq.* (West 1978)); New York (N.Y. PUB. HEALTH LAW §§ 2803 *et seq.* (McKinney 1984)); Washington (WASH. REV. CODE ANN. tit. 70, ch. 39); West Virginia (W. VA. CODE ch. 16, art. 29B (1983)); Wisconsin (WIS. STAT. §§ 20.441 *et seq.* (amended 1983-85)); Vermont (VT. STAT. ANN. tit. 26, §§ 1952 *et seq.* (1983)). *See also* AMERICAN HOSPITAL ASSOCIATION, STATE RATE-SETTING LEGISLATION: LEGAL ISSUES IN THE NEGOTIATION AND IMPLEMENTATION OF A STATUTE, State Legal Initiatives, Legal Developments Report No. 3, Jan. 1984.

23. ME. REV. STAT. ANN. tit. 22, §§ 381 *et seq.*

24. *See, e.g.,* WASH. REV. CODE ANN. tit. 70, ch. 39. The Rate Review Commission in Washington is required by law to permit any hospital subject to its provisions to charge reasonable rates and to permit hospitals to render necessary effective services. WASH. REV. CODE ANN. § 70.39.150(2).

25. W. VA. CODE § 16-29B-20.

26. CONN. GEN. STAT. ANN. § 19a-151 (West 1984).

27. *See* OR. REV. STAT. § 442.410 (1983); WIS. STAT. §§ 20.441 *et seq.* (amended 1983-85); FLA. STAT. ANN. § 395.5085 (West); W. VA. CODE § 16-29B-25.

28. *See* W. VA. CODE ch. 16, art. 29B-4.

29. *See* discussion of certificate-of-need laws at the beginning of this chapter.

30. *See, e.g.,* FLA. STAT. ANN. § 395.005(1)(5) (West).

31. *See* Hill-Chinn, *supra* note 3.

32. *See, e.g.,* 35 PA. CONS. STAT. ANN. § 448.101 (Purdon); WASH. REV. CODE ANN. § 70.38.105; ME. REV. STAT. ANN. tit. 22, §§ 303 *et seq.*

33. 35 PA. CONS. STAT. ANN. § 448.101 (Purdon).

34. *See, e.g.,* Kansas, Florida, Virginia, and Pennsylvania. KAN. STAT. ANN. § 65-427; FLA. STAT. ANN. § 395.003(1)(a) (West); W. VA. CODE § 16-5B-1; 35 PA. CONS. STAT. ANN. §§ 448.802a; 448.806 (Purdon).

35. *See, e.g.,* Pennsylvania. 35 PA. CONS. STAT. ANN. § 448.808(b) (Purdon). No separate license is required for different services within a single health care facility, except home health care or intermediate nursing care. Separate licenses are required for home health and intermediate nursing care. In Florida, separate licenses are required for separate nursing facilities maintained in separate premises, even though operated under the same management. FLA. STAT. ANN. § 400.062 (West).

36. *E.g.,* Maine excludes private physician's offices from the definition of an ambulatory surgical center for licensure purposes. ME. REV. STAT. ANN. tit. 22, § 303.

37. W. VA. CODE § 16-15B-1.

38. *E.g.,* Pennsylvania and Florida. 35 PA. CONS. STAT. ANN. § 448.802a (Purdon); FLA. STAT. ANN. §§ 400.461 *et seq.* (West).

39. *E.g.,* West Virginia and Florida. W. VA. CODE §§ 16-5D-6 *et seq*; FLA. STAT. ANN. §§ 400.601 *et seq.* (West).

40. *E.g.,* Pennsylvania and Texas. 35 PA. CONS. STAT. ANN. § 448.802(a) (Purdon); TEX. HEALTH & SAFETY CODE ANN. tit. 71, art. 4437f-3, § 4(a) (Vernon).

41. *E.g.,* Kansas, Florida, and Pennsylvania. KAN. STAT. ANN. § 65-428; FLA. STAT. ANN. § 395.005(1)(f) (West); 35 PA. CONS. STAT. ANN. § 448.808(a)(5) (Purdon).

42. *E.g.,* Maine and Pennsylvania. ME. REV. STAT. ANN. tit. 22, § 30312A; 35 PA. CONS. STAT. ANN. § 448.603 (Purdon).

43. *E.g.,* Connecticut and Pennsylvania. CONN. GEN. STAT. ANN. § 19a-30 (West 1984); 35 PA. CONS. STAT. ANN. §§ 2153, 2154 (Purdon).

Chapter 6. Regulatory Concerns

Notes

44. FLA. STAT. ANN. § 395.009 (West).

45. *E.g.*, Connecticut, Pennsylvania, Maine, and Washington. CONN. GEN. STAT. ANN. § 19a-155 (West 1984); 35 PA. CONS. STAT. ANN. § 448.603 (Purdon); ME. REV. STAT. ANN. tit. 22, § 30312A; WASH. REV. CODE ANN. § 70.38.105. Washington's statute exempts such acquisitions by HMOs.

46. Pub. L. No. 93-222 (amending 42 U.S.C. §§ 300e *et seq.*).

47. *See, e.g.*, the Minnesota Health Maintenance Act. MINN. STAT. ANN. §§ 62D.01 *et seq.* (West).

48. States that do not have HMO statutes are Alabama, Alaska, District of Columbia, Louisiana, Mississippi, Montana, New Mexico, Rhode Island, Wisconsin, and Wyoming. AMERICAN HOSPITAL ASSOCIATION, STATE REGULATION OF PREFERRED PROVIDER ORGANIZATIONS: A SURVEY OF STATE STATUTES, State Legal Initiatives, Legal Developments Report No. 4, Mar. 1984, at 11 n.10 [hereinafter cited as AHA PPO SURVEY].

49. *E.g.*, Maine. ME. REV. STAT. ANN. tit. 22, § 303.

50. Washington. WASH. REV. CODE ANN. § 70.38.105.

51. *E.g.*, California, Florida, Minnesota, Virginia, Wisconsin, and Indiana.

52. Colorado, Michigan, and Utah have considered but have not passed PPO legislation. Utah has promulgated regulations pertaining to PPOs under the authority of its insurance code. UTAH ADMIN. R. 81-82 (1981). *See* AHA PPO SURVEY, *supra* note 48, at 12 n.11.

53. California's regulation only extends to EPOs (exclusive provider organizations). Indiana's statute, which became effective on December 31, 1984, authorizes the insurance commissioner to regulate EPOs established pursuant to the statute. IND. CODE ANN. § 27-8-11 (Burns 1984). *See generally* AHA PPO SURVEY, *supra* note 48, at 5.

54. *See*, discussion of state insurance regulation in the AHA PPO SURVEY, *supra* note 48, at 6-8.

55. AHA PPO SURVEY, *supra* note 48, at 6.

56. CAL. INS. CODE § 10133.5 (West).

57. VA. CODE §§ 38.1-347.2, 38.1-813.4 (1983).

58. IND. CODE ANN. § 27-8-11 (Burns 1984).

59. MINN. STAT. ANN. § 72A.20(15)(4) (West 1973, amended 1984).

60. *See, e.g.*, California Environmental Quality Act of 1970 (CEQA), CAL. PUB. RES. CODE §§ 21000-21176 (West) (every public agency is required to receive and consider an environmental impact report prior to the approval of any project that affects the environment). *See* Friends of Mammoth v. Board of Supervisors, 8 Cal. 3d 247, 502 P.2d 1049, 104 Cal. Rptr. 761 (1972); Juanita Bay Valley Community Ass'n v. Kirkland, 9 Wash. App. 59, 510 P.2d 1140 (1973).

61. *See, e.g.*, 14 CAL. ADM. CODE § 15151; Greenbaum v. City of Los Angeles, 153 Cal. App. 3d 391, 409, 200 Cal. Rptr. 237 (1984). *See also* In re Spring Valley Dev., 300 A.2d 736 (Me. 1973); *In re* Maine Clean Fuels, Inc., 310 A.2d 736 (Me. 1973); *In re* Barker Sergent Corp., 132 Vt. 42, 313 A.2d 669 (1973).

62. *See, e.g.*, CAL. PUB. RES. CODE §§ 21080(c), 21152(b) (West); 14 CAL. ADM. CODE §§ 15060, 15083. *See also* Gabric v. Rancho Palos Verde, 73 Cal. App. 3d 183, 140 Cal. Rptr. 619 (1977); No Oil, Inc. v. Los Angeles, 13 Cal. 3d 68, 529 P.2d 66, 118 Cal. Rptr. 34 (1974); McGlore v. Inaba, 636 P.2d 158 (Haw. 1981); Center Square Ass'n. v. Corning, 105 Misc. 2d 6, 430 N.Y.S. 2d 953 (1980); Gardner v. Pierce County Board of Comm'rs, 27 Wash. App. 241, 617 P.2d 743 (1980).

63. It may be known as the *master plan, comprehensive plan, development plan, municipal plan,* or in some statutes merely *the plan*. *See* Haar, *In Accordance with a Comprehensive Plan*, 68 HARV. L. REV. 1154 (1955). The master plan is a long-term outline of a general form of development, and zoning is a tool to implement the broader plan. *See, e.g.*, IND. CODE ANN. § 18-7-5-46 (Burns 1974); WIS. STAT. § 62.23(c) (1961); MICH. COMP. LAWS ANN. § 125.39 (1967). *See also* Dalton v. Honolulu, 51 Haw. 400, 462 P.2d 199 (1969).

64. *See, e.g.*, Devereux Foundation Inc. Zoning Case, 351 Pa. 478, 41 A.2d 744, *appeal dismissed*, 326 U.S. 686 (1945).

65. *See, e.g.,* R.N.R. Assoc. v. Zoning Board of Review, 100 R.I. 7, 210 A.2d 653 (1965); Brown v. Beuc, 384 S.W.2d 845 (Mo. Ct. App. 1964).

66. Booe v. Zoning Board of Appeals, 151 Conn. 681, 202 A.2d 245 (1964). *But see* Williams v. Kuehart, 243 Ark. 746, 421 S.W.2d 896 (1967) (unless the zoning ordinance specifically requires a showing of unnecessary hardship, a variance might be permissible if the planning agency chooses to permit it).

67. The National Historic Preservation Act of 1966, 80 Stat. 915, 16 U.S.C. §§ 470 *et seq.*, establishes a national register of historic sites. It imposes no duties on state or local government to preserve the sites and does not guarantee preservation. Hence, parties hoping to preserve historic or architecturally important structures must take their claims to court. *See, e.g.,* Kent County Council for Historic Preservation v. Romney, 304 F.Supp. 885 (W.D. Mich. 1969); Maher v. New Orleans, 371 F.Supp. 653 (E.D. La. 1974), *aff'd*, 516 F.2d 1051 (5th Cir. 1975). A number of localities have landmark preservation ordinances. *E.g.,* N.Y. CITY CHARTER & ADMIN. CODE ch. 8A (1971). *But see* Lutheran Church in America v. City of New York, 35 N.Y.2d 121, 359 N.Y.S.2d 7, 316 N.E.2d 305 (1974) (refused to preserve a building designated as a landmark under the ordinance).

68. Financing commitments for many building projects usually expire if the loan is not processed within a certain time. Also, interest expense accumulated while construction is delayed can be fatal to the financial feasibility of a project.

Chapter 7: Reimbursement Concerns

Medicare Reimbursement
    Primary Care and Urgent Care Centers
    Emergency Centers
    Hospital Outpatient Care Centers
    Ambulatory Surgical Centers
        Freestanding Centers
        Hospital-Affiliated Centers
    Comprehensive Outpatient Rehabilitation Facilities
    Hospice
    Clinical Laboratories
    Diagnostic Radiology Services
    Preferred Provider Organizations
    Health Maintenance Organizations and Competitive Medical Plans
    Home Health Care Agency
    Durable Medical Equipment
Reimbursement by Other Third-Party Payers

Chapter 7. Reimbursement Concerns

Of great concern in any health care enterprise, including joint ventures, is reimbursement: who pays for services provided by health care facilities and practitioners, and how are these payments made? The health care market is unique in that the consumers of health care services often are not responsible for payment. Moreover, the health care financing market is dominated by large private and governmental payers who exercise considerable influence on the manner and amount of reimbursement. Thus, to compete in the marketplace, health care joint ventures must not only attract consumers by providing high-quality care, but they must also be able to provide such care in a cost-effective way if they are to survive economically in an increasingly competitive environment.

For many health care joint ventures, the most important of the third-party payers is the federal government's Medicare program. An estimated 29 million elderly Americans are served by Medicare each year,[1] and that number is growing. Other payers whose reimbursement policies are important factors in the decision-making process are large insurance companies and employers.

Medicare Reimbursement

The Medicare program affects an economic joint venture in two different ways. First, the reimbursement mechanism and the total amount of reimbursement available for the treatment of Medicare patients can be important considerations in structuring the joint venture. Second, the participants in an economic joint venture who provide services to Medicare or Medicaid beneficiaries are subject to statutory prohibitions against fraud and abuse under these programs. In addition to situations clearly involving fraud, such as billing for services not actually provided, the Medicare antifraud and abuse statutes govern such matters as patient referrals to enterprises in which the provider or practitioner holds an ownership interest. The first consideration, reimbursement, is the subject of this chapter. The second consideration, relating to the antifraud and abuse laws, is treated in chapter 8.

Medicare reimbursement is especially important to those joint ventures in which Medicare and Medicaid patients represent a significant part of the market that the new enterprise aims to serve. Such joint ventures must be structured to take into account the changing reimbursement system. Even so, the organizers of any health care joint venture, whether or not they intend to serve a large number of Medicare or Medicaid patients, must become familiar with Medicare reimbursement practices because many private payers often follow Medicare policies in their private programs.

Historically, the Medicare program reimbursed hospitals and other providers of inpatient care on the basis of the lesser of their reasonable costs or reasonable charges. Physician services and other nonhospital outpatient care were reimbursed on the basis of reasonable charges. As federal expenditures for health care services increased, critics focused on reimbursement mechanisms as a means to control costs. The cost-reimbursement system was criticized on the grounds that it encouraged hospitals to incur additional costs in order to increase reimbursement. The reasonable charge system, under which the maximum amount payable by Medicare is based on prevailing charges, was also criticized because it provides an incentive for practitioners to raise their fees to increase maximum allowable reimbursement.

In response to these concerns, Congress and the Health Care Financing Administration (HCFA) have adopted several changes to the Medicare reimbursement system. Perhaps the most significant change has been the enactment of the *prospective pricing system* (PPS) for inpatient hospital services.[2] Under PPS, the method by which the federal government pays for inpatient care provided to Medicare beneficiaries has changed from a cost-based reimbursement system to a system based on *diagnosis-*

related groups (DRGs).[3] Inpatient hospital services are paid by Medicare on the basis of prospectively determined rates that are applied on a per-discharge basis.[4]

Because of PPS, health care providers and practitioners must question the financial feasibility of certain joint ventures in view of the prospectively determined amount of Medicare reimbursement available for services that are required to treat particular diagnosed illnesses. Unlike the cost-based reimbursement system, PPS puts the hospital provider at risk for cost overruns that may result from providing inpatient services. If the costs a provider incurs in furnishing inpatient services for a particular DRG are lower than the prospectively determined rate, the provider may keep the difference between that rate and its operating costs. However, the provider receives no reimbursement for any operating costs that exceed its payment rate for any diagnosis.[5]

The provider may not charge a Medicare beneficiary any additional amount over the PPS rate for Medicare-covered services even if the provider's expenses for providing those services exceed the amount of the PPS payment.[6] Moreover, under the PPS system, a provider cannot obtain additional reimbursement by *unbundling* services, that is, contracting for the provision of certain services by related or unrelated practitioners or providers.[7] The provider remains responsible for the provision of required services for its inpatients.

As a result of such PPS restrictions, joint ventures based on the potential for increased reimbursement for inpatient services are no longer feasible. However, hospitals should continue to investigate joint ventures that enable the hospital and its medical staff to provide inpatient services more efficiently. Through such joint ventures, the provider may maximize its return under PPS.

The current reimbursement environment is more conducive to joint ventures for outpatient and noninstitutional services than for inpatient services. In recent years, Congress has expanded Medicare coverage for various noninstitutional services, such as those offered by ambulatory surgical centers, and outpatient rehabilitation services.[8] Moreover, the Medicare reimbursement for many of these services continues to be made on the basis of reasonable cost. Even such services that are subject to a prospectively determined rate, such as ambulatory surgical center services,[9] or to a fee schedule, such as diagnostic laboratory services,[10] appear to have a greater potential for profit maximization in the outpatient setting than in the inpatient setting.

As Congress and HCFA gain experience in working with new types of providers and as health care providers adjust to the PPS system, providers will encounter fewer opportunities to realize a profit solely by structuring a joint venture to obtain a favorable reimbursement mechanism. Indeed, observers anticipate that all health care services under the Medicare program may eventually be reimbursed under a PPS or a fee schedule.[11] Despite diminishing opportunities, economic joint venture participants should become familiar with reimbursement principles to ensure that:

- The venture is eligible for Medicare reimbursement.
- The venture is structured so that it can obtain reimbursement under the most favorable reimbursement mechanism available.
- The venture mechanism selected will ensure maximum reimbursement for the joint venture.

A complete reimbursement strategy should also take into account the reimbursement implications of providing services through a joint venture as distinguished from other structural alternatives, such as the hospital's providing such services directly. Maximization of total Medicare reimbursement is one goal to be considered in selecting a project or a structure for a joint venture.

The initial concern in developing a joint venture that is dependent on Medicare reimbursement for a large part of its operating revenue is whether the service offered by the joint venture is covered under the program. Typically, some time elapses between the introduction of new technology and the availability of reimbursement for services rendered using that technology. Joint ventures employing new technology should ascertain whether Medicare coverage exists. For example, reimbursement is available for only a limited number of services rendered in an ambulatory surgical center.[12] Therefore, participants in a joint venture to establish an ambulatory surgical center for particular specialty services should ascertain whether those services are covered under Medicare.

After establishing that the services to be provided are covered under Medicare, the joint venture participants should determine the reimbursement mechanism or mechanisms that are available to the venture. The reimbursement mechanism for a service rendered under the Medicare program is determined by the type of facility in which that service is rendered as well as by the nature of the service itself. In some instances, the same service can be reimbursed under two or more different mechanisms. For example, ambulatory surgical procedures rendered in the outpatient department of a hospital are currently reimbursed on a reasonable-cost basis.[13] The identical services rendered in a Medicare-certified ambulatory surgical center are reimbursed under the prospective system uniquely applicable to ambulatory surgical centers.[14] When both alternatives are available, and assuming a significant Medicare volume is anticipated, the hospital should do a financial comparative analysis to determine which alternative provides maximum Medicare reimbursement. However, such analysis should be subject to a caveat: Medicare reimbursement levels are not static and are likely to change, and as a result, the structure selected for joint ventures should rarely depend primarily on Medicare reimbursement considerations.

In making the decision to enter into a joint venture, the participants must determine whether available reimbursement mechanisms enable the joint venture participants to accomplish their financial goals. Under PPS, joint ventures involving inpatient services must be carefully considered, because Medicare pays only the hospital's prospective rate for inpatient services.[15] If alternative reimbursement mechanisms that are more favorable to the facility are available, the joint venture participants may structure the venture to take advantage of such mechanisms. For example, current Medicare regulations offer an incentive to provide certain outpatient surgery in ambulatory surgical centers because physicians rendering services in such facilities receive 100 percent, rather than 80 percent, of reasonable charges if they accept assignment under Medicare.[16] In other instances, the reimbursement mechanism may be more favorable for services, such as outpatient rehabilitation services, that are performed in physicians' offices or outpatient centers rather than in hospital outpatient settings.

In addition, participants in a joint venture must determine whether Medicare provides reimbursement, also known as a facilities fee, for the joint venture's technical component (use of facility, equipment, supplies) as opposed to reimbursement solely for professional services rendered in the facility. For example, with respect to eligible services rendered in a Medicare-certified ambulatory surgical center, both the physician rendering the services and the facility itself are reimbursed.[17] The physician's reimbursement is a professional fee. Reimbursement for the facility is by means of a facilities fee.

As of 1986, outpatient facilities other than ambulatory surgical centers, such as primary care centers, urgent care centers, and emergency centers, are not entitled to receive a facilities fee for the technical component of Medicare-covered services rendered to beneficiaries. Only the practitioner rendering services in these facilities is paid the professional fee, and the costs associated with providing the facility supplies and personnel have to be absorbed within that professional fee. Consequently, if a hospital owns part of a joint venture for a facility such as an urgent care center, it receives only a part of the professional fee that is reimbursed to the facility by

Medicare. If the hospital is a supplier of services to the outpatient facility, acting in essence as a service bureau, it is also paid by the facility for the services it renders. Because payment for the technical component is not always available under Medicare, the participants must ascertain whether the venture is eligible to receive a facilities fee if such reimbursement is important to the success of the venture.

The potential ability to obtain Medicare reimbursement through a facilities fee may be an increasingly significant factor in determining how to structure a joint venture, especially in view of the government's efforts to reduce increases in the levels of prevailing physicians' charges. A freeze was imposed on physicians' prevailing-charge levels beginning on July 1, 1984, and continuing through December 31, 1986, for physicians who did not elect to participate in the program before May 1, 1986. For physicians who elected to participate prior to the May 1, 1986, deadline, the freeze ended on April 30, 1986. However, the ability to update prevailing charges is limited to certain classes of physicians.[18] This policy of seeking to limit physician fees can adversely affect the establishment of office-based outpatient and other freestanding primary care and emergency facilities because any limitation on the fees for physicians' services may prevent a facility that is not entitled to a technical component under Medicare from recovering its full costs for Medicare patients.[19]

Even though the service to be rendered is a Medicare-covered service and the technical component of rendering the service is reimbursable to the joint venture through a facilities fee, the joint venture must be structured to meet the requirements for Medicare certification and reimbursement. The regulations addressing each type of facility eligible for a facilities fee set forth the particular requirements applicable to the facility. Typically, the requirements relate to such matters as the governing body of the facility, documentation of the treatment plan, and ability to provide covered services. In addition, when the characteristics of the facility or equipment can affect the quality of care, such as in ambulatory surgical centers and outpatient rehabilitation centers, the regulations may also set forth minimum standards relating to the facility and its equipment.[20]

For the most part, how the joint venture is structured has no material effect on whether the facility meets requirements for certification. However, joint venture participants should be aware that conflicts of interest may affect certification and reimbursement. For example, a home health agency may not be reimbursed for services rendered to a Medicare beneficiary when the physician who prepares treatment plans holds a significant financial interest or contractual relationship in the home health agency.[21] Given current concerns about antifraud and abuse violations, similar standards may be adopted for other facilities (see chapter 8).

With these general considerations in mind, this chapter now discusses particular reimbursement mechanisms for facilities that are potential candidates for joint ventures. Participants considering a particular type of joint venture must keep in mind that Medicare statutes and regulations are frequently amended to refine the program or change prevailing incentives.

Primary Care and Urgent Care Centers

Primary care centers provide medical services similar to those provided in a private physician's office. *Urgent care centers* provide care for minor injuries and illnesses and sometimes have additional equipment that a private physician's office may not have.

Neither primary care centers nor urgent care centers have been recognized as distinct providers under Medicare. Therefore, the health care providers in the facility must meet the conditions for participation for individual practitioners. Alternatively, a primary care or urgent care center operated under a hospital license can meet the qualifications for reimbursement as a hospital outpatient department.

Unless the primary care or urgent care center qualifies as a hospital outpatient department, the center itself is not entitled to receive a facilities fee. Physicians practicing at a primary or urgent care center that is not recognized as a hospital outpatient department are reimbursed for most services on the basis of the reasonable charge for a private office visit, which is subject to a deductible.[22] A portion of the physicians' charges may be disallowed if they reflect a higher cost of providing care at a primary or urgent care center than in a private office setting. Efforts by the federal government to limit increases in physicians' fees may also have an effect on reimbursement for this type of center.

Emergency Centers

Emergency centers are health care facilities that have been established to provide an alternative for patients who do not need care in a hospital emergency department or who are unable to see a private physician in his or her office. Typically, emergency centers are open for longer hours than physicians' offices, and they accept walk-in patients. The waiting time is often shorter than in the hospital emergency department, and the cost is usually less.

Although a concerted lobbying effort seeks to obtain facilities fees for emergency centers, emergency centers have not yet been recognized as distinct providers of services under the Medicare program. However, services rendered at emergency centers may be reimbursed as physician services or, if applicable, as services provided by a hospital outpatient department. Under Medicare Part B, practitioners in an emergency center are reimbursed on the basis of 80 percent of the reasonable charges for providing services in the private office setting.[23]

Hospital Outpatient Care Centers

A hospital-owned or affiliated emergency or other outpatient care center may receive facility reimbursement separate from reimbursement for physicians' professional services if the center is organized as a hospital outpatient department.[24] To be reimbursed as a hospital outpatient department, the center must be operated under the hospital's license and be closely integrated with other hospital services. In some states, outpatient departments may include facilities that are geographically separate from the hospital, and these facilities may obtain separate Medicare reimbursement if they are closely integrated with other hospital services.

Reimbursement for physicians' services rendered in a facility organized as a hospital outpatient department is typically less than reimbursement for the same services performed in a physician's office setting. Under regulations in effect in 1986, the *prevailing charge* for services routinely furnished in physicians' offices is limited to only 60 percent of the private office rate, reflecting the fact that in the outpatient department setting the hospital pays the overhead costs assumed by the physician in the private office setting.[25] For services not routinely provided in physicians' offices, such as ambulatory surgical services, the 60 percent limitation does not apply.[26]

In either case, the physician receives only 80 percent of the allowable charge for most services; the remaining 20 percent is a copayment from the patient.[27] Thus, if a physician's prevailing charge for a service routinely provided in the private office setting is $100, the physician is reimbursed $48 by Medicare (100 x 0.60 x 0.80) for the same service performed in an outpatient department and is entitled to a $12 copayment. If the service is not routinely provided in a private office setting and is subject to the copayment, the physician is entitled to $80 from Medicare and $20 from the patient.

The participants in a joint venture of this nature need to determine whether the ability of the hospital to obtain cost-based reimbursement for services and supplies in addition to a professional fee for providing physicians' services outweighs the decrease in reimbursement for those physicians' services as a result of providing them in a hospital outpatient department. In most cases, the disadvantage of a reduced professional fee is probably offset by the ability of a hospital outpatient department to obtain reimbursement for overhead costs. If receiving the separate facilities fee is sufficiently important, a hospital outpatient department may be the appropriate structure, particularly as the physicians are not able to increase their reimbursement under the Medicare program by raising their rates to reflect the additional overhead.

Of course, these considerations are only important if the joint venture participants anticipate that a large number of Medicare patients will be using the facility. For instance, a proposed freestanding clinic located near a retirement community is likely to serve a large number of Medicare patients, and consequently the amount of Medicare reimbursement is a major consideration in the decision on the location of the clinic and the structure of the joint venture. However, an office-based clinic for the treatment of sports-related injuries is not dependent on Medicare reimbursement.

Ambulatory Surgical Centers

Medicare regulations make several options possible in a joint venture to establish an out-of-hospital surgical center. The center can be established as a hospital outpatient department, a freestanding ambulatory surgical center (ASC), or a hospital-affiliated ambulatory surgical center (HAASC). The principles applicable to hospital outpatient departments are discussed in the previous section. This section focuses on ASCs and HAASCs.

Freestanding Centers

The most important feature of the *freestanding ambulatory surgical center* (ASC) from the reimbursement perspective is that, unlike other freestanding centers treated as physicians' offices, the government is authorized to reimburse an ASC separately for both the technical and the professional components of the services it provides. In addition, physicians who *accept assignment*, that is, accept Medicare reimbursement as payment in full, are reimbursed at 100 percent of their reasonable charges for specified surgical procedures conducted in the ASC.

An ASC is defined in the regulations as any distinct entity that:[28]

- Operates exclusively for the purpose of providing surgical services to patients who do not require hospitalization
- Agrees to participate as an ASC for Medicare-reimbursement purposes
- Complies with the terms of the regulations

The ASC must be *distinct*, that is, it must be separated physically from the hospital or from any other facility in which it is located. This requirement has been interpreted to mean that although it may be located in the same building as another health care facility, it must be located in a separate room or suite that is distinct from the rest of the facility.[29] In other words, an ASC cannot share space with another facility at the same time, although it could possibly share a common space at nonoverlapping times. The Medicare regulations do not specifically state whether a nonoverlapping sharing arrangement complies with the requirements for an ASC.

In addition, the ASC must comply with the various requirements in the regulations for ASCs. For instance, it must comply with applicable state licensure laws.[30]

Medicare Reimbursement
Ambulatory Surgical Centers

Significantly, compliance with such laws does not necessarily require that the ASC be licensed by the state as an ASC before it can be Medicare certified. For example, a physician's office can be certified by Medicare as an ASC if a state's licensure law permits the services to be provided in a physician office setting.

As an additional requirement imposed by the regulations, the ASC must be able to transfer, without delay, patients who require hospitalization. It must either have a written transfer agreement with a Medicare-participating hospital, or physicians performing surgery at the center must have staff privileges at such a hospital.[31] Furthermore, the center must comply with other specific regulations with respect to the quality of surgical services, staff, and corollary services.[32]

Only those surgical procedures specified on the government's list of covered procedures are reimbursed when performed in an ASC. No services or items other than those that are specifically covered or are furnished in connection with listed covered surgical procedures, such as nursing services, technician services, drugs, surgical dressings, and related diagnostic services, are covered when rendered in an ASC.[33] As of 1986, more than 100 procedures are eligible for reimbursement in the ASC setting. This number is likely to increase as technology enables more procedures to be performed safely in an outpatient setting.

Participating ASCs are paid a fixed facility services rate for each specified procedure. This fixed rate is intended to cover all facility service costs, including overhead, nursing and other personnel services, drugs, supplies, and diagnostic and therapeutic services.[34] The rate does not cover physicians' services, which are reimbursed separately under Medicare Part B. The rates are divided into four levels of payment depending on the complexity of the procedure and the estimated facilities' costs associated with it. Medicare beneficiaries pay no deductible for ambulatory surgical center services.

The professional component of surgical services performed in an ASC is reimbursed at 100 percent of the reasonable charge for the service if the physician performing the surgery has agreed to comply with Medicare regulations, that is, has accepted assignment under Medicare.[35] In this case, no deductible or coinsurance payment is required of the beneficiary. However, if the physician has not accepted assignment, his or her charges are reimbursed generally under Medicare Part B at 80 percent of reasonable charges. This portion of reimbursement is separate from the facility reimbursement. The facility reimbursement for a service remains the same whether or not the physician performing the service has accepted assignment.

Hospital-Affiliated Centers

Hospital-affiliated ambulatory surgical centers (HAASCs) have the option of being reimbursed on a reasonable-cost basis, like a hospital outpatient department, or under the payment system applicable to freestanding ASCs. No difference exists between an HAASC and an ASC with respect to physician reimbursement (see discussion in the preceding section with respect to physician reimbursement for ASCs).

To be treated as an ASC for reimbursement purposes, the HAASC must be a separately identifiable entity from other hospital departments or operations, financially as well as administratively. It must also meet all of the requirements established in the regulations for ASCs, including the requirement that the facility be used *exclusively* for ambulatory surgical purposes.[36]

However, to be treated as a hospital outpatient department, and thus reimbursed on a cost basis, the HAASC must be an integral part of the hospital and must operate with other hospital departments under a common license and under the same professional supervision. If an HAASC opts to be treated as a hospital facility, it cannot be certified as an ASC.

In deciding whether to be treated as an ASC or as a hospital outpatient department, the HAASC generally chooses the structure that maximizes total Medicare reimbursement. If the HAASC chooses to be treated as a hospital outpatient department, it is reimbursed by Medicare on the basis of its reasonable costs for all surgical and nonsurgical procedures performed at the center, whether or not they are on the approved list of procedures developed for ASCs. On the other hand, if it opts for ASC treatment, it must limit its practice to procedures on the approved list or forego reimbursement from Medicare for facility costs associated with those procedures that are not on the Medicare approved list.[37]

The HAASC must also evaluate whether cost-based reimbursement is more advantageous than the prospectively determined ASC reimbursement for the services eligible for such ASC reimbursement. Although in the long run this factor becomes less crucial as the approved list of procedures for ASCs is expanded, in the short run it can be an important consideration: is it better to have 100-percent prospective ASC reimbursement for some procedures or to limit procedure offerings to those on the Medicare list, or is it better to have 80-percent reimbursement for the reasonable cost of all procedures?

This 100-percent reimbursement gives ASCs a certain marketing advantage over HAASCs that have elected to be treated as hospital outpatient departments. An ASC can advertise to the public that it performs *no-cost surgery* because, even if it is reimbursed according to the PPS, that reimbursement constitutes payment in full for the covered surgery.[38] The Medicare beneficiary pays nothing. Although an HAASC treated as a hospital outpatient center may receive higher reimbursement for the procedure under the cost-based system, it may also lose patients to a competing ASC because in the HAASC the patient or the patient's coinsurer is responsible for 20 percent of the cost of the surgery. Of course, the HAASC can waive the 20 percent payment for beneficiaries, but this practice may constitute a violation by the HAASC of antifraud and abuse provisions of the Medicare statute.[39]

Although structuring the joint venture as an HAASC may be desirable from a Medicare reimbursement point of view because of the flexibility that the facility has initially in terms of opting for the most advantageous form of reimbursement, the HAASC structure is not feasible in some cases. In many states, HAASCs must obtain a certificate of need (CON) because they are operated by or on behalf of a hospital, whereas ASCs owned by parties unrelated to a hospital may not be subject to CON review. Moreover, those ASCs sponsored by physicians may also escape CON review because they are viewed as an extension of the physician's office.[40] Because the CON application process can be lengthy and expensive and because the application may be denied, this factor can be the determining one, irrespective of Medicare reimbursement, in the decision to structure the joint venture as an ASC (see chapter 6).

Comprehensive Outpatient Rehabilitation Facilities

Medicare has special reimbursement regulations applicable to *comprehensive outpatient rehabilitation facilities* (CORFs). To qualify, a CORF must be a nonresidential facility established and operated exclusively for the purpose of providing diagnostic, therapeutic, and restorative services on an outpatient basis at a single location to patients who have a significant potential for restoration or improvement of lost or impaired function. In addition, a CORF must comply with all applicable state and local laws with respect to licensure.[41] Also, a CORF must meet certain minimum standards with respect to services, staff, and administration.[42]

Covered services in a CORF include certain physicians' services, physical therapy services, occupational therapy services, speech-language pathology services, respiratory therapy services, prosthetic device services, orthotic device services, social services, psychological services, nursing services, drugs and biological products, supplies, equipment appliances, and a home environment evaluation.[43] To be reimbursed for covered services, a physician must certify that:

- The patient requires skilled rehabilitation services.
- A treatment plan has been established and will be reviewed.
- The services are furnished while the patient is under the care of a physician.

Reimbursement for CORF services is based on reasonable cost.[44] In addition to the Medicare Part B deductible, a CORF may charge beneficiaries an additional amount of up to 20 percent of the customary charges. After subtracting the deductible, a CORF is reimbursed at the lesser of 80 percent of the remaining reasonable cost or the remaining reasonable cost minus 20 percent of reasonable charges. Providers may be increasingly interested in CORFs because a CORF is an entity that readily lends itself to joint venture development.

Hospice

Another entity that traditionally was not deemed a provider of services under the Medicare law but is now covered under Medicare is the *hospice*.[45] Hospice benefits are available only to Medicare beneficiaries who are terminally ill, that is, who have been medically diagnosed as having a life expectancy of six months or less.[46]

To participate in Medicare, a hospice must be licensed under applicable state law. In addition, a hospice must demonstrate management capability and employ a physician as its medical director. The hospice must be able to demonstrate that it can provide Medicare-covered services pursuant to a written plan of care. The hospice must designate an interdisciplinary group to supervise care and is obliged to conduct an ongoing quality assurance program. Several other administrative standards must also be met.[47] To be reimbursed, the hospice must enter into a contractual arrangement with HCFA.

The Medicare patient elects hospice care in lieu of other Medicare benefits and can receive varied services, including physician services, nursing care, medical and social services, counseling services, medical supplies such as drugs and home health equipment, and physical or occupational therapy.[48] The time for which benefits are available to the individual patient is two 90-day periods and a subsequent 30-day period.

Hospice providers are reimbursed on a payment system that is cost related, prospective, and subject to a maximum threshold. Physicians' services are reimbursed under Medicare Part B if the physician is *not* employed by the facility. Services of physicians who are part of the hospice staff are reimbursed under Medicare Part A as hospice services.[49]

Generally, Medicare reimbursement for hospice services has been spartan and is not likely to be substantially increased in the foreseeable future. As a result, most hospices have had to rely on volunteer contributions or subsidies from their sponsor to sustain their existence.

Clinical Laboratories

Medicare reimbursement may also affect the structuring of a *clinical laboratory* joint venture. Medicare reimbursement for laboratory services presently differs, depending on who performs the tests, for whom they are performed, and where they are performed. Clinical laboratories affiliated with a hospital are treated differently under Medicare than are so-called independent clinical laboratories and laboratories maintained as part of physicians' offices. Services furnished by hospital-affiliated laboratories are currently reimbursed on a reasonable-cost basis. Services furnished by laboratories in physicians' offices for those physicians' patients are currently reimbursed as part of the fee for physicians' services.[50]

Fees for diagnostic tests performed at independent clinical laboratories are reimbursed according to an areawide fee schedule to be established by the Secretary of Health and Human Services.[51] *Independent clinical laboratories* are defined in the regulations as being independent of both hospitals and attending physicians' offices.[52] Services furnished by an out-of-hospital laboratory under the direction of a hospital staff pathologist are within this definition if the facility is available to other physicians for the performance of diagnostic tests. However, a laboratory maintained by a physician for the performance of tests only for the convenience of his or her patients is not within the definition unless that laboratory accepts 100 or more specimens in any category and in any year on referral from other physicians. In that case, it is deemed independent for purposes of the regulations.

To be reimbursed as an independent laboratory, the facility must comply with all of the conditions set forth in the regulations.[53] Physicians have a choice of accepting or not accepting assignment with respect to laboratory services. When assignment is accepted, payment is the lesser of 100 percent of the fee-schedule amount or the actual charges. When assignment is not accepted, payment is the lesser of 80 percent of the fee-schedule amount or the actual charges.

As of 1986, the fee schedule is set at 60 percent of the prevailing-charge level for similar diagnostic laboratory tests performed during the year beginning July 1, 1984, and is adjusted annually according to changes in the consumer price index.[54] The fee schedule for tests performed by a hospital laboratory for hospital outpatients is set at 62 percent. In addition, a nominal fee to cover the cost of collecting samples is allowed. The statute in effect in 1986 provides that the fee schedule for laboratory tests performed in a physician's office or by a laboratory other than a hospital laboratory for outpatients will be established on a nationwide basis by 1987. Unless the statute and the regulations interpreting it are further modified, reimbursement for a hospital laboratory for outpatients will apparently revert to a reasonable-cost basis before the end of 1987.

This area of laboratory reimbursement is in a state of flux, and further changes in reimbursement patterns can be expected. Any joint venture project involving a clinical laboratory should take these potential changes into account and ideally should remain as flexible as possible to adapt readily to future adjustments in Medicare reimbursement patterns.[55]

Diagnostic Radiology Services

Hospitals and physicians may enter into joint ventures for the purpose of establishing *diagnostic radiology centers*. A joint venture diagnostic radiology center may be beneficial to the hospital because the center can provide the hospital with readily available access to such services and may be a potential source of referrals. The physicians can benefit to the extent that the hospital contributes capital, facilities, and personnel to finance and staff the center.

Diagnostic radiology centers are not recognized as distinct providers under Medicare. A radiology center that is part of a hospital is reimbursed in the same manner as an outpatient department. However, a radiology center that is separate and independent from a hospital and is owned and directed by a physician is treated as a physician's office for reimbursement purposes. Of course, in either situation, the equipment must also meet safety standards set forth in the regulations.

Diagnostic radiology services rendered by physicians in other than a hospital setting are reimbursed on a reasonable-charge basis as physicians' services.[56] Services of technicians are also reimbursed under Medicare Part B if that technician is an employee and the physician supervises and retains responsibility for the tests performed.

Physicians are reimbursed for radiology services furnished in a hospital at a reasonable charge that is calculated not to exceed 40 percent of the prevailing charge for similar services provided in a nonhospital setting.[57] This limitation applies to services rendered to hospital outpatients as well as to inpatients.

Preferred Provider Organizations

A *preferred provider organization* (PPO) is a network of hospitals and providers who contract with employers or insurance carriers to provide certain health care services on a negotiated fee-for-service payment basis while providing financial incentives to patients using the PPO. Medicare does not recognize PPOs as distinct providers. To obtain reimbursement, institutional providers or individual practitioners must each meet conditions for participation.

The participating practitioners of a PPO who provide medical services to Medicare enrollees are reimbursed directly by Medicare for their reasonable charges under Part B of the Medicare program. Similarly, institutional providers are reimbursed under Medicare in accordance with the principles applicable to the particular institutions and services. The PPO may assist the providers and practitioners administratively in obtaining such reimbursement, but the Medicare program does not reimburse the PPO for its administrative costs of processing these Medicare claims.

Health Maintenance Organizations and Competitive Medical Plans

Institutional providers and practitioners participating in a *health maintenance organization* (HMO) that has not directly contracted with HCFA for Medicare reimbursement may be reimbursed in the manner described in the previous section with respect to providers and practitioners in a PPO setting. Alternatively, HMOs, as well as nonhospital clinics and physicians, can be reimbursed on a reasonable-charge basis for Medicare Part B medical services that they and their practitioners render to Medicare beneficiaries. Such a charge-based reimbursement plan may also be acceptable to an *individual practice association* (IPA), a type of HMO that pays its physicians and other practitioners on a fee-for-service basis. However, group or staff model HMOs may have difficulty obtaining reimbursement under this formula, as their physicians are not typically compensated on a fee-for-service basis. Under this reimbursement methodology, HMOs and other prepayment plans are not compensated for the administrative, marketing, or enrollment costs of providing care to Medicare beneficiaries.

Until 1985, the federal government gave HMOs no real incentive for participating in Medicare. Under previous regulations, a provider had the choice of two types of reimbursement contracts with the government: an *at-risk contract* or a *cost contract*. Those HMOs opting for a cost contract were reimbursed on a reasonable-cost basis in the same manner as traditional private practitioners. This system was contrary to the HMO operating philosophy of cost control. Those HMOs with at-risk contracts were reimbursed on a capitation basis, which is similar to prepayments made by non-Medicare HMO patients except that Medicare payments were made retroactively. In addition, HMOs had to share with the government any savings to be had under the at-risk contract but were expected to absorb all losses.

Regulations adopted in 1985 allow HMOs and similar entities to enter into more traditional HMO-like risk contracts.[58] Section 1876 of the Social Security Act sets forth a definition of organizations eligible to enter into these risk-based contracts with Medicare. An *eligible organization* under Section 1876 is a federally qualified HMO or a competitive medical plan (CMP) that is organized under state law as an entity with the following characteristics:[59]

- It provides certain basic health care services through arrangements with physicians.
- It assumes full financial risk on a prospective basis, with certain exceptions.
- It is compensated by enrollees on a basis other than fee for service.
- It provides adequate protection against the risk of insolvency.

In addition, although duplicative of federal HMO qualification requirements, eligibility under Section 1876 requires both federally qualified HMOs and state-regulated CMPs to:[60]

- Possess administrative capability to manage the plan
- Establish grievance procedures and quality assurance programs
- Enroll a representative portion of the population
- Ensure that enrollees and potential enrollees are not refused on the basis of health status
- Provide Medicare covered services, including emergency care, on an available and accessible basis

In addition, an HMO or CMP must conduct an annual open enrollment for persons eligible for Medicare benefits. Unless a waiver is obtained, no more than 50 percent (up to 75 percent with a waiver) of the plan's enrollees may be entitled to Medicare or Medicaid benefits. Except in nonurban areas, contracts for reimbursement on a risk-sharing basis are limited to eligible organizations with at least 5,000 enrollees.[61] In addition, to be eligible for a risk-based reimbursement contract, an HMO or CMP must have at least 75 Medicare enrollees or have a plan for achieving a Medicare enrollment of 75 within two years.

An HMO or CMP that enters into a risk-sharing contract with HCFA is paid, in advance, a monthly per capita amount for each Medicare enrollee.[62] The monthly amount equals 95 percent of the organization's *adjusted average per capita cost* (AAPCC). The AAPCC is a prospectively calculated actuarial estimate by Medicare of the average amount per enrollee that Medicare would have paid for the covered services to providers other than an HMO or CMP.

The HMO or CMP is at risk for the amount by which the actual cost of providing services to Medicare enrollees exceeds 95 percent of the AAPCC. However, the HMO or CMP does not have to share with Medicare any savings based on the difference between the Medicare payment at 95 percent of the AAPCC and the actual cost of providing covered services to Medicare enrollees. Nevertheless, it must use a portion of those savings to benefit Medicare enrollees with, for example, additional health care benefits or reduced copayment or deductibles.

The amount of savings that the HMO or CMP must use to benefit Medicare enrollees is the difference between Medicare payments to the HMO or CMP and the *adjusted community rate* (ACR).[63] The ACR, which is essentially the organization's premium for providing services covered by Medicare, is adjusted for differences in utilization and complexity of services for Medicare beneficiaries as compared with other patients. Significantly, the ACR calculation apparently includes a profit component to be retained by the organization if it correctly estimates the actual costs of providing services to Medicare enrollees.

An HMO or CMP may elect to have HCFA directly reimburse participating hospitals for services covered under Part A of Medicare.[64] The amount estimated for payments to hospitals and the administrative costs incurred in making such payments are then deducted by HCFA from the organization's monthly payment. Under this method, the HMO or CMP remains at risk for hospital charges.

Medicare also allows HMOs and CMPs to participate on a cost-based reimbursement contract basis. Under regulations in effect in 1986, the organization must have at least 1,500 enrollees as a condition of eligibility for a cost-based contract. These regulations also require that the HMO or CMP have at least 75 Medicare enrollees or a plan for achieving a Medicare enrollment of 75 within two years. By the fourth year of a cost-based reimbursement contract, 250 of those persons enrolled in the HMO or CMP have to be Medicare enrollees.

In general, cost-reimbursement principles applicable to eligible organizations operating under a cost-based reimbursement contract are the same as cost-reimbursement principles generally applied with respect to other providers, such as hospitals.[65] In addition to the costs of providing covered medical and hospital services to Medicare beneficiaries, some specific costs that are allowable to HMOs and CMPs under regulations applicable in 1986 to cost-based reimbursement contracts include:

- Enrollment and marketing costs incurred in connection with marketing to Medicare beneficiaries, conducting an open enrollment, and providing other special member services[66]
- Membership costs incurred in connection with maintaining and servicing subscriber contracts, including maintaining statistical, financial, and other data on enrollees[67]
- Reasonable costs of reporting individual Medicare enrollment accretion and deletion data[68]
- Return on equity for owners of proprietary organizations[69]

Under a cost-based reimbursement contract, HCFA pays an eligible organization an interim monthly per capita amount. The amounts paid to an eligible organization under such a cost-based reimbursement contract are subject to retroactive adjustment during the interim and final settlements.[70]

As of January 1, 1986, HCFA has limited total payments under Section 1876 cost-based reimbursement contracts to 95 percent of the AAPCC, which is the same as the reimbursement limit for risk-based HMOs.[71] As of mid-1986, HCFA was not entering into any new cost-based reimbursement contracts.

Because the new regulations have broad applicability and encompass different types of delivery systems, of which the federally qualified HMO is only one, the federal government hopes that more Medicare beneficiaries enroll in these types of prepaid health plans. As a result of these incentives, many more physicians may be willing to align themselves with group practices or other alternative delivery relationships, possibly through joint ventures, to attract Medicare patients.

Home Health Care Agency

A *home health care agency*, which is defined in the regulations as an entity primarily engaged in providing skilled nursing and other therapeutic services,[72] is eligible for Medicare reimbursement if it meets the conditions of participation contained in the regulations. These conditions of participation include compliance with state and local laws governing such types of agencies as well as requirements for treatment plans, record keeping, and other administrative services.[73] Only services to eligible beneficiaries are covered. These beneficiaries are Medicare patients who are confined at home and who are under a physician's care and in need of either skilled nursing services or physical or speech therapy.[74]

A certified home health care agency is reimbursed for covered services at the rate of 100 percent of the lesser of its reasonable costs or charges on a cost-per-visit basis.[75] The coverage is limited when the treating physician is an officer or director of or partner in the home health care agency. For example, a physician who has a direct or indirect ownership interest of 5 percent or more in a home health care agency cannot establish or review a plan of treatment for a potential patient of the home health care agency.[76]

A home health care agency may be affiliated with a hospital. In such an instance, the agency is reimbursed for services provided by interns or residents of the hospital.[77] Without such affiliation or common control, these services are not covered home health care services. To receive reimbursement for an affiliated home health care agency, the hospital must have made written arrangements with the home health care agency that specify the services to be provided, administrative control, and delegation of responsibility for patient care.[78]

Durable Medical Equipment

Medicare beneficiaries may also be reimbursed for certain *durable medical equipment* (DME) if the equipment meets the following qualifications:[79]

- It can withstand repeated use.
- It serves primarily a medical purpose.
- It is not generally useful in the absence of an illness or injury.
- It is appropriate for use in the home.

In addition, the item must be medically necessary for the particular individual.[80]

Common examples of Medicare-covered DME are oxygen units, wheelchairs, and canes. Other items of equipment may also be designated as DME by individual carriers for the Medicare program under Medicare Part B. For certain items, reimbursement may be available for the equipment itself,[81] but not for delivery or maintenance.[82]

Medicare Part B reimburses for DME at 80 percent of reasonable charges. Thus, reimbursement cannot be higher than either the supplier's usual charge for that item (the customary charge) or the amount charged by most suppliers of the item in the locality (the prevailing charge). The remaining 20 percent of the supplier's charge is paid by the beneficiary as a copayment or by a third-party insurer pursuant to a Medicare supplemental coverage contract.[83] Some suppliers may reduce the coinsurance requirement, but if this becomes a common practice of the supplier, the amount of reimbursement from Medicare is reduced to 80 percent of the amount the supplier actually charges its Medicare customers. In addition, a waiver of a coinsurance requirement may be a violation of the Medicare antifraud and abuse statute (see chapter 8).

In certain circumstances, the reasonable charge is determined to be the lowest charge level at which the piece of equipment is usually available or is most consistently available in the particular locality.[84] This decision is made if, in the opinion of the Secretary of Health and Human Services (HHS), an item of DME, such as a standard wheelchair or hospital bed, does not vary significantly in quality from one supplier to another. The Consolidated Omnibus Budget Reconciliation Act of 1985 authorized the Secretary of HHS to issue regulations for determining a reasonable charge for DME and other services that takes into account the inherent reasonableness of reported charges that seem grossly excessive or deficient.[85]

The beneficiary has the choice of either renting or purchasing an item of DME.[86] The total amount of reimbursement allowable for a leased item may be limited by its reasonable cost or charge.[87] If the equipment is purchased or rented from a supplier, the supplier is reimbursed under Medicare Part B at 80 percent of reasonable charges. If the equipment is furnished by a provider, such as a hospital, a skilled nursing facility, or a home health care agency, reimbursement is made to the provider under Part A of Medicare on a reasonable-cost basis.[88]

Reimbursement by Other Third-Party Payers

Various payers other than the federal government have reimbursement policies that either encourage or discourage certain types of health care facilities. The policies of the private plans vary considerably, and it is not possible to discuss the variations in detail. However, some general developments should be noted.

First, at least one state has passed legislation that requires insurers to negotiate with hospitals to establish prospective pricing arrangements that provide financial incentives for the containment of hospital costs. Prior to March 1, 1987, each hospital in the state of Florida must negotiate with each health insurer a prospective pricing arrangement that represents 10 percent or more of the private-pay patients of the hospital.[89] Compliance with this requirement is to be taken into account when the hospital budget is approved or disapproved by state authorities.[90] Each pricing system must contain a maximum prepayment amount for individual hospital products, services, and diagnoses; utilization reviews for appropriateness of treatment; and preadmission screening for nonemergency surgery.

Second, a few major insurers have created some reimbursement incentives to encourage the use, when possible, of freestanding ambulatory surgical centers and outpatient facilities. For instance, some plans may reimburse surgical procedures performed on an outpatient basis at 100 percent with no deductible but only reimburse at 80 percent if the same procedure is performed in an inpatient setting. Other incentives may include additional payments to physicians or facilities when selected procedures are performed in the physicians' offices or in a freestanding facility. Nevertheless, many insurance companies and other private third-party payers do not reimburse services provided in a joint venture facility that is not licensed as a hospital or as a physician's office.

Finally, a number of large insurers have entered into agreements with hospitals and providers to establish alternative delivery systems. These systems introduce cost savings programs and usually entail some sort of prepaid amount designed to pay for all covered health care for their beneficiaries.

All of these changing reimbursement patterns offer incentives for the creation of new out-of-hospital facilities and alternative delivery systems. Such systems may be formed by means of joint ventures among insurers, hospitals, and various other providers of health care. Because third-party reimbursement may be vital to the financial feasibility of a venture, participants should analyze the availability of and requirements for such reimbursement carefully in the financial planning stages of the venture.

Notes

1. *See* WASHINGTON REPORT ON MEDICINE & HEALTH PERSPECTIVES, Feb. 11, 1985, at 1.

2. Title VI, Social Security Amendments of 1983, Pub. L. No. 98-21. *See* 42 C.F.R. §§ 412.1 *et seq.*

3. 42 C.F.R. § 412.2(a). Psychiatric hospitals, rehabilitation hospitals, long-term hospitals, hospitals outside the 50 states and the District of Columbia, and hospitals reimbursed under special arrangements are still reimbursed under the cost-reimbursement rules. 42 C.F.R. § 412.23.

4. 42 C.F.R. § 405.470. Capital-related costs are still reimbursed on a cost basis as a pass-through exception to the DRG system. However, both HCFA and Congress are considering various alternative approaches to the control of capital expenditures under the DRG system. OFFICE OF ASSISTANT SECRETARY FOR PLANNING AND EVALUATION, DEPARTMENT OF HHS, HOSPITAL CAPITAL EXPENSES: A MEDICARE PAYMENT STRATEGY FOR THE FUTURE, Mar. 1986.

Chapter 7. Reimbursement Concerns

Notes

5. 42 C.F.R. § 412.2(a).
6. 42 C.F.R. § 412.2(b).
7. 42 C.F.R. § 412.20.
8. *See, e.g.,* 42 C.F.R. §§ 416.1 *et seq.;* 42 C.F.R. §§ 405.1730 *et seq.*
9. *See* 42 C.F.R. § 416.120.
10. 42 U.S.C. § 1395l.
11. *See Lids on Health Care Fees Counter Reagan Focus on Deregulation and Split Business Community,* Wall St. J., Jan. 10, 1985, at 60, col. 1, indicating that reliance on a particular type or amount of reimbursement is even more foolhardy in light of current deficit-trimming proposals that affect both Medicare and Medicaid programs.
12. 42 C.F.R. § 416.65.
13. 42 U.S.C. § 1395l.
14. 42 C.F.R. § 416.125.
15. 42 C.F.R. § 412.20.
16. 42 C.F.R. § 416.110.
17. 42 C.F.R. §§ 416.110, 416.120.
18. Pub. L. No. 99-272, § 9301 (Apr. 7, 1986).
19. *Id.* at § 9305. Section 9305 of the Consolidated Omnibus Budget Reconciliation Act provides for the establishment of a Physician Payment Review Commission and directs the commission to make recommendations regarding adjustments to reasonable charge levels. Section 9305 further instructs the Secretary of HHS to develop a relative-value scale for physician services.
20. *See* 42 C.F.R. §§ 416.42, 416.44, 416.46.
21. 42 C.F.R. § 405.1633(d).
22. 42 C.F.R. §§ 405.240, 405.245.
23. *Id.*
24. 42 C.F.R. § 405.1032.
25. 42 C.F.R. § 405.502(f).
26. 42 C.F.R. § 405.502(f)(3).
27. 42 C.F.R. §§ 405.240, 405.245.
28. 42 C.F.R. § 416.2.
29. *Id. See* HCFA INTERPRETIVE GUIDELINES AND SURVEY PROCEDURES, AMBULATORY SURGICAL SERVICES.
30. 42 C.F.R. § 416.40.
31. 42 C.F.R. § 416.41.
32. *See* 42 C.F.R. §§ 416.42-416.49.
33. 42 C.F.R. § 416.61.
34. 42 C.F.R. § 416.120.
35. 42 C.F.R. § 416.110.
36. 42 C.F.R. § 416.2. *See* HCFA INTERPRETIVE GUIDELINES AND SURVEY PROCEDURES, AMBULATORY SURGICAL SERVICES.
37. *See* 42 C.F.R. §§ 416.60 *et seq.*
38. Kant & Ramansky, *One Day Surgery,* MODERN HEALTHCARE, Sept. 1984, at 95.
39. Social Security Act § 1877(b)(1), 42 U.S.C. § 1395nn(b)(1). This issue is discussed in chapter 8 of this book.
40. *See, e.g.,* CAL. HEALTH & SAFETY CODE § 437.10(b) (West). Other states require a CON for ambulatory surgical centers irrespective of ownership. *See also* discussion in chapter 6 of this book.
41. 42 C.F.R. § 485.54.
42. *See generally* 42 C.F.R. §§ 485.56-485.70.
43. 42 C.F.R. § 405.260.
44. 42 C.F.R. § 405.401.

Chapter 7. Reimbursement Concerns

Notes

45. 42 C.F.R. §§ 418.50 *et seq.*; Pub. L. No. 99-272, § 9123 (Apr. 7, 1986).
46. 42 C.F.R. § 418.22(b).
47. 42 C.F.R. §§ 418.50 *et seq.*
48. 42 C.F.R. § 418.24.
49. 42 C.F.R. § 418.202.
50. 42 C.F.R. § 405.515.
51. 42 U.S.C. § 1395l(h).
52. 42 C.F.R. § 405.1310(a).
53. *See* 42 C.F.R. §§ 405.1311-405.1312.
54. An adjustment is also made for bona fide emergency laboratory tests and certain low-volume and high-cost tests that require sophisticated equipment or skilled personnel to ensure high-quality care.
55. HCFA is apparently considering the possibility of purchasing laboratory services on a competitive-bid basis. However, under the Consolidated Omnibus Budget Reconciliation Act of 1985, the Secretary of HHS is precluded from conducting demonstration projects relating to competitive bidding until Jan. 1987. *See* Pub. L. No. 99-272, § 9303 (Apr. 7, 1986).
56. 42 C.F.R. § 405.555.
57. 42 C.F.R. § 405.555(c).
58. 42 C.F.R. §§ 417.400 *et seq.*
59. 42 C.F.R. § 417.407.
60. 42 C.F.R. §§ 417.410-417.418.
61. 42 C.F.R. § 417.413.
62. 42 C.F.R. § 417.584.
63. 42 C.F.R. § 417.592.
64. 42 C.F.R. § 417.586.
65. 42 C.F.R. § 417.413.
66. 42 C.F.R. § 417.538.
67. 42 C.F.R. § 417.540.
68. 42 C.F.R. § 417.550(b)(1).
69. 42 C.F.R. § 417.536(1).
70. 42 C.F.R. §§ 417.574, 417.576.
71. *Payment Changes Could Hurt HMOs,* HOSPITALS, Mar. 20, 1986, at 78.
72. 42 C.F.R. § 405.1201.
73. *See generally* 42 C.F.R. §§ 405.1220-405.1229.
74. *See* 42 C.F.R. §§ 405.1234-405.1239.
75. 42 U.S.C. § 1395d(a)(3).
76. 42 C.F.R. § 405.1633(d).
77. 42 C.F.R. § 409.40.
78. 42 C.F.R. § 405.1221.
79. 42 U.S.C. § 1395x.
80. 42 U.S.C. § 1395n(a)(2); 42 C.F.R. § 405.250(b).
81. MEDICARE CARRIERS' MANUAL HIM, at § 5110.
82. MEDICARE CARRIERS' MANUAL HIM, at § 5105.
83. 42 U.S.C. § 1395x(s); 42 U.S.C. § 1395l.
84. 42 U.S.C. § 1395u(b)(3); 42 C.F.R. § 405.511.
85. Pub. L. No. 97-272, § 9304 (Apr. 7, 1986).
86. 42 C.F.R. § 405.514.
87. *See* 51 Fed. Reg. 5276 (Feb. 18, 1986); HCFA, PROVIDER REIMBURSEMENT MANUAL, Part 1, § 110. Section 9304 of the Consolidated Omnibus Budget Reconciliation Act of 1985 could be interpreted to permit HCFA to limit reimbursement for leased equipment only in

circumstances in which the total charges are grossly excessive.

88. Reimbursement for the provision of DME by a home health care agency was more generous in the past, and the Medicare beneficiary frequently paid no coinsurance for equipment acquired from the home health care agency. Changes in the law within the past five years have generally reduced the amount of available reimbursement, and there is now a coinsurance requirement.

89. FLA. STAT. ANN. § 395.515 (West).

90. *Id. See* discussion of rate review in chapter 6 of this book.

Chapter 8
Business Practices and Ethical Considerations

Corporate Practice of Medicine and Fee Splitting
    Unlicensed Entity
    Employment of Physicians
    Fee Splitting
State Laws on Self-Referrals
    Ownership Interest
    Medicaid Antikickback Laws
Medicare-Medicaid Antifraud and Abuse Statutes
    Regulations and Advisory Opinions
    Case Law
    Problem Areas
        Self-Referrals
        Waiver of Coinsurance
        Captive Referral Situations
Ethical Restrictions of American Medical Association

Chapter 8. Business Practices and Ethical Considerations

Corporate Practice of Medicine and Fee Splitting

Various business practices of joint venture enterprises can lead to potential ethical problems for the participants and for the venture itself. For instance, a venture between a licensed medical practitioner and lay parties can lead to so-called corporate practice issues. Also, compensation schemes of joint venture participants may lead to potential liability for illegal referrals.

The very nature of a joint venture and the motives for entering into such a transaction may invite problems because a joint venture is an enterprise between two or more legally separate entities who usually retain other business interests beyond the scope of the venture. For example, a corporation that is the parent of a hospital as well as the participant in a joint venture may act at odds with the best interests of the hospital in favor of the joint venture enterprise or vice versa. Conflicts can also arise between the financial interests of joint venture participants and the best interests of their patients. Other troublesome areas are business practices to achieve economies of scale or discounts and efforts to secure referrals to the new enterprise. The area of compensation of the owners of a joint venture entity, especially of those owners who are in a position to provide services or to make referrals to the enterprise, is particularly worrisome.

A joint venture may encounter at least four key legal or ethical restrictions. First, the arrangement between the parties may involve the corporate practice of medicine or the splitting of fees derived from the practice of medicine with nonpractitioners. Second, under some state laws, a health care practitioner who is in a position to refer patients to a facility in which he or she, or his or her immediate family, has a financial interest must disclose that interest to the patient prior to making any such referral. Third, any venture that intends to provide services to either Medicare or Medicaid beneficiaries must take care not to inadvertently violate any of the rules and regulations encompassed within the Medicare-Medicaid antifraud and abuse laws. Fourth, the American Medical Association has ethical rules prohibiting various practices by its members that give the appearance of a bribe or kickback or that put the physician in a position of placing his or her own financial interest over the best interests of the patient. This chapter discusses all of these problems and explores ways in which they may be avoided.

Corporate Practice of Medicine and Fee Splitting

Whenever a lay party is a part of a health care joint venture, the joint venture may risk violating state laws prohibiting the so-called *corporate practice of medicine*. The corporate practice of medicine involves the following two situations:

- A lay entity holds itself out to the public as offering health care services.
- A lay entity has physicians as employees.

A number of states forbid any lay entity from holding itself out to the public as offering health care services. Only licensed practitioners may do this.[1] Sometimes, hospitals and other not-for-profit charitable entities are exempted. However, these exemptions for unlicensed entities are occasionally limited to those institutions that do not charge for professional services rendered to patients.[2]

Only in California and Texas is the employment of physicians viewed as suspect. Moreover, even in those states, medical professional corporations, which by law may be composed of only licensed persons, are exempted from the prohibition.[3] State restrictions also do not apply to federally qualified HMOs because they are exempted by federal statute.[4]

The reasons behind the corporate-practice restriction with respect to the employment of physicians is a desire on the part of the state to protect the public from unscrupulous practices. Allowing lay parties to make decisions relating to the provision of medical care, as might be the case in an employer-employee relationship, can arguably lead to a breakdown in ethical standards[5] or the commercial exploitation of sick people and of the patient-physician relationship.[6]

The attitude of legislatures and courts against both the involvement of lay entities in the practice of medicine and the employment of physicians is being relaxed, and the Federal Trade Commission (FTC), for one, is actively promoting the removal of these restrictions in those states that still have them.[7] In the meantime, if a joint venture is planned in a state that still strictly enforces corporate practice prohibitions, such as California, the participants must take such restrictions into consideration. Sanctions for not doing so can be severe, including possible revocation of the license of the physicians who are a part of the joint venture and an injunction against further business operations by the enterprise.

Three major issues are relevant to this discussion with respect to hospital-physician joint ventures. First, can an unlicensed entity, such as an ambulatory health clinic, offer health care services for a profit, especially when all of the participants in the venture are licensed health care practitioners and hospitals? Second, can the venture employ physicians to staff it? Third, can a service bureau entity that furnishes services to physicians as part of the joint venture receive as compensation a percentage of the gross fees of physicians or of the net income from the enterprise?

Unlicensed Entity

In those states that have a stricture against the corporate practice of medicine, an unlicensed entity owned partially by lay persons is not able to hold itself out as a health care facility and provide health services directly to the public without violating the law. California is an example of such a state. In a recent case, a California appeals court held that a vision center, which was an unlicensed lay entity, was engaged in the unlicensed practice of optometry.[8] The California attorney general likewise has recently rendered an opinion that an industrial medical center operated by a corporation owned by nonprofessionals was in violation of the law when it contracted directly with employers to furnish medical services to employees.[9]

The situation may differ if the unlicensed entity is owned entirely by licensed entities. Arguably, a center, albeit not itself licensed, ought not to be bound by the same restrictions if it is operated by licensed parties (a hospital and physicians). In most states, this argument prevails. For instance, a joint venture entity owned by a hospital can acquire a physician practice and operate it. However, in one or two jurisdictions, such as California, a hospital can arguably not buy a physician's office practice and operate it as its own practice, either under contract or through a joint venture with physicians.[10] Joint ventures in California have to use alternative means to achieve the same purpose.

For example, if the lay party retains an ownership interest in the facility or in administration aspects of the operation but leaves control of the professional aspects of the operation to the owner-physicians, the arrangement may withstand scrutiny. This situation is analogous to that of the middleman or lay business manager hired by a physician group practice. Even in California, which appears to be the most onerous state with regard to corporate-practice issues, courts have long held that a licensed person may engage a lay manager to handle advertising, bookkeeping, billing, and purchasing.[11] The key in a state where corporate practice is a concern is that the lay person does not interfere with the physicians' professional practice.[12] The licensed health care practitioners must at all times retain control over all aspects of patient care.

Employment of Physicians

In many joint ventures, the easiest way to handle the staffing of the facility is to employ physicians to provide the medical services offered by the enterprise. Yet, this simple solution may violate the corporate-practice rule in several states.[13] The California attorney general, for instance, has rendered an opinion that even a hospital is engaged in the unauthorized practice of medicine when it contracts with a physician to operate one of its departments because that physician serves as the hospital's employee.[14]

To avoid this problem, then, the parties may be required to structure the arrangement between the physicians and the facility as something other than that between an employer and employee. For example, an independent contractor arrangement avoids the problem. The California attorney general has provided several guidelines to indicate whether a prohibited employer-employee relationship exists:[15]

- Is the physician's judgment as to the necessity and appropriateness of medical diagnostic equipment limited by his or her agreement with the facility?
- Is the physician required to assist in various activities at the direction of the lay owners of the facility?
- Is the physician required to perform free services, such as consulting services, on behalf of the enterprise?
- Are the physician's work hours set by lay parties?
- Who determines the amount of malpractice insurance the physician must carry?
- Do lay entities have approval power over the amount of the physician's fees and the collection of those fees?
- Do lay entities receive a percentage of the physician's gross fees?

Another means of testing whether an employer-employee relationship exists is the federal *common-law employee test*. This test ascertains the *economic reality* behind the relationship and determines the *right of control* over work conditions. To determine the economic reality, courts scrutinize the challenged relationship by looking at elements traditionally associated with an employer-employee relationship. In ascertaining the right of control, the courts consider such factors as to whom the individual reports, how this reporting is done, who sets the rules and regulations for work, how much supervision the individual requires, whether the compensation more closely resembles a salary arrangement or a contractual arrangement, and whether the relationship is for a definite term (suggesting an independent contractor relationship) or for an indefinite duration (suggesting an employer-employee relationship). See the section on employee leasing in chapter 5.

The key issue to a finding of corporate practice is lay interference with respect to medical judgment. A fine line separates a corporation (a lay entity) that employs physicians who remain independent in their medical judgment from a partnership of physicians who employ other physicians and a lay manager who does not participate in medical decisions. Little difference exists between the two, except for the fact that the former is prohibited under corporate-practice statutes while the latter is not.

Fee Splitting

Related to the corporate practice issue is that of fee splitting. Many states have some sort of law prohibiting the sharing of any portion of a physician's professional fees with a nonprofessional.[16] This restriction can affect the structuring of the compensation scheme of a joint venture enterprise. In states that prohibit fee splitting, a suspect situation would be one in which all owners, lay and physician, receive, on an equal basis, a percentage of the net income collected from patients for physician's services.[17]

However, not all revenue-sharing schemes are prohibited. If this were the case, then many joint ventures would be unable to operate. In general, many percentage-of-profits schemes that merely compensate the lay entity out of gross income are considered legitimate as long as a reasonable relationship exists between the compensation and the item provided. For example, payment to a lay entity for services, such as those provided by a service bureau,[18] or for furnishing facilities[19] is not prohibited.

State Laws on Self-Referrals

Of great concern when evaluating the compensation scheme of a joint venture enterprise is the so-called self-referral problem, which is related to the fee-splitting issue that is discussed in the previous section of this chapter. Simply stated, the question is whether a physician who has an ownership interest in a health care facility can refer patients to that facility. If the answer to this first question is yes, the next question to be asked is whether the physician can accept a fee or any form of compensation in return for that referral.

Ownership Interest

In some states, a physician may not participate as an owner in certain types of joint venture projects. For instance, some states prohibit physician ownership of pharmacies.[20] The perceived risk is that the physician would always choose to refer patients to that particular pharmacy even if such a referral were not in the best interests of the patients from either a health care or financial perspective.

In most cases, however, physicians may make legitimate investments in various medical service establishments. To protect patients' interests, a few states do have laws or regulations requiring disclosure of those ownership interests to the patients prior to the making of any such referrals.[21]

For example, California's law, which is fairly far-reaching, prohibits specified licensed medical practitioners from referring patients to clinical laboratories in which the licensee has any membership, proprietary interest, or co-ownership in any form or has any profit-sharing arrangement without first making a written disclosure of that interest to the patient. The disclosure must clearly indicate that the patient has the right to choose any clinical laboratory to perform the necessary work.[22] Therefore, a participant in a clinical laboratory joint venture is able to refer patients to the enterprise, but only after telling the patients about interests that the practitioner has in the enterprise.

This disclosure law was recently broadened to make it unlawful for a licensed practitioner to bill a patient on behalf of or refer a patient to any organization in which the practitioner, or his or her immediate family, has a "significant beneficial interest," unless the licensee first gives a written disclosure to the patient of such interest and advises the patient that alternative services are available and that the patient is free to choose any organization to obtain the services ordered by the practitioner.[23] *Immediate family* can include the husband or wife of the physician as well as parents, parents of the physician's spouse, children, or children's spouses. *Significant beneficial interest* is defined as any financial interest in an enterprise that is 5 percent or more of the total interests held in the business or $5,000, whichever is less.[24]

The more difficult problem when dealing with the self-referral issue is whether the physician can accept a fee for such referrals. In states that prohibit bribes or kickbacks, a straight fee to a physician as payment for a referral is prohibited.[25] Such payments are also clear violations of the Medicare antifraud and abuse statutes (see the section "Medicare-Medicaid Antifraud and Abuse Statutes" later in this chapter). Less clear, however, is whether various profit-sharing schemes of a joint venture fall within the scope of antikickback laws. Physicians are generally not prevented from making a profit from their investments in health care enterprises. However, some arrangements that are tied to the amount of business the owners have brought in look like remuneration for referrals.

The laws can be fairly inclusive. For example, California defines an unlawful fee as "any rebate, refund, commission, preference, patronage dividend, discount, or other consideration, whether in the form of money or otherwise, as compensation or inducement for referring patients."[26] Thus, it covers more than just a flat fee.[27] Any fee that is even remotely connected with an actual or a hoped-for referral is prohibited.[28] The statute's purpose is to prevent referrals from being made that would be contrary to the best interests of the patient.[29]

Thus, in a joint venture enterprise, such as an ambulatory surgical center, the following practices are probably in violation of the law. First, any return of dividends to the physician-owner that are measured by the number or value of his or her referrals is prohibited.[30] Second, other rewards to the owners based on the amount of business that they generate for the facility, such as credits for free or reduced-rate services from the facility or at the facility's expense, may be disallowed. Such credits would be no different from patronage dividends.[31] Third, any other benefits to the physician, such as reduced rent for the use of the facility's operating rooms, for example, are also illegal if the benefits bear a direct relationship to the physician's referrals.

To be legitimate, compensation to the owners on account of their ownership of the facility should be based *solely* on the percentage of their ownership interest or the amount of capital contributed to the enterprise. This situation is true regardless of the fact that the physicians would nevertheless benefit financially, albeit indirectly, from self-referrals. To hold otherwise would effectively prohibit the physician from referring to any facility in which he or she has an interest and, except in limited cases,[32] such restraint is not generally required by state antikickback laws.[33]

Medicaid Antikickback Laws

Under local antikickback laws, various state health care agencies and attorneys general have challenged suspect ownership and compensation schemes. Enforcement has been particularly severe with respect to state Medicaid antifraud and abuse statutes.[34]

For example, in the state of Pennsylvania, the law specifically provides that a physician who treats Medicaid patients may not in any case refer that patient to any health care facility or service business in which he or she has an ownership interest.[35] Even if no payment is made to the physician, such a referral violates the law, and the physician would be subject to prosecution simply by referring the patient to the facility, even if the physician deems the referral to be in the best interests of the patient. If a violation is found, the physician is not permitted to participate further in the state Medicaid program and has to pay back to the state all amounts received by the physician from the state on behalf of Medicaid patients.[36] A Medicaid task force composed of representatives from the Federal Bureau of Investigation (FBI), the U.S. Department of Health and Human Services (HHS), the state of Pennsylvania, and the U.S. attorney's office in Philadelphia cooperated in investigations that resulted in the convictions of several physicians for fraud under the Medicaid antikickback statute between 1983 and 1985. Moreover, staff attorneys from that task force have traveled around the country to participate in seminars and training programs that explain to prosecutors how to obtain such convictions. Such cooperation among prosecuting departments is apparently standard procedure.[37]

Because of the aggressiveness with which state governmental authorities are scrutinizing physician ownership of health care facilities, the feasibility of physician involvement in economic joint ventures is being carefully examined. The pronouncements of the California attorney general have made it clear, however, that in that state at least, physicians may own interests in health care facilities. In most instances they may refer patients to those same facilities, but in their dealings, they must scrupulously avoid the appearance of impropriety. Absolutely no relationship can exist between any return to the physician-owners from the enterprise and the number or potential profitability of patients referred there by those physician-owners.

Medicare-Medicaid Antifraud and Abuse Statutes

Any health care provider that receives reimbursement under either the Medicare or Medicaid program is subject to the antifraud and abuse provisions of the Social Security Act. This statute prohibits, among other things, the knowing or willful solicitation or receipt of any payment (including any kickback, bribe, or rebate) in return for referring a patient to any provider for an item or service for which payment may be made under Medicare or Medicaid.[38] If a violation of the statute is found, criminal sanctions, including both substantial fines and imprisonment, may be imposed.[39]

The prohibitions contained in the Medicare antifraud and abuse statute do not apply to "any amount paid by an employer to an employee (who has a bona fide employment relationship with such employer) for employment in the provision of covered items or services."[40] Unfortunately, the statute does not provide an explanation of the term *employee*. It is therefore an open question whether an *employment relationship*, as the term is used in the statute, can include within its scope, for example, an independent contractor relationship or a consulting relationship that a joint venture entity may have with its participants. No interpretive regulations or cases explain the limits of the employee exclusion from the provisions of the Medicare antifraud and abuse law.

Courts may interpret the statutory provision narrowly and require that, to be included within the exclusion, the relationship must be similar to that of a common-law employee under federal labor law.[41] On the other hand, because the Medicare antifraud and abuse statute is a criminal statute and therefore should be interpreted to give the greatest benefit of the doubt to the defendant, the term *employee* may be construed to apply to the broad range of persons or entities who may provide services on an ongoing basis to the joint venture entity. It is at least arguable that Congress intended this broad interpretation of the language when it enacted the antifraud and abuse statute.[42]

Because of the lack of precision in the antifraud and abuse statute and because it is worded broadly, it may encompass within its scope various economic joint venture business practices. The statute was enacted prior to the recent upsurge in economic joint ventures and consequently does not take into account how it can hamper these new ways of doing business, including those that the government may want to encourage. For instance, many joint ventures offer physicians financial incentives to increase their use of the joint venture facility. If a health care provider receives money from the joint venture facility and at the same time refers patients to it, any payments received by the provider could appear to be a bribe or kickback under the law.

The main problem with the Medicare antifraud and abuse statute as it applies to joint ventures is that no clear guidelines on its application exist. First, no regulations or advisory opinions from governmental agencies having authority over administering the Medicare program exist to help a health care provider decide whether a proposed joint venture complies with the antifraud and abuse laws. The Department of Health and Human Services (HHS), the agency that administers the Medicare antifraud and abuse program, has no authority to issue opinions.[43] The only administrative guidelines available are in several directives issued by the Health Care Financing Administration (HCFA) that relate to payments for referrals to manufacturers and suppliers of medical equipment.[44] Second, there are relatively few cases interpreting the law under the Medicare antifraud and abuse statute. The cases that may be relevant offer some clue as to how stringently the law will be interpreted, but have fairly egregious facts.[45] Moreover, these cases are not directly applicable to many of the problems that the antifraud and abuse statute raises for joint ventures and their participants.

Regulations and Advisory Opinions

Being able to obtain an opinion or ruling on the legality of an enterprise or scheme from the governmental authority charged with enforcing the statutes would be most helpful to prospective participants in a joint venture. However, HHS has no authority to issue binding opinions pertaining to the interpretation of this statute to the public as the Internal Revenue Service does with respect to the tax law.[46] The Medicare antifraud and abuse statute is a criminal statute and only the U.S. Department of Justice, which is the prosecuting arm of the federal government, has discretion to determine violations of criminal statutes. The Department of Justice has also refused to provide any formal advance guidance as to the types of business practices that may violate the Medicare antifraud and abuse law.[47] The Department of Justice will only scrutinize a transaction once the possible violation has already occurred.

Consequently, joint venture participants cannot receive any opinion of an advisory nature regarding the legality of a proposed scheme, nor can they obtain any sort of *no-action letter* reassuring them that the government will not take action against them for an arrangement that is of questionable legality under the statute. The only reassurance that joint venture participants may receive as to the legality of a proposed transaction is the assurance from those persons enforcing the Medicare antifraud and abuse program that the law's intent is not to penalize legitimate business transactions.

At one time, representatives from the Office of the Inspector General of HHS, the Office of General Counsel, and HCFA formed a task force to study related issues under the antifraud and abuse statute and to explore approaches to establishing uniform guidelines for doing business within the confines of the law.[48] But none of the advisory notices cautioning against practices that would be subject to criminal prosecution that the task force hoped to issue, were forthcoming during the existence of the task force. In the absence of any such advisory notices, participants in joint ventures must examine their payment arrangements on their own in the light of what legal advice is available. The vagueness of advice that is available and the refusal of governmental authorities to take a firm stand on certain practices will most probably have a chilling effect on many joint venture arrangements.

Case Law

The cases that have considered the Medicare and Medicaid antifraud and abuse statutes have generally taken a broad approach in interpreting them. The case that may have the greatest chilling impact on joint venture payment schemes is *United States v. Greber*.[49] Dr. Greber was an osteopathic physician who owned an entity that provided diagnostic services to cardiac patients. Whenever the diagnostic entity performed tests for referring physicians, it would forward a portion of the Medicare reimbursement that it received for the test to the referring physician. This payment was ostensibly for interpretations by the referring physicians. In upholding Dr. Greber's conviction under the Medicare antifraud and abuse statute, the court held that any payment to a referring physician violates the statute if a purpose of the payment is to induce a referral. The fact that the payment could also be viewed as compensation for health care services was irrelevant.[50]

The broad language in the *Greber* case is sufficient to cause some concern for potential joint venture participants who, as a consequence of this decision, may be hesitant in entering into arrangements in which compensation paid to them could be viewed as a payment for a referral. Although this case and several other cases interpreting the Medicare and Medicaid antifraud and abuse statutes have egregious fact situations in which the defendants arguably had an intent to violate the law, the broad language that the courts used in deciding these cases is certain to have a chilling effect on many joint ventures.[51]

Problem Areas

Certain practices within the joint venture structure may invite scrutiny:

- Self-referrals and payments for referral fees, including referral fees or mandatory referral requirements for joint venture participants; sharing of venture proceeds in proportion to referrals; bonuses or incentive programs that provide remuneration for increasing utilization; and kickbacks, rebates, and commissions
- Waiver of coinsurance and deductibles
- Captive referral situations

Self-Referrals

The referral problem under the Medicare-Medicaid statutes is similar to that posed under the state antikickback laws considered earlier in this chapter. Certain referral payment schemes almost certainly raise problems. An analysis of the cases that have considered referral situations indicates several facts that can help determine whether a payment scheme is legitimate remuneration or an illegal kickback. A legitimate scheme has the following attributes:

- *The payment is made for actual performance of services, and those services are medically necessary.* Payments made by a joint venture entity to those who are in a position to refer patients to it are particularly suspect if those payments are not made in exchange for actual services. Those services must also be medically necessary. For example, a payment to a physician who refers patients to a facility in exchange for supervisory services will be scrutinized to determine that those services are necessary to the treatment of the facility's patients. In *Greber*, payments were made to the physicians even when they failed to perform any "interpretation services" provided for in their contracts.[52] Other payment schemes that are suspect because they indicate that no real service has been rendered are handling fees,[53] fees for consulting services,[54] and administrative salaries.[55]
- *A direct correlation exists between the value of the payment and the value of the services rendered.* A payment will also be examined to determine that a correlation exists between the payment and the value of the services rendered. If

the amount of the payment is greater than the value of the services, part of that payment could be a fee for a referral. For example, if a laboratory pays a management company owned by doctors a fee for services, such as collecting specimens and supplying forms, and the value of the services is substantially less than the compensation that the management company receives for those services, a court may well presume that part of that compensation is a disguised fee to the physician-owners for referrals to the laboratory.[56]

- *There is no tie-in between the payment and the amount of Medicare reimbursement anticipated for the service.* Arrangements in which the amount of the fee for the services rendered by the referring party is directly tied to the amount of Medicare reimbursement that the health care facility receives are also suspect. A court may assume that the fee is actually a rebate paid in return for patient referrals. For example, in the *Greber* case, the court noted that the fee was 40 percent of the Medicare payment.[57] To avoid suspicion, fees should not depend on the amount of Medicare reimbursement. Instead, they should be based, for example, on an hourly rate or a fixed rate according to the type of service.

To determine in any individual case whether a payment is in actuality a fee for a referral, courts look for any of the above elements and generally examine the substance, and not merely the form, of the payment scheme as a whole. An example of how a court examines payment arrangements is the case of *United States v. Universal Trade and Industries*[58] under the Medicaid antifraud provisions.[59] A large medical laboratory established a smaller facility on the premises of a medical clinic. This on-site laboratory was owned by a separate corporation in which the clinic and staff physicians owned stock (although they had invested no capital). A percentage of gross revenues from the laboratory operations was paid to the clinic as an incentive for referring work to the on-site laboratory. Physicians who staffed the clinic also received a percentage of the profits as administration salaries. The laboratory was used almost exclusively by patients of the clinic. As a result of this exclusive use, the payments to the clinic under the percentage arrangement would always be directly related to the number of tests ordered by the clinic. The court found the arrangement to be a kickback scheme that violated the antifraud and abuse statute.

The situation in this case is extreme because of the peculiar facts surrounding the payments. First, the physicians who received a percentage of profits from the laboratory were listed as part owners even though they had invested no capital in the enterprise. Second, neither the clinic nor any staff physicians performed any administrative duties or rendered any services of any sort to the laboratory in return for the percentage-based salaries. Third, the on-site laboratory was provided at no cost to the clinic and was used almost exclusively by it. Fourth, the payments were made on the basis of a percentage of gross revenues and were thus directly related to the number of tests referred by the clinic to the laboratory. Such an accumulation of suspicious facts invites scrutiny under the antifraud and abuse statute.

The obvious cases do not pose great dangers to the average joint venture because most attorneys for health care providers are aware that physicians cannot base their compensation from a facility in which they have an interest on the number of referrals that they make to that facility. This practice is prohibited by state and federal law in most instances. However, the *Greber* case is more worrisome. In that case, the court stated that payments to a referring physician are in violation of the statute if *one* purpose of the payment is to induce a referral even if the payments are also compensation for health care services rendered to patients.[60] Decisions such as *Greber* cause some fear that arrangements having sound economic reasons totally unrelated to referrals may fall within the scope of the statute and may invite prosecution, depending on the whims of the prosecutor.

Chapter 8. Business Practices and Ethical Considerations

Medicare-Medicaid Antifraud and Abuse Statutes
Problem Areas

An example of such a sound economically motivated scheme is a payment scheme included in a joint venture proposal to attract investment capital. In a partnership between a hospital, as a general partner, and physicians, as limited partners, to operate an ambulatory surgical center, a typical scheme for paying out profits may be the following: of the first $50,000 of gross profits, 75 percent would go to the general partner; of the second $50,000, 50 percent would go to the general partner; and of the next $50,000, 25 percent would go to the general partner; all amounts in excess of $150,000 would go entirely to the limited partners. The limited partners, all of whom are physicians, also work in the center and are in a position to refer patients to it. The business reasons for this particular payout scheme are to reimburse the general partner at an early stage in the venture for any start-up costs incurred. In such a circumstance, the general partner is usually entitled to such an early payout. Moreover, such a payout scheme is a common way of structuring many limited partnerships. The reasons for this type of payout scheme may be totally unrelated to the potential for referrals from limited partners. However, the more business that the center has (that is, the more referrals that physician-owners send there), the more money the limited partners make. Does this scheme violate the Medicare fraud and abuse laws?

This particular scheme can be challenged, despite its sound business purposes, because so few legal guidelines exist and because the HHS Office of the Inspector General seems willing to challenge any payments made to a health care provider who is in a position to refer patients, regardless of whether or not the payments constitute valid compensation for services or supplies.[61] Consequently, all compensation schemes of joint venture enterprises should probably be carefully reviewed in light of the Medicare antifraud and abuse statutes for the possibility that owner-physicians are being remunerated for referrals.

Of greater concern to the feasibility of physician involvement in joint ventures is the issue of whether a physician-owner of a health care facility may refer patients at all without violating the statute. The *Greber* decision certainly gives substance to this fear.[62] The Medicare antifraud and abuse statute does not specifically prohibit physicians from owning health care facilities or from referring patients to any facility in which they have an ownership interest. However, the statute clearly prohibits any remuneration in return for referrals. Although no cases under this statute have looked at this specific issue, the government may take the position that any equity distributions from the business to owner participants on the basis of relative utilization of the business are of questionable legality. The government would probably take such a position because this type of distribution is ultimately made on the basis of the number of referrals that the physicians make to the facility rather than on the actual ownership interest that each physician has in it. Such equity distributions would therefore constitute payment for referrals, which is prohibited by the statute.[63]

The larger problem is this: because physician-owners benefit financially from self-referrals, the profit distributions they receive from the enterprise can be characterized in all cases as illegal kickbacks or referral fees even though no compensation is paid to a physician directly on the basis of any of those referrals and even though the benefits distributed by the enterprise are shared by all owners of the facility. Until this issue has been clarified, physician participation in any venture must be structured to avoid even the appearance of impropriety.

Consequently, in the case of a joint venture facility, such as an emergency center, to which a physician would be likely to refer Medicare or Medicaid patients, the participants should structure physician disbursements from the center as a percentage of gross fees based on the physicians' respective ownership interests in the facility or as legitimate compensation for substantive services rendered to the facility by the physician. Under no circumstances should there be a requirement that physicians or any other party refer patients to the facility. If this restriction is not possible to meet, then the parties should consider a joint venture that does not accept Medicare patients. Even then, however, the facility could not operate in some states without complying with the similar state restrictions with respect to referrals[64] (see the discussion on state antikickback laws earlier in this chapter).

Another self-referral issue that can arise in a joint venture setting is whether *discounts* offered to a joint venture participant from the facility constitute a fee for referrals. For example, a hospital and a group of physicians set up a medical pavilion joint venture. Physician participants are encouraged to lease space in the pavilion for satellite offices. To induce physicians into the pavilion, the joint venture offers a reduced rental to those physicians. Even though the joint venture agreement does not have a written requirement that physicians receiving such a rental reduction refer patients to other pavilion services, such as the pharmacy, laboratory services, or health clinic services, is it in violation of the Medicare antifraud and abuse statute? There is no specific answer to this question.

A similar situation is discussed in a recent legal memorandum from the Office of Legal and Regulatory Affairs of the American Hospital Association.[65] The hypothetical example used in this report was a discounted office building lease. The task force argued that if the hospital providing the rent reduction willfully and knowingly reduced the amount of the fee in return for a referral or if either party knew that the primary purpose of the rate reduction was a referral or hoped-for referral, then an antifraud and abuse violation had occurred. Similarly, in this example, the parties have probably violated the antifraud and abuse statutes if such referrals are expected or are an implied requirement even though no written agreement requires physicians to refer patients to other clinic services.

Waiver of Coinsurance

Other potential violations of the Medicare antifraud and abuse statute can arise in the joint venture setting. One issue that can tangentially arise in connection with a joint venture is the waiving of Medicare coinsurance and deductibles to attract Medicare patients. For example, a hospital participates with medical staff members to establish a hospital outpatient surgery center. The center competes directly with a nearby freestanding facility. The competing facility receives 100 percent reimbursement from Medicare for specified services provided to Medicare beneficiaries and so advertises in local newspapers that it provides no-cost surgery.[66] The hospital outpatient center is only reimbursed for 80 percent of its costs. The Medicare patient or an insurance company has to pay the remaining 20 percent. To compete, the outpatient department waives the 20 percent coinsurance payment. Has the joint venture violated the statute by willfully and knowingly soliciting Medicare patients?

The Office of the Inspector General has received several inquiries regarding this practice, which is apparently becoming prevalent as competition in the health care industry increases. Officials at HCFA have told some health care attorneys that no antifraud and abuse violation has occurred because the waiver of the Medicare deductibles and coinsurance does not cost the Medicare program any additional money and may save Medicare patients some expense.[67] The government's primary concern in enforcing the Medicare antifraud and abuse provisions is to take action against those practices that have a potential for increased costs to the Medicare-Medicaid system. The government seems less willing to take action against a practice that is not detrimental to the government, as in the case of waivers of coinsurance requirements.[68]

In this connection, the Inspector General of HHS requested the Department of Justice to publicly state that the Department of Justice would not prosecute in cases of routine waivers of coinsurance and deductibles because such practices cause no harm to the federal government and because the Department of Justice had declined to prosecute all such cases referred by HHS. The Department of Justice declined to make such a public statement because such business practices are nevertheless a technical violation of the law.[69] As a result, this area of application of the Medicare antifraud and abuse statute remains unclear.

Captive Referral Situations

Another potential problem is that of so-called *captive referrals.* A situation involving captive referrals might occur, for example, when a hospital participates with a manufacturer of health care products in a home health care joint venture. As part of the terms of the agreement, the hospital encourages its patients at the time of their discharge from the hospital to buy the products of the joint venture enterprise. Every time a certain amount of such equipment is purchased as a result of the hospital's referral efforts, the hospital's purchase price for inpatient equipment is reduced through some mutually agreed-upon formula. This arrangement presents a serious risk of a violation of the antifraud and abuse provisions. The hospital is in effect receiving a payment from the manufacturer based on the number of patients referred by the hospital to the home health care enterprise. Quite probably these payments could be seen as a fee for referrals.[70]

Efforts to shield the illegal payments from the scope of the law by means of labels that have no true economic substance, such as calling them fees for "administrative services" rendered by the hospital, will not work. The government looks at the reality of the situation to determine whether the payment is reasonable for services actually performed.[71] For instance, if a supplier pays regular fees to a health care practitioner, those fees are suspect unless the practitioner has rendered an actual, substantive service to the supplier, other than offering mere consultation or administrative services.[72]

This situation was the topic of a series of intermediary letters issued by HCFA. The government initially found that a service agreement in which a respiratory therapist referred patients to a supplier of durable medical equipment and received payments for setting up and maintaining the equipment was illegal.[73] The argument that the payments were only for services rendered and not referrals was initially rejected by HCFA. Creating an opportunity to generate a fee was determined by HCFA to be sufficient to make a remuneration illegal if the remuneration is intended to induce patient referrals. In a subsequent letter superseding the earlier opinion, HCFA modified this harsh language, stating that payment by a DME supplier of any fee as an inducement for a referral of Medicare patients to the supplier is illegal. In removing the reference to the opportunity for a referral, HCFA noted that it unduly prejudiced certain arrangements without due consideration of all relevant factors.[74]

A joint venture might protect itself somewhat from scrutiny under the antifraud and abuse provisions in various ways. First, the enterprise and all participants should always make clear to patients that the ultimate choice of care provider (or supplier in the case of equipment, supplies, or drugs) belongs to the patient. Second, medical services provided by the facility should be medically necessary, and this fact should be well documented. Third, all fees should be reasonable. No requirement whatsoever should exist with respect to referrals, and no percentage distributions should be made on the basis of facility utilization. All fees should be based on arm's-length contracts.

Ethical Restrictions of American Medical Association

As a final restraint on joint venture activities, the American Medical Association (AMA) prescribes various rules with respect to physician ownership of health care facilities and physician participation in joint ventures. These AMA guidelines permit physician ownership of health care facilities, such as for-profit hospitals, nursing homes, or freestanding surgery centers. Such an ownership interest does not provide an irresoluble conflict of interest as long as the physician discloses his or her ownership interest to patients prior to referring them to the facility and the physician *always* places the patient's well-being above his or her own financial interests.[75]

Medical ethics do prohibit any payment or fee in return for the referral of patients. Payments that are not tied to referrals but merely represent a return on investment or payment for services actually rendered do not constitute any ethical violation.[76]

The AMA will probably also scrutinize the various MeSH-type joint ventures, in which physicians and hospitals participate in risk-sharing arrangements with respect to Medicare reimbursement. Some of these schemes allow hospitals and their medical staffs to share losses and gains from discharges above or below the DRG allowance. Such arrangements raise the issue of whether they contain an inherent conflict for physicians between what may be best for the patient (for example, an extra day in the hospital) and a potential profit from early discharge of patients and curtailment of customary hospital services. This conflict may be avoided by having a separate entity, such as the integrated health care corporation (IHCC) discussed in chapter 1, in which both physicians and the hospital are participants, oversee DRGs, patient admissions, and discharges. At any rate, such a conflict is inherent in any alternative delivery system, such as an HMO, and is inherent in most present-day relationships between hospitals and medical staffs even when no MeSH or IHCC exists. Such a conflict between financial concerns and the patient's best interests are inherent in the prospective pricing system itself.

The AMA has proposed several new guidelines for physician involvement in ventures such as MeSH, including the restriction that all staff physicians must be invited to participate.[77] However, final guidelines had not been issued as of mid-1986.

Notes

1. *See, e.g.,* CAL. BUS. & PROF. CODE § 2400 (West) (prohibits the practice of medicine by nonprofessional corporations and other artificial legal entities); COLO. REV. STAT. § 12-36-117(1)(m).

2. *E.g.,* CAL. BUS. & PROF. CODE § 2400 (West). *But see* CAL. BUS. & PROF. CODE § 2401 (West) ("notwithstanding Section 2400, a clinic operated primarily for the purpose of medical education by a public or private nonprofit university medical school which is approved by the Division of Licensing of the Board of Osteopathic Examiners may charge for professional services rendered by licensers who hold academic appointments on the faculty of such university, if such charges are approved by the physician in whose name the charges are made"). The state of Ohio applies the corporate-practice restriction to both for-profit and not-for-profit corporations. OPS. OHIO ATT'Y GEN. No. 82 (1963).

3. *See, e.g.,* CAL. BUS. & PROF. CODE § 2402 (West).

4. Federal Health Maintenance Organization Act of 1973, 42 U.S.C. § 300e-10. *See also* CAL. BUS. & PROF. CODE § 2411 (West); MINN. STAT. ANN. § 62D.22, Subdiv. 3 (West).

5. *See, e.g.,* Dr. Allison, Dentist, Inc. v. Allison, 360 Ill. 638, 196 N.E. 799, 800 (1935).

6. *See, e.g.,* County of Los Angeles v. Ford, 121 Cal. App. 2d 407, 413, 263 P.2d 638 (1953); McMurdo v. Getter, 298 Mass. 363, 10 N.E.2d 139 (1937).

7. *See, e.g.,* Letter from Carol Crawford, Director, Bureau of Consumer Protection, to Theresa Donahue, Director of Sunset Department of Regulatory Agencies, for the State of Colorado (June 22, 1984), which urges that state to repeal corporate-practice restrictions or allow such laws to expire.

8. California Ass'n of Dispensing Opticians v. Pearle Vision Center, Inc., 143 Cal. App. 3d 419, 191 Cal. Rptr. 762 (1983).

9. 65 OPS. CAL. ATT'Y GEN. 223 (1982).

Chapter 8. Business Practices and Ethical Considerations

Notes

10. *But see* Blank v. Palo Alto-Stanford Hosp. Center, 234 Cal. App. 2d 377, 44 Cal. Rptr. 572 (1952) (hearing denied), in which the court held that the doctors retained freedom of action in their practice and so the corporate hospital was not engaged in the practice of medicine. In Oregon, hospitals are not subject to the corporate practice restriction and could therefore directly employ physicians. See OPS. OR. ATT'Y GEN. No. 7230 (1975).

11. Messner v. Board of Dental Examiners, 87 Cal. App. 199, 204, 262 P. 58 (1927) (lay manager exercised no control or direction over the professional work performed in the office).

12. Complete Service Bureau v. San Diego County Medical Soc'y, 43 Cal. 2d 201, 272 P.2d 497 (1954) (rehearing denied). *But see* Pacific Employers Ins. Co. v. Carpenter, 10 Cal. App. 2d 592, 52 P.2d 992 (1935); People v. Pacific Health Corp., 12 Cal. 2d 156, 82 P.2d 429 (1938).

13. *See, e.g.,* Painless Parker v. Board of Dental Examiners, 216 Cal. 285, 14 P.2d 77 (1932) (rehearing denied). *See also* 58 OPS. CAL. ATT'Y GEN. 883 (1975) (a corporation that supervised a hospital laboratory and employed a pathologist as its representative could not require the pathologist to perform any medical functions, or the corporation would be practicing medicine).

14. *See* 55 OPS. CAL. ATT'Y GEN. 103 (1972).

15. *Id.*

16. *See, e.g.,* CAL. BUS. & PROF. CODE § 2264 (West) (a physician may not aid or abet any unlicensed person to engage in the practice of medicine or in any other mode of treating the sick that requires a license); VT. STAT. ANN. tit. 26, §§ 1354(2),(15); OHIO REV. CODE ANN. § 47321.22(B)(13) (Page). *See also* 55 OPS. CAL. ATT'Y GEN. 103 (1972).

17. *See, e.g.,* CAL. BUS. & PROF. CODE § 650 (West).

18. *See, e.g.,* Complete Service Bureau v. San Deigo County Medical Soc'y, 43 Cal. 2d 201, 272 P.2d 497 (1954) (rehearing denied).

19. *See, e.g.,* Blank v. Palo Alto-Stanford Hosp. Center, 234 Cal. App. 2d 377, 44 Cal. Rptr. 572 (1965) (hearing denied); Letsch v. Northern San Diego County Hosp. District, 246 Cal. App. 2d 673, 55 Cal. Rptr. 118 (1966).

20. *See, e.g.,* CAL. BUS. & PROF. CODE § 4080.5 (West).

21. *See, e.g.,* VT. STAT. ANN. tit. 26, § 1354(13).

22. CAL. BUS. & PROF. CODE § 654.1 (West).

23. CAL. BUS. & PROF. CODE § 654.2(a) (West) (added 1984, effective 1/1/85), *as amended* Stats. 1985, ch. 1542, 1986 Cal. Legis. Serv.

24. CAL. BUS. & PROF. CODE § 654.2(c) (West), *as amended* Stats. 1985, ch. 1542, 1986 Cal Legis. Serv.

25. *E.g.,* CAL. BUS. & PROF. CODE § 650 (West); OHIO REV. CODE ANN. § 4731.22(B)(4) (Page).

26. CAL. BUS. & PROF. CODE § 650 (West). *See also* FLA. STAT. ANN. § 395.0185 (West); CONN. GEN. STAT. ANN. § 19a-30(f) (West 1984) (prohibits inducements through rebates, fee schedules, billing methods, personnel solicitation, or payment to the practitioner for consultation or assistance or for scientific, clerical, or janitorial services).

27. *See* Mason v. Hosta, 152 Cal. App. 3d 980, 199 Cal. Rptr. 859 (1984) (a $250 fee to a hospital administrator for referrals of a physician for emergency department services to other hospitals was considered compensation for a referral).

28. For instance, even courtesy services rendered by one health care practitioner to another may be illegal if they can be viewed as an inducement for referrals, depending on the facts. *See* 63 OPS. CAL. ATT'Y GEN. 89, 94 (1980).

29. *See* Magan Medical Clinic v. California State Board of Medical Examiners, 249 Cal. App. 2d 124, 57 Cal. Rptr. 256 (1967).

30. *See, e.g.,* OPS. CAL. ATT'Y GEN. No. 84-806 (Feb. 1985) (a physician may refer patients to a clinical laboratory in which he or she owns a limited partnership interest if the physician's return on his or her investment in the limited partnership is not measured by the number or value of his or her referrals).

31. *See, e.g.,* 16 OPS. CAL. ATT'Y GEN. 24 (1950).

32. *E.g.,* CAL. BUS. & PROF. CODE § 654 (West) (prohibits a physician from referring patients directly or indirectly to a registered dispensing optician for the filling of a

prescription for ophthalmic lenses and related products if that physician has an ownership or coownership interest in or a profit-sharing arrangement with the optician).

33. CAL. BUS. & PROF. CODE § 650 (West) (expressly provides that "it shall not be unlawful for any person licensed under this division to refer a person to any laboratory, pharmacy, clinic, or health care facility solely because such licensee has a proprietary interest or coownership in such laboratory, pharmacy, clinic, or health care facility . . . [unless there was] no valid medical need for such referral").

34. These are generally similar to the federal antifraud and abuse laws (42 U.S.C. § 1396h(b)) that are discussed in this chapter. *See, e.g.*, the Pennsylvania fraud and abuse statute, 62 PA. CONS. STAT. ANN. § 1407 (Purdon 1984).

35. 55 PA. CONS. STAT. ANN. § 1101.51(c)(5) (Purdon 1984).

36. 55 PA. CONS. STAT. ANN. § 1101.77(a)(i) (Purdon 1984).

37. Telephone conversations of Carol R. Boman, Esq., with Peter Smith, Esq., head of the criminal division at the United States Attorney's Office in Philadelphia, PA (Apr. 25, 1985).

38. Social Security Act § 1877(b)(1), 42 U.S.C. § 1395nn(b)(1) provides that if an individual:

knowingly and willfully solicits or receives any remuneration (including any kickback, bribe, or rebate) directly or indirectly, overtly or covertly, in cash or in kind

 (A) in return for referring an individual to a person for the furnishing or arranging of any item or service for which payment may be made in whole or in part [by the Medicare or Medicaid programs] or

 (B) in return for purchasing, leasing, ordering, or arranging for or recommending purchasing, leasing or ordering any good, facility, services or item for which payment may be made in whole or in part [by the Medicare or Medicaid programs],

he shall be guilty of a felony. . . .

Section 1909(b) of the Social Security Act, 42 U.S.C. § 1396h(b), contains identical antifraud and abuse provisions relating to the Medicaid programs.

39. Upon conviction for a violation of the antifraud and abuse statute, the provider is subject to a maximum fine of $25,000 and/or imprisonment for no more than five years. 42 U.S.C. §§ 1395nn(b)(1), 1396h(b). The same sanctions can be applied to an individual who "knowingly and willfully offers or pays any remuneration (including any kickback, bribe or rebate) directly or indirectly, overtly or covertly, in cash or in kind to any person to induce the person" to commit such a fraud or abuse violation. 42 U.S.C. § 1395nn(b)(2). Because the statute covers both the offer and payment and the solicitation and receipt of such illegal remuneration, all parties to a suspect transaction risk liability.

40. Social Security Act § 1877(b)(3)(B), 42 U.S.C. § 1395nn(b)(3)(B).

41. *See* discussion of the common-law employee question in chapter 5.

42. When the Medicare antifraud and abuse provisions were considered in the House of Representatives, Rep. Dan Rostenkowski, D-IL, then a member of the House Ways and Means Subcommittee on Health, stated that the committee intended "to exempt only those payments that represented payments for legitimate employment." However, he went on to state as an example of such "legitimate employment" a situation in which a distributor of equipment "pays a retailer on a commission basis for the use of his store to sell a product" because the retailer is "a legitimate agent employed in a traditional manner to sell a product." 123 CONG. REC. 30279 (1977) (Statement of Rep. Rostenkowski).

43. In a recent exchange of correspondence between the Inspector General of HHS and the Department of Justice, Justice instructed HHS that HHS was prohibited from issuing any advisory opinions as to whether any particular course of conduct violates the antifraud and abuse provisions. *See* Letter from the Honorable Richard P. Kusserow, inspector general, Department of Health and Human Services, to Stephen S. Trott, assistant attorney general, Criminal Division, Department of Justice (Apr. 17, 1985), and Letter from Stephen S. Trott to the Honorable Richard P. Kusserow (Oct. 30, 1985) [hereinafter cited as HHS-Justice Letters].

44. *See Payments of "Finders" or "Referral" Fees to Respiratory Therapists by Durable Medical Equipment Suppliers*, ILB No. 94-9 (Sept. 1984), superseded by Program Memo (Carriers) No. B-85-2 (Apr. 1985).

45. *See, e.g.,* United States v. Greber, 760 F.2d 68 (3d Cir. 1985), *cert. denied*, _____ U.S. _____, 106 S. Ct. 396 (1985); United States v. Universal Trade and Indus., 695 F.2d 1151 (9th Cir. 1983).

46. *See* HHS-Justice Letters, *supra* note 43.

Chapter 8. Business Practices and Ethical Considerations

Notes

47. *Id.*

48. Letter from the Honorable Richard P. Kusserow, Inspector General, Department of Health & Human Services (HHS), to Ross E. Stromberg, Esq. (Oct. 9, 1984) [hereinafter cited as Kusserow Letter].

49. 760 F.2d 68 (3d Cir. 1985), *cert. denied,* _____ U.S. _____, 106 S. Ct. 396 (1985).

50. United States v. Greber, 760 F.2d at 71.

51. *See also* United States v. Hancock, 604 F.2d 999 (7th Cir. 1979), *cert. denied,* 444 U.S. 991 (1979); United States v. Porter, 591 F.2d 1048 (5th Cir. 1979); United States v. Lipkis, 770 F.2d 1447 (9th Cir. 1985); United States v. Universal Trade and Indus., 695 F.2d 1151 (9th Cir. 1983).

52. 760 F.2d 68 (3d Cir. 1985), *cert. denied,* _____ U.S. _____, 106 S. Ct. 396 (1985).

53. *See, e.g.,* United States v. Hancock, 604 F.2d 999 (7th Cir. 1979), *cert. denied,* 444 U.S. 991 (1979); United States v. Porter, 591 F.2d 1048 (5th Cir. 1979); United States v. Lipkis, 770 F.2d 1447 (9th Cir. 1985).

54. *See* United States v. Ruttenberg, 625 F.2d 173 (7th Cir. 1980); United States v. Tapert, 625 F.2d 111 (6th Cir. 1980), *cert. denied,* 449 U.S. 952 (1980).

55. *See* United States v. Universal Trade and Indus., 695 F.2d 1151 (9th Cir. 1983).

56. *See* United States v. Lipkis, 770 F.2d 1447 (9th Cir. 1985).

57. United States v. Greber, 760 F.2d at 70.

58. 695 F.2d 1151 (9th Cir. 1983).

59. Identical to the Medicare antifraud and abuse statute. Section 1909(b) of the Social Security Act, 42 U.S.C. § 1396h(b).

60. United States v. Greber, 760 F.2d at 72 (emphasis added).

61. The Inspector General of HHS, Richard Kusserow, stated in a published interview that, when health care providers are "bribed," by means of fees that could be on account of referrals, into making treatment decisions that may not be best for the particular patient, he "will nail every one of the [blackguards]. . . ." HEALTHSPAN, May, 1985, at 13 (brackets in the original).

62. United States v. Greber, 760 F.2d 68 (3d Cir. 1985), *cert. denied,* _____ U.S. _____, 106 S. Ct. 396 (1985).

63. *See* Kusserow Letter, *supra* note 48.

64. *See, e.g.,* the Pennsylvania fraud and abuse statute, 62 PA. CONS. STAT. ANN. § 1407 (Purdon).

65. AMERICAN HOSPITAL ASSOCIATION: MEDICARE-MEDICAID ANTIFRAUD AND ABUSE AMENDMENTS: APPLICATION TO HOSPITAL ACTIVITIES UNDER THE MEDICARE PROSPECTIVE PAYMENT SYSTEM (Select Legal Advisory Committee on Medicare, Feb. 1985), at 9 [hereinafter cited as AHA ANTIFRAUD MEMORANDUM]. This paper resolves some of the issues raised by the antifraud and abuse provisions but does not address a number of sensitive areas in the health care field, particularly those relating to joint ventures.

66. *See* discussion in chapter 7, with respect to Medicare reimbursement of freestanding and hospital affiliated ambulatory surgical centers (HAASCs).

67. *See* AHA ANTIFRAUD MEMORANDUM, *supra* note 65, at 16-17.

68. The Inspector General stated that prosecuting someone when no injury to the government has occurred is not easy. HEALTHSPAN, May 1985, at 9.

69. *See* HHS-Justice Letters, *supra* note 43.

70. *See* AHA ANTIFRAUD MEMORANDUM, *supra* note 65, at 19-20, for a similar situation.

71. *See, e.g.,* United States v. Greber, 760 F.2d 68 (3d Cir. 1985), *cert. denied,* _____ U.S. _____, 106 S. Ct. 396 (1985).

72. *See* U.S. v. Ruttenberg, 625 F.2d 173, 174 (7th Cir. 1981).

73. *See Payments of "Finders" or "Referral" Fees to Respiratory Therapists by Durable Medical Equipment Suppliers and the Illegal Remuneration Provisions of the Social Security Act,* ILB No. 84-9 (Sept. 1984).

74. *See* Program Memo (carriers) No. B-85-2 (Apr. 1985).

75. Current opinions of the Judicial Council of the American Medical Association, Section 4.04.

76. *Id.* at Sections 3.02 and 6.03.

77. *See* California Hospital Association (CHA) Insight (Mar. 1985).

Chapter 9 Labor Law Issues

Collective Bargaining
    Successor Employers
        Continuity of the Enterprise
        Continuity of the Work Force
        Appropriateness of Collective Bargaining Unit
    Duty to Bargain
        Subcontracting
            Service Bureau
            Leased Employees
        Partial Closing
    Single-Employer or Joint-Employer Status
        Single-Employer Status
        Joint-Employer Status: Employee Leasing
    Accretion
State Employment Laws
    Traditional Concept of Employment-at-Will
    Statutory Limitations
    Theories behind Wrongful Discharge Cases
        Wrongful Discharge in Violation of Public Policy
        Good Faith and Fair Dealing
        Implied Contract
        Promissory Estoppel
    Avoiding Liability for Bad-Faith Dealings

One major consideration in forming any joint venture is staffing and other personnel matters. When a hospital or other health care provider enters into an agreement with outside investors to set up an out-of-hospital health care center, such as a birthing center, major decisions must be made about whether to staff the new facility with professional and other staff from the hospital, staff members presently employed by another participant in the venture, newly hired personnel, or leased employees.

These decisions affect not only the new facility but also the employee relations of the venture participants. For instance, the formation of the new enterprise may involve mergers of two or more existing entities and acquisitions of new entities; the closing or relocation of a department or facility; the sale or transfer of businesses; the subcontracting for services with outside parties, such as a service bureau; and employee leasing. All of these organizational changes within an existing business have labor law implications.

The major labor and staffing issues that must be considered in the joint venture situation are collective bargaining and state laws governing treatment of employees by employers. The first section of this chapter, on collective bargaining considerations, is the most extensive because the most heavily regulated businesses, from the labor law perspective, are those that enter into such agreements with their employees or in which union activity takes place. Nevertheless, no employer, unionized or not, is immune from labor law considerations. Every joint venture participant should be aware that many states require employers to treat their employees fairly.

Collective Bargaining

Labor law concerns weigh most heavily on health care and health supply providers whose employee relations are governed by collective bargaining agreements at the time that they participate in the joint venture. The terms and conditions of these agreements may determine, to a lesser or greater extent, the staffing arrangements of the new venture enterprise.

Many questions are raised by the decision to participate in a joint venture. For instance, if a hospital participant uses its own staff for the new center, would those staff members continue to be covered by the hospital's collective bargaining agreement, or would the venture facility be viewed as a new employer of the staff members, thereby possibly leading to the negotiation of a separate union contract? More difficult questions involve staff members who divide their time between the hospital and the new facility and the situation in which the center is staffed by employees of both the hospital and another participant. For instance, in a birthing-center joint venture, midwives who are employed by a group obstetric practice participant and are not covered by a collective bargaining agreement may staff the center along with obstetric nurses who are employed by the hospital participant and are covered by a collective bargaining agreement.

Other problems may be encountered if each hospital in a joint venture has a different collective bargaining agreement with its employees, such as in the magnetic resonance imaging (MRI) joint venture described in appendix B. Do the existing agreements cover the employees who are working in the new facility, or is a new agreement necessary? Also, if the venture participants decide to hire new personnel for the clinic, present employees of either participant may have grounds to complain, particularly if one participant closes a department or reduces staff when it becomes part of a joint venture for a similar facility.

The failure of joint venture participants to consider and properly apply pertinent principles of labor law when making staffing decisions can result in the filing of unfair labor practice charges and civil suits by disgruntled employees. For example, a hospital may enter into a joint venture for a referral laboratory with another hospital. The new facility is to be staffed with newly hired personnel. At the same time, the hospital reduces the operations and staff at its present pathology laboratory, which is subject to a collective bargaining agreement. Those employees who are laid off as a result of the reductions in the work force may bring suit against the hospital on the grounds of unfair labor practice under the labor agreement.

Several collective bargaining principles are particularly relevant whenever a significant change in an employer's structure or staffing needs occurs as the result of a joint venture. These principles are:

- The law of successor employers
- A duty to bargain arising out of a change in an employer's business operations
- Issues relating to whether the employer is considered a joint or single employer
- Accretion issues

Successor Employers

A change in ownership or control of a business raises the question of whether the new employer, such as a newly created joint venture entity, is bound by the collective bargaining agreements to which the prior employer was a party. Labor law provides for a presumption of successorship if the new employer conducts essentially the same business as the former employer and has as a majority of its work force former employees of the previous employer. For instance, if a hospital reorganizes its pathology department in the course of a joint venture with staff physicians so that ownership of the pathology laboratory resides in a new entity, that new entity may be deemed a *successor employer* to the hospital if the laboratory performs basically the same services as the in-house laboratory and if the hospital transfers most of its unionized laboratory personnel to staff the new facility.

The implication of the designation of successorship is that if the laboratory employees were represented by a union while employed by the hospital, support for that union among those employees is presumed to continue after the change in ownership. As a result, the new employer, in this case the reference laboratory, has a duty to recognize and bargain with that union.[1] The underlying rationale is that a mere change in ownership alone is not likely to affect employee attitudes toward representation.

Of course, several considerations in this analysis may determine whether successorship, with its concomitant duty to bargain, is found. These considerations include:

- Continuity of the enterprise
- Continuity of the work force
- Continued appropriateness of the collective bargaining unit

Continuity of the Enterprise

In making a judgment as to whether *continuity of the enterprise* exists, the National Labor Relations Board (NLRB) considers several factors, including whether:[2]

- There has been substantial continuity of the same business operations.
- The new employer uses the same plant or facility.
- Substantially the same work force is employed.
- The same jobs exist under the same working conditions.
- Supervisory personnel are the same.

- The same machinery, equipment, and methods of production are used.
- The same services are offered.

No one of these factors by itself is controlling. The main focus of the inquiry is on whether the change in working conditions has affected employee expectations of continuity in representation.[3]

Many joint ventures typically involve a substantial change in the provision of health care services. For instance, a new physical plant, such as an ambulatory surgical center, or new personnel or equipment, such as an MRI unit, may change the way a service is offered or may entail offering a different service. New ownership, control, and payment mechanisms also result in changes. In these situations, successorship is not likely to be found because there is insufficient continuity of the enterprise. However, a joint venture that involves merely a change in ownership, as in the reorganization of the pathology laboratory just described, can be deemed a successor entity. In that example, the laboratory continues to operate in the same locale with basically the same services, the same staff, including supervisory personnel, and the same equipment. The only change is in the ownership and the internal management, and the average employee is hardly aware of such changes. In this instance, the joint venture laboratory is likely to be deemed a successor to the hospital pathology laboratory.

However, significant operational changes do not always preclude a finding of successorship. In a recent case, a corporate purchaser of a Mom and Pop printing operation was required to bargain with the union representing the 19 employees of the predecessor despite the fact that the purchaser had extensive plans to transform the small business into a large national enterprise.[4] Even though the purchaser had in fact moved to a larger facility and eventually more than tripled the size of the work force, a finding of successorship was enforced.

Continuity of the Work Force

Even though a finding of successorship as the result of the requisite continuity of the enterprise has been made, an obligation to bargain with the collective bargaining representative recognized by the predecessor entity does not automatically follow. The next inquiry is whether the successor has, in fact, taken on enough of the employees of its predecessor so that these employees constitute a majority of the successor employer's work force. The area of contention most often encountered in this analysis is the question of *when* the successor's employees should be counted: at the time the new successor entity has hired its full complement of employees or at the time the union that was recognized by the predecessor makes its demand on the successor for recognition.

The *full-complement standard* gives to as many of the successor's employees as possible the opportunity to choose their own bargaining representative while at the same time ensuring that the employees have representation as soon as possible.[5] This standard, which is employed by most courts, serves to reduce the likelihood that the new employer will be deemed a successor, because its application can delay the measurement of the employer's work force until such time as the number of new employees reduces the contingent of the predecessor entity's employees to a minority.[6]

Not all cases use the full-complement standard.[7] In a recent case, the court used a *union-demand standard* to allow the NLRB to determine whether it was the appropriate time to bargain by examining the work force when the successor had hired "merely a substantial and representative complement" of its employees.[8] Relevant factors were whether the job classifications designated for the operation were filled or substantially filled, whether the operation was in normal or substantially normal production, what the size of the complement on the date of normal production was, what time was expected to elapse before a substantially larger complement was at work, and what was the relative certainty of the employer's expected expansion. The court concluded that the employer's work force would be measured on the date of the union's demand for recognition, notwithstanding the employer's definite and accurate prediction that it would triple its predecessor's work force and thereby under the full-complement standard be relieved from having to bargain with the union recognized by its predecessor.[9]

Because this area of successorship law is uncertain, the more cautious course for a new joint venture entity to follow is to recognize and bargain, to an impasse if necessary, with the previously recognized representative of the employees. Doing so avoids the possibly onerous remedies that the NLRB is empowered to grant if the employer wrongfully refuses to bargain. However, at the time of formation of the joint venture entity, the venture participants should consult with competent labor counsel regarding this issue. Proper guidance from counsel may point out ways to avoid following this cautious course.

Appropriateness of Collective Bargaining Unit

Even though an employer has been found to be a successor entity because of the application of the first two criteria, continuity of the enterprise and continuity of the work force, it may still argue that the collective bargaining unit of the predecessor's employees is not appropriate to the new entity. Generally, a union is *irrebuttably* presumed to represent those employees for a period of one year following the union's certification[10] and is *rebuttably* presumed to represent them following that year.[11] In other words, for one year after a union has been certified to represent a particular group of employees, that union's status as their representative may not be challenged. After that one year has passed, the union's status may be challenged, in certain instances, even by a new entity that has in the interim become a successor to the former employer of those employees. The successor entity may bring such a challenge, and thereby extinguish its duty to bargain with that union representative, if it can show that the union in fact no longer represents a majority of the members of the bargaining unit or that the employer has a reasonable good-faith doubt as to continued majority support.[12]

A decertification petition by the employees themselves is always the best indication that the union no longer enjoys majority status. In the absence of such an indication, other objective considerations may lead to a good-faith doubt as to the union's continued majority status so that the employer may reasonably assert that the employees' attitudes toward union representation have changed.[13]

Courts vary as to what objective considerations are deemed a sufficient basis for an employer's good-faith doubt. They are generally more certain as to what considerations by themselves will *not* be sufficient. These considerations include the union's continued solicitation of authorization cards,[14] mere expressions of dissatisfaction with the union by employees, or a diminished work force because of employee turnover.

If the employer does have serious doubts about the union's status among its staff, it can petition for a new election.[15] In a recent decision, the NLRB determined that an employer who admitted its successor status and who had even voluntarily entered into negotiations with the union when it first took over the company was entitled to abandon those negotiations and move to have the union decertified. While in the course of negotiations, the employer received a petition, apparently signed by a majority of its employees, stating that they did not wish to be represented by that union. The employer used that petition as an excuse to withdraw from the negotiations. The NLRB upheld the employer's decision, stating that a successor employer may walk away from the bargaining table even after voluntary recognition if it in good faith begins to doubt its employees' desire for continued representation by that union.[16]

Duty to Bargain

Participating in an economic joint venture often involves staffing changes in a participant's present business operations. For instance, work, such as data processing, that is presently performed by a participant's own staff may be referred to a service bureau. Also, new staffing needs arising from participation in the joint venture may be met by means of leased employees. The joint venture participant may decide to partially close an existing facility or to consolidate its operations. All of these actions can lead to changes in staffing. However, the employer whose relationship with its employees is governed by a collective bargaining agreement may not be able to unilaterally make such decisions involving changes in business operations. In some instances, that employer has a *duty to bargain* with its workers' union representative.[17] This duty arises only if contemplated changes in operations constitute a "mandatory subject of bargaining."[18] In general, changes require such mandatory bargaining if they will "radically alter the status of bargaining union employees"[19] and the union, once notified of the pending change, makes a timely request for such bargaining.[20]

One controversy surrounding this duty to bargain is with respect to the timing of the notice of the proposed change to the union representative. Courts and the NLRB commonly distinguish between *decision bargaining* and *effects bargaining*. Once the employer has decided to enter into a venture, it must notify the union before implementing that decision in order to allow the union to negotiate concerning the *effects* of the decision on the employees who are represented by that bargaining unit. This kind of bargaining is effects bargaining, which is bargaining with respect to the impact of the change on the employee. Subjects to be discussed in such bargaining are the impact of the decision to participate in the joint venture on seniority rights, accrued benefits (from vacation to health care and pension plans), severance pay, and transfers. Where controversy may arise is with respect to decision bargaining: Does the employer have a duty to notify the union that it is considering entering into a joint venture and to bargain with union representatives about the actual *decision* to participate in the venture?

This section on duty to bargain considers this controversy as it may arise in the joint venture situation, particularly with respect to two areas: the subcontracting of work, either by means of a service bureau or leased employees, and the partial closing or complete shutdown of a facility or department as a result of a joint venture.

Subcontracting

A duty to bargain with union representatives exists when a change in operations involves the subcontracting of work that had previously been performed by union employees, even though there may be legitimate business reasons for the decision to subcontract.[21] However, such a duty is imposed only insofar as the employer's freedom to manage its own business is not "significantly abridge[d]."[22] For example, a hospital would probably be violating its duty to bargain if it were to unilaterally alter its nursing services by replacing certain of its own nurses who are protected by a collective bargaining agreement with nurses from a leasing agency who would then perform the same work under similar employment conditions.

Generally, the right of the employees to protection from practices altering the terms and conditions of their employment is balanced against the right of the employer to make "managerial decisions, which lie at the core of entrepreneurial control."[23] As one court recently held, the employer has a duty to bargain only if the benefits to the employees and to "labor-management relations . . . outweighs the burden placed on the" right of the employer to unencumbered decision making in "the conduct of the business."[24] This balancing depends on the facts of the specific situation.

Two hypothetical examples illustrate this approach in the context of a joint venture enterprise. The first example involves a decision to use a service bureau; the second involves leased employees.

Service Bureau

Health Care Maintenance Organization is a health maintenance organization (HMO) that has decided to participate in a joint venture with a data service company to consolidate operations and form a new jointly owned data service company.

The administrative employees of the HMO, including those in its data processing department, are subject to a collective bargaining agreement. As a result of the joint venture, all of the data services presently performed by the HMO's employees will be taken over by the new data service company. The union representatives were not consulted before the HMO made the decision to participate in the joint venture. The union is now arguing that this decision should be the subject of mandatory bargaining.

Whether or not the HMO had a duty to bargain depends on whether the decision to form a data service bureau and turn all data service work presently performed by union employees over to the service bureau involves a fundamental change in the nature or direction of the business or a desire to reduce labor costs.[25] If labor costs are the pivotal factor in the decision, then the representative of the employees has to be consulted before that decision is made.[26] If the decision represents a fundamental change in the nature or the direction of the enterprise, it is not subject to union negotiations.

Of relevance in this instance is the fact that the present data processing department of the HMO is inefficient, for example, or that it is inadequate to meet new needs of the HMO as a result of its expansion into new service areas. The fact that the new data service bureau serves a larger clientele than the single HMO did is also important. As an independent enterprise that is greatly expanded over the existing department, the new venture requires a significant infusion of capital from both of the joint venture participants. Courts and the NLRB are sensitive to the fact that decisions involving the investment of capital or the scope of the enterprise are not in themselves decisions about "conditions of employment."[27] Consequently, even if labor costs may have "stimulated the evaluation process which generated the decision,"[28] there is no duty to bargain if the decision itself did not hinge on labor costs.[29]

The NLRB has arrived at such a conclusion even when cost savings and overall reduction in overhead expenses are the primary motivation behind an employer's decision to turn part of its operations over to a subcontractor, with the resulting layoff of four of the employer's five employees in that division.[30] The NLRB noted there that even though labor costs are a component in the overhead costs that the employer intends to reduce, the basic decision to use a subcontractor is based on a significant change in the direction of its business: in this case, the abandonment of that particular operation.

Leased Employees

To compete more effectively with commercial laboratories, Memorial Hospital spins off its clinical laboratory as part of a joint venture with staff physicians to create a referral laboratory. The hospital retains control over laboratory operations through a newly formed, wholly owned subsidiary.

As part of the transaction, the hospital enters into an agreement with a leasing agency. Under the terms of this agreement, leased employees perform laboratory services formerly performed by hospital employees. The union charges that the hospital has committed an unfair labor practice by failing to bargain with union representatives regarding the decision to subcontract. One consequence of this subcontract is that a number of hospital laboratory employees are to be laid off.

Again, in determining whether the hospital had a duty to bargain, the NLRB assesses whether the decision to use leased employees is based on a change in the nature or direction of the business or on labor costs. Once the decision to use leased employees has been made, the union is entitled to negotiate with the hospital concerning the effect of the reorganization and the use of leased employees on union employees. However, the union is arguing that the decision itself to use leased employees is a matter for negotiation.

In an NLRB decision containing facts similar to this one,[31] the NLRB held that the decision of a restaurant operator to transfer its shrimp processing work to an independent contractor did not go to "the very core of entrepreneurial control,[32] and hence was a suitable subject for collective bargaining. Thus, such a cost-saving decision involving the transfer of work from union employees to an independent contractor by itself does not substantially alter the nature of an employer's business and hence is not immune from a decision-bargaining duty.[33] However, a decision involving the complete closing of a department, such as the hospital's pathology department,[34] or the complete restructuring of a business, including the expansion of its scope or a large infusion or restructuring of capital, is not an appropriate subject for collective bargaining.[35]

Because this area of the law is unclear, with decisions made on the basis of the facts in specific cases, prospective venture participants should review the proposed joint venture with labor counsel and plan strategies accordingly. When in doubt as to whether decisions on the structure of the joint venture could be the subject of collective bargaining, joint venture participants should engage in decision bargaining with union officials at the outset. Although this bargaining may seem to be not without risk and an unnecessary burden, the risk is slight when compared with the remedies that the NLRB could impose if it found an unfair labor practice. For example, the NLRB may rule that back pay must be paid to all union employees wronged from the time the joint venture participants first made their decision. Moreover, when contemplating a joint venture decision that could involve negotiations with union representatives, health care providers should take care to consistently document the cost, efficiency, and marketability considerations that underlie the venture decision.

Partial Closing

As a general rule, the decision of an employer to close or partially close part of its business solely for economic reasons is not a proper subject of negotiation with collective bargaining representatives.[36] This prerogative of employers is deemed to be too important to the freedom and flexibility that they need to respond to changing business environments to be hampered by labor-management negotiations.[37] Consequently, the decision of a hospital to close an inpatient facility, such as its pathology laboratory, when participating in a joint venture for an out-of-hospital enterprise, such as a referral laboratory, generally does not create problems under collective bargaining agreements even if that decision can adversely affect hospital employees. Of course, the hospital still has a duty to bargain with union representatives as to the *effects* of the closure on the employees.[38]

However, if the partial closing, or any other business decisions made in the course of the joint venture, has the purpose and effect of chilling unionism, that is, is motivated by "anti-union animus," it will constitute an unfair labor practice.[39] As the Supreme Court has stated, "[a]n employer may not simply shut down part of its business and mask its desire to weaken and circumvent the union by labeling its decision 'purely economic.'"[40]

Employee representatives who are frustrated by their inability to thwart the joint venture by other means may charge discrimination. For example, such a challenge may occur and a discriminatory motive may be found if an employer has transferred its operations to a new entity following a frustrated attempt by employees to unionize, or if the employer has expressed dissatisfaction with the union in an internal memorandum or other documentation.[41]

One factor that courts examine carefully when seeking a discriminatory motive is whether the employer, by taking action against unionized employees, gains some future benefit from other employees. For instance, if a union had recently attempted to organize the staff in a hospital pathology laboratory and the hospital subsequently closed its in-house laboratory and referred its laboratory work to a joint venture commercial facility but continued to provide all other health care services previously offered, the union could charge, and a court might find, that the hospital had closed its laboratory to discourage unionization in the remainder of the facility.[42] The closing of an entire business ends the employer-employee relationship, but a partial closing has repercussions on what remains of the enterprise. The effect may be to discourage unionizing efforts by the remaining employees.[43]

This future benefit need not be from employees of the same facility that was closed, and for this reason a joint venture entity may itself be at risk of being held liable for unfair labor practices. The integration of the two businesses is not necessary to find such an unfair labor practice. If the employer who is laying off employees does so for antiunion reasons and that employer has any interest in any other business, such as a joint venture enterprise, that is substantial enough to benefit from the discouragement of the unionization of that business, then an unfair labor practice may be found. This situation is limited, however, to one in which an employer lays off its present employees in order to discourage unionization of the new joint venture facility and has such influence in the new business that its employees can reasonably fear that the joint venture business may also be closed if they engage in union activities.[44]

In brief, an unfair labor practice case requires the presence of:

- Discrimination against employees because of their union activity
- Relationship of power within the joint venture by the employer who lays off the employees
- Reasonable foreseeability that new employees at the joint venture facility will fear a similar closing if they engage in union activities
- Motivation on the part of the employer to provoke such fear in the new employees

Even though the presence of these factors may be difficult to prove, a court can still impose severe remedies, including reinstatement with back pay for aggrieved union members if the court were to make a negative ruling. Such a result is undesirable. Early consultation with labor counsel is the best safeguard against a discrimination charge.

Single-Employer or Joint-Employer Status

In most joint ventures, staffing the new facility requires the participation of at least two entities, often with the additional presence of an employee leasing organization. Under such circumstances, labor law may place an obligation on the joint venture participants to recognize a union that has an existing collective bargaining relationship with one of the parties as the representative of the employees of the newly created facility. Liability for unfair labor practices and a duty to collectively bargain can follow. Such a duty depends in part on whether the joint venture participants or a venture participant and an employee leasing company constitute a *single employer* or a *joint employer*, terms of art referring to the legal status of the entities as determined by their interrelationship and their dealings with the employees of the new facility.

Single-Employer Status

Employers are viewed as a single employer if two nominally separate entities are deemed to be one entity for employment law purposes. In the event of such a finding, employees of both entities may be treated as being in the same bargaining unit. Such a possibility exists, for example, in the occupational medicine center described in appendix C, the alternative delivery system joint venture described in appendix D, and the phased reference laboratory joint venture described in appendix E. In each of these hypothetical cases, reorganizations nominally transfer control of an existing facility from a hospital or foundation to a newly created entity. In responding to a charge by a union representing employees at one facility that it is being wrongfully denied recognitional status at the other, the NLRB investigates the two employing units to determine whether they, in reality, constitute one integrated enterprise.[45] The NLRB recognizes four factors as being relevant to the single-employer inquiry:[46]

- Functional integration of operations
- Centralized control of labor relations
- Common management
- Common ownership

Careful avoidance of common ownership is not sufficient to escape single-employer status. The venturing entities should also attempt to decentralize control of employment relations as much as is feasible without jeopardizing the agreement among the parties with respect to control. By reducing somewhat the degree of centralization and common control, the relationship between the venture and its owners sufficiently resembles arm's-length interrelationships ordinarily existing among unintegrated companies to survive, and so the venture can survive scrutiny as to single-employer status.[47]

Joint-Employer Status: Employee Leasing

A popular practice in the health care industry is *employee leasing:* An employer contracts with an outside agency to provide it with a certain number of employees in addition to any regular employees it may have or in place of any regular employees. The employer is thus relieved of responsibility for negotiating individual contracts with many groups of employees and with the expense and trouble of recruiting, hiring, and firing. This practice is ideal for the large employer with fluctuating staffing needs. This employer can obtain staff for short-term needs without being obliged to make long-term employment commitments. Employee leasing is also ideal for the small employer who can lease virtually all of its staff, including supervisory personnel, and thus be relieved of the bookkeeping and other paperwork that are required if it maintains its own staff.

One problem that can result from the practice of employee leasing occurs when the employer and the leasing organization are viewed as joint employers for federal labor law purposes. Although such a finding often results in similar obligations regarding collective bargaining and unfair labor practice liability, a finding of joint-employer status depends on considerations distinct from the four factors that are determinative of single-employer status. The joint-employer concept does not focus on the integration of the enterprises involved; rather it assumes that the entities are what they purport to be—legally independent. Nevertheless, the joint-employer analysis includes an inquiry into the degree to which two or more separate entities share or codetermine essential terms and conditions of employment.[48] Parties to a joint venture may be deemed a joint employer regardless of their organizational ties to each other. What is necessary to such a finding is a showing that the joint venture participant meaningfully participates in establishing the terms and conditions of the employment relationship, including hiring, firing, discipline, supervision, and direction.[49]

An inquiry into joint-employer status is especially relevant in those joint venture situations in which staffing is accomplished by means of an agreement with an employee leasing firm. Although the lessor supplies the work force, the extent to which the joint venture participant establishes the terms and conditions of the leased employees' employment is crucial for joint-employer status and its incumbent liability and obligations. The greater the role that the employer plays with respect to the employment conditions of the leased employees, the more likely it is to be considered a joint employer.[50]

A finding that a party to the venture is a joint employer subjects that party to obligations vis-a-vis any union that has gained recognition as the representative of the leased employees. As such, the joint employer has a duty to bargain with the union and is precluded from making unilateral changes in the terms of employment. Moreover, the joint employer cannot unilaterally terminate its leasing contract in the event of an attempt to unionize the leased employees or in the case of a labor dispute. The joint employer is obliged to treat the affected employees as its own. Because part of the reason for entering into a leasing arrangement is to gain flexibility in employee relations, the purposes of the joint venture participants are thwarted if the arrangement results in a joint-employer designation, with the resultant loss of that flexibility.

To avoid a joint-employer designation, the joint venture participants must relinquish certain control over the leased employees. The leasing contract should provide that the essential terms and conditions of employment for the leased employees are the sole responsibility of the company,[51] particularly in the following areas:

- *Hiring.* The employer should not attempt to assert any influence over hiring decisions of the leasing company. If one of the joint venture participants will be terminating some employees when the venture is formed, that participant should not insist that the leasing company take on its former employees. If the leasing company does hire any of these former employees to staff the new joint venture facility, the joint venture participant should terminate all aspects of the former employment. It should pay any accrued sick leave and vacation instead of attempting to transfer these items to the new employer.
- *Supervision.* To avoid joint-employer status, the employer should leave the daily direction and control over work assignments of leased employees, as well as the assessment of their job performance, to the leasing company. Although one recent NLRB opinion stated that routine supervision of leased employees by the employer did not justify a finding of joint-employer status,[52] this theory has not been tested in the courts. Therefore, routine supervision and direction of the leased employees or other employment matters should be left to the leasing company if such action is possible within the scope of the facility license and is permitted by malpractice insurance carriers. Standards of care can be drafted into the leasing contract. All investigations of employee misconduct or inadequate job performance should be conducted by the leasing company personnel managers, not by the employer. In no event should the joint venture participant engage in firing or disciplining leased employees.[53]
- *Salaries, benefits, and other conditions of employment.* Salaries and benefits are best handled by the leasing organization for business as well as legal reasons. All

salaries and other payments, including expense reimbursement, to leased employees should be paid by the leasing company. The employer should not attempt to influence the leased employee's wage rates, hours of work, vacation, pension, or other benefits. These items should be determined by the leasing company exclusively because these items are generally the essential ones negotiated in collective bargaining agreements. Control or participation in establishing their terms can alone be sufficient to establish joint-employer status.

In short, the design, negotiation, and implementation of the leasing arrangement should divest the joint venture participant of as much control over the daily operations of the employees as is practical from a business perspective.

Accretion

All of the hypothetical ventures described in the appendixes present the issue of representational rights of employees of one party to the joint venture being extended to employees of the newly established remote facility. This extension of rights is known as *accretion,* and it must be considered by any health care providers engaged in a joint venture enterprise.

The NLRB employs a multifactor analysis to determine whether a newly established or newly acquired enterprise constitutes an accretion to the existing operations of an employer. If an accretion exists, any collective bargaining relationship covering employees at the existing operations of the employer is extended to the operations of the newly acquired or formed facility and its employees, irrespective of the desires of those employees and notwithstanding the fact that no election has taken place. In fact, a finding of accretion can bar a requirement that a representational election take place at the new facility.

The NLRB and the courts have established definite criteria for determining whether accretion has occurred. These criteria, which emphasize the common control and interests of the two operations, include:

- Common supervision of employees
- Degree of transfer and interchange of employees between facilities
- Geographical distance between facilities
- Degree of integration of the operations
- Similarity of working conditions, skills, and functions of the employees
- Common control over labor relations
- Centralized administrative control
- Collective bargaining history
- Comparative number of employees in new operation versus existing operation

No set formula is available for determining whether existing collective bargaining relationships in any given situation will be automatically extended to the new operation. However, the factors that the NLRB emphasizes are the degree of interchange of employees between the affiliated operations and the extent to which the different groups of employees are commonly supervised on a day-to-day basis.[54] In addition, accretion is unlikely when the group sought to be accreted far outnumbers the existing contingent of employees.[55]

The issue of control is likely to be of paramount concern for the parties to the joint venture. One participant in a joint venture may have officers, directors, or partners in common with the new clinic, laboratory, or pavilion. If it does, then a certain degree of centralization of administrative functions, managerial oversight, and clerical services is difficult to avoid. However, common control of general policy alone does not result in a finding of accretion.

In a recent decision, the NLRB refused to make a finding of accretion in spite of the following facts:[56]

- The two enterprises had both common ownership and management at the policy-making level.
- The common president formulated the labor policies for both groups of employees.
- The employees possessed common skills and used similar, and at times the same, tools and equipment.
- The two facilities were located across the street from each other.

The NLRB determined that the nonunion employees of the new enterprise were not accreted into the existing bargaining unit, which was made up of union employees of the other enterprise. The NLRB based this decision on the fact that there was no common immediate supervisor and no day-to-day contact between the two groups of employees. More important, there was no evidence of actual interchange or regular contacts between the two sets of employees and "the daily operations of the facilities were separate and autonomous." Moreover, "day-to-day control and supervision of matters of interest to the employees were handled entirely within each of the facilities by the respective service managers."[57] Without these elements, the NLRB hesitated to find accretion because it did not wish to eliminate the basic right of employees to select their own bargaining representative.[58]

By decentralizing day-to-day supervision, joint venture participants can insulate themselves against having to extend recognition to existing unions for employees at newly created entities. The responsibility for recruiting, hiring, and disciplining employees should be the principal responsibility of the supervisory personnel of the remote facility rather than shared with or controlled by the management of the hospital or other joint venture participant. Personnel used at the new entity should not continue to have duties at the hospital, and separate personnel policies should be maintained. The more the management of the two entities' employment relations is blurred, the greater the likelihood that the new employees will be accreted into an existing unit. The end result is the extension of recognitional status to employees who may not otherwise demand union representation. This discussion assumes that a newly established entity is wholly owned and operated by an existing hospital or health care foundation. This circumstance may arise in some joint venturing models, such as the hypothetical situation described in appendix A. A more common situation involves two or more separate entities jointly establishing, equipping, and staffing a new facility. Problems of accretion also can raise the question of whether the joint venture is a single employer or a joint employer.

State Employment Laws

A joint venture is a separate business and as such is subject to all federal laws and the laws of the state in which the joint venture does business. Many states have statutes and case law that determine to a great extent how an employer works with its employees. Parties to a joint venture should be aware of these laws and should take them into consideration when making decisions affecting the staffing of the venture enterprise.

Under the laws of a few states, a joint venture or the parties to the joint venture may be liable to employees if any participant, as a consequence of entering the venture, adversely changes the terms and conditions of the employment of such employees. For example, an employer may close down operations in an existing facility and lay off its employees when it enters into a venture to form a new enterprise. A joint venture participant whose employees are protected by collective bargaining agreements is limited by federal labor law with respect to what it can do to those employees. Although not all employees of health care providers are covered by such agreements, some states have developed case law that limits the way in which employers can treat their employees. In those states, the employer may not be able to terminate an employee or reduce such employee's wages, benefits, or seniority if, for example, such action is motivated in bad faith[59] or is in violation of company policy.[60]

Traditional Concept of Employment-at-Will

The traditional relationship between an employer and an employee in this nation is that of *employment-at-will:* in the absence of a written contract that states otherwise, either party may terminate the employment relationship with or without notice. Many American employees, including employees in health care fields, are employed on an at-will basis. These employees are not governed by the labor law principles discussed in the preceding section on collective bargaining agreements.

In most states, employers who are not governed by collective bargaining agreements have basically an unfettered right to hire and fire employees who are not hired for a definite term. However, the federal government and a number of states have statutes that prohibit the discharge of employees for certain specified reasons.[61] Courts in a few states have also created exceptions to the employment-at-will doctrine to protect employees in certain limited instances. These laws can have an impact on a joint venture when certain employees' conditions of employment are changed and those employees can also show that, in their particular cases, the reason for the discharge was not really the joint venture but rather some other unjustified motive.[62]

Statutory Limitations

Statutes that protect employees range from so-called fair employment laws to civil rights statutes. Among these are laws that protect employees from discrimination on account of their sex,[63] for example, or their age.[64] So-called *whistle-blower statutes* protect employees from retaliation for reporting employer violations of statutory safety and environmental standards.[65]

Any of these statutes can become relevant if an employee falling under their protection is discharged, even if that discharge is related to the employer's participation in a joint venture. For example, a former hospital employee was recently found to be the victim of age discrimination when her position as director of the hospital outpatient department was eliminated in the course of a hospital reorganization. The hospital's decision to eliminate the employee's position before the reorganization was considered evidence that it was discriminating against the employee on account of her age. If the hospital had no purpose of discriminating, the jury determined that the hospital should have offered the employee the newly created position of associate director of nursing for ambulatory care.[66] Joint venture participants should be aware that the result may have been the same if the employee's position had been eliminated as a result of the hospital's participation in a joint venture instead of a reorganization.

Theories behind Wrongful Discharge Cases

Courts have prevented the discharge of employees in certain instances on any of the following theories:

- Wrongful discharge in violation of public policy
- Breach of an implied covenant of good faith and fair dealing
- Breach of an implied-in-fact covenant to terminate only for good cause
- *Promissory estoppel*, that is, detrimental reliance by the employee on a representation of the employer

Wrongful Discharge in Violation of Public Policy

Cases that have prevented an employer from discharging an employee on public policy grounds have often relied on the provisions of one of the so-called *whistle-blower* statutes. In some states, the courts only recognize an employee complaint on this ground if there is statutory authority.[67] Other states go beyond statutes to find sources of public policy.[68]

The public policy reasons for refusing to allow a discharge of an employee are varied. For example, an employer may be prevented from discharging an employee who refuses to engage in illegal activities[69] or who reports wrongdoing by his or her employer.[70] For example, if a health care employee in a clinic were to refuse to administer a drug that state authorities had prohibited and was subsequently discharged when the clinic was closed to allow the owners to participate in a joint venture clinic, that employee could claim wrongful discharge according to the laws of some states.[71] Similarly, a hospital participating in a joint venture should be careful in its treatment of an employee who, for instance, reported to state authorities the fact that the hospital was turning away indigent patients in contravention of state law.

The public policy theory is not all-encompassing, however. Many courts are reluctant to recognize this type of action in the absence of a specific statute.[72] Most courts have not applied the public policy exception from the at-will rule to the discharge of employees making statements against or refusing to participate in legal business activities. For example, a pharmaceutical company was found to be justified in dismissing an employee who protested company-conducted research on a controversial drug.[73] Unfortunately, foreseeing when a court will determine that public policy overrides the employer's right to discharge an employee is not always easy. Although the state of California generally demands that the public policy be based on a statute, a court in that state nevertheless decided that an employee was unlawfully discharged for protesting working conditions that might have created a health hazard.[74] In that case, the employee demanded to be placed in a work area that was free of cigarette smoke. The court based its decision loosely on the Occupational Safety and Health Act.[75]

Good Faith and Fair Dealing

In a very few states, courts have held that the employer's right to discharge an employee is limited by an implied requirement that the employer use "good faith and fair dealing" in its treatment of all of its employees, whether they have a written employment contract or not.[76] If an employer has developed policies for the benefit of its employees, fair dealing means that the employer must apply those policies to all employees in a just and even-handed manner.[77] Before disciplining an employee, the employer must at least give the employee some notice of the proposed disciplinary action and an opportunity to respond to the charges.[78]

In states that apply the fair-dealing requirement, participants in a joint venture must be careful that termination or other decisions with respect to the employment of individual employees that result from or are on account of the joint venture are not made in bad faith. Caution is particularly advisable because in many instances when bad faith is found, courts have allowed not only contract damages in favor of the employee (that is, reinstatement) but also compensatory damages (back pay) and punitive damages.[79]

Implied Contract

A number of states have also determined that a contract of employment limiting the right to discharge an employee may be implied from certain oral or written assurances from the employer. For example, statements of policy, such as supervisors' manuals or personnel manuals, can create contractual rights for employees.[80] In one case, a head nurse in a hospital was discharged in spite of protections in an employee handbook. The court inferred from the language in the handbook that once an employee completed a probationary period at the hospital, he or she could no longer be terminated without cause.[81]

However, most states do not go so far in implying rights for employees. The majority still take the position that personnel policies are merely unilateral expressions of company policy and nothing more.[82] Employers doing business in those states should nevertheless proceed with caution in dealing with their employees. Any court, given appropriate facts, may find that a fixed company policy creates an implied contract in favor of an employee who has been unfairly discharged.

Promissory Estoppel

Even in those states that do not recognize any implied contract that protects at-will employees from wrongful discharge, a court may still protect the employee who has relied on the employer's statements to his or her detriment. At least one state has applied the theory of *promissory estoppel* to employment situations.[83] Under that theory, a nonbinding agreement may be transformed into a binding agreement if one party has relied to his or her detriment on statements of another party and if that reliance is reasonable. For example, if a prospective employee resigns a position in reliance upon an offer of employment from a joint venture organization that is being formed and then does not receive the employment because of a last-minute change in the structure of the venture, that prospective employee may be able to force the organization to hire him or her under a promissory estoppel theory.[84]

Avoiding Liability for Bad-Faith Dealings

Potential liability for bad-faith dealings can be minimized for participants in a joint venture if they take certain basic precautions. First, when forming the joint venture, the participants should make a clear decision from the outset on whether they want to establish a contractual relationship with the employees of the newly formed organization. If they decide that they want to maintain an at-will relationship with the joint venture's employees, they should take affirmative steps to provide for that at-will relationship. For example, in recruiting and hiring new employees, persons responsible for interviewing and communicating with prospective employees should guard against statements that can be relied on by those prospective employees or interpreted as guaranteeing continued or permanent employment.

Second, the persons responsible for writing the joint venture's employment applications, employee handbooks, and other policy manuals should avoid any language that can create a presumption of permanent employment. These documents should name the classifications of employees for which they have been written. All such communications with employees should expressly state that all employees are considered to be at-will employees. Ideally, the understanding that an at-will employment relationship is being created should be put in writing, such as in the employment application, and signed by the prospective employee.[85]

Third, participants in a joint venture should be scrupulous in their dealings with their own employees. Thus, the formation of a joint venture should not be construed as a good opportunity to eliminate marginal employees or employees who are viewed as troublemakers in the workplace. Such a practice can lead to liability to those employees. Thus far, no case has held that an employer cannot lay off employees, provided there is no contract, express or implied, prohibiting such a layoff. However, if, for instance, a joint venture participant were to act without notice to its employees or in violation of company policies, stated or implied, with respect to the treatment of employees, then those employees who believe that they were treated unfairly may sue for a breach of the employer's implied covenant of good faith and fair dealing and, in certain states, may well win their case.

Any joint venture participant who assumes that employees' concerns are inconsequential is taking a serious risk of liability. By contrast, timely consultation with legal counsel can ensure a smooth transition from one form of business operation to another. By addressing potential employment problems at the outset, the joint venture participants can avoid costly delay and litigation and form a more secure enterprise for every concerned party: venture participants, venture entity, employees, and patients.

Notes

1. NLRB v. Burns Int'l Security Servs., Inc., 406 U.S. 272 (1972); Premium Foods, Inc., 260 N.L.R.B. 708 (1982), *enforced,* 709 F.2d 623 (9th cir. 1983).

2. Premium Foods, Inc., 260 N.L.R.B. 708 (1982).

3. *Id. See also* NLRB v. Jeffries Lithograph Co., 752 F.2d 459 (9th Cir. 1985).

4. NLRB v. Jeffries Lithograph Co., 752 F.2d 459 (9th Cir. 1985).

5. NLRB v. Pre-Engineered Building Prods., Inc., 603 F.2d 134, 136 (10th Cir. 1979).

6. *Id. See also* NLRB v. Hudson River Aggregates, Inc., 639 F.2d 865 (2d Cir. 1981); Pacific Hide & Fur Depot, Inc. v. NLRB, 553 F.2d 609 (9th Cir. 1977). In the event, however, of a refusal to hire certain of the predecessor's employees because of antiunion animus, the earlier, date-of-demand measurement of the successor employer's work force may be used. *See, e.g.,* NLRB v. Houston Distribution Servs., Inc., 573 F.2d 260 (5th Cir. 1978), *cert. denied,* 439 U.S. 1047 (1978).

7. NLRB v. Jeffries Lithograph Co., 752 F.2d 459 (9th Cir. 1985).

8. *Id.* at 467.

9. *Id.* at 468.

10. Brooks v. NLRB, 348 U.S. 96, 35 L.R.R.M. 2158 (1954); NLRB v. Edjo, Inc., 631 F.2d 604 (9th Cir. 1980).

11. *E.g.,* Zim's Foodliner, Inc. v. NLRB, 495 F.2d 1131 (7th Cir. 1974), *cert. denied,* 419 U.S. 838 (1974); Nazareth Regional High School v. NLRB, 549 F.2d 873 (2d Cir. 1977).

12. *E.g.,* NLRB v. World Evangelism, Inc., 656 F.2d 1349 (9th Cir. 1981).

13. Virginia Sportswear, Inc., 226 N.L.R.B. 1296, 94 L.R.R.M. 1411 (1976); NLRB v. Tahoe Nuggett, Inc., 584 F.2d 293 (9th Cir. 1978), *cert. denied,* 442 U.S. 921 (1979).

14. Premium Foods, Inc. v. NLRB., 709 F.2d 623 (9th Cir. 1983).

15. Tahoe Nugget, Inc. v. NLRB, 584 F.2d 293 (9th Cir. 1978). *See also,* Zim's Foodliner, Inc., v. NLRB, 495 F.2d 1131 (7th Cir. 1974), *cert. denied,* 419 U.S. 838 (1974).

16. Harley-Davidson Transportation Co., Inc., 373 N.L.R.B. 192, 118 L.R.R.M. 1204 (1985).

17. Section 8(a)(5) of the National Labor Relations Act provides that an employer's refusal to bargain with the representative of his employees is an unfair labor practice cognizable by the National Labor Relations Board. 29 U.S.C. § 158(a)(5).

18. *See* NLRB v. Borg-Warner Corp., 356 U.S. 342, 42 L.R.R.M. 2034 (1958).

19. Houston Shopping News Co., 223 N.L.R.B. 1133, 1134, 92 L.R.R.M. 1074 (1976), *enforcement denied*, 554 F.2d 739, 95 L.R.R.M. 2801 (5th Cir. 1977).

20. *See, e.g.,* City Hosp. of East Liverpool, Ohio, 234 N.L.R.B. 58, 97 L.R.R.M. 1125 (1978).

21. Fibreboard Paper Products Corp. v. NLRB, 379 U.S. 203, 57 L.R.R.M. 2609 (1964).

22. *Id.* at 213.

23. *Id.* at 223 (Stewart, J. concurring). *See also* First National Maintenance Corp. v. NLRB, 452 U.S. 666, 107 L.R.R.M. 2705 (1981).

24. First National Maintenance Corp. v. NLRB, 452 U.S. at 679.

25. Otis Elevator Company, 115 L.R.R.M. 1281 (1984).

26. *Id.* at 1283.

27. *Id.*, quoting from Fibreboard Paper Products Corp. v. NLRB, 379 U.S. at 223 (concurring opinion of Stewart, J).

28. Otis Elevator Co., 115 L.R.R.M. 1281 (1984).

29. Gar Wood-Detroit Truck Equip., Inc., 274 N.L.R.B. No. 23 (Feb. 19, 1985).

30. *Id.* at pp. D-2–D-3. The decision to abandon an operation could lead to charges of an unfair labor practice. *See* discussion in section on partial closing.

31. Bob's Big Boy Family Restaurants, 264 N.L.R.B. No. 178, 111 L.R.R.M. 1354 (1982). The composition of the NLRB was different when this decision was handed down than when the *Gar Wood* case was decided. 274 N.L.R.B. No. 23 (Feb. 19, 1985).

32. Bob's Big Boy Family Restaurants, 264 N.L.R.B. No. 178, 111 L.R.R.M. at 1356.

33. *Id.*

34. First National Maintenance Corp. v. NLRB, 452 U.S. 666, 107 L.R.R.M. 2705 (1981). *But see* Edward Hines Lumber Co. of Oregon v. Lumber & Sawmill Workers Local 2588, 764 F.2d 631 (9th Cir. 1985): an employer cannot close a facility because of poor economic conditions and then seek to reopen it, subcontracting out work done previously by employees. Although the subcontracting policy is not stated in the collective bargaining agreement, the employer is bound to abide by its past practice, thereby limiting its right to subcontract.

35. Gar Wood-Detroit Truck Equip., Inc., 274 N.L.R.B. No. 23 (February 19, 1985).

36. First National Maintenance Corp. v. NLRB, 452 U.S. 666, 107 L.R.R.M. 2705 (1981).

37. *Id.* at 679.

38. *Id.* at 686.

39. According to Section 8(a)(3), it is an unfair labor practice "by discrimination in regard to hire or tenure or employment or any term or condition of employment to encourage or discourage membership in any labor organization. . . ." 29 U.S.C. § 158(a)(3).

40. First National Maintenance Corp. v. NLRB, 452 U.S. at 682.

41. *See* NLRB v. New Madrid Mfg. Co., 215 F.2d 908, 914 (8th Cir. 1954).

42. *See, e.g.,* NLRB v. Savoy Laundry, 327 F.2d 370 (2d Cir. 1964).

43. Textile Workers Union v. Darlington Mfg. Co., 380 U.S. 263, 275 (1965): "we are constrained to hold . . . that a partial closing is an unfair labor practice under § 8(a)(3) if motivated by a purpose to chill unionism in any of the remaining plants of the single employer and if the employer may reasonably have foreseen that such closing would likely have that effect."

44. *Id.* at 275-76.

45. NLRB v. Browning, Ferris Indus., 691 F.2d 1117, 111 L.R.R.M. 2748 (3d Cir. 1982).

46. Radio Union v. Broadcast Serv. of Mobile, Inc., 380 U.S. 255, 58 L.R.R.M. 2545 (1965); Parklane Hosiery Co., Inc., 203 N.L.R.B. 597, 83 L.R.R.M. 1630 (1973).

47. Local No. 627, Int'l Union of Operating Engineers, AFL-CIO v. NLRB, 518 F.2d 1040, 1046-47, 90 L.R.R.M. 2321, 2325-26 (D.C. Cir. 1975), *aff'd in pertinent part, sub nom.*

South Prairie Constr. Co. v. Local No. 627, Int'l Union of Operating Engineers, AFL-CIO, 425 U.S. 800, 92 L.R.R.M. 2507 (1976).

48. NLRB v. Browning-Ferris Indus., 691 F.2d 1117, 111 L.R.R.M. 2748 (3d Cir. 1982); Boire v. Greyhound Corp., 376 U.S. 473, 55 L.R.R.M. 2694 (1964).

49. TLI, Inc., 271 N.L.R.B. No. 128, 117 L.R.R.M. 1169, 1170 (1984); Laerco Trans. and Warehouse, 269 N.L.R.B. No. 61, 115 L.R.R.M. 1226 (1984).

50. Browning-Ferris Indus., Inc., 259 N.L.R.B. 148, 108 L.R.R.M. 1285 (1981), *enforced sub nom.* NLRB v. Browning-Ferris Indus., 691 F.2d 1117, 111 L.R.R.M. 2748 (3d Cir. 1982). *But see* TLI, Inc., 271 N.L.R.B. No. 128, 117 L.R.R.M. 1169 (1984).

51. *Id.*

52. TLI, Inc., 271 N.L.R.B. No. 128, 117 L.R.R.M. 1169 (1984).

53. *See* discussion of alternate rulings, *supra* note 50.

54. Mac Towing, 262 N.L.R.B. 1331, 110 L.R.R.M. 1537 (1982); Save-It Discount Foods, 263 N.L.R.B. 689, 111 L.R.R.M. 1110 (1982).

55. Renaissance Center Partnership, 239 N.L.R.B. 1248, 100 L.R.R.M. 1121 (1979).

56. Towne Ford Sales, 270 N.L.R.B. No. 55, 116 L.R.R.M. 1067 (1984).

57. *Id.* at 1067-1068.

58. *Id.* at 1067.

59. *See, e.g.,* Tameny v. Atlantic Richfield Co., 27 Cal. 3d 167, 610 P.2d 1330, 164 Cal. Rptr. 839 (1980).

60. *See, e.g.,* Hepp v. Lockheed-California Co., 86 Cal. App. 3d 714, 150 Cal. Rptr. 408 (1978); Greene v. Howard Univ., 412 F.2d 1128 (D.C. Cir. 1969).

61. More than half of the states now recognize some exception to the employment-at-will rule. Examples of such statutes are fair-employment laws and so-called whistle-blower statutes. *See* discussion later in this chapter.

62. *See, e.g.,* Jennings v. Lenox Hill Hosp., 84 Civ. 1081 (S.D.N.Y. 1986) (when a director of the outpatient department at a hospital was discharged in the course of a reorganization, the court held that the hospital employer had willfully discriminated against the employee on account of her age because it refused to hire her for a newly created position). *See also* discussion later in this chapter.

63. *See, e.g.,* Title VII of the Civil Rights Act of 1964, as amended, 42 U.S.C. §§ 2000e *et seq.* (providing protection against discharges based on race, color, religion, sex, or national origin) and similar state statutes.

64. *See* the Age Discrimination in Employment Act of 1967, as amended, 42 U.S.C. §§ 621-634.

65. Federal statutes include the Occupational Safety and Health Act of 1970, 29 U.S.C. § 660(c), and the Federal Water Pollution Control Act, 33 U.S.C. § 1367. New York has recently enacted a statute prohibiting discharges in retaliation against employees for disclosing an activity of an employer that is in violation of a law when the violation creates a danger to public health and safety or for refusing to participate in an activity that is such a violation. 1984 N.Y. Laws, § 741-7, art. 20-C, as enacted by ch. 660-L (1984) (effective Sept. 1, 1984).

66. Jennings v. Lenox Hill Hosp., 84 Civ. 1081 (S.D.N.Y. 1986).

67. *E.g.,* California. CAL. LAB. CODE § 1102.5 (West). *See, e.g.,* Shapiro v. Wells Fargo Realty Advisors, 152 Cal. App. 3d 467, 199 Cal. Rptr. 613 (1984) (public policy of "job security and stability in the community" was insufficient grounds to prevent discharge). *See also* Rachford v. Evergreen Int'l Airlines, Inc., 596 F. Supp. 384 (N.D. Ill. 1984) (under Illinois law, a cause of action for retaliatory discharge is available to an at-will employee when his termination is in violation of an Illinois statute, not a federal law); Murphy v. American Home Products Corp., 58 N.Y.2d 293, 448 N.E.2d 86, 461 N.Y.S.2d 232 (1983) (court refused to allow a suit for wrongful discharge in violation of public policy because there was no statute giving it authority to do so).

68. *See, e.g.,* Kalman v. Grand Union Co., 183 N.J. Super 153, 443 A.2d 728 (App. Div. 1982) (professional code of ethics).

Chapter 9. Labor Law Issues

Notes

69. *See, e.g.,* Tameny v. Atlantic Richfield Co., 27 Cal. 3d 167, 610 P.2d 1330, 164 Cal. Rptr. 839 (1980); Petermann v. International Brotherhood of Teamsters, 214 Cal. App. 2d 155, 29 Cal. Rptr. 399 (1959).

70. *See* Kalman v. Grand Union Co., 183 N.J. Super. 153, 443 A.2d 728 (App. Div. 1982) (the court recognized that a pharmacist may have been wrongfully discharged for notifying state authorities that the pharmacy section of a supermarket did not have a pharmacist on duty at all times that the pharmacy was open to public access as required by state law).

71. O'Sullivan v. Mallon, 160 N.J. Super. 416, 390 A.2d 149 (Law Div. 1978).

72. *See, e.g.,* Parnat v. Americana Hotels, Inc., 65 Haw. 370, 652 P.2d 625 (1982) (no cause of action for dismissal that rendered an employee unavailable for investigation of federal antitrust charge); Martin v. Platt, 179 Ind. App. 688, 386 N.E.2d 1026 (1979) (no cause of action for dismissal following executive employee's complaints to supervisor of officer's solicitation and receipt of kickbacks); Geary v. United States Steel Corp., 456 Pa. 171, 319 A.2d 174 (1974) (no cause of action for wrongful discharge when employee salesman attempted to have allegedly unsafe product withdrawn from market and complained about supervisor).

73. Pierce v. Ortho Pharmaceutical Corp., 84 N.J. 58, 417 A.2d 505 (1980). *See also* Warthen v. Toms River Community Memorial Hosp., 118 L.R.R.M. 3179 (N.J. App. Div. 1985); Suchodolski v. Michigan Consolidated Gas Co., 412 Mich. 692, 316 N.W.2d 710 (1982); Keneally v. Orgain, 186 Mont. 1, 606 P.2d 127 (1980).

74. Hentzel v. Singer Co., 138 Cal. App. 3d 290, 188 Cal. Rptr. 159 (1982). *But see* Ohlsen v. DST Industries, 111 Mich. App. 580, 314 N.W.2d 699 (1981).

75. Occupational Safety and Health Act of 1970, 29 U.S.C. § 660(c).

76. California is one such state. *See* Cleary v. American Airlines, 111 Cal. App. 3d 443, 168 Cal. Rptr. 722 (1980). Only one or two other states have recognized the implied covenant of good faith. *See, e.g.,* Fortune v. National Cash Register Co., 373 Mass. 96, 364 N.E.2d 1251 (1977). New Hampshire requires the employee to show that the employer was motivated by bad faith and that the discharge resulted from a refusal to engage in an action that public policy condemns or from the employee's engaging in an action that public policy encourages. Cloutier v. Great Atlantic & Pacific Tea Co., 121 N.H. 915, 436 A.2d 1140 (1981); Monge v. Beebe Rubber Co., 114 N.H. 130, 316 A.2d 549 (1974). Most other states do not presently recognize an implied covenant of good faith and fair dealing, but such a theory could be adopted in a number of states if a case offered appropriate facts. *See, e.g.,* English v. Fischer, 660 S.W.2d 521 (Tex. 1983) (concurring opinions).

77. *See, e.g.,* Khanna v. Microdata Corp., 170 Cal. App. 3d 250, 215 Cal. Rptr. 860 (1985); Rulon-Miller v. IBM, 162 Cal. App. 3d 1181b, 208 Cal. Rptr. 524 (1984); Cleary v. American Airlines, Inc., 111 Cal. App. 3d 443, 168 Cal. Rptr. 722 (1980).

78. Pugh v. See's Candies, Inc., 116 Cal. App. 3d 311, 171 Cal. Rptr. 917, 927 n.25 (1981).

79. *See, e.g.,* Seaman's Direct Buying Serv., Inc. v. Standard Oil of California, 36 Cal. 3d 752, 686 P.2d 1158, 206 Cal. Rptr. 354 (1984); Canceller v. Federated Department Stores, 672 F.2d 1312 (9th Cir. 1982), *cert. denied,* 459 U.S. 859 (1982). In Smithers v. Metro-Goldwyn-Mayer Studios, Inc., 139 Cal. App. 3d 643, 189 Cal. Rptr. 20 (1983), the jury initially awarded the wronged employee $300,000 for the breach of the covenant of fair dealing, $500,000 for breach of contract, $200,000 for fraud, and $2,000,000 in punitive damages. The employer had threatened to blacklist the employee unless he agreed to forego certain rights to compensation that he had under his contract. The court later reduced but did not overturn the damages that the employee received.

80. *See* Toussaint v. Blue Cross/Blue Shield of Michigan, 408 Mich. 579, 292 N.W.2d 880 (1980); Damrow v. Thumb Cooperative Terminal, Inc., 126 Mich. App. 354, 337 N.W.2d 338 (1983); Southwest Gas Corp. v. Ahmad, 668 P.2d 261 (Nev. 1983); Pine River State Bank v. Mettille, 333 N.W.2d 622 (Minn. 1983).

81. Walker v. Northern San Diego County Hosp. Dist., 135 Cal. App. 3d 896, 185 Cal. Rptr. 617 (1982).

Notes

82. *See, e.g.,* Heidick v. Ken General Hosp., Inc., 446 A.2d 1095 (Del. 1982); Beidler v. W.R. Grace, Inc., 461 F.Supp. 1013 (E.D. Pa. 1978), *aff'd,* 609 F.2d 500 (3d Cir. 1979); Johnson v. National Beef Packing Co., 220 Kan. 52, 551 P.2d 779 (1976).
83. Grouse v. Group Health Plan, Inc., 306 N.W.2d 114 (Minn. 1981).
84. *Id.*
85. *See* Gianaculas v. Trans World Airlines, Inc., 761 F.2d 1391 (9th Cir. 1985).

Chapter 10 Antitrust Law

Per Se Rule and Rule of Reason
Problems Associated with Formation and Structure
    Overinclusiveness
        Merger-Type Ventures
        Ventures That Compete with Venture Participants
        Potential Market Entrants
    Underinclusiveness
    Legitimate Purpose of the Venture
Problems Associated with Operations
    Ancillary Restraints
    Spillover Collusion
    Problems Arising from the Venture Practices
        Exclusive Dealing
        Tying Arrangements
        Discriminatory Pricing

Another legal consideration that may affect many joint ventures is the need to comply with antitrust laws. The formation and operation of a health care joint venture may result in scrutiny from those governmental authorities charged with enforcing the antitrust statutes. No clear guidelines are presently available to establish for participants in such an enterprise which forms or types of activities are antitrust violations and which are not.

Two reasons exist for this lack of clarity, beyond the general confusion that seems to surround the application of antitrust laws. First, relatively few cases have dealt with joint venture situations in any industry. This paucity of case law stems primarily from the nature of the joint venture. No specific definition of a joint venture exists for antitrust purposes. Whenever two or more parties join together for any purpose, they can call their enterprise a joint venture. Because of this broadness in the definition, different antitrust analyses may be required, depending on the nature of the participants' activities.[1] Further, this type of arrangement often involves a number of side agreements, called *ancillary agreements,* which on their own may trigger antitrust scrutiny.

Second, although there has been a recent upsurge in cases applying antitrust principles to the health care industry in general, only one case has specifically considered any arrangement calling itself a joint venture.[2] Most health care antitrust cases have involved hospital mergers, denials of medical staff privileges, or exclusive arrangements between hospitals and certain staff members.[3]

Not every joint venture that may restrain trade is proscribed by antitrust laws. The formation of a health care joint venture is not of itself an antitrust violation despite the potential reduction in competition that may result from it. Recent cases and statements by Department of Justice officials recognize that a bona fide joint venture is a legitimate business practice that should not be discouraged by overzealous enforcement of the antitrust laws.[4] Because a joint venture usually involves a union of two parties who may be competitors in their separate businesses to work for a common purpose, problems with antitrust issues may arise.

Per Se Rule and Rule of Reason

When analyzing an agreement or form of joint action between parties, courts have consistently held that only unreasonable restraints are unlawful.[5] Whether a restraint is unreasonable depends on its purpose and effect. In assessing reasonableness under the statutes, courts use two different analyses. Certain types of arrangements have been shown by experience to be inherently anticompetitive. These arrangements are deemed to be unlawful as a matter of law, without any further analysis and are called *per se antitrust violations.*[6]

When no per se violation exists, courts look at the arrangement according to the *rule of reason.* The rule of reason permits them to assess the situation by balancing all of the circumstances surrounding the activity, including the type of industry involved, the market in which the parties do business, the nature of the restraint, and the condition of the market before and after such restraint is imposed.[7] When analyzing a joint venture under the rule of reason, certain factors are examined, including the size of each joint venture participant, its share of the market, its contributions to the venture, the overall benefits derived from the venture, and the likelihood that in the absence of the joint venture, one or both parties would undertake a similar project alone or with another firm in the market.[8]

Antitrust problems for a joint venture can occur when it is first structured, because federal antitrust laws prohibit the formation of joint ventures that substantially lessen competition. Antitrust problems can also affect the venture after it is established if the business enterprise operates in a manner that restrains trade unnecessarily.

Problems Associated with Formation and Structure

Several statutes may affect the formation of a joint venture enterprise. These statutes are Sections 1 and 2 of the Sherman Act and Section 7 of the Clayton Act. Of these, Section 7 of the Clayton Act is probably the most important in determining whether a proposed joint venture restrains competition unnecessarily. Section 1 of the Sherman Act prohibits all contracts, combinations, and conspiracies in restraint of trade,[9] and Section 2 prohibits monopolies or attempts to monopolize.[10]

In most cases involving the formation of a joint venture, Section 7 of the Clayton Act, which dicusses mergers and acquisitions,[11] is also applicable. This statute, which has consistently been interpreted by courts to apply to a wide range of affiliations, including joint ventures, is more restrictive than the other two.[12] Consequently, if a situation passes muster under Section 7, it is almost always held to be legal under Sections 1 and 2. Conversely, an arrangement that is disallowed under Section 7 probably also fails under the other two statutes.

Three potential problems are associated with the formation of a health care joint venture:

- Overinclusiveness, that is, the reduction of competitors in the marketplace
- Underinclusiveness, that is, the exclusion of potential participants to render them unable to compete effectively
- Illegitimate purposes, that is, the creation of a venture as a conduit for illegal activity

These problems are generally analyzed under the rule of reason discussed in the previous section.

Overinclusiveness

Overinclusiveness may be a problem in three potential joint venture situations:

- Merger-type ventures, in which potential competitors consolidate operations to create a new facility to carry on together a business that they had previously conducted separately
- Ventures that compete with venture participants and that involve competitors who, while still continuing the same line of business, open up a separate new facility to engage in the same or similar activities
- Potential market entrants, which involve competitors who participate in a joint venture activity in which only one or neither had previously participated

The first type merges two or more competitors and hence removes actual competitors or potential competitors from the market. The second, which is similar to the first, creates a new market entrant that must compete with its owners and operators. The third removes one or more potential competitors from the market.

Merger-Type Ventures

Joint ventures in which parties consolidate operations that they had previously conducted separately can restrain competition because they represent the joining of two or more competitors to achieve some common purpose. As a result, a competitor is removed from the market. The question for purposes of antitrust analysis is whether this type of venture restrains competition too much. In other words, what effect does the combining of these two competitors in one enterprise, and the resultant elimination of one of them, have on the market? For example, if two hospitals in an area close down their psychiatric departments and form a joint venture to acquire or establish a consolidated psychiatric facility, the anticompetitive effect could be too great if, as a result of the venture, the new facility creates a monopoly for psychiatric care in the area.[13]

The analysis for this type of venture is the same as for a merger under Section 7 of the Clayton Act. In each case, the assessment of this arrangement for a potential antitrust violation looks at whether the merger lessens competition substantially in a particular market. This analysis requires not only a close examination of the geographic area that is affected by the arrangement and the amount of concentration in the market before and after the transaction as indicated by the Herfindahl-Hirschman Index (HHI), but also other relevant factors contained in the merger guidelines. Among these factors are:[14]

- Changing conditions in the relevant market.
- Financial condition of one or both parties to an affiliation.
- Ease of market entry. If new competitors can readily enter a market, the potential adverse impact of a merger is decreased.
- Efficiencies, including economies of scale, better integration of production facilities, and plant specialization.

In the health care industry, this type of analysis is appropriate to the creation of a preferred provider organization (PPO) joint venture. This type of arrangement has antitrust implications because it represents a consolidation of many potential competitors in a given area into one entity. If it includes too many such health care providers, the venture may be successfully challenged under antitrust laws because it overly restrains competition.[15]

The test is whether the PPO joint venture ties up such a substantial percentage of hospital and physician providers that it is difficult for competing health care delivery arrangements to do business. This test has several applications. The fact that the restraint on the market is substantial can be determinative in and of itself that an antitrust violation has occurred. However, no clear guidelines on this issue are available. Recent statements by representatives of the Department of Justice indicate that a PPO joint venture containing no more than 20 percent, or in some instances perhaps 25 percent, of the total number of providers in a given area would probably survive antitrust scrutiny. If more than 20 or 25 percent were involved in the PPO, the participants have greater cause for concern. Certainly, a joint venture containing 70 percent of the health care providers in the area presents a greater risk of a finding of an antitrust violation.[16] Those persons charged with enforcing antitrust statutes are looking closely at PPOs and will take action against any arrangement that they think too tightly restricts the market.[17]

If the situation is marginal, one factor to be considered is the *exclusivity* of the arrangement. If the providers participating in the PPO are restricted from entering into other arrangements and if these providers represent a relatively large number of the providers in the community, then the arrangement runs a greater risk of being treated as potentially harmful from an antitrust point of view than if the providers are free to participate in other joint ventures. An exclusive arrangement reduces competition in the market by impairing entry into the market by other potential alternative delivery service companies that desire to contract with the same providers. However, an arrangement that is not exclusive merely adds to the alternative delivery service market one more competing entity among others, including not only hospitals but also insurance companies such as Blue Cross/Blue Shield, other PPOs, and health maintenance organizations (HMOs). When no significant market restraint and no substantial anticompetitive effect exist, the arrangement can probably withstand scrutiny unless it is formed for illegitimate purposes.

A PPO that is generally kept on a relatively small scale should not encounter difficulties; it may well be seen as procompetitive. By limiting the number of participants in the PPO, the parties ensure the availability of participants in competing networks and health care delivery systems. Also by limiting the number of providers in the one system, the PPO ensures that no provider excluded from the arrangement has any more difficulty in competing in the market served by the new PPO than it would have if that PPO did not exist.

Other procompetitive effects of the PPO that could act to balance potential restraints on competition are the efficiencies created by this new structure. When assessing a proposed joint venture that serves to eliminate potential competitors in the marketplace, one factor weighing in the balancing is whether, by forming the venture, efficiencies are produced that cannot otherwise be obtained.[18] In the PPO example, the parties can probably demonstrate how this type of enterprise can achieve economies of scale with resultant cost savings to the consumer. Because of the affiliation between several hospitals as well as a number of physicians and the consequent tendency to refer patients to other providers within the system for specialized care, the PPO provides health care that patients may not otherwise receive and supplies it at a reasonable cost.

Ventures That Compete with Venture Participants

Even though a new venture entity created by competitors who continue to compete in their separate business activities adds a potential new competitor to the market, it nevertheless has potential antitrust problems. The major concern is that the new entity may not operate in a truly competitive fashion in the same market with its parent; too great a risk for collusion between the parents and their new subsidiary exists in this situation. Because of this concern, this type of venture may be disallowed, depending on the size of the respective venturers and their market share. If it is permitted, various assurances or guarantees from the parties against anticompetitive activity may be required.

An example of such a joint venture is the new health care data service company described in appendix D. In that example, an HMO, with an existing, albeit inefficient, data system enters into a venture with the sole owner of a data service company to form a new data service company to provide data services to HMOs. The existing data service company continues in operation after the transaction is consummated and, apparently, competes with the new joint venture enterprise.

Such a venture can be structured in two different ways so as to reduce the potential restraint on competition. First, the new enterprise can provide a product or a service somewhat different from that provided by its owners. For example, the existing data service company can continue to provide the services that it has been offering, while the new business can offer a different type of service not presently offered by the existing business and perhaps more specifically suited to the needs of HMOs and similar health care providers. However, offering similar services but to different clients may not be wise. Continuing to offer similar services but to different clients is, in effect, a division of the marketplace among competitors, an act specifically forbidden by antitrust law.[19] The differences in the companies must be in the services that they offer and not in the clients that they serve.

A second means of avoiding anticompetitive effects in this joint venture situation is to include as part of the transaction a *merger* between a subsidiary of the HMO's parent and the existing data service company. In that case, one legal entity, the HMO's parent, controls both the new data service company and the existing data service business. The two data service companies are now brother-sister enterprises. Although the two entities offer the same services to potentially the same clients, thereby opening the door to collusion and other anticompetitive activities by the subsidiaries, they are *subsidiaries* of an integrated single entity, in other words, in the same corporate family, as opposed to being owned by several competing participants in a joint venture.

A recent United States Supreme Court decision, *Copperweld Corp. v. Independence Tube Co.*,[20] holds that a parent and wholly owned subsidiary are not able to conspire with each other as a matter of law; only enterprises that are independent of each other are capable of the concerted action to restrain trade required by Section 1 of the Sherman Act. The Supreme Court noted that, for purposes of Section 1, the coordinated activity of a parent and its wholly owned subsidiary must be viewed as that of a single enterprise.

Following this reasoning, the activities of two wholly owned subsidiaries of a single parent can also be viewed as those of a single entity.[21] Even if the subsidiaries are not wholly owned by a single parent, cooperation between them may not lead to an antitrust violation, depending on the amount of control that the alleged conspiring parent exercises over management and operations of the subsidiary. With substantial control, that is, less than 100 percent but more than 50 percent ownership in the subsidiary enterprise, cooperation between the two companies would probably not be viewed as anticompetitive.[22] In *Copperweld*, the Supreme Court noted that in a prior decision, in which a conspiracy to restrain trade had been found, the parent did not own a majority interest in either subsidiary and did not control them.[23] Therefore, a joint venture that is not wholly owned, or at least controlled by a particular participant, might be held liable under Section 1 of the Sherman Act for conspiracy to restrain trade. Whether this suggested merger would pass muster under Section 7 of the Clayton Act depends on the market analysis. However, at least one decision since *Copperweld* has relied on *Copperweld* to liberally assess various cooperative business efforts, such as a joint venture, under the rule of reason. The court in that case stated, "[a]ntitrust law is designed to ensure an appropriate blend of cooperation and competition, not to require all economic actors to compete full tilt at every moment."[24]

Potential Market Entrants

A more serious antitrust problem affecting joint ventures arises under the so-called *potential market entrant doctrine*.[25] This doctrine has been applied in the joint venture context when two noncompeting companies form a new company that will offer a product or service neither party or only one of the parties has previously offered. The question is whether one or both of the participants would have entered the market separately and would have thereby created two new market entrants instead of just the one represented by the joint venture. An example of this type of venture is the one described in appendix B, in which two hospitals form a partnership to purchase and operate a magnetic resonance imaging (MRI) facility.

In applying antitrust analysis to this type of joint venture, the courts have asked whether:[26]

- Either venture participant was perceived by existing firms as a potential independent entrant into the market (the so-called perceived potential entrant theory).
- The venture had an actual restraining impact on the competitive conduct of existing competitors.
- The market was concentrated.
- The venture participant was one of few likely entrants into the market.

The courts have noted that if the joint venture participants are only potential entrants into the market by means of the proposed joint venture structure, then the joint venture presents no threat to competition. Likewise, if the created entity has no impact on the activities of others in the market, no restraint on competition exists.

Furthermore, if the market is not concentrated, the activity of the perceived potential entrant would not significantly affect other parties in that market. Finally, if the market has many potential entrants, the loss of one would have no real impact on competition.

In the MRI example (appendix B), either hospital may decide independently to acquire the equipment and provide MRI services in the community. However, more information is required to gauge the anticompetitive effect of the venture. Investigators would want to know the number of other potential entrants into the market and the impact of the venture on their plans. Simply saying that by constructing the facility, the two joint venture participants are probably dampening plans of other local health care providers is not sufficient. The exact composition of the market must also be gauged.

The venture participants could argue, for instance, that because the enterprise is limited to only two hospitals and perhaps a few staff physicians, a significant number of other potential competitors remain in the market. Any remaining hospitals, non-participating radiologists, and other physicians may also offer competing MRI services. Furthermore, to a significant extent, the MRI facility faces competition from existing computed tomography (CT) scanners, which perform many of the same functions as MRI equipment. In this respect, the joint venture is adding a new competitor to the existing market for diagnostic services and is therefore increasing rather than decreasing competition.

The parties to the joint venture should examine the need for MRI services in the particular community in which the new center is to be located. The resolution of the antitrust question in this situation depends on whether the area to be served by the joint venture could economically support more than one MRI facility. If the community can support no more than one MRI facility, it makes little difference from the point of view of potential competition who owns it. Competition is restrained because of natural market forces and not because of the proposed joint venture, and therefore antitrust problems are not at issue. However, if the market could economically support several such facilities, this joint venture could have antitrust problems. Before embarking on such a venture, the parties should consult legal counsel about the application of antitrust law to their particular situation.

Underinclusiveness

Another argument that a challenger may make to a joint venture arrangement is that it is underinclusive, that is, it excludes competitors who might have wished to join and who, as a result of the exclusion, are unable to compete effectively. An example of a joint venture that can come under attack as being underinclusive is the PPO. Such an enterprise includes some health care providers and excludes others. It must exclude some providers, or it would be subject to attack as being overinclusive (see the discussion earlier in this chapter on overinclusiveness). However, it may also be attacked if it excludes too many providers. An agreement among horizontal competitors, such as the hospital providers or the physician providers in a PPO, to decline to do business with one or several other providers in an area, such as a medical equipment supplier or radiologist, may come under attack as a concerted refusal to deal. A *concerted refusal to deal* is a form of exclusive dealing between competitors that is deemed to be per se unlawful because it is so inherently anticompetitive (see the discussion earlier in this chapter on the per se rule and rule of reason).

Outside the joint venture context, a violation of antitrust laws exists if one or more hospitals, for instance, agree with a health insurance payer that the payer will refuse to purchase services from a specified hospital in the area. However, within a legitimate joint venture, conduct having a potentially anticompetitive effect or **agreements** that would otherwise be per se unlawful are analyzed under the rule of **reason**.[27] Under the rule of reason, the trier of fact looks at all of the circumstances surrounding an agreement to determine the effects that a refusal to deal has on the health care market. As a result, this type of underinclusive arrangement in the joint venture context does not represent a major problem in most instances, despite its theoretical potential for antitrust liability.

In challenging such an arrangement under the rule of reason, plaintiffs must meet the so-called *essential-facilities* or *bottleneck test*. Under this theory, the excluded party must show that the venture creates a significant competitive advantage for members, that those excluded are denied that advantage and thereby cannot compete effectively in the marketplace, that they cannot practically duplicate this competitive advantage without access to the venture, and that no legitimate business reason for the exclusion exists.[28] Few, if any, cases have successfully applied this doctrine to the health care industry. In order to overcome the essential-facilities hurdle, the challenger must demonstrate that the facility or access to a service is truly essential, and doing so is difficult. For example, in the scenario of a joint venture between the only hospital in a rural setting and a group of physicians to purchase and operate expensive medical equipment, privileges for the use of the equipment would be granted to all but a few of the physicians in the area. The excluded physicians would have to argue not only that they had been denied access to a service that was too expensive to be readily acquired by them without the cooperation of the hospital, but also that they could not compete at all as physicians unless they were able to offer that service to their patients. In other words, the physicians would have to demonstrate that access to the equipment was *essential* to them. Such an argument may be difficult to prove.

In fact, the contrary argument prevails in most instances. Being excluded provides the excluded party with sufficient incentive to create a facility to compete with the one from which he or she is excluded. With respect to health care joint ventures, authorities on the subject indicate that not only *may* a joint venture, such as a PPO, limit participation, but it will be *required* to do so in most instances.[29] So long as its business purposes are legitimate, the PPO has every right to limit the size of its membership.[30]

Legitimate Purpose of the Venture

Another potential antitrust problem that can affect the formation of a joint venture is the purpose behind it, its raison d'etre. The formation of a joint venture enterprise is analyzed under the rule of reason unless that enterprise was formed for an anticompetitive purpose. The main question posed at the outset in antitrust analysis is whether the venture serves a legitimate business purpose or whether it is merely a conduit for illegal activity.

If the venture serves a legitimate purpose, then any threat that it imposes to competition, any restraints that it contains are judged under the rule of reason. However, the final test for determining antitrust violations is the *purpose of the venture*. If the venture is viewed as a mere vehicle to enable competitors to engage in an anticompetitive activity, such as price fixing, then its structure will be disregarded, and the restraints that it imposes will be judged as per se violations.[31] Calling an arrangement a joint venture does not protect it from scrutiny.

The PPO joint venture exemplifies this problem. A legitimate PPO has a myriad of functions, such as utilization review or economies of scale. Any of these functions gives legitimacy to its existence. However, if a group of physicians forms a joint venture that ostensibly performs PPO-type functions but whose real purpose is to fix minimum or maximum price levels for the group members' private practices, the fact that the group calls itself a joint venture would be disregarded because the arrangement has no real purpose aside from that of fixing prices.[32] Consequently, when establishing a joint venture, the parties should be careful to define legitimate purposes for it at the outset. Any restraints on competition resulting from the arrangement should be necessary or important to the functioning of the enterprise.

Problems Associated with Operations

Other antitrust considerations become important once the joint venture has been formed. These other considerations are:

- Ancillary restraints, which are necessary to the functioning of the joint venture enterprise as a business entity
- Spillover collusion, which arises from practices of venture participants
- Antitrust problems that can result from business operations of the venture, such as exclusive dealing or predatory pricing

Ancillary Restraints

In the course of structuring a joint venture, the participants at times need to enter into side agreements to facilitate the transaction. If these agreements restrain competition, they can be subject to antitrust scrutiny. Generally, unless these agreements are themselves the purpose of the arrangement, they are analyzed under the rule of reason. If the agreements are ancillary, that is, reasonably necessary or important to the functioning of the venture, they will be upheld (see the discussion earlier in this chapter on the per se rule and the rule of reason).[33] In determining the real reason behind such agreements, courts consider whether the restraint:

- Is reasonably necessary to the legitimate primary purpose of the arrangement and has no broader scope than is reasonably necessary
- Does not unreasonably affect competition in the marketplace
- Is not imposed by a party or parties with monopoly power

In essence, the courts look at the venture with and without the ancillary agreements and decide whether the venture has a procompetitive purpose without considering the effect of the ancillary restraint.

An example of an ancillary restraint is an agreement among the joint venture participants to fix minimum or maximum price levels for the enterprise. For instance, in a venture for an ambulatory surgical center between a hospital and physicians, the parties may fix what rates the center will charge without encountering antitrust problems even though, outside of the joint venture, price fixing among competitors is a per se antitrust violation. In such a joint venture, the physicians, "who would otherwise be competitors [have pooled] their capital and [are sharing] the risks of loss as well as the opportunities for profit."[34] The ambulatory center is viewed as a single entity that may legitimately set the prices to be charged.

A different situation arises when physicians join together to form a foundation and collectively set prices. If the physicians in the group do not really integrate their practices and if in other respects they still compete against one another, a court will look at the situation as a whole with and without the price-fixing element and determine whether the so-called joint venture had any purpose other than to set prices. If not, a per se antitrust violation will have occurred.[35]

Somewhere in between these two extremes are other joint ventures among health care providers, such as the PPO. Within the PPO structure, groups of physicians may wish to set fees on a collective basis. These physicians need to know whether the

PPO will be deemed a sufficiently integrated entity to avoid antitrust complications. Under a literal reading of the *Maricopa* opinion, a physician-controlled entity whose major function is only the establishment of a uniform fee structure, utilization review, and joint claims administration is perhaps not sufficiently integrated to legitimately set its own prices. To achieve sufficient functional integration, the venture participants have to pool some capital, probably more than a minimum amount to cover start-up costs and administrative expenses, and share the risk or be financially interdependent.[36]

However, officials of the Antitrust Division of the United States Department of Justice have taken a contrary position. For instance, in a 1985 speech, the head of this division announced that PPOs and other similar physician groups may achieve sufficient integration to legitimately engage in collective price setting without undertaking significant risk sharing.[37] Under this interpretation, a physician-controlled PPO is not subject to prosecution if the physicians agree to:

- Treat patients on a fee-for-service basis at reduced levels or pursuant to a fee schedule
- Abide by some form of utilization review
- Administer claims and market the venture jointly
- Limit the group to no more than approximately 20 percent of the area's physicians

Abiding by these requirements may not be sufficient for such a joint venture to avoid any antitrust claims either by governmental agencies or competing claimants. Also, a court of law may not follow this more lenient view; it may just as likely follow the stricter approach.

Spillover Collusion

Other antitrust problems can arise because of dealings with joint venture participants outside of the context of their mutual interest in the joint venture. By its very nature, the joint venture is conducive to so-called *spillover collusion* among the parties. Spillover collusion occurs when joint venture participants, who may be competitors outside of the venture, act jointly or appear to act jointly with respect to their separate business activities. The result of this collusion lessens the competition among the participants in areas not related to the venture. As one court has noted, "the joint venture puts the parents, particularly if they are competitors, in dangerous proximity to discuss and act jointly on aspects of their business apart from the joint venture and creates an aura of cooperative team spirit which is apt to dampen competitive fires between the firms involved."[38]

The temptation to take advantage of the joint venture relationship to reduce competition between the participants in other areas is always present. For instance, the participants may decide to allocate territories among themselves; or as they fix the rates to be charged by a joint venture ambulatory surgical facility, they may also agree on minimum or maximum fees that they will charge in their outside practices. They may also decide to use in their separate business activities confidential information that they have obtained about each other through the joint venture. In any of these instances, the venture participants could be charged with an antitrust violation.

The general rule in approaching this problem is that agreements made lawfully within the ambit of the joint venture may not spill over into other areas in which the participants continue to compete. For instance, a parent corporation, such as an occupational medicine franchisor, can allocate a particular market to each of its subsidiary franchisees without antitrust repercussions. However, for the separate participants in that venture to allocate markets among themselves in their separate capacities is an antitrust violation.[39] Likewise, the setting of prices by an integrated facility is a legitimate activity, but the setting of prices between competitors is a per se violation of antitrust laws.[40] Consequently, even when the joint venture is not itself anticompetitive, the participants must be scrupulous in their own behavior, both with respect to the venture and to each other as competitors outside of the venture context to avoid any appearance of collusion or anticompetitive practice in their separate business decisions.

Problems Arising from the Venture Practices

Once the joint venture enterprise has begun operations, it is treated under the law as a single business enterprise. It cannot conspire with itself,[41] but it is nevertheless not immune from the application of the antitrust laws. As a business, it is subject to all laws and regulations applicable to any other industry or health care provider, including normal constraints imposed on businesses by the antitrust laws. Antitrust problems do not cease to exist merely because the venture has escaped scrutiny at the moment of its formation. Compliance is an ongoing function that should be closely monitored by the management of the new venture enterprise.

Certain business practices of the venture entity itself or between the venture entity and venture participants are particularly relevant in the antitrust analysis. The most common practices for a health-care-related business are exclusive dealing, tying, and discriminatory pricing.

Exclusive Dealing

Because exclusive-dealing arrangements place certain limitations on the ability of market participants to work with whom they please in a free and unfettered manner, such arrangements may have potential antitrust implications. An exclusive-dealing arrangement between two horizontally related entities, such as two hospitals, may be deemed a concerted refusal to deal and as such a per se antitrust violation. However, when challenged under the antitrust laws, exclusive-dealing arrangements between vertically related entities, such as between hospitals and physicians or hospitals and suppliers, as opposed to horizontally related entities are normally analyzed under the rule of reason and not the per se rule.[42] Such challenges generally are brought under Section 1 of the Sherman Act, which prohibits contracts or conspiracies that unreasonably restrain trade[43] or Section 3 of the Clayton Act, which makes it unlawful to prevent a buyer from purchasing a competitor's goods when the effect is to reduce competition substantially or to tend to create a monopoly.[44]

The standard of Section 3 prohibits many more arrangements than does Section 1 because Section 1 requires an *actual*, substantial anticompetitive effect, whereas under Section 3, so long as an exclusive arrangement *tends to* lessen competition substantially, it is unlawful, regardless of its actual effect. Consequently, most challenges to exclusive-dealing arrangements are brought under Section 3 rather than under Section 1. However, because Section 3 covers only agreements involving goods or commodities, it is inapplicable to most arrangements among health care providers, which mainly deal with services.

To assess whether an exclusive-dealing arrangement is unlawful under the rule-of-reason analysis, its anticompetitive effects must be determined. In this analysis, the relevant geographic and product market must be assessed to determine how much of it is being tied up as a result of the exclusive-dealing arrangement.[45] Because many factors are involved, pinpointing a threshold beyond which an arrangement is likely to be struck down is impossible. As a general rule, the greater the percentage of the market involved, the more likely that an exclusive-dealing arrangement will be condemned. Under Section 1, an exclusive arrangement may withstand a challenge if it includes even as much as 50 percent of the market, whereas a challenge to such an arrangement under Section 3 may be successful even if only 5 percent of the market is involved.[46]

An example of an exclusive-dealing arrangement within the joint venture context is an agreement between a PPO and an employer in the PPO's service area whereby the employer agrees not to offer its employees the services of any other PPO as a health care benefit option. Whether this agreement is legal under the rule-of-reason analysis depends on how much of the market is tied up and what the justification for the arrangement is. The geographic market and the size of the employer are also relevant factors in the determination. In a large city, such an agreement with even a large employer would probably be upheld, but a different result may be obtained in a rural area when the arrangement is with the region's largest employer.[47]

Tying Arrangements

A tying arrangement results when a party provides a service or sells a product to another only on condition that the other party also purchase a second product or service (the tied product) from the seller or from someone designated by the seller. A tying arrangement is illegal per se in most instances if the seller has the so-called market power to oblige a purchaser to buy something that the purchaser would not necessarily buy in a freely competitive market.[48] As one court has noted, "the essential characteristic of an illegal tying arrangement lies in the seller's exploitation of its control over the tying product to force the buyer into the purchase of a tied product that the buyer either did not want at all, or might have preferred to purchase elsewhere on different terms."[49]

However, a tying arrangement is only condemned if anticompetitive consequences may arise from it. If the party is forced to take a tied item in only one or several isolated instances, the impact on competition is not deemed to be severe enough to merit antitrust scrutiny. Courts will refuse to find an arrangement to be illegal unless "a substantial volume of commerce is foreclosed thereby."[50]

Likewise, the situation warrants scrutiny only when a likelihood exists that the seller has the market power and is using it to restrain competition. Evidence of such power is present when the seller has a large market share of the tying product or when the product is so unique that competitors cannot easily offer it.

Because of these restrictions, few, if any, situations in the health care industry are deemed to be illegal tying arrangements. In a recent case, for instance, the court found that, although in theory, the use of a hospital's operating room facilities could be tied to anesthesiology services because the two items are distinguishable in the eyes of patients, the hospital's linking of the two as a package to surgery patients was not *illegal* tying because the hospital did not coerce patients to purchase the services. The hospital lacked sufficient market power to force any recalcitrant purchaser to accept both. Even the control by the hospital of 30 percent of the market in its area was not sufficient reason because 70 percent of the persons in the area went elsewhere for operating room services.[51]

Discriminatory Pricing

Another antitrust issue is raised if a joint venture grants to certain favored customers special prices that are lower than the company's usual charges. This practice is prohibited by the Robinson-Patman Act if such a pricing policy adversely affects competition.[52] Certain health care providers, such as not-for-profit hospitals, nursing homes, and not-for-profit HMOs, may be exempt from application of the provisions of the

Robinson-Patman Act by reason of the Non-Profit Institutions Act[53] if the products purchased are for the charitable institution's own use.[54] As a general rule, if a not-for-profit joint venture, such as an HMO, supplies drugs or medical equipment as well as clinical services to patients, the drugs and equipment may be considered to be for the institution's own use for purposes of the Non-Profit Institutions Act. Sales at a discount or at cost by a hospital or other not-for-profit entity to a not-for-profit subsidiary joint venture would probably also be exempted from scrutiny under the Robinson-Patman Act.[55] However, the law is not clear with respect to the situation in which one of the partners in the joint venture is a for-profit corporation or the joint venture purchases items from a not-for-profit partner.

Notes

1. *See* J. VAN KALINOWSKI, ANTITRUST LAWS AND TRADE REGULATION § 17.08(1) (1986).

2. In Arizona v. Maricopa County Medical Soc'y, 457 U.S. 332 (1982), the court found that what was involved was a mere illegal price-fixing agreement, not a bona fide joint venture.

3. *See, e.g.*, United States v. Hospital Affiliates Int'l, Inc., [1980-81] Trade Cas. (CCH) ¶63,721 (E.D. La. 1981) (involves a preliminary injunction against a proposed merger of two psychiatric hospitals); City of Fairfax v. Fairfax Hosp. Ass'n, 562 F.2d 280 (4th Cir. 1977), *cert. granted, vacated and recorded*, 435 U.S. 992 (1978) (the acquisition of one acute care hospital by another could violate Sections 1 and 2 of the Sherman Act). *See also* Jefferson Parish Hosp. Dist. No. 2 v. Hyde, 466 U.S. 2, (1984) (involves an arrangement between a hospital and certain staff members for exclusive rights).

4. *See, e.g.*, Polk Bros., Inc. v. Forest City Enterprises, Inc., 776 F.2d 185 (7th Cir. 1985). *See also* Speech by J. Paul McGrath, assistant attorney general, Antitrust Division, U.S. Department of Justice, National Health Lawyers Association Conference, Washington, DC (Jan. 22, 1985), *cited in* HEALTH LAW. NEWS REP., National Health Lawyers Association (Feb. 13, 1985) [hereinafter cited as McGrath Speech]. *See generally* Brodley, *Joint Ventures and Antitrust Policy*, 95 HARV. L. REV. 1521, 1535 (1982).

5. *See* Board of Trade of City of Chicago v. United States, 246 U.S. 231 (1917).

6. *See* Arizona v. Maricopa County Medical Soc'y, 457 U.S. 332 (1982).

7. *See* Board of Trade of City of Chicago v. United States, 246 U.S. at 238 (1917).

8. Berkey Photo, Inc. v. Eastman Kodak Co., 603 F.2d 263, 302 (1979).

9. Section 1, Sherman Act, 15 U.S.C. § 1.

10. Section 2, Sherman Act, 15 U.S.C. § 2.

11. 15 U.S.C. § 18 (1976).

12. *See* United States v. Penn-Olin Chemical Co., 378 U.S. 158 (1964) (applies Section 7 to the joint venture situation).

13. *See, e.g.*, United States v. Hospital Affiliates Int'l, Inc., [1980-81] Trade Cas. (CCH) ¶63,721 (E.D. La. 1981) (preliminary injunction against a proposed merger of two psychiatric hospitals); City of Fairfax v. Fairfax Hosp. Ass'n, 562 F.2d 280 (4th Cir. 1977), *cert. granted, vacated and recorded*, 435 U.S. 992 (1978) (the acquisition of an acute care hospital by another could violate Sections 1 and 2 of the Sherman Act).

14. MERGER GUIDELINES OF THE DEPARTMENT OF JUSTICE (June 4, 1984).

15. PPOs are treated as "combinations" to restrict free trade under Section 1 of the Sherman Act, 15 U.S.C. § 1.

16. *See* Arizona v. Maricopa County Medical Soc'y, 457 U.S. 332 (1982).

17. On Oct. 12, 1984, the Department of Justice announced that it would take action against Stanislaus Foundation Preferred Provider Organization on antitrust grounds. When the PPO subsequently dissolved, the department dropped its action.

18. *See* United States v. Columbia Pictures Indus., 507 F. Supp. 412 (S.D.N.Y. 1980).

Notes

19. *See, e.g.,* Timken Roller Bearing Co. v. United States, 345 U.S. 593 (1951).
20. 467 U.S. 752 (1984).
21. Century Oil Tool, Inc. v. Production Specialties, Inc., [1984-2] Trade Cas. (CCH) ¶66,370 (5th Cir. 1984); Hood v. Tenneco Texas Life Ins. Co., [1984-2] Trade Cas. (CCH) ¶66,515 (5th Cir. 1984).
22. Magnum Force Distributors v. Bon Bon Co., No. 84-2629 (E.D.N.Y. 1984) (unreported decision rendered from the bench, *cited* in Van Kalinowski, ANTITRUST REPORT, Apr. 1985, at 10).
23. 467 U.S. at 771, *citing* Timken Roller Bearing Co. v. United States, 345 U.S. 593 (1951).
24. Polk Bros., Inc. v. Forest City Enterprises, Inc., 776 F.2d 185, 188 (7th Cir. 1985).
25. United States v. Penn-Olin Chemical Co., 378 U.S. 158 (1964).
26. *Id.* at 173-74. *See also* United States v. Siemens Corp., 621 F.2d 499 (2d Cir. 1980).
27. Jefferson Parish Hosp. Dist. No. 2 v. Hyde, 466 U.S. 2 (1984).
28. *See, e.g.,* United States v. Realty Multi-List, Inc., 629 F.2d 1351 (5th Cir. 1980); MCI Communications v. American Telephone & Telegraph Co., 708 F.2d 1081, 1102-33 (7th Cir. 1983), *cert. denied,* 464 U.S. 891 (1983).
29. *See* Zimmerman, *Adventures in Jointness,* 1968 ABA ANTITRUST L.J. 125; OP. OHIO ATT'Y GEN., [1985 Transfer Binder: New Developments] TRADE REG. REP. (CCH) ¶65,796.
30. *See* Mid-South Grizzlies v. National Football League, 720 F.2d 772 (1983).
31. *See* Arizona v. Maricopa County Medical Soc'y, 457 U.S. 332 (1982).
32. *Id.*
33. *See, e.g.,* Timken Roller Bearing Co. v. United States, 345 U.S. 593 (1951); Polk Bros., Inc. v. Forest City Enterprises, Inc., 776 F.2d 185 (7th Cir. 1985).
34. Arizona v. Maricopa County Medical Soc'y, 457 U.S. at 356 (1982).
35. *Id.* at 356-57. In *Maricopa,* the United States Supreme Court found a medical foundation of otherwise competing physicians, whose only activities were the promulgation of a fee schedule, billing, collection, and peer review, to be in violation of antitrust law. The court applied the per se rule because the physicians did not need to set prices to perform the other administrative activities of the foundation.
36. *Id.* at 356. *See generally,* Stromberg, Duncheon & Goldman, *PPOs and the Antitrust Laws,* HOSPITALS, Oct. 16, 1983, at 65.
37. *See* McGrath Speech, *supra* note 4.
38. Northern Natural Gas Co. v. Federal Power Comm'n, 399 F.2d 953, 972, *citing* Brodley, *Oligopoly Power Under the Sherman and Clayton Acts—From Economic Theory to Legal Policy,* 19 STAN. L. REV. 285, 333-34 (1967).
39. Timken Roller Bearing Co. v. United States, 341 U.S. 593 (1951).
40. Arizona v. Maricopa County Medical Soc'y, 457 U.S. 332 (1982).
41. *See* Copperweld Corp. v. Independence Tube Corp., 467 U.S. 752, (1984).
42. *See, e.g.,* Tampa Electric Co. v. Nashville Coal Co., 365 U.S. 320 (1961). *But see* discussion earlier in this chapter of underinclusiveness and exclusive-dealing arrangements (concerted refusals to deal) between horizontally related entities and discussion *infra* note 46.
43. 15 U.S.C. § 1 *et seq.*
44. 15 U.S.C. § 12.
45. In Jefferson Parish Hosp. Dist. No. 2 v. Hyde, 466 U.S. 2 (1984), the exclusive contract situation was recently analyzed in the context of an agreement granting use of a hospital's operating rooms to a group of four anesthesiologists. A rival anesthesiologist complained that the contract stifled competition. The court agreed but held that such a restraint on trade would only be unreasonable if a significant number of competitors were frozen out of the market by the exclusive deal. The court found that an arrangement that was narrow in scope, such as one in which a single hospital dealt exclusively with a single group of anesthesiologists, posed no such threat.

Chapter 10. Antitrust Law

Notes

46. An exclusive-dealing arrangement between horizontal competitors such as two hospitals agreeing, for example, to deal with certain suppliers only is a concerted refusal to deal and is per se illegal unless ancillary to a legitimate venture. *See* the section on ancillary restraints in this chapter.

47. *See* discussion of Stanislaus Foundation, *supra* note 17.

48. *See* United States Steel Corp. v. Fortner Enterprises, Inc., 429 U.S. 610 (1977).

49. Jefferson Parish Hosp. Dist. No. 2 v. Hyde, 466 U.S. 2, 9 (1984).

50. *Id.* at 7. *See also* United States Steel Corp. v. Fortner Enterprises, 394 U.S. 495, 501-502 (1969); Will v. Comprehensive Accounting Corp., 776 F.2d 665 (7th Cir. 1985).

51. Jefferson Parish Hosp. Dist. No. 2 v. Hyde, 466 U.S. at 17. *See also* Will V. Comprehensive Accounting Corp., 776 F.2d 665 (7th Cir. 1985).

52. 15 U.S.C. § 13(a).

53. 15 U.S.C. § 13(c).

54. *See* Abbott Laboratories v. Portland Retail Druggists Ass'n, 425 U.S. 1 (1976).

55. *See* FTC *Advisory Opinion to St. Peter's Hospital,* [1977] FTC COMPLAINTS AND ORDERS, ¶21,316 (June 10, 1977), *cited* in Johnson, *Joint Ventures in the Home Health Field,* CAPITAL FINANCE AND JOINT VENTURES, The National Health Lawyers Association Conference, Washington DC (Jan. 22, 1985).

Chapter
11 Conclusion

Summary
Beyond Joint Ventures

Chapter 11. Conclusion

Summary

This book has considered various legal and business issues arising out of economic joint ventures in the health care industry. Joint venturing is the creation of a new enterprise by two or more legally independent parties, an enterprise that is jointly owned by such parties and in which the economic risk or reward is shared among the venture participants. The two basic types of health care joint ventures are the special-project joint venture and the alternative delivery system joint venture. Although other means, such as more traditional mergers or contractual arrangements, can accomplish the same goals, joint ventures may at times be the most practical tool for parties who want to achieve some mutual purpose while retaining their legal independence from each other in other respects.

Joint ventures are popular for several reasons. Among these are the fact that such enterprises present opportunities for:

- Opening up new sources of capital
- Containing costs and achieving economies of scale
- Meeting the demands of a changing population for new types of delivery systems better suited to their needs, such as home health care services, hospices for the elderly, sports medicine clinics, and birthing centers
- Acquiring and maintaining newly developed, expensive medical equipment
- Developing systems with which to meet increased competition from other health care providers

Joint ventures take on a myriad of forms. Six types of joint venture projects that are currently being undertaken and the potential problems that they may face are illustrated in the six appendixes:

- Ambulatory surgical center joint venture (appendix A)
- Magnetic resonance imaging (MRI) center joint venture (appendix B)
- Occupational medicine center joint venture (appendix C)
- Alternative delivery system joint venture (appendix D)
- Reference laboratory joint venture (appendix E)
- Medical pavilion joint venture (appendix F)

In each of these examples, the various options for structuring the venture and the potential participants are discussed. Options for the ambulatory surgical center include a partnership or a corporation formed by a hospital and staff physicians. The MRI joint venture is formed as a partnership between two tax-exempt hospitals. The occupational medicine center involves a general partnership with an entrepreneur and the licensing of individual local centers. In the alternative delivery system joint venture, the parent of an HMO forms a PPO with several hospitals and a physician practice group. The HMO also participates in a joint venture with a local entrepreneur for a data service center. The reference laboratory joint venture occurs in phases, over time, with each phase acquiring greater complexity as more outside parties, including a national investment company, participate. The medical pavilion joint venture involves a hospital and a hospital investment corporation in a large-scale venture to attract various health care providers to one locale.

All of these possible joint ventures face potential practical and legal problems that have to be resolved before the venture can be formed. Among the legal issues are general corporate law questions; securities law issues; potential franchise issues; tax questions; potential ERISA problems; issues arising out of health care regulations, such as certificate of need and licensing; Medicare and other reimbursement concerns; potential Medicare-Medicaid antifraud and abuse problems, as well as other legal and ethical concerns; labor law questions; and potential antitrust problems.

Before undertaking a joint venture, the potential participants must balance all of these legal considerations in an effort to choose a structure that best accomplishes their goals. This book explores various structure options and discusses certain steps to be taken to turn a joint venture idea into an actual legal entity. However, this discussion only serves as a guideline. Readers wishing to undertake their own joint ventures should consult with competent legal counsel and financial planners at the outset so that they can determine whether the project that they have in mind is feasible from an economic or practical point of view as well as from a legal point of view. With the help of counsel, they can set up a venture structure that accomplishes their particular goals while maximizing legal and financial benefits and avoiding running afoul of any of the myriad laws and regulations that can affect the venture.

Beyond Joint Ventures

The health care industry is rapidly changing as the needs and concerns of practitioners, patients, and payers change. To meet these needs, providers must keep themselves flexible and, like the proverbial reed, must be capable of bending with the wind, which in this case represents the many factors, economic and otherwise, currently affecting health care services.

Within the next several years, the health care industry will continue to take on different appearances than it has today or had a decade ago. For instance, the future of the health care industry may lie in the greater consolidation of the number of providers and in the development of large megasystems that result from the horizontal and vertical integration of hospitals, physicians, and insurance financing mechanisms. Regional and national systems will continue to grow. Consolidation and system building are the way of the future for health care.

These new health care systems will be geographically disbursed in the service region and comprehensive in the array of services and benefit packages offered either directly by the central entity or through its affiliates. The systems will concentrate on alternative delivery system products in the form of indemnity products, PPOs, and HMOs; and these products, rather than hospitals, will increasingly be the source of revenues, as the system shifts from fee for service to contractual arrangements with third-party payers.

Physician providers will also be organized in various ways and affiliated, whether on an exclusive basis or not, with such central regionalized systems, either through contracts or through ownership or both. Hospitals will be integrated into the system along with other preacute and postacute institutional providers. Other partners, such as insurance companies, health maintenance organizations, and entrepreneurs, may also be integrally linked within the system by contract or by ownership interest. To capture a share of new markets or obtain new sources of revenue, the system may likely also have to participate in several joint ventures or outreach programs.

Some charitable foundation components will also be part of this system in order to capture potential donations, assuming that changes in the tax laws have not reduced incentives for such donations. This charitable entity will serve to support activities such as care of the indigent, medical research, and education, that would otherwise be difficult to provide economically within a cost-effective price-competitive health care system. The entire system or network will be held together under some central entity, such as a parent holding company.

These new joint venture system developments raise many novel legal and regulatory issues. Some of these issues will probably be similar to those discussed in this book. However, other issues may arise, possibly in response to these new system developments.

Chapter 11. Conclusion
Beyond Joint Ventures

Hospitals and physicians are in the forefront of these new developments, which are rapidly changing the nature of health care services. Joint ventures have an important role in accomplishing these changes and helping the health care industry to adapt to the new environment in which it must operate, an environment composed of individuals who are aware both of the cost of medical care and the need for high-quality care. If parties interested in joint ventures remember to consider carefully all of the many legal and business factors that contribute to the feasibility of any venture, they can form new entities that will be sound and well-managed and will be in compliance with present regulations. With such solid building blocks, joint ventures will pave the way for a changed but economically viable health care industry in the coming years.

Appendix A: Ambulatory Surgical Center Joint Venture

Description of the Venture
Structure Options
Legal Considerations
    Licensing and Certificate of Need
    Corporate Practice Issues
    Tax Concerns
    Reimbursement
    ERISA Issues
    Referral Issues
Outcome

Appendix A

Description of the Venture

Establishing and operating an ambulatory surgical center is a common special-project joint venture.

Description of the Venture

Memorial Hospital, a not-for-profit, tax-exempt corporation, is considering an economic joint venture with physician staff members to establish an ambulatory surgical center in a local medical office building. All members of the medical staff of the hospital will be eligible to invest in the center. The participants hope to create a viable enterprise that will enhance their short-stay surgery market share and develop revenue that the hospital and the physician investors can share.

Both the hospital and the physicians plan to participate in the ownership, governance, and control of the project. All participants see this venture as a means of minimizing potential unnecessary competition among them. In addition, the parties think that the venture will bring them a fair return on their investment, which would preferably be tax free for the tax-exempt hospital and which could provide some tax-sheltering opportunities for the physician investors. The parties want to avoid obtaining either a separate license for the venture's clinic operations or a certificate of need. However, they want the clinic to be certified as an ambulatory surgical center under Medicare.

Structure Options

The parties are considering the following ways to structure this project:

- A partnership, composed of the hospital and physician partners, to lease a site for the facility, install the improvements, purchase equipment, and operate the clinic. As a variation of this structure, the venture can be organized as a limited partnership, with the hospital and certain staff physicians as general partners and other physicians who are interested in a passive investment as limited partners.
- A business corporation, owned by the hospital and physician shareholders, that would own and operate the facility.
- A lease of a facility, with the hospital or a subsidiary of the hospital as lessor and owner of the facility and a partnership of physicians, as lessee, to operate it. The hospital may also lease equipment to the physician entity, or the physician partnership may either purchase the necessary equipment on its own or lease it from a general or limited partnership of investor physicians.

In the first and second structure options, the hospital, as a general partner in the operating partnership or as a shareholder in the corporation, can exercise a significant amount of control over the management and operation of the enterprise. In the third option, the hospital loses this control over day-to-day operations but can participate indirectly through its facilities' lease. By means of conditions, covenants, and restrictions (CC&Rs) contained in this lease, the hospital can actually exert considerable control over the operations of the ambulatory surgical center. For instance, it can require that the facility be operated solely as an ambulatory surgical center in compliance with all laws and the fundamental policies of the hospital. It can also require that all hospital staff physicians who meet certain minimum standards must receive privileges to use all center facilities. In addition, the hospital can participate in the revenue from the project by setting the rental amount, in whole or in part, as a percentage of the gross receipts from center operations. As a variation of this third option, the hospital, or a subsidiary entity, can also act as a service bureau to provide services to the clinic by means of a management or service contract.

Legal Considerations

In discussing their proposal with legal counsel, the parties are concerned about several legal issues that can arise from the structuring and operation of this particular type of joint venture. The following are among the most important:

- Licensing and certificate of need
- Corporate practice issues
- Tax Concerns
- Reimbursement
- ERISA issues
- Referral issues

Following is a brief description of these legal considerations. A more detailed analysis of these and other legal issues that arise in the joint venture context can be found in specific chapters of this book.

Licensing and Certificate of Need

Depending on the particular state in which the center is to be operated, it may require some sort of license. For instance, to avoid the allegation that it is illegally practicing medicine, any lay operating entity jointly owned or controlled by the hospital and physicians may have to be considered an extension of the hospital's outpatient license in some states or an extension of a physician's office practice. Some states provide by statute for the separate licensure of ambulatory surgical centers (see the discussion of state licensing laws in chapter 6).

Licensing and other regulatory issues can be important considerations for this type of joint venture. Licensing questions may trigger certificate-of-need (CON) requirements, which can cause delays and unforeseen expenses that can seriously impede and even in some cases halt a proposed project (see chapter 6). On the other hand, certifying the facility pursuant to CON review may lend legitimacy to the company for purposes of avoiding scrutiny under laws prohibiting the corporate practice of medicine. Consequently, when such laws apply, venture participants need to ascertain at the outset how to structure the venture to obtain any necessary licenses or other certificates, such as a CON, without any undue delay.

Corporate Practice Issues

Another factor that must be weighed is the issue of the corporate practice of medicine. Depending on how the facility is organized, it could be holding itself out as offering health care to the public without a license. This practice is prohibited in some states by statute of case law. If the facility is organized and operated by a partnership of physicians, as in the first structure option, the physicians could operate the facility in most states under their own licenses as an extension of their office practice.

If the hospital is involved in the operation either through a corporation or a partnership, the corporate practice issue would probably not arise in most states. However,

Appendix A
Legal Considerations
Tax Concerns

a business corporation that is owned by a for-profit subsidiary of a hospital and physicians and is not licensed or certified in its own right, may not be allowed to operate in those states that adhere to the corporate practice doctrine (see chapter 8). In many states, the corporate practice issue does not arise, and no one in those states would challenge the right of such a business corporation to offer medical services.

Tax Concerns

Participation in the venture also raises various tax problems, depending on how the project is structured. The hospital's tax-exempt status may be questioned if the hospital participates in the operation of the facility, either alone or through a new entity jointly owned by it and staff physicians. In addition, income to the hospital as a result of its participation in center operations may be considered to be derived from a trade or business unrelated to the charitable purposes of the exempt hospital. These tax consequences can be somewhat minimized if a taxable subsidiary of the hospital or the hospital's parent, rather than the hospital, participates in the operation of the facility (see chapter 4). Further, start-up capital or services furnished to the taxable joint venture enterprise, unless provided by the hospital in exchange for reasonable consideration, may lead to private inurement, that is, significant benefit to private investors from hospital services, and thus jeopardize the hospital's tax exemption.

Other tax consequences to the other venture participants can result from the way in which this venture is structured. If the physicians form a partnership to acquire equipment, they may benefit from an investment tax credit (ITC) and accelerated depreciation, although they have to comply with certain tax rules applicable to leases of equipment by persons other than corporations.[1] However, these potential tax benefits may be reduced or even eliminated in certain cases, such as with respect to the ITC, if tax reform proposals before Congress in 1986 become law.[2] If the physicians lease the equipment to the tax-exempt hospital, other rules relating to the so-called tax-exempt use of the equipment can apply.[3] The rules relating to tax-exempt use can result in a reduction of potential tax benefits. The eventual tax consequences of this joint venture depend entirely on the actual structure selected for the venture and the relationship of the parties with each other. The Internal Revenue Service (IRS) judges each situation on its own particular facts. To be sure of a certain tax treatment, the participants may wish to request a private letter ruling from the IRS on these issues (see chapter 4).

Reimbursement

A major goal of the participants in establishing an ambulatory surgical center is to obtain reimbursement from Medicare and other third-party payers for facility utilization fees that are separate and apart from the professional fees of physicians performing services at the center. As a general practice with respect to freestanding health care facilities, Medicare and other payers include fees for facility utilization within the professional service fees for services rendered in a physician office setting.[4] However, an ambulatory surgical center can be reimbursed by Medicare for both the *technical component* (use of facility, equipment, and supplies) and the *professional component* (physicians' professional fees) of health care services.

Under Medicare regulations, a *distinct entity* that operates exclusively as an ambulatory surgical center may qualify for reimbursement for separately stated facility utilization charges[5] if the center enters into an agreement with the Health Care Financing Administration (HCFA) and meets the conditions of its regulations.[6] In addition, reimbursement is provided to such qualified centers only for procedures stipulated by

HCFA. This list of covered services is constantly updated by HCFA. An ambulatory surgical center that is affiliated with a hospital may currently elect Medicare reimbursement as a freestanding center or reimbursement on a reasonable-cost basis as a hospital outpatient department.[7]

ERISA Issues

Depending on how the entity operating the surgical center is organized, problems can arise with respect to pension and other employee benefit plans of venture participants. All tax-qualified plans are subject to the provisions of the Employee Retirement Income Security Act (ERISA). One of the basic precepts of ERISA is that a tax-qualified plan must cover substantially all the employees of an employer and may not discriminate in favor of owner-employees or highly compensated persons in comparison with rank-and-file staff members.

As a result of the application of certain affiliated service group (ASG) rules, which are designed to prevent venture participants from using related entities to avoid various ERISA coverage and antidiscrimination requirements, physician participants in joint venture operations may unwittingly jeopardize the tax-qualified status of benefit plans maintained by them or their professional corporations. Under the ASG rules, distinct and separate entities that are related or affiliated must be treated as one employer for purposes of testing compliance with ERISA.[8] These rules apply to plans of physicians, or their professional corporations or partnerships, who acquire ownership interests in the ambulatory surgical center and who also perform services either for it or for their patients in association with the center, such as by performing surgery there.

Unless all of the plans maintained by such physicians or their professional corporations or partnerships are fairly similar, the application of the ASG rules may have the effect of causing some plans to violate the antidiscrimination or other rules of ERISA. Compliance with ERISA in the case of an ASG with a fairly large number of dissimilar plans can be determined only by means of an actuarial study, and noncomplying plans revealed through such a study must be amended.

Whenever possible, avoiding the application of the ASG rules is preferable. For example, a single, existing, fully integrated physician group could operate the center, or if permissible from a corporate practice point of view, the center could be operated as a business corporation and therefore possibly be exempted from the application of the ASG rules. According to temporary proposed regulations governing the application of the ASG rules, a business corporation, that is, a corporation that is not a professional service corporation (as this term is defined in the regulations), will not be viewed as a service organization subject to the ASG rules,[9] unless a significant portion of that corporation's business is the performance of services for another professional service organization and 10 percent or more of the shares in the corporation are held by officers, highly compensated employees, or owners of that professional service organization.[10]

Despite this exception, which was created in the proposed regulations for business corporations, a business corporation formed by and owned entirely by physicians for the purpose of offering health care services to the public would likely be viewed by the Internal Revenue Service (IRS) as a disguised professional service corporation. If the business corporation has other shareholders, such as a for-profit subsidiary of a hospital or a hospital holding company, the corporation's owners have a stronger argument that the corporation is not a professional service corporation of the type envisioned by the ASG rules and therefore should not be affiliated with other groups.

Unfortunately, these ASG rules are exceedingly complex, and no generally applicable guidelines exist to assist in the planning process. The actual participants in any such joint venture, the current business relationships they may have, and the general nature of any plans maintained by them or for their benefit determine how the project should be structured (see chapter 5).

Referral Issues

Additional legal risks can occur when physicians are involved as owners of a health care facility in which they may be treating their own patients or to which they may make referrals. Both the Medicare and the Medicaid statutes contain language that prohibits gain to physicians from referrals. In addition, certain states have laws that either prohibit referrals to centers in which physicians have a financial interest or require disclosure of this interest (see chapter 8).

Outcome

In this particular venture, the participants explored several structure options. They considered three options: a corporation owned by the hospital and physicians, a partnership, composed of the hospital and physicians, or a partnership composed solely of physicians. In the first two options, the corporation or partnership would own and operate the ambulatory surgical center; in the third option, the physician partnership would operate the facility leased from the hospital. As variations on these structures, the participants considered having the physicians form a limited partnership that would own the facility and the equipment and lease these to the operating entity or purchase only the equipment to be used at the facility and lease it to the operating group. Venture participants also explored the possibility of the hospital's leasing the facility to the physician operating partnership as well as leasing equipment to it.

In light of the certificate-of-need and licensing laws of the state and in view of ERISA issues that can arise if a physician partnership engages in the operation of the ambulatory surgical center, the participants decide to structure the venture so that the center is operated by a business corporation owned by a hospital holding company and the physicians. A limited partnership composed of physicians participates by leasing equipment and the facility to the corporation. The hospital provides certain management and administrative support services. The hospital will also ground lease to the corporation the land on which the facility will be built. Figure 4, next page, illustrates the structures the participants have selected for this venture.

This plan offers certain advantages. First, the facility can become a participating ambulatory surgical center, thereby obtaining Medicare reimbursement for both the technical and professional components of its costs.

Second, the hospital has a certain amount of control over the operation of the facility through the ownership interest that the hospital holding company has in the corporation that operates the surgery center and also through the service agreement to provide management and administrative support. If the hospital holding company is a tax-exempt entity, the dividends received on account of its ownership interest are tax-exempt income to it, except to the extent that it borrowed money to acquire that ownership interest. The hospital holding company can also receive tax-free rents from the ground lease of the real property to the operating company. Provided that the hospital holding company does not wholly own and control the corporation that operates the ambulatory surgical center, there should be no risk to the tax-exempt status of either the hospital holding company or the hospital itself.

Keeping the ownership of the business corporation that operates the facility in the tax-exempt hospital holding company and the physicians will probably avoid

Appendix A

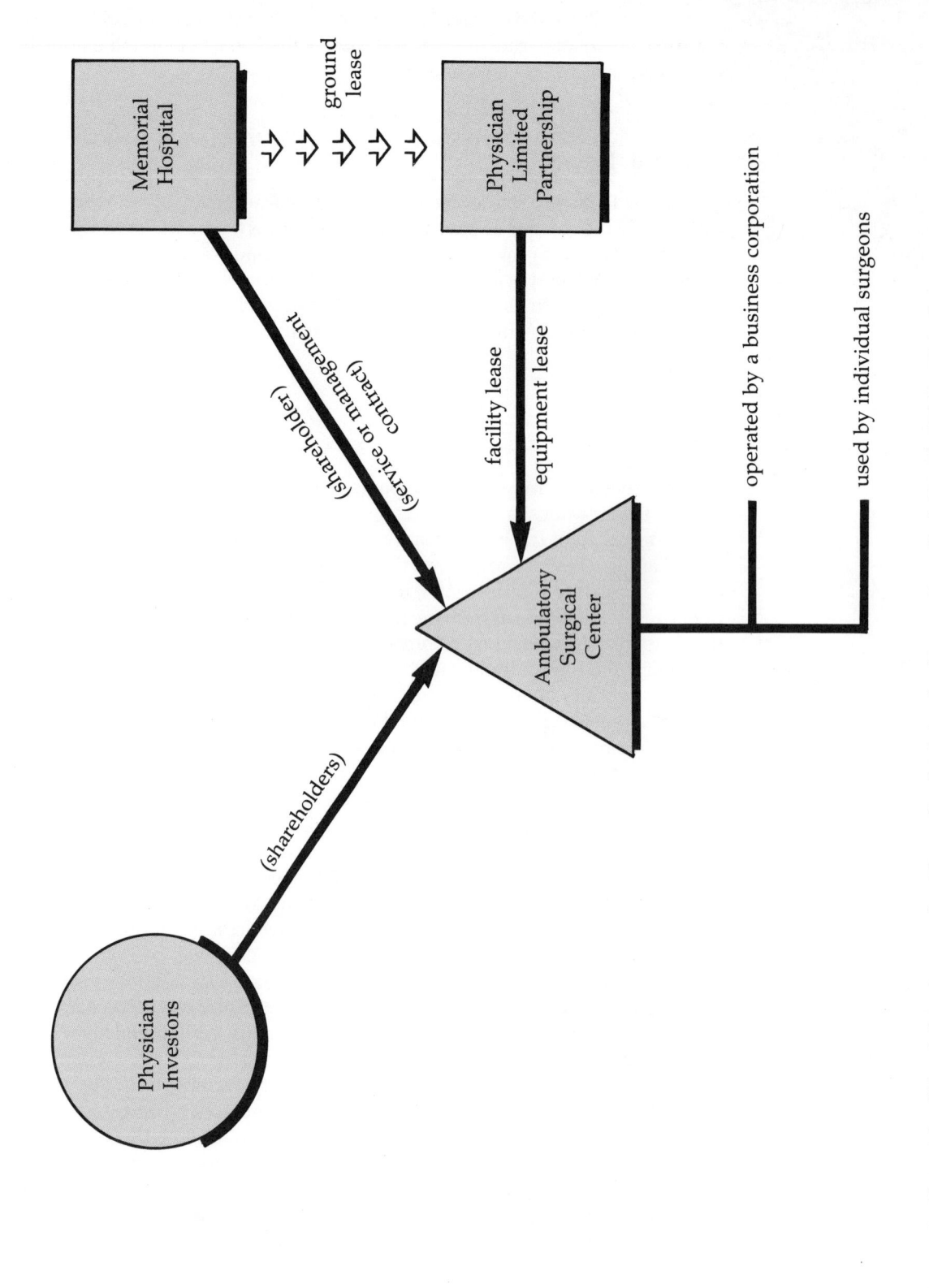

Figure 4. Organizational Structure of a Hypothetical Ambulatory Surgical Center Joint Venture

potential corporate practice problems that may arise in some states. The risk of a corporate practice problem is greater if the entity is owned by a for-profit subsidiary of the hospital and physicians. In a few states, the ambulatory surgical center will have to obtain a separate license and may have to meet certificate of need requirements.

The physician participants also benefit from this arrangement through the limited partnership that acquires the equipment and leases it to the operating corporation. By building the facility and leasing it to the operating company along with necessary medical equipment, the limited partnership can avail itself of certain potential tax benefits, which in turn may be used by the individual physician limited partners to the extent of their investment in the enterprise to offset income from other sources. By leasing real property to the company along with the equipment, the partnership avoids certain limitations on ITC that may otherwise be available. The partnership is also able to enjoy further tax benefits by depreciating the real property.

The participants in the joint venture have structured the entity that will operate the ambulatory surgical center as a business corporation owned by the hospital holding company and physicians instead of a partnership of physicians or a professional service corporation. The participants hope in this manner to avoid the application of the ASG rules that require aggregation of the qualified benefit plans of all of the participants in the joint venture (see earlier discussion on ERISA issues).

Notes

1. *See* Peterson v. Comm'r, 44 T.C.M. 674 (1982). *See also* discussion of noncorporate lessor rules in chapter 4.

2. *See* discussion of the two tax reform proposals before Congress in chapter 4, note 1.

3. *See* I.R.C. §§ 48(a)(4),(5); 168(j). *See also* chapter 4.

4. 42 C.F.R. § 405.231. *See also* chapter 7.

5. *See* 42 C.F.R. § 416.2. Reimbursement for separately stated facility utilization fees can be obtained only if the operating entity is organized as a distinct entity that exclusively operates an ambulatory surgical center. Thus, if a single, existing, fully integrated physician group is to act as the operating entity, the rules relating to reimbursement require this group to be reincorporated as another entity, although with the same members, that would operate the center exclusively. Group activities not related to center operation can continue to be undertaken through the original group entity.

6. 42 C.F.R. §§ 416.42-416.49.

7. 42 C.F.R. § 416.2. *See* further discussion of reimbursement issues in chapter 7.

8. I.R.C. § 414(m); Proposed Treas. Reg. §§ 1.414(m)-1 *et seq.* (1984). *See* discussion of these rules in chapter 5.

9. Proposed Treas. Reg. § 1.414(m)-1(c) (1984).

10. I.R.C. § 414(m)(2).

Appendix B
Magnetic Resonance Imaging Joint Venture

Description of the Venture
Structure Options
Legal Considerations
    Licensing and Certificate of Need
    Tax Concerns
    ERISA Issues
    Labor Law
    Unlicensed Practice of Medicine
    Securities Laws
Outcome

Appendix B
Description of the Venture

This special project joint venture is a hypothetical case study between several health care participants to acquire and use sophisticated and expensive medical equipment, such as a magnetic resonance imaging (MRI) unit or a lithotripter. The participants in this type of venture can vary widely. Several hospitals may acquire the equipment together, or physicians may join them in the transaction. Equipment manufacturers or suppliers may also be participants. A joint venture is, of course, not the only means of acquiring such equipment. A hospital may decide to purchase it on its own, or a group of physicians may do so without entering into a joint venture with the hospital. However, the joint venture form offers various possibilities for this particular type of transaction.

Description of the Venture

The participants in this joint venture are Memorial Hospital, a not-for-profit, tax-exempt corporation; Community Hospital, a not-for-profit, tax-exempt corporation; and staff radiologists from both hospitals. Memorial Hospital and Community Hospital are located in the same city. Because of the need to achieve economies of scale and because of certificate-of-need laws applicable in the state in which they are located, the two entities plan to acquire, on a joint basis, an MRI unit to be installed in a center physically separate from either hospital but convenient to both. Staff radiologists are also participants in the venture in some capacity. The parties plan to lease employees to perform staff functions from a local medical staff leasing agency.

Structure Options

The parties examine the following possible ways of structuring this particular joint venture:

- A not-for-profit corporation or partnership between the hospitals, which would own and operate the MRI center. In this instance, physicians would perform professional services at the center on a contract basis.
- A partnership, with other physicians as limited partners. The partnership would lease the facility from the two hospitals. The hospitals would supply management and other services on a contract basis, as a service bureau entity.
- A new joint venture entity, composed of hospital and physician participants, to own and operate the center.
- Variations of the three basic structure options:
  - The operating partnership or corporation would lease the equipment from a separate physician leasing partnership.
  - The physicians and the hospitals would form a separate joint venture service bureau to provide all equipment, personnel, management, and professional direction to the operating entity.
  - The operating entity acquires limited management and professional services from a separate service bureau.

The hospitals are in favor of the first option, in which they form their own entity, because they would then have control over center operations. Any structure that involves physicians on other than a contract basis means relinquishing part of this control. In the second option, which involves the physicians leasing the facility from the hospital partnership, ultimate control over operations resides with the physician group because the center is operated by a physician partnership. Of course, the hospitals can in the facilities' lease impose certain controls, such as a requirement that the center be available to patients of nonparticipating physicians who are on the staff of either hospital. The third option, in which both hospitals and physicians own a single entity that operates the enterprise, requires that the parties share all the burdens and risks of ownership and jointly control the operation, with such division of control probably to be commensurate with their respective ownership interests.

Legal Considerations

The parties and their legal counsel spotlight certain legal concerns with respect to each of the above three options that must be weighed in selecting the final structure for the venture. Among these are:

- Licensing and certificate of need
- Tax concerns
- ERISA issues
- Labor law
- Unlicensed practice of medicine
- Securities laws

Following is a brief description of these legal issues. A more detailed analysis of these and other issues that can arise in the joint venture context can be found in specific chapters of this book.

Licensing and Certificate of Need

Licensing and other regulatory considerations depend on the law of the particular state in which the center is to be located. Some states require a certificate of need for the acquisition of equipment, such as MRI units, only when a hospital is the party that acquires it. Other states now require certificate-of-need evaluation no matter who is involved (see chapter 6). In those states, having a physician group alone acquire the equipment is not enough to avoid certificate-of-need requirements.

If the hospitals decide to adopt the first option and set up the center through their partnership, then possibly the center can operate under the license of one of the hospitals, depending on how the transaction is structured. Of course, this decision should be reviewed by legal counsel. If the equipment is acquired by a venture entity composed of both the hospitals and physician participants, as in the third option, legal counsel can determine whether the operator of the center must be licensed and whether the new entity created qualifies for such a license. Counsel also has to determine the applicability of certificate-of-need laws.

Tax Concerns

Depending on how this joint venture is structured, the tax-exempt hospitals can risk the loss of their tax-exempt status and the treatment of income from the enterprise as unrelated business income. However, these risks may be minimized. For example, if the exempt hospitals form a partnership to own and operate the facility, they may be able to avoid the unrelated business income tax on income from center operations.

No cases or other interpretive rulings of the Internal Revenue Service (IRS) clearly decide this issue, but generally, private letter rulings have said that even when not-for-profit hospitals are involved with for-profit enterprises in a health-care-related business, the income to the not-for-profit entity is not always taxable.[1] Thus, the hospitals may find it to their advantage to form a partnership that then passes on the tax-free income earned by the center to them. The result may not be the same if the two hospitals form a subsidiary corporation to own and operate the facility. This new entity may not qualify for Section 501(c)(3) status under the tax code but instead could be denied an exemption altogether or could be forced into Section 501(e), which has narrow parameters as to what activities the enterprise is then able to undertake.[2] Before the hospitals enter into such an enterprise, they may consider seeking a private letter ruling to clarify this issue.

Different tax results ensue if the parties choose one of the other two possible options. If a physician entity acquires and operates the equipment, it benefits fully from an investment tax credit (ITC) and other credits and depreciation allowances that may be available, without worrying about tax-exempt property restrictions.[3] Of course, tax reform proposals before Congress in 1986 may limit or even eliminate these tax benefits (see chapter 4). The hospitals' participation through their facilities lease generally does not result in unrelated business income to them. An equipment-leasing partnership of physicians has to comply with tax rules applicable to noncorporate lessors in order to obtain ITC.[4] Alternately, the physician leasing partnership may pass available credits on to the physician operating group.[5]

The creation of a new entity owned by both hospitals and physicians may lead to the income from the hospitals' participation in the venture being treated as income derived from an unrelated trade or business. However, the IRS is generally fairly liberal as long as the new enterprise provides health care to members of the community served by the hospitals. The hospitals may also decide to act as a service bureau for the new entity without adverse tax consequences.[6] If the hospitals' participation does not constitute an unrelated trade or business and if the venture is structured as a partnership or other pass-through entity, the ownership interests of the hospitals may cause a portion of the MRI and other equipment to be deemed *tax-exempt-use property*. This designation results in the loss of a portion of tax credits and possibly extends the period over which such assets may be depreciated.[7]

ERISA Issues

If the venture is structured so that two or more physicians, or existing physician groups, form a new group for purposes of owning and operating the MRI center, affiliated service group (ASG) rules are potentially applicable. If this proves to be the case, employee benefit plans maintained by group members can be disqualified. Consequently, the rules strongly favor operation of the center by an existing practice group. The two groups can undertake an actuarial study, which can lead to developing comparable plans between the two groups and thereby avoid the adverse effects of the ASG rules.

An additional problem is presented if the participants decide to staff the center with employees leased from a medical leasing agency. For purposes of testing the lessee's employee benefit plans for ERISA compliance, ERISA provisions require that leased employees be treated as employees of the lessee if such leased employees have performed services, of a type historically performed by employees, pursuant to an agreement with the lessee, on a substantially full-time basis for a period of at least one year.[8] An exception is made under the tax code for leased employees covered by a pension plan that is maintained by a leasing company and that meets certain requirements of the statute as to amounts of coverage.[9]

Labor Law

This particular venture may also have labor law problems, particularly if any employees of either hospital are covered by a collective bargaining agreement. If the hospitals form a partnership to create and operate the MRI center, a question arises as to whether one or the other of the collective bargaining agreements covering the employees of the hospitals is effective in the new facility. If leased employees are used in the center, other so-called joint-employer issues are raised, depending on how much control the MRI center has over the terms and conditions of employment (see chapter 9).

Unlicensed Practice of Medicine

The choice of structure for the MRI center may also depend on the applicable state law regarding the unlicensed practice of medicine. In most states, either the hospital partnership or the physician group can operate the facility under their respective licenses without encountering restrictions against the practice of medicine by unlicensed persons. However, in some states, such as California, the center has to be operated solely by physicians or solely by the hospitals but probably not by a combination of the two without securing a separate license.[10]

Securities Laws

If the parties choose to acquire the equipment or to operate the MRI center through a limited partnership of physicians, they may have to register the limited partnership interests as securities under either federal or state securities laws, unless an exception, such as a so-called limited-offering exemption, applies. Chapter 3 discusses the impact of securities laws on joint ventures.

Outcome

Because the hospitals wish to retain control over the venture, they decide to form a partnership that establishes a facility and acquires and operates the MRI equipment. Because of tax-exempt-use rules, physician investors decide not to form a leasing partnership to acquire the equipment and lease it to the hospitals. Instead, they form a group practice that supplies professional services to the center under contract with the hospital partnership. Figure 5, next page, illustrates the structure the participants have selected for this venture. Before commencing further with the enterprise, however, the hospitals are considering having their tax counsel seek a private letter ruling from the IRS regarding whether income from center operations would constitute unrelated business income for the participants.

Appendix B

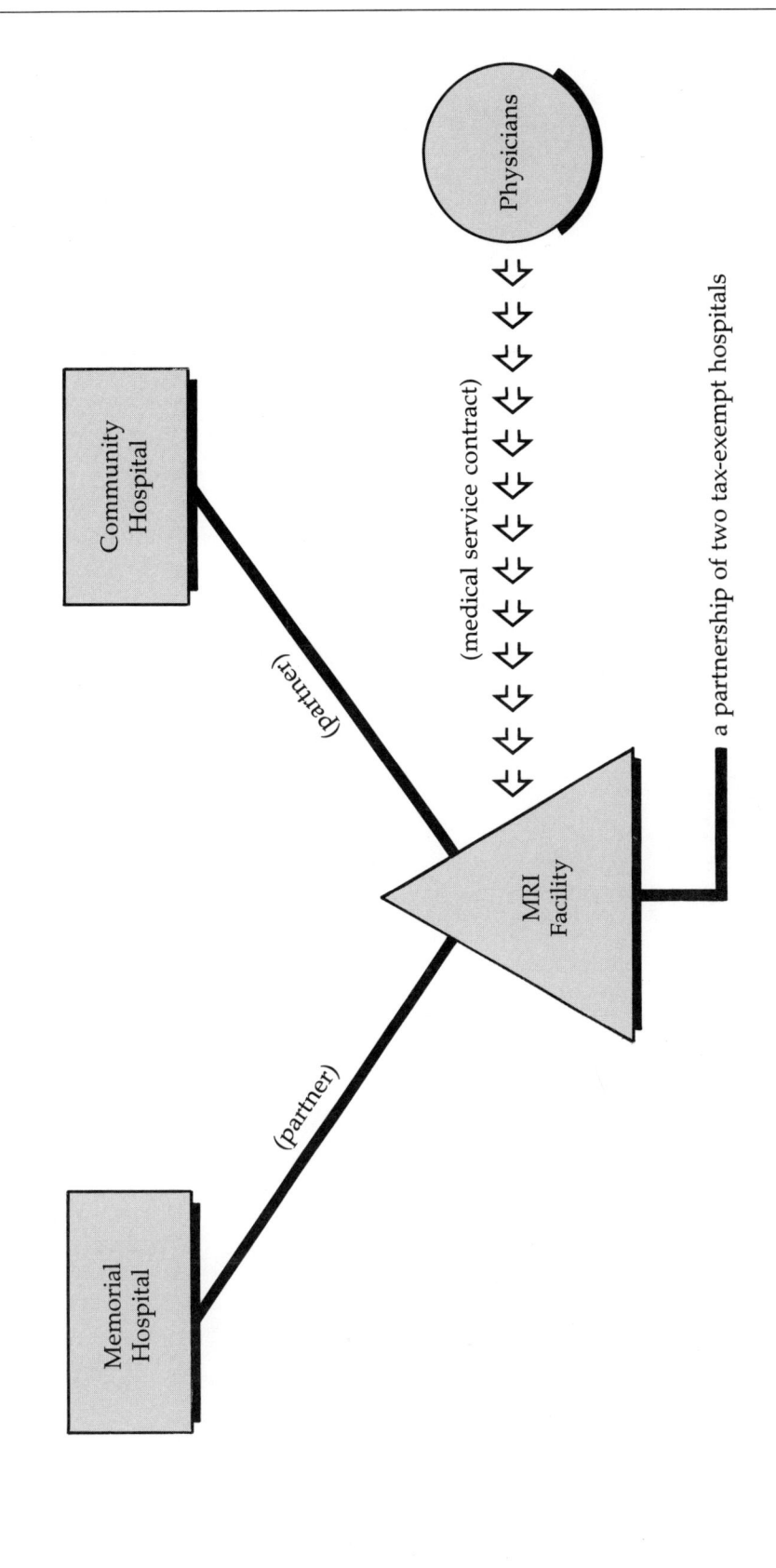

Figure 5. Organizational Structure of a Hypothetical Magnetic Resonance Imaging (MRI) Joint Venture

Notes

1. *See, e.g.,* Private Letter Ruling 8504060 (Oct. 30, 1984).

2. A Section 501(e) corporation is treated as a tax-exempt entity if it performs a limited number of services—such as purchasing, data processing, billing, industrial engineering—solely for two or more tax-exempt hospitals. *See* I.R.C. § 501(e).

3. *See* I.R.C. §§ 48(a)(4),(5); 168(j). *See also* chapter 4.

4. I.R.C. § 46(e)(3). *See* Peterson v. Comm'r, 44 T.C.M. 674 (1982). *See* discussion of tax aspects in Appendix A and of noncorporate lessor rules in chapter 4.

5. I.R.C. § 48(d).

6. *See* Private Letter Ruling 8504060 (Oct. 30, 1984).

7. I.R.C. §§ 48(a)(4), (5), 168(j). *See* discussion of this issue in chapter 4.

8. I.R.C. §§ 414(n)(1), (2).

9. I.R.C. § 414(n)(5). *See* discussion of these issues in chapter 5.

10. *See, e.g.,* CAL. BUS. & PROF. CODE §§ 2400, 2264 (West). *See also* discussion of this issue in chapter 8.

Appendix C
Occupational Medicine Center Joint Venture

Description of the Venture
Structure Options
Legal Considerations
    Franchise Law
    Securities Laws
    ERISA Issues
    Labor Law
Outcome

Appendix C

Description of the Venture

This particular hypothetical joint venture describes a special project joint venture for more than one facility.

Description of the Venture

The participants in this joint venture are:

- Memorial Hospital, a not-for-profit, tax-exempt corporation that is a subsidiary of Medical Facilities Corporation (the parent corporation)
- Medical Facilities Corporation, a not-for-profit corporation and parent of Memorial Hospital and Outpatient Facilities Corporation (Outpatient Corporation)
- Outpatient Facilities Corporation (Outpatient Corporation), a for-profit corporation that is a subsidiary of the parent corporation
- Occupational Medical Supplies, Inc. (Medical Supplier), a for-profit corporation
- Occupational Health Centers Associates (Health Centers Associates), a general partnership of Outpatient Corporation and Medical Supplier
- Local clinics licensed by Health Centers Associates as local occupational medicine centers

Memorial Hospital decides to form a joint venture with Medical Supplier to establish and equip two occupational medicine centers in the region in which the hospital is located. Figure 6, next page, illustrates the proposed structure for this venture. Medical Supplier is an entrepreneurial corporation engaged in the business of equipping occupational medical centers throughout the nation. Because the parties want to quickly develop a presence in a market that is new to both of them, they envision forming some sort of franchise or franchise-type venture with two local clinics that have been providing services similar to those to be offered by the new occupational medicine centers.

Structure Options

The parties are considering a combination of the following possible structures for this venture:

- Corporate reorganization to form a parent corporation to Memorial Hospital and two brother-sister corporations as subsidiaries of the parent corporation: Memorial Hospital, as a not-for-profit corporation, and Outpatient Corporation, as a for-profit corporation. In addition to the parent corporation, outside investors may possibly own an interest in Outpatient Corporation.
- General partnership, Health Centers Associates, to improve the clinic space, acquire equipment, and provide administrative and other services as well as personnel to the two local facilities selected. The managing partner would be Medical Supplier.
- Franchise or licensing-royalty arrangement with certain local facilities to be equipped as local occupational medicine centers.

Legal Considerations

The parties consult their legal counsel, who advises them about various legal considerations that may affect decisions with respect to the structuring, operation, and

Appendix C

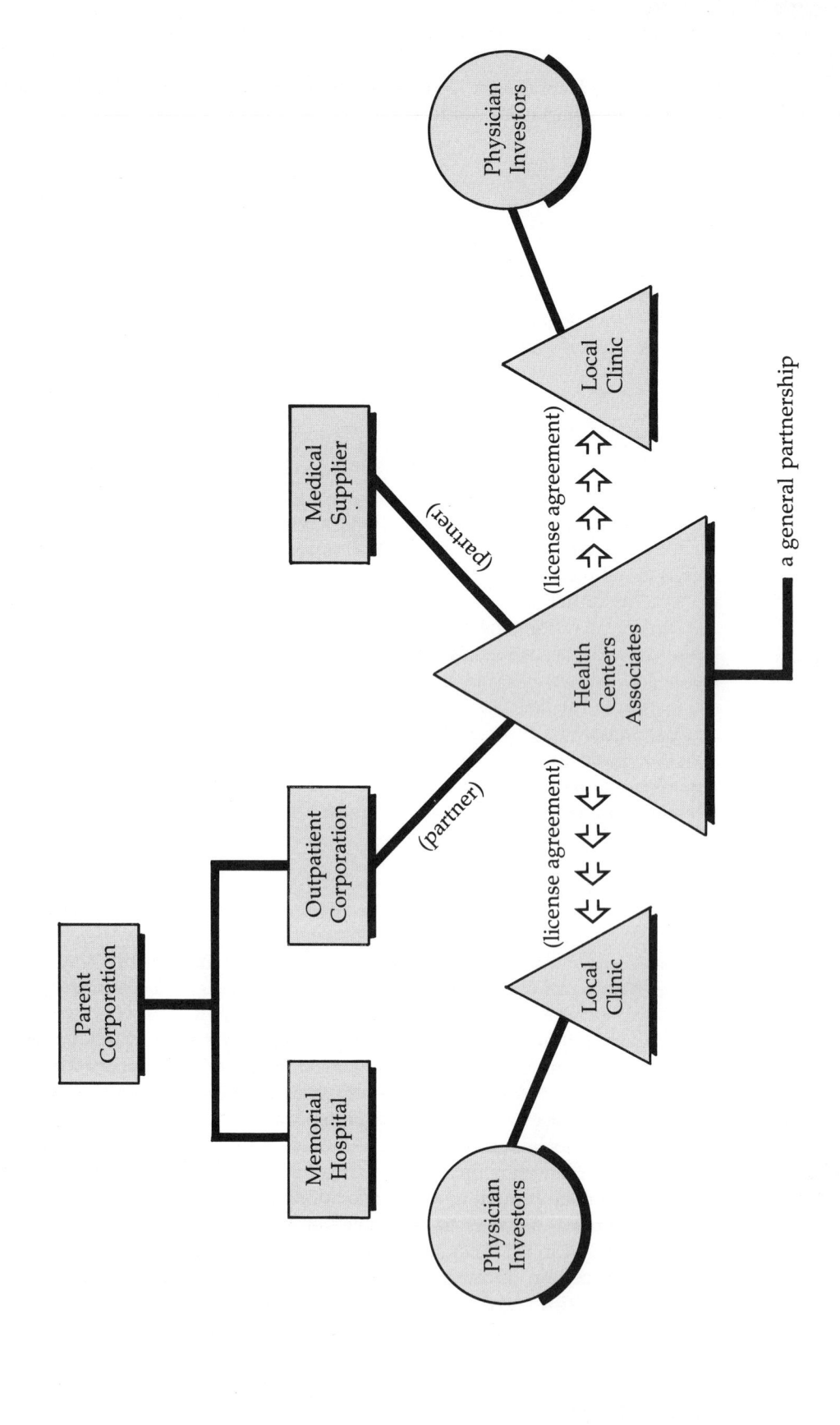

Figure 6. Organizational Structure of a Hypothetical Occupational Medicine Center Joint Venture

staffing of the local clinics. Counsel suggests that the following legal considerations can affect this particular venture:

- Franchise law
- Securities laws
- ERISA issues
- Labor law

Following is a brief description of these legal issues. A more detailed analysis of these considerations and other legal problems affecting the joint venture can be found in specific chapters of this book.

Franchise Law

Franchises are subject to extensive regulation by many states as well as by the Federal Trade Commission.[1] Franchisors must register their arrangements as well as provide extensive disclosure forms to prospective franchisees. To avoid the burden of the franchise laws, the relationship between Health Centers Associates and the local occupational medicine centers might better be structured through licensing-royalty agreements rather than actual franchises. However, the parties must be careful in structuring such licensing-royalty arrangements because even an agreement labeled otherwise may be treated as a franchise if it contains key elements defined in the statutes: a uniform plan of business, a prescribed marketing plan, and substantial association of the licensee's business with the licensor's logo or trademark. To avoid being designated a franchise, the licensing agreements should not contain any semblance of these key elements. Furthermore, the parties should be wary in their business dealings with each other not to give the appearance of a franchisor-franchisee relationship (see chapter 3).

Securities Laws

Many joint ventures may be subject to state or federal securities laws if they involve the formation of a for-profit corporation or a limited partnership. Any interest sold or offered that can be called a security under the law must be registered, unless an exception, such as a limited-offering exemption, applies (see chapter 3).

A question that arises with respect to the structure of the occupational medicine center joint venture is whether an interest in the general partnership, Health Centers Associates, might be considered a security under federal or state securities laws and consequently subject to registration and regulation as such. This issue does not arise if the sole partners in Health Centers Associates are Outpatient Corporation and Medical Supplier. However, Memorial Hospital may want to invite certain staff physicians, who will be providing services in the new local centers, into the partnership. If these additional partners have no decision-making power in the partnership and are not involved in the operation of the business, their interest may be considered a security in certain instances. This determination depends on their own level of sophistication with respect to business investments and their rights under the partnership agreement (see chapter 3).

ERISA Issues

The formation of this joint venture can trigger an application of the complex tax rules that relate to affiliated service groups (ASGs). Depending on the role that Health

Centers Associates plays in the venture vis-a-vis the local centers, its partners may be affiliated with the two local centers for purposes of qualification of their pension plans (see chapter 5).

Labor Law

How the parties structure their relationship with the two local centers may also raise labor issues (see chapter 9). Staffing problems can arise if the services to be offered by the local centers under the terms of their agreements with Health Centers Associates are similar to services previously offered by these facilities. By the terms of their agreements with the partnership, the existing local centers may need to modify their labor contracts with existing employees or hire new staff members. The existing facilities may have to be restructured as new businesses to become the type of entity required by the licensing agreement. In such an instance, the "new" local center may face limitations on the extent to which it can ignore existing agreements with staff members.

Outcome

After considering all the issues involved, the parties decide to carry out their original plan with some modifications. Memorial Hospital begins its corporate reorganization. The new for-profit company, Outpatient Corporation, enters into the general partnership with Medical Supplier. Physician staff members are not invited to join this general partnership because of potential problems with securities laws. However, the assets of the two local centers to be licensed by the general partnership are to be sold to a limited partnership in which some of these interested physicians are invited to participate. Because the number of these investors remains small, the parties expect to obtain an exemption from securities registration. Once the local centers are acquired, they enter into licensing agreements with Health Centers Associates to begin operations as occupational medicine centers.

Note

1. *See* 15 U.S.C. §§ 41 *et seq.*

Appendix D
Alternative Delivery System Joint Venture

Description of the Venture
Structure Options
Legal Considerations
    Conversion to For-Profit Status
    Antitrust Considerations
    Labor Law
    Other Corporate Law Issues
Outcome

Appendix D
Description of the Venture

This hypothetical situation explores the second basic type of joint venture: the alternative delivery and financing system joint venture.

Description of the Venture

The participants in this joint venture are:

- Health Care Foundation, a not-for-profit health maintenance organization (HMO) to be converted to for-profit status
- Health Care Physicians Associates (Associates), a not-for-profit physician practice group
- Memorial Hospital, a not-for-profit, tax-exempt hospital
- Community Hospital, a not-for-profit, tax-exempt hospital
- Health Care Services, Inc. (Parent Corporation), a for-profit corporation that is the parent of HMO and Health Care Providers, a preferred provider organization
- Health Care Providers, a preferred provider organization (PPO)
- John Smith, owner of Data Services Company (a sole proprietorship)
- Health Care Data Services, Inc. (HCDS), a for-profit corporation, owned jointly by Parent Corporation and John Smith

The HMO was formed as a not-for-profit corporation several years ago by two unrelated hospitals (who are not participants in this joint venture except through the HMO) and the physician practice group, Associates. At present, the HMO is operating at a deficit and is searching for additional capital and exploring several potential sources. First, it is considering forming a limited partnership and selling interests to outside investors. Second, it has been approached by several venture capitalists and is considering some sort of transaction in that market. Third, it has received an offer from two hospitals in nearby cities, Memorial Hospital and Community Hospital, who want to buy into the enterprise. Finally, it is considering a public stock offering.

Structure Options

The following actions are being considered by the HMO:

- Memorial and Community hospitals have proposed a joint venture with the HMO in which they would acquire some partial ownership interest in the HMO as well as participate in its governance and share in the revenue. On the one hand, the HMO wants the best price for its stock and hopes to give up as little control as possible. On the other hand, the opportunity to enter into a venture with Memorial and Community hospitals is appealing because the HMO would then be able to move rapidly into new markets, namely, the service areas of the two hospitals, something that the HMO has been wanting to do for some time. The two hospitals are respected comprehensive hospitals, and an association with them would bolster the credibility of the HMO as it seeks increased enrollment. All in all, the HMO is willing to give up some of its stock in order to obtain that opportunity.
- Before the HMO enters into any agreements with outside parties, it is considering a corporate reorganization to create the for-profit Parent Corporation. First, although the HMO has been losing money over the past few years since

its formation, this next year it will likely operate at a profit. Any arrangement into which it enters now would be facilitated if it were a for-profit enterprise instead of a not-for-profit entity. It is therefore seriously thinking of converting to for-profit status at the time of this reorganization. Parent Corporation, rather than the HMO, would participate in the venture with the hospitals to form a preferred provider organization, the PPO. In the course of the reorganization, Associates, the physician practice group, would also become a for-profit entity.

- As a long-range project, the HMO is also reviewing its management structure and has determined that it does not have a good data system. With the new venture for the PPO in the offing, the HMO is exploring ways of improving its data base. A small local company, Data Services Company, owned and managed by John Smith, has been operating as a service bureau for several HMOs in the region. Smith is a brilliant young manager who was formerly with a major insurance company. Representatives from management of the HMO have approached Smith with a proposal that together they set up a company to be owned partially by Parent Corporation and by either John Smith as an individual or by Data Services Company. This new company, HCDS, would provide services for Parent Corporation, the HMO, and the PPO, the new preferred provider joint venture, as well as for other interested clients. As an enticement to persuade Smith to enter into the joint venture, the HMO would also provide capital to Smith's company, Data Services Company.

The parties are concerned about several potential problems that have arisen in the course of their negotiations. First, they want to work out an agreement whereby Smith does not offer certain competing services through Data Services Company that are to be offered by HCDS. They also want to agree as to which potential clients in the region are in the "territory" of Data Services Company and which will "belong" to HCDS. Second, the HMO would like Smith to agree not to compete with HCDS in seeking new markets. Finally, the parties are trying to set parameters on the freedom of the HMO and Smith or Data Services Company to participate in joint ventures with other parties for projects similar to the proposed data service venture.

Legal Considerations

This joint venture proposal is complex and, unlike many special-project joint ventures, is envisioned to take place in stages over a relatively longer period than most special-project joint ventures. In addition to the health care regulations and tax laws that can have an impact on any joint venture in this area, legal counsel for the participants raises several specific legal issues that may affect this particular venture. These issues are:

- Conversion to for-profit status
- Antitrust considerations
- Labor law
- Other corporate law issues

Following is a brief description of these potential problems. A more detailed analysis of these considerations and other legal problems affecting the joint venture can be found in specific chapters of this book.

Conversion to For-Profit Status

One major problem that may frustrate the HMO's intention to convert to for-profit status is the so-called charitable-trust doctrine applicable in many states (see chapter 3). Under this doctrine, a corporation that designates itself as a not-for-profit corporation for charitable purposes is deemed to hold its assets in trust for the furtherance of those purposes. Before granting permission to such a corporation to convert its status to that of a for-profit enterprise, many states require that the entity donate the value of those assets held in trust to charitable purposes. The exact value of those assets can be the subject of extensive negotiations with state authorities.

In this case study, the HMO is legitimately worried that if it negotiates with Memorial Hospital and Community Hospital with respect to a purchase by the hospitals of a portion of the stock of the HMO, the value that the parties place on the stock, which the HMO would naturally want to be high, would be the value attached to it by the attorney general of the particular state in which the venture is to be located for charitable trust purposes when it proceeds with the conversion. Consequently, the HMO hopes to convert before conducting serious negotiations with the two hospitals. On the other hand, if the HMO waits too long, the hospitals may explore other markets, and the HMO will miss the opportunity of a potentially lucrative enterprise.

Antitrust Considerations

Because of the involvement of a number of parties that would otherwise be competitors, this joint venture raises serious antitrust problems that the parties must take into account in structuring their enterprise. Antitrust statutes prohibit conspiracies in restraint of trade. The statutes also prevent mergers and other combinations that would have the effect of lessening competition. Several of the proposals suggested in this hypothetical example invite scrutiny, including the arrangement between the HMO and Memorial and Community hospitals to buy into the HMO, the proposed joint venture to form the PPO, and the various agreements being considered between HCDS, the new data service company, and John Smith.

The agreement in which the hospitals acquire some interest in the HMO will pass muster under antitrust law unless the result of the arrangement is to significantly reduce competition in the area. The pros and cons of the situation must be balanced against each other. One primary consideration is whether the hospitals would have formed a new HMO in the area to compete with the HMO if they were not involved in the proposed arrangement.

A similar balancing approach is used with respect to the new PPO to be formed. The major worry with any PPO is that it be neither too inclusive nor too exclusive. Apparently, a PPO that does not permit its members to enter into similar provider arrangements is given closer scrutiny than one that permits free association by its members.

By itself, the formation of the data service company should present no antitrust problem, unless the new venture has no legitimate business purpose other than to prevent John Smith from offering his services to competing HMOs. However, the various arrangements that the parties are considering may raise legal questions. For instance, an allocation of the market for data services between Smith and a competing company may lead to an antitrust suit from other competitors. Such an allocation by HCDS, as an integrated company, of its clients and the clients of a sister or parent corporation would not be an antitrust violation. Under recent case law any such *ancillary* allocation would probably pass muster if scrutinized for violations of antitrust law,[1] but the parties do not want to take any risks in this area. An agreement between Smith, as the owner of his separate company, and HCDS not to compete in the market may still be a violation of antitrust laws. This situation is an example of a case in which a legitimate business restraint within the joint venture spilled over into the participants' separate business relationships as competitors (see chapter 10).

Labor Law

Whenever entities with collective bargaining agreements with their own employees enter into arrangements with hospitals or with other parties with similar agreements, some question of accretion arises, that is, whether these agreements are applicable to the new company and to what extent. In this hypothetical joint venture, problems with respect to the formation of the data service joint venture depend on whether:

- The HMO closes down its own data service department when it enters into the venture.
- The new entity is staffed primarily by the HMO's employees or employees of Smith.
- Some of the employees of the new enterprise divide their time between the new company and their former employer.
- Leased employees are used.

For a detailed discussion of possible labor law problems, see chapter 9.

Other Corporate Law Issues

Several federal and state legal principles need to be considered in this type of joint venture. Various laws and regulations relating to federally qualified HMOs may be applicable both to the investment of the two hospitals into the HMO and the establishment of the joint venture PPO. For instance, a regulation requires that a consumer representative sit on the board of a federally qualified HMO. Additional requirements prohibit a federally qualified HMO from also operating a PPO. The proposed transactions have to be structured to account for these and other applicable requirements.[2]

Outcome

After meeting with counsel to resolve potential legal problems, the parties decide to undertake the transaction in the following way (figure 7, next page):

- The HMO is reorganized as a for-profit organization. Thus, the HMO becomes a subsidiary owned by the newly formed for-profit corporation, Parent Corporation, and, eventually, by other outside investors. Memorial and Community hospitals and the HMO enter into an option contract under which the hospitals acquire an interest in Parent Corporation that is less than 50 percent. By acquiring shares of Parent Corporation, instead of the HMO, the hospitals will have some control over the PPO to be formed. By transferring an ownership interest in Parent Corporation to the hospitals, the parties also hope to avoid the impact of a low valuation of stock in the HMO by the state attorney general. On the other hand, this valuation is still important for purposes of the reorganization. Stock in the HMO is valued, by the terms of the option agreement, at whatever value is set for it by the state for charitable-trust purposes. The balance of the investment by the hospitals is made in the form of subordinated debt, which may later be forgiven or converted to preferred stock.

Appendix D

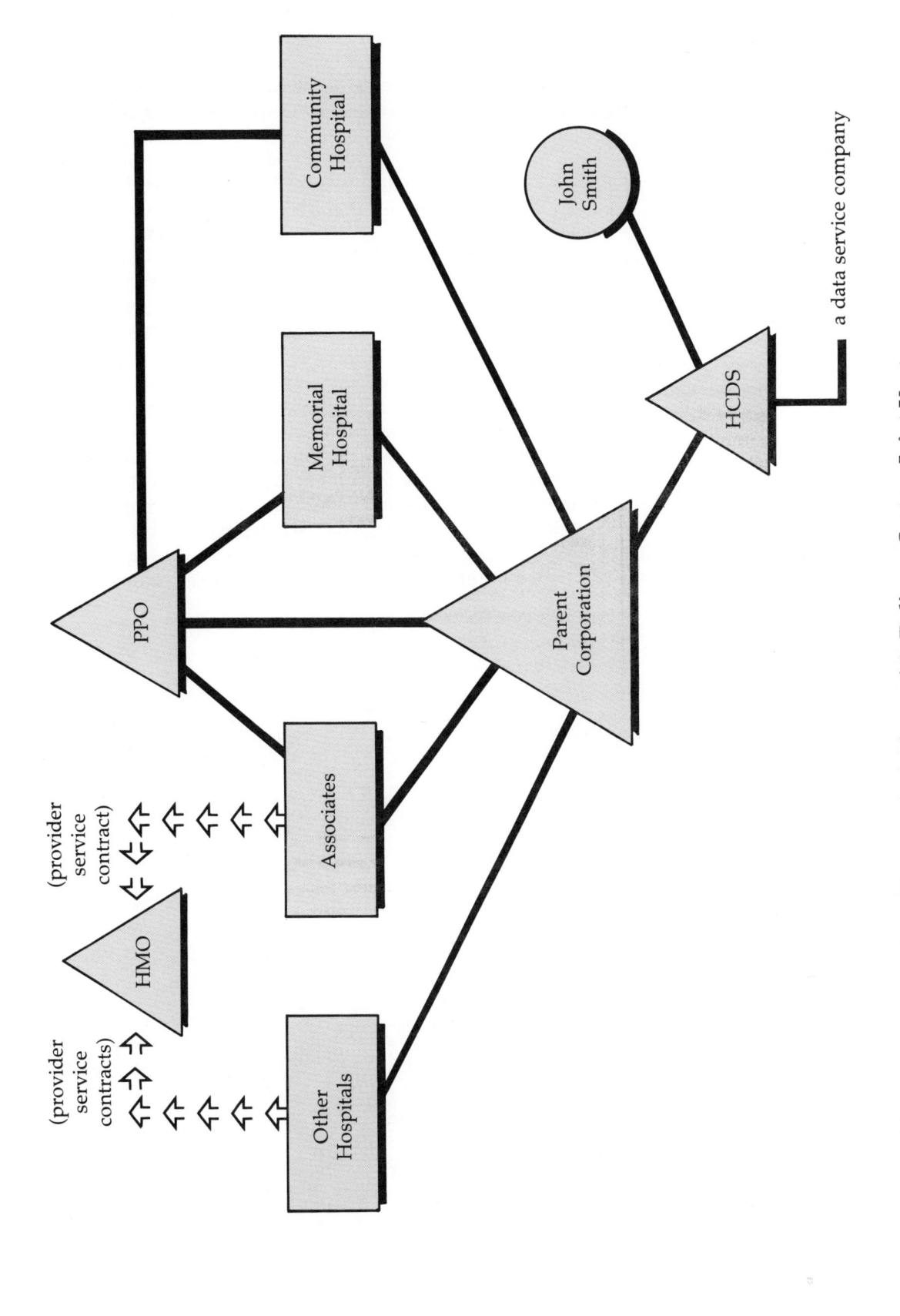

Figure 7. Organizational Structure of a Hypothetical Alternative Delivery System Joint Venture

- As part of its agreement with Memorial and Community hospitals, Parent Corporation also forms a joint venture PPO with them and with Associates, the physician practice group. By entering into the joint venture with Parent Corporation, instead of with the HMO, the parties avoid the federal requirements that a consumer representative be placed on the governing board. The consumer representative sits only on the HMO's board, as is required, and is not involved in the joint venture transactions with the HMO's parent. By working with the parent, the parties likewise avoid the federal prohibition against a federally qualified HMO operating a PPO.[3]
- John Smith, as an individual, and Parent Corporation also enter into a joint venture to form the data-base service bureau, HCDS. The capital for start-up costs and the initial expenses of the new company are provided by Parent Corporation. Smith's major contribution to the enterprise is in the form of services. To prevent antitrust implications, HCDS limits itself to providing data services to HMOs and similar health care providers. Smith's company, Data Services Company, continues to provide data services to HMOs that have been its clients but will expand into other areas. To prevent conflict-of-interest problems, the parties agree that, although Smith has considerable control over operations and systems management within HCDS, marketing and business development are to be the primary responsibility of an independent manager to be selected by the HMO and over whom Smith has no control.

Notes

1. *See* Polk Bros., Inc. v. Forest City Enterprises, Inc., 776 F.2d 185 (7th Cir. 1985).
2. *See, generally,* 42 U.S.C. §§ 300e *et seq.*; 42 C.F.R. §§ 110.111 *et seq.*
3. *Id.*

Appendix E: Phased Joint Venture for a Reference Laboratory

Description of the Venture
Evolution of the Venture Structure
    First Evolution: Internal Reorganization
    Second Evolution: Spin Off
    Third Evolution: Regional Enterprise
    Final Evolution: Network of Laboratories
Legal Considerations
    Tax Concerns
    Labor Law
    Referral Issues
    Franchise Law
Outcome

Appendix E

Description of the Venture

Some joint ventures evolve over time as needs change and new opportunities present themselves. The following phased joint venture for a reference laboratory is an example of the evolution of a joint venture enterprise in the face of the need to adopt new structures to meet changing situations and new developments.

Description of the Venture

The participants in this joint venture are:

- Memorial Hospital, a not-for-profit, tax-exempt hospital
- Health Care Services, Inc. (Parent Corporation), a not-for-profit corporation that is the parent of Memorial Hospital, Outpatient Services Corporation (Outpatient Services), and Corp. Ventures, Inc. (Ventures)
- Outpatient Services Corporation (Outpatient Services), a not-for-profit, tax-exempt corporation that is a subsidiary of Parent Corporation
- Corp. Ventures, Inc. (Ventures), a for-profit corporation that is a subsidiary of Parent Corporation and a parent of Joint Venture Reference Lab (Reference Lab)
- Joint Venture Reference Lab (Reference Lab), a for-profit corporation that is a subsidiary of Ventures
- Hospital staff physicians
- Local laboratories, which are licensed by Reference Lab
- National Health Care Ventures, Inc. (National), a national for-profit corporation that was organized for the purpose of investing in promising health care entities
- Central Reference Laboratory, Inc. (Central Lab), a for-profit corporation

Several years ago, Memorial Hospital had a reference laboratory that was part of its department of pathology, and it had a contract with a group of pathologists who provided clinical direction. All employees, space, equipment, and supplies were owned and controlled by the hospital, which billed its "customers," the referring physicians, directly for services rendered. This situation was unsatisfactory in several respects. First, other commercial laboratories were offering prices lower than the prices Memorial Hospital could offer. Second, the hospital believed that its reference laboratory services were too hospital and inpatient oriented and that it was missing new opportunities in the reference laboratory market. Because laboratory employees were members of the hospital staff, they were paid regular hospital wage rates and were subject to the same policies and procedures as other hospital employees. This situation put the hospital laboratory at a competitive disadvantage. With the advent of the Medicare prospective pricing system (PPS), the situation became more serious.

Evolution of the Venture Structure

First Evolution: Internal Reorganization

To resolve these problems, Memorial Hospital first underwent a corporate reorganization (figure 8, next page). This move permitted it to expand its revenue sources by capturing more reference laboratory business while retaining the tax-exempt status of the laboratory and avoiding certificate of need and rate review. Hence, Health Care Services, Inc. (Parent Corporation) was formed. The not-for-profit Parent

Appendix E

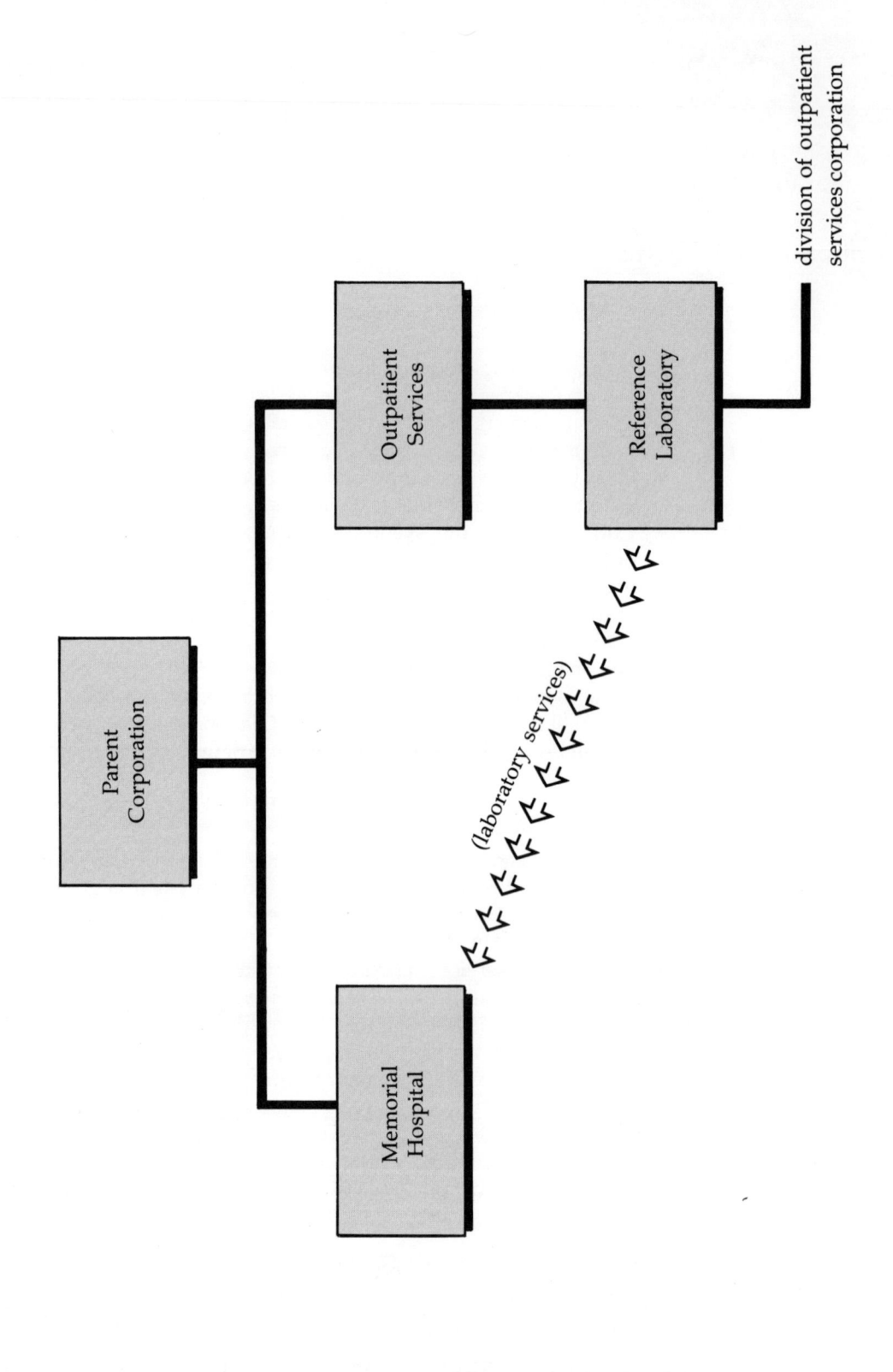

Figure 8. Organizational Structure for a Hypothetical Phased Joint Venture for a Reference Laboratory: First Evolution

- Parent Corporation
  - Memorial Hospital
  - Outpatient Services
    - Reference Laboratory (division of outpatient services corporation)

(laboratory services)

Corporation had Memorial Hospital and Outpatient Services Corporation (Outpatient Services), a tax-exempt entity, as its wholly owned subsidiaries. The reference laboratory became a division of Outpatient Services and was physically separated from licensed hospital activities. Major laboratory equipment was transferred to the reference laboratory. Although staff pathologists were under contract with Outpatient Services for clinical direction of the laboratory, all employees, space, equipment and supplies were either owned or leased by Outpatient Services. The reference laboratory obtained a separate license as a pathology laboratory. However, it still provided a high volume of services to the hospital.

As a result of the reorganization, the laboratory gained a potentially enhanced ability to be price competitive with the commercial laboratories in the region. It was able to maintain an image distinct from that of the hospital, and this new image enhanced its marketing ability with physicians and other hospitals. Its space, its personnel policies, and its hours of coverage allowed it to compete effectively with the commercial laboratories. Moreover, the space in the hospital that had been used for the pathology laboratory was now available for other patient services.

Second Evolution: Spin Off

In the course of time, other problems arose. The reference laboratory proved to be a profitable enterprise. In fact, it was so profitable that Outpatient Services' tax exemption was endangered. Moreover, physicians were anxious to participate in the equity of the enterprise. Other hospitals in the region were not using the facility as much as they could, and Outpatient Services assumed that these other hospitals could be enticed to use the laboratory more if they received an equity participation in it. Generally, the enterprise wanted to expand its market.

Consequently, Parent Corporation decided to spin off the reference laboratory from Outpatient Services to permit Outpatient Services to maintain its tax-exempt status (figure 9, next page). A separate, for-profit entity, Corp. Ventures, Inc. (Ventures), was formed as a subsidiary of Parent Corporation. In turn, Ventures formed a subsidiary corporation, Joint Venture Reference Lab (Reference Lab), which was the reference laboratory. A majority of the stock in Reference Lab was owned by Ventures. The balance was owned by hospital pathologists, customer hospitals, and local physicians. The reference laboratory employees were transferred to Reference Lab, which contracted with the pathologists for clinical services. Equipment and space were owned by a partnership of physicians and leased to Reference Lab, which continued to furnish laboratory services to the hospital.

Third Evolution: Regional Enterprise

As the laboratory became better known, it was approached by pathologists and hospitals in other areas who were interested in acquiring the expertise of the Reference Lab system but wished to retain local autonomy. They conceived of a scheme of licensing a series of local laboratories in other areas.

Everyone agreed that Reference Lab would furnish the new laboratories with start-up operational direction and access to capital markets. The new laboratories were also entitled to use Reference Lab's logo, which was well known in the medical community. The individual laboratories were to be owned by Reference Lab as well as by local investors composed of local hospitals and physician groups. By means of this device of licensing local laboratories, Reference Lab was able to avoid selling stock in Reference Lab itself.

Appendix E

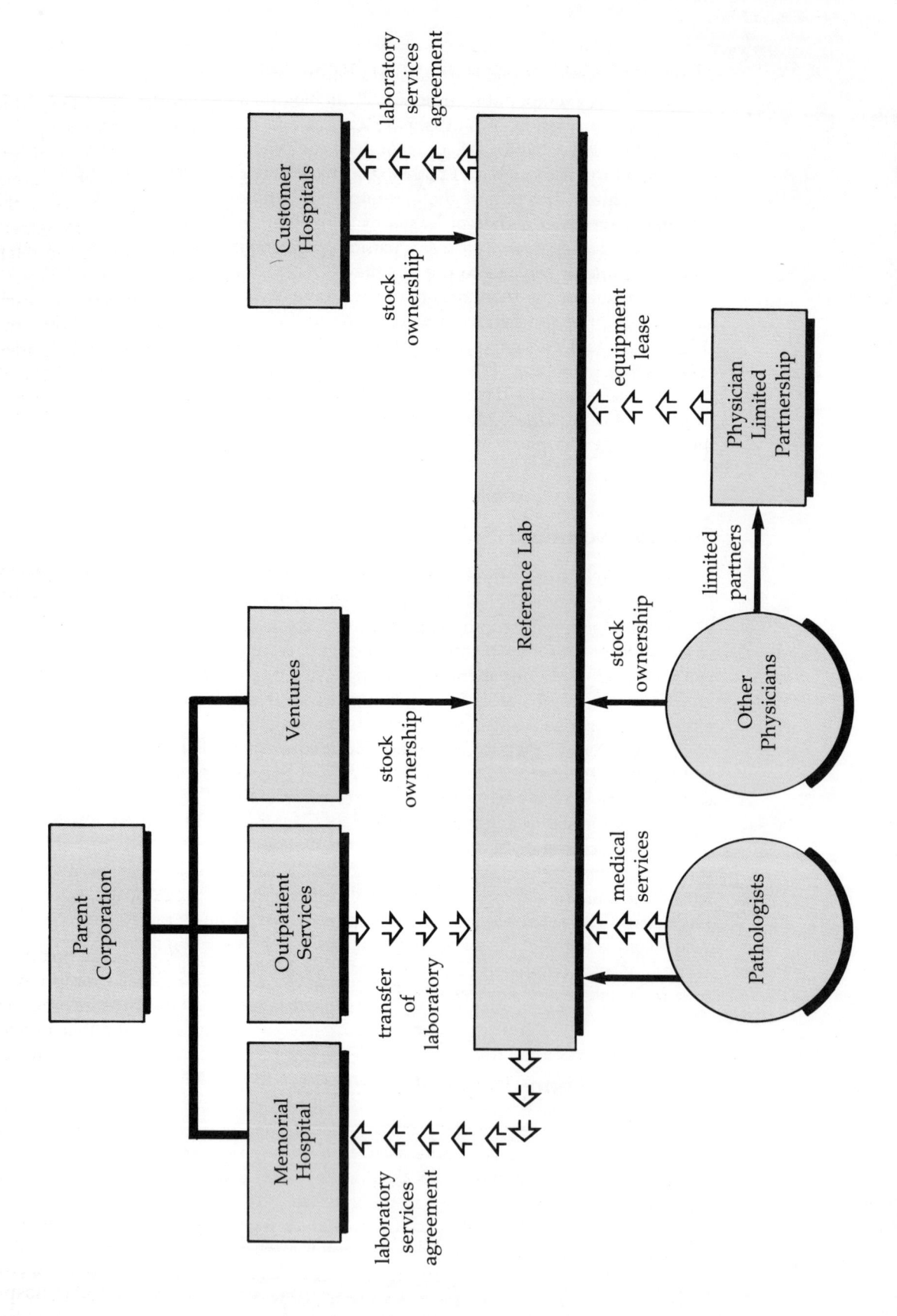

Figure 9. Organizational Structure for a Hypothetical Phased Joint Venture for a Reference Laboratory: Second Evolution

Final Evolution: Network of Laboratories

As the reference laboratory business grew, the joint venture participants decided to expand their program on a large regional or even national basis (figure 10, next page). To secure the substantial capital resources required for such an ambitious goal, the company decided to participate in a joint venture with a national company, National Health Care Venturers, Inc. (National), or to go public, or both. National offered the potential of sound management expertise and other resources needed to implement and operate the network strategy. This particular venture would permit the reference laboratories to achieve economies of scale by pooling high volume and esoteric laboratory services on a centralized and regional basis; to link local outlets, for example, drawing stations and local laboratories, to a regional and central network; and to use existing transportation systems. The company especially hoped that by undertaking this venture and giving up equity in the new national enterprise to National, it would secure substantial economic recognition of Reference Lab's research and development expertise and good will.

Legal Considerations

The evolution of the enterprise in this hypothetical example occurred to some extent as a response to the various concerns raised by legal counsel. Some of the issues that the parties had to consider are:

- Tax concerns
- Labor law
- Referral issues
- Franchise law

Following is a brief description of these problems. A more detailed analysis of these considerations and other legal problems affecting this joint venture can be found in specific chapters of this book.

Tax Concerns

One of the principal reasons for spinning off the reference laboratory in the first place is the potential risk that the laboratory subsidiary would lose its tax exemption or that income from the enterprise would be treated as unrelated business income (see chapter 4). As the laboratory served a larger percentage of the general public in relation to hospital patients, the hospital chose to separate itself not only physically but also legally from this enterprise to avoid any risk to its own tax exemption. As other investors became involved in the enterprise, other tax questions, such as the availability of tax benefits, also became important.

Labor Law

One key issue that became important as the reference laboratory gradually distanced itself from hospital operations was whether employees of the new reference laboratory remained subject to the collective bargaining agreements governing other hospital employees (see chapter 9). When the reference laboratory first separated from the hospital, a question arose as to whether the hospital would be entitled to close down its in-house pathology department and dismiss employees staffing it while opening

Appendix E

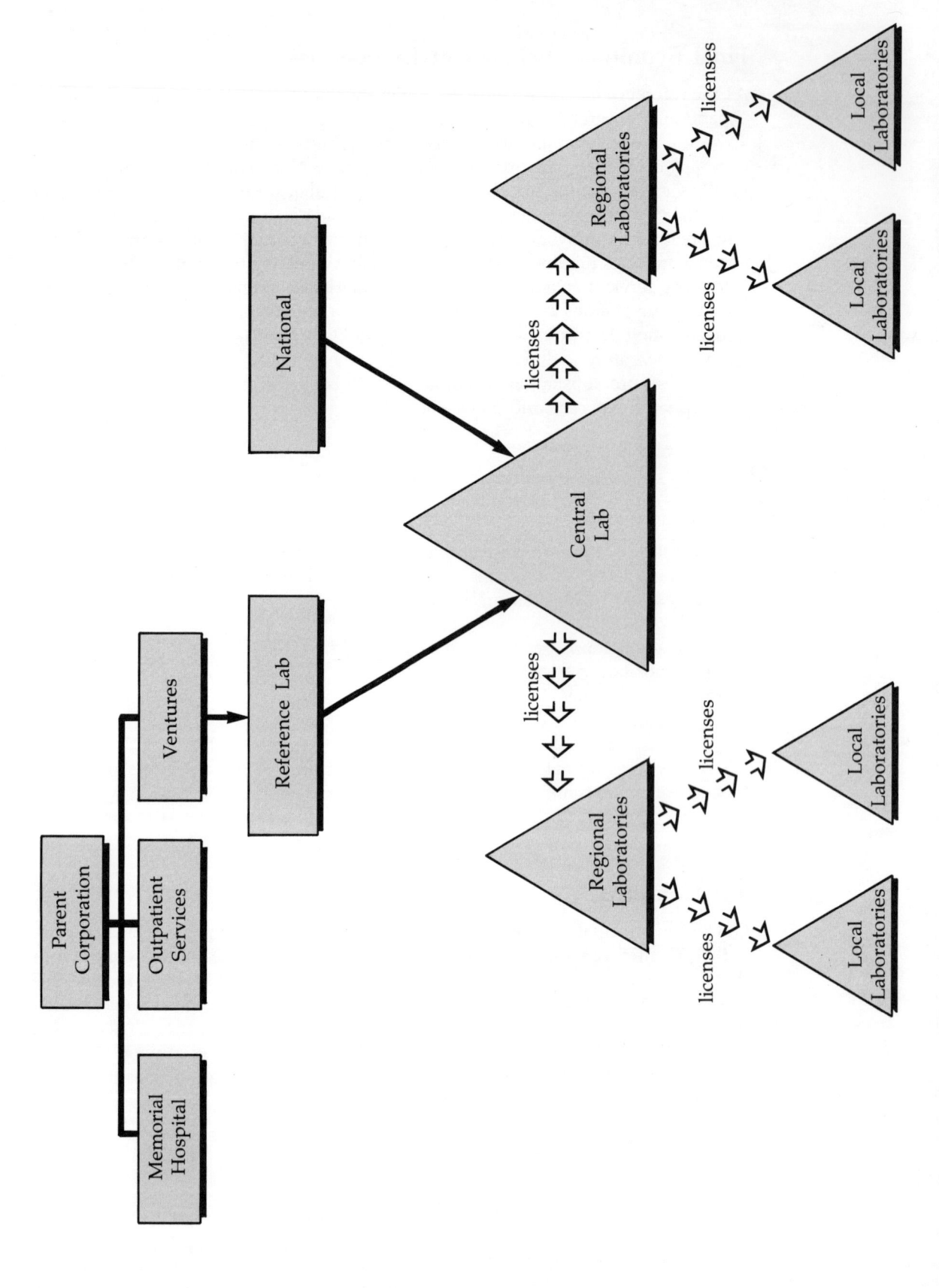

Figure 10. Organizational Structure for a Hypothetical Phased Joint Venture for a Reference Laboratory: Final Evolution

a reference laboratory in an outpatient setting. Depending on what agreements governed the hospital employees, this act might be viewed as employment discrimination or some other violation of labor laws. To avoid the problem, the parties chose initially to continue the employment of those laboratory staff members who wished to remain. Eventually they were absorbed by a leasing agency, which then staffed the facility.

Referral Issues

As the venture evolved and physician investors became involved, another legal issue became important: the problem of referrals to the laboratory by physician-owners (see chapter 8). In structuring compensation schemes for these physicians, the parties, on the advice of legal counsel, were careful not to base any sharing of profits from the enterprise on the percentage of patients referred to it by any particular owner. To have done otherwise could have violated the so-called antifraud and abuse statutes applicable to Medicare and Medicaid participants as well as various state disclosure laws and the restraints of the American Medical Association.

Franchise Law

As the venture evolved from a single reference laboratory to a regionally based entity, the potential application of franchise law to the venture became an issue (see chapter 3). If the agreement between the parties falls within the definition of a franchise, it is subject to state and federal disclosure laws. For this reason, the parties structured the arrangement as a licensing-royalty agreement and carefully avoided those characteristics, such as a centralized marketing plan, that would bring it within the scope of franchise law.

Outcome

Two corporations, Reference Lab and National, form a new laboratory network, Central Reference Laboratory, Inc. (Central), which is a for-profit corporation consisting of a centralized laboratory, clusters of regional laboratories, and local laboratories operating under separate licensing-royalty agreements. Reference Lab will transfer all or part of its resources and programs to Central in exchange for substantial stock. The remainder of the stock in Central is held by National and other investors to be obtained through a public offering that will generate additional capital required for the venture. Different functions are to be assigned centrally, regionally, and locally and are linked into existing transportation systems.

Appendix

F Medical Pavilion Joint Venture

Description of the Venture
Structure Options
Legal Considerations
    Licensing and Certificate of Need
    Reimbursement
    Ethical Concerns and Corporate Practice Issues
    ERISA Issues
    Antitrust Considerations
Outcome

Appendix F

Description of the Venture

This hypothetical venture illustrates the various opportunities for joint ventures in a changing health care environment.

Description of the Venture

The participants in this joint venture are Medical Building Associates (Associates), a general partnership, and Memorial Hospital, a not-for-profit, tax-exempt hospital. The general partner, Associates, is an unrelated real estate developer that specializes in exploring real estate opportunities in the health care market and managing such real estate projects. Associates has proposed to Memorial Hospital that together they enter into a joint venture to create a health care center that will offer a wide range of medical services in one of the new downtown office complexes. The center will be called the Medical Pavilion. The two parties will form a partnership that will both enter into a master lease for space in the building and improve it to create this general health care facility. Physicians and others can participate in the venture as limited partners. Figure 11, next page, illustrates the proposed venture.

Structure Options

The participants envision that various enterprises will sublease space in the pavilion on a concession basis. For instance, part of the space is to be used as a pharmacy. A reference laboratory and an ambulatory surgical clinic will also be located in the pavilion. Memorial Hospital has already negotiated with one of the large companies in the building to set up an emergency health care clinic to service employees of that company and other tenants in the building. To maximize use of the space, treatment rooms in the clinic may be subleased to health care practitioners on a time-share basis. The pavilion would also offer a variety of services to pavilion sublessees. These services, including secretarial, billing, clerical, data processing, and other support services, would combine the general office services sometimes offered by a landlord to building tenants with those services supplied by a medical service bureau. Because these services have the potential of being very profitable to the partnership, the venture participants are considering a requirement that all tenants of the pavilion use at least some of these services.

In addition, the participants want to establish a physician's office practice in the pavilion. One physician who is retiring is interested in selling his practice to the partnership or to the hospital. The partners are also considering buying the assets of other office practices and leasing the space and equipment to physicians for satellite offices on a time-share basis. The physicians themselves would remain independent, but as an enticement to take advantage of this option, the partnership is willing to guarantee an income to new physicians in a certain amount for a maximum of one year. To benefit other tenants in the pavilion, the participants would like to require that all physicians leasing space in the pavilion refer their patients to other pavilion tenants, such as the pharmacy or the reference laboratory.

Legal Considerations

Because this fact pattern presents novel methods of practicing medicine, it is unclear whether it would conform with laws regulating the practice of medicine as well as other regulations. Key issues include:

Appendix F

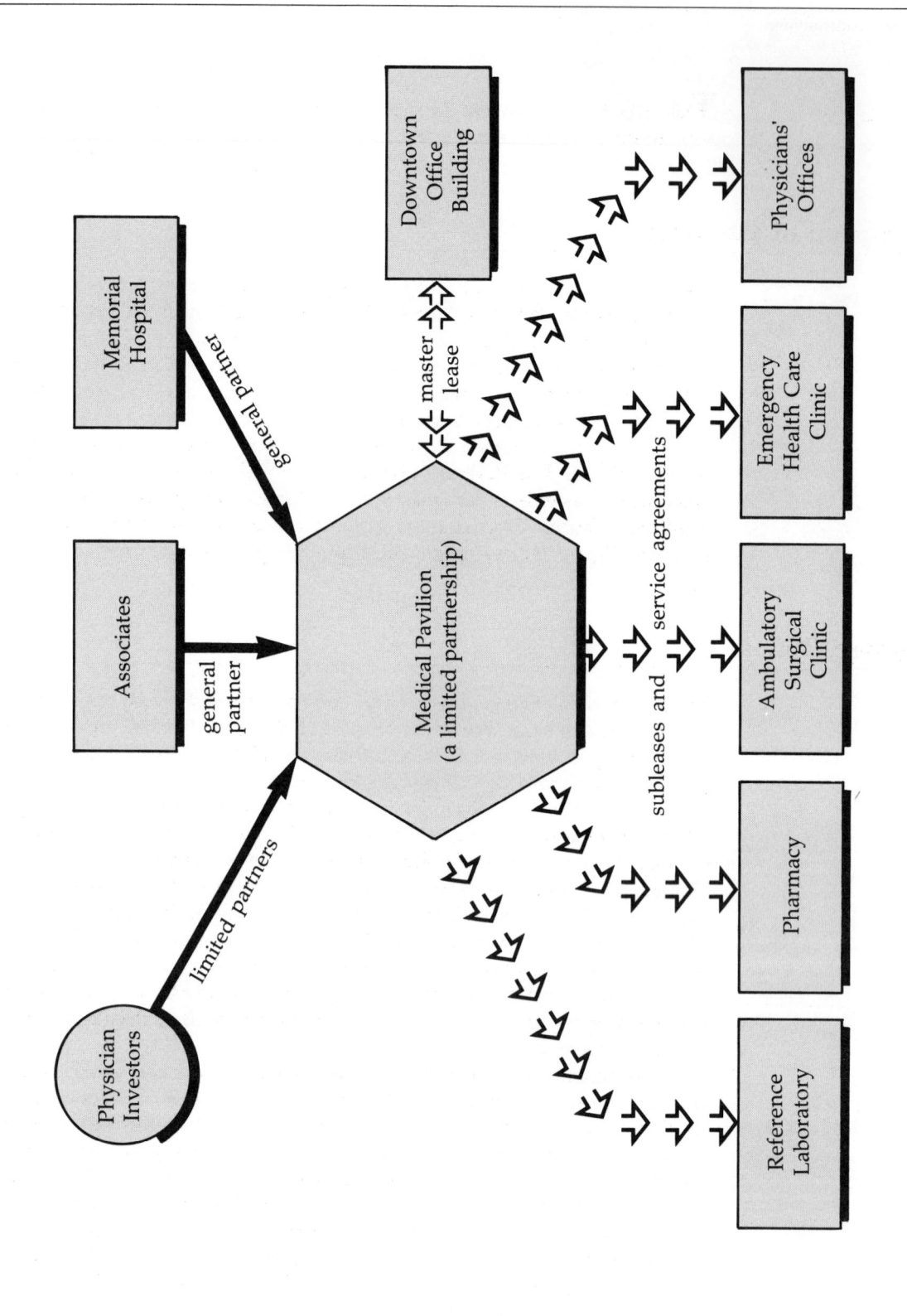

Figure 11. Organizational Structure for a Hypothetical Medical Pavilion Joint Venture

- Licensing and Certificate of Need
- Reimbursement
- Ethical concerns and corporate practice issues
- ERISA issues
- Antitrust considerations

Licensing and Certificate of Need

The parties are concerned about the requirements for licensing the pavilion or for a certificate of need (see chapter 6). Answers to these concerns depend on the law of the particular state in which the pavilion is to be located. One threshold question that must be answered is whether the pavilion is to be treated as a single integrated facility, with the various clinics and other providers within it viewed as departments. In this instance, the pavilion probably requires some type of licensure in some states. However, if the pavilion is seen merely as a site in which various providers are located for convenience purposes, licensing and certificate-of-need requirements vary depending on the type of facility in question and its owners.

Reimbursement

This particular scenario raises several questions with respect to Medicare reimbursement policies. For instance, would the various ambulatory clinics be reimbursed as physicians' offices under Medicare or as hospital outpatient departments? Would the fact that certain of the facilities are to be used on a time-share basis affect reimbursement? This latter question is not particularly important in the case of shared physicians' office space, because physicians' offices do not receive separate facilities-use reimbursement under Medicare. However, if the ambulatory surgical center located in the facility were to lease out its operating rooms to various providers, including a hospital for use by its outpatient surgery department, some question of reimbursement would arise if one user was not hospital-affiliated and was reimbursed as a distinct surgical center. Because these questions arise from a rather novel situation, no clear answers are available in the Medicare regulations (see chapter 7).

Ethical Concerns and Corporate Practice Issues

Several problems of an ethical nature arise out of this particular grouping of health care providers. First, the fact that the pavilion's administration provides staffing, service bureau, and other services to the various lessees within the center raises the issue of the unlicensed practice of medicine. If those services are paid by the lessees on the basis of their reasonable cost to the pavilion, no problem exists. However, if the lease payment to the pavilion were to permit the pavilion to participate in a percentage of each lessee's profits, there could be problems.

Second, additional corporate practice issues arise if the pavilion buys a physician's practice, because the physician's practice would be then owned in part by Associates, a lay party. In some states, the hospital alone may be able to purchase the practice, but in a number of states even this type of arrangement may not be permitted. A requirement that physicians leasing space in the pavilion refer patients to other pavilion tenants may also raise legal, or at least ethical, questions. Under corporate practice laws of a number of states, and under guidelines of the American Medical Association, this requirement may be viewed as too great a restriction on the physicians' independent medical judgment. If the physicians also have an ownership interest in the pavilion, they may also be prosecuted for illegal referrals under some states' antikickback laws.

Third, an ethical problem arises if the pavilion guarantees income to a physician to entice him or her to establish a satellite office in the pavilion. This practice may be a violation of the Medicare antifraud and abuse statutes, which prohibit illegal fees or kickbacks for practitioners treating Medicare or Medicaid patients. However, no specific legal opinion has settled this issue. Many rural communities use such income-guarantee schemes to attract physicians, presumably with the acquiescence of the Medicare program, but the situation here is different. In the rural setting, physicians are needed to provide health care in the community. The motives in the case of the pavilion are not so community centered: the participants' main purpose in providing the income guarantee is to attract physicians for the purpose of economic gain. Consequently, no one knows how the government will react to such a scheme (see chapter 8).

ERISA Issues

Even though no real integration between the various providers leasing space in the pavilion exists, the fact that the pavilion offers various services, including technical staff and secretarial services, can trigger application of various ERISA rules. This situation is even more likely if providers leasing space in the pavilion and using various pavilion services also have some ownership interest in the pavilion itself or in pavilion facilities (see chapter 5).

Antitrust Considerations

Besides being a potential source of dissatisfaction for pavilion tenants and therefore a bad marketing strategy, the requirements that the participants are considering with respect to referrals to other pavilion tenants and to the use of the partnership's medical service bureau could lead to potential challenges on antitrust grounds. If, for example, the sublease for physicians requires that they use data processing services offered by the pavilion service bureau, the physicians may be able to contest this lease provision by claiming that such a requirement constitutes *tying*, which in certain cases can be a violation of antitrust law. If the pavilion controls a significant portion of the market for medical office space in the area and the physicians do not want the data processing services or can obtain them cheaper elsewhere (such as by using their own personal computer program), the pavilion could be found by a court to be in violation of antitrust laws (see chapter 10).

Outcome

Memorial Hospital and Associates decide to form a limited partnership to acquire, improve, and lease space in the pavilion, with Associates as managing general partner. Physician staff members are invited to invest in the venture. Physician staff members may also invest in the various health care facilities that will lease space in the pavilion. However, because of potential legal and ethical problems, the participants decide to place no requirements on pavilion tenants to refer patients to other health care providers in the pavilion or to use any pavilion services.

The parties negotiate leases with various providers, including a local pharmacist and several local physicians. Memorial Hospital participates with its staff members to establish an ambulatory surgical clinic. An emergency care clinic for employees of a large company leasing space in the building is also to be located in the pavilion.

Memorial Hospital and Associates form a separate for-profit corporation to act as a medical service bureau within the pavilion. On its own, Memorial Hospital purchases the assets of one physician's office practice rather than the practice itself to avoid corporate practice issues in the state where the pavilion is located and offers contracts to interested physicians for the use of the facility in the pavilion on a time-share basis.

Glossary

[**Note:** The use of an asterisk (*) at the end of a definition indicates that the definition comes from *Hospital Administration Terminology*, 2d edition, by the American Hospital Association Resource Center (Chicago: AHA, 1986).]

AAPCC. See *Adjusted average per capita cost.*

Accelerated cost recovery system (ACRS). System devised by the tax code to enable a purchaser to more rapidly depreciate, that is, recover, the cost of assets out of taxes owed than would be the case if the taxpayer had to divide the cost of each asset by the number of its useful years.

Accelerated depreciation. See *Accelerated cost recovery system.*

Accredited investor. Investor defined in the federal securities laws as an institutional investor, which is an organization exempt from federal taxation under I.R.C. § 501(c)(3) and with assets of more than $5 million. An institutional investor may also be a director, executive officer, or general partner of the issuer of the stock.

Accretion. Principle of labor law under which representational rights of employees are extended to the employees at a facility newly established by an employer. The newly hired employees are added to the existing bargaining unit.

ACR. See *Adjusted community rate.*

ACRS. See *Accelerated cost recovery system.*

Acquisition indebtedness. Amount of debt incurred in order to acquire property.

Adjusted average per capita rate (AAPCR). Prospectively calculated actuarial estimate by Medicare of the average amount per enrollee that Medicare would have paid for the covered services to providers other than a health maintenance organization (HMO) or competitive medical plan (CMP).

Adjusted community rate (ACR). Organization's premium for providing services covered by Medicare. The ACR is adjusted for differences in utilization and complexity of services for Medicare beneficiaries as compared with other parties.

Affiliated service group (ASG). Under ERISA, an aggregation of several organizations, which must include a first-service organization (FSO) and either an A-organization

(A-ORG) or a B-organization (B-ORG) or any combination of A-ORGs and B-ORGs. See also, *First service organization, A-organization,* and *B-organization.*

Aggregation. Grouping together of several organizations under the affiliated service group (ASG) rules of ERISA.

Alternative delivery and financing system. Health care delivery and financing mode, such as health maintenance organizations (HMOs), preferred provider organizations (PPOs), and competitive medical plans (CMPs), that serves as an alternative to traditional fee for service by integrating financing issues with patient care services.*

Alternative delivery system. Health care delivery mode, such as ambulatory care, hospice, home care, and preventive services, that provides an alternative to traditional fee for service by integrating financing issues with patient care services.*

Alternative system joint venture. Joint venture in which two or more participants form an alternative delivery and financing system. See also *Joint venture* and *Alternative delivery and financing system.*

Ambulatory care. Health services rendered to patients who are not confined to an institutional bed as inpatients during the time services are rendered.*

Ambulatory care center, freestanding. Facility with an organized professional staff that provides various medical treatments on an outpatient basis only. A freestanding ambulatory care center may be one of three types, depending on the level of care it is equipped to provide: freestanding emergency center, freestanding urgent care center, or primary care center.*

Ambulatory care center, hospital-based. Organized hospital facility providing nonemergency medical and/or dental services to patients who are not assigned to a bed as inpatients during the time services are rendered. Services provided to nonemergency patients in the emergency department do not constitute an organized ambulatory care program.*

Ambulatory health clinic. See *Ambulatory care center, freestanding,* and *Ambulatory care center, hospital-based.*

Ambulatory surgical center. Distinct entity that operates exclusively for the purpose of furnishing outpatient surgical services to patients and that enters into an agreement with the Health Care Financing Administration (HCFA) to do so. See also *Hospital-affiliated ambulatory surgical centers (HAASC).*

Ancillary restraints. In antitrust law, restrictions that are imposed on parties to a joint venture. Such restrictions are supplemental to or in addition to the main agreement between the parties.

Antifraud and abuse laws. See *Medicare-Medicaid antifraud and abuse statute.*

Antitrust. Laws prohibiting unfair competition and combinations between competitors that tend to create a monopoly.

A-organization (A-ORG). Under ERISA, a service organization that is a shareholder or partner in a first service organization (FSO) and that regularly performs services for the FSO or is regularly associated with the FSO in performing services for third parties. See also *First service organization.*

Articles of incorporation. The organizational and operative document of the corporation. The articles of incorporation must be filed with the authorities of the state in which the corporation is formed.

ASG. See *Affiliated service group.*

Glossary

Assignment. Acceptance by a physician of Medicare payment as full payment for services rendered.*

Basis. In the tax law, the amount that a taxpayer has invested in an asset. Basis is determined by adding to the amount that the taxpayer originally paid for an item the amount of capital expended on it, and by subtracting from that total the amounts deducted from otherwise taxable income on account of the item, such as for depreciation and the amount of any debt incurred to acquire the item that was subsequently forgiven.

Benefit plan. Under ERISA, a plan maintained by an employer that provides for certain benefits, such as retirement, profit-sharing, or stock options, in addition to the wages or salary earned by the employees.

Bond rating. Classification given to bonds by a rating service, such as Standard & Poor's or Moody's. The classification given depends on the creditworthiness of the bond issuer. A rating by Standard & Poor's of AAA+ indicates that the issuer of the bonds is extremely creditworthy and likely to make timely payment on its debt. A rating of B indicates that the issuer is less creditworthy.

Bond. Certificate of the indebtedness of a public or private entity. A holder of a bond is entitled to interest at the rate stated on the bond. Bonds are usually secured by a lien on particular assets.

B-organization (B-ORG). Under ERISA, any organization other than a first-service organization (FSO) or an A-organization (A-ORG), but not necessarily a service organization, that has as a significant portion of its business the performance of services for the FSO, for A-ORGs, or both of a type historically performed by employees in the service field of the FSO or the A-ORGs and that has 10 percent or more of the interests in its organization held by persons who are officers, highly compensated employees, or common owners of the FSO or A-ORGs.

Bottleneck test. Antitrust theory under which a party challenging an arrangement between other parties that excludes that party must show that the arrangement creates a significant competitive advantage for members, that the excluded parties are denied that advantage and thereby cannot compete effectively in the marketplace, that the excluded parties cannot practically duplicate this competitive advantage without access to the arrangement, and that no legitimate business reason for the exclusion exists.

Brother-sister control. Under ERISA, control over several corporations that exists when five or fewer individuals own, all together, at least 80 percent or more of two or more organizations and the smallest interest held by each of such individuals in any of the organizations aggregates to more than 50 percent.

Brother-sister corporations. Two or more corporations that are subsidiaries of the same parent corporation. See also *Brother-sister control.*

Bylaws. Governing document of a corporation that contains the basic rules for the conduct of corporate affairs. Bylaws are generally more detailed as to the ownership and governance of the corporation than are the articles of incorporation. See also *Articles of incorporation.*

Capital pools. Arrangement in which two or more otherwise independent entities commingle funds into pools to enhance access to capital by the participants.

Capitation. Method of payment for health care services in which an individual or institutional provider is paid a fixed, per capita amount for each person served without regard to the actual number or nature of services provided.*

CAT. See *Computed tomography service.*

C corporation. Corporation to which the provisions of Subchapter C of the tax law apply.

Certificate of need (CON). Certificate of approval usually issued by a state health planning agency to health care facilities that propose to construct or modify a health care facility, incur a major capital expenditure, or offer a new or different health care service.*

C.F.R. See *Code of Federal Regulations.*

Charge. See *Customary charge, Prevailing charge,* and *Reasonable charge.*

Charitable trust doctrine. Doctrine holding that charitable or not-for-profit corporations hold their assets in trust for the benefit of the public.

Clayton Act. Federal antitrust law that prohibits unreasonable restraints on competition.

Close corporation. Small corporation owned by a relatively small group of persons who maintain active control over the management of corporate affairs.

Closely held corporation. In the tax law, a corporation in which at least 50 percent of the value of its outstanding stock is owned by no more than five individuals.

Closing. Finalization of a transaction, such as the purchase of property, the formation of a partnership, or the borrowing of money. At the closing, all documents are signed and exchanged and funds are simultaneously transferred.

Closing date. Date fixed for the closing of a transaction.

CMP. See *Competitive medical plan.*

Code of Federal Regulations (C.F.R.). Publication containing all federal administrative rules and regulations except federal taxation materials, which are published in separate Treasury Regulations.

Collective bargaining. In labor law, the negotiations between a union representing employees and the employer to resolve such issues as wage rates, benefits, hours, and working conditions. These negotiations usually result in a contract. See also *Collective bargaining agreement.*

Collective bargaining agreement. Contract between an employer and its unionized employees. Such agreements result from the collective bargaining process.

Common-law employee. Under federal law, an employee of an employer who has real responsibility for that employee and controls the employment conditions of that employee, such as supervision, payroll records, recruitment, job assignments, compensation, and employee discipline.

Common stock. Capital stock in a corporation. Common stock has no priority or preference over other kinds of stock. Rights of common shareholders are fixed by statute and by the corporate bylaws. Generally, only holders of common stock have the right to elect directors.

Community of interest. Element of a franchise, under some definitions, that gives the parties to the arrangement a joint or common interest in the operational and financial success of the franchisee's business.

Community rating procedure. Rating system used by health maintenance organizations (HMOs) to set premium rates. The HMO's premium rates may not vary from group to group on the basis of individual health service utilization experience.

Competitive medical plan (CMP). A type of health maintenance organization (HMO) that pays its physicians and other practitioners on a fee-for-service basis.

Compensatory damages. Amount of damages given by a court to a party to make up for injury or loss that the party has suffered. See also *Damages*.

Computed tomography (CT) scanner. See *computed tomography service*.

Computed tomography service. Service providing diagnosis of disease through visualization of internal body structures by means of computer synthesis of x-ray particles.*

CON. See *Certificate of need*.

Concerted refusal to deal. In antitrust law, an exclusive-dealing arrangement between horizontally related entities who refuse to do business with, for instance, a certain supplier in an area. A concerted refusal to deal represents such a restraint on competition that it is deemed to be a per se antitrust violation. See also *Exclusive dealing* and *Per se rule*.

Conditions, covenants, and restrictions (CC&Rs). Restrictions placed on the use of property by its developer. By agreeing to purchase a parcel of property, a purchaser also agrees to abide by the CC&Rs that have been placed against it.

Contract. Legally binding agreement between two or more parties whereby one of the parties changes position in some respect or agrees to a change in position in return for something of value (consideration).

Contractual relationship. Relationship existing between parties by reason of a contract. See also *Contract*.

Convenience rule. Principle devised by the Internal Revenue Service (IRS) and tax courts that allows an exemption for income earned from products or services that were provided for the convenience of a tax-exempt organization's "members," such as patients, students, or staff.

Corporate practice of medicine. Principle referred to in the statutes of some states that prohibits an unlicensed entity from holding itself out to the public as a medical practitioner. This principle may also refer to the employment of physicians by corporations or other lay entities.

Corporate reorganization. Restructuring of a corporation or of a related group of corporations to create, for example, a parent corporation and its subsidiaries.

Corporation. Entity created, pursuant to statute, by one or more persons to act as a single legal person.

Cost-based reimbursement. Payment by a third-party payer to a hospital of all allowable costs incurred by the hospital in the provision of services to patients covered by the contract.*

Cost-based system. See *cost-based reimbursement*.

Credit base. Amount used by an investor to purchase an asset with credit.

Creditor relationship. Relationship of one party to another in which the first party has loaned money to the second and is thereby the creditor of the second.

CT. See *Computed tomography service*.

Customary charge. Fee that a physician or provider usually charges.

Damages. Pecuniary compensation or indemnity, which may be recovered in the courts by any person who has suffered loss, detriment, or injury, whether to his or her person, property, or rights, through the unlawful act or omission or negligence of another. [Derived from *Black's Law Dictionary*, 4th revised edition, p. 467.]

Debenture. Certificate of a debt that is backed by the general credit of the issuer.

Debt-financed rules. Rules in the tax code that deny a tax exemption for income earned by a tax-exempt entity through passive investments, such as the purchase of stock in a corporation, if the tax-exempt organization borrowed money with which to purchase the stock.

Decision bargaining. In labor law, negotiations between an employer and the union representing that employer's employees with respect to a decision of the employer to change its business practices, such as relocating its operations, closing a plant, or expanding its operations.

Deed of trust. Document by which one party conveys real property to a neutral third party to hold in trust as security for the benefit of a second party who has made a loan to the first party. See also *Mortgage*.

Depreciation allowance. Allowance a taxpayer is permitted to take against taxes owed to account for the gradual decrease in value of certain assets of the taxpayer that are used by the taxpayer in the production of income, such as rental property.

Diagnosis-related group (DRG). Patient classification system that relates demographic, diagnostic, and therapeutic characteristics of patients to length of inpatient stay and amount of resources consumed, that provides a framework for specifying hospital case mix, and that identifies 468 classifications of illnesses and injuries for which Medicare payment is made under the prospective pricing program.*

Discriminatory pricing. In antitrust law, the prohibited practice of granting to favored customers special prices that are lower than the company's usual charges, thereby adversely affecting competition.

Disqualified lease. In the tax law, any lease of real estate to a tax-exempt organization from which tax benefits may not be available because of tax-exempt use property restrictions. A lease is disqualified for purposes of determining whether tax-exempt use property restrictions apply if the portion of the property leased to the tax-exempt entity is more than 35 percent of the entire property. Other limitations are also applicable.

Dividend. Distribution of profits by a corporation to its shareholders based on the pro rata interest that the shareholders have in the corporation. Preferred shareholders may have a right to receive dividend distributions prior to holders of common stock.

Double taxation. Refers to the taxation of the same profits twice. The corporation pays income taxes on its profits, and the shareholders in that corporation also pay taxes on distributions of those same profits to them.

Durable medical equipment (DME). Equipment, such as walkers, canes, beds, oxygen, commodes, respirators, and wheelchairs, that is designed to assist the injured or ill. Medicare and third-party payers will reimburse for use of DME in the home setting only if the physician approves of such use. For private-pay patients, DME is a discretionary purchase.

Economic joint venture. See *joint venture*.

Effects bargaining. In labor law, negotiations between an employer and the union representing that employer's employees with respect to the effect that a decision to change business operations may have on the employees. Some areas to be negotiated may be seniority rights, accrued benefits, severance pay, and transfers.

Emergency center. Facility that is designed, organized, equipped, and staffed to provide medical care on a 24-hour per day basis for injuries and illnesses, including those that are life-threatening, that provides laboratory and radiographic services and has established arrangements for transporting critical patients or patients requiring hospitalization once stabilized, and that does not provide continuity of care but treats episodic, emergency, and primary care cases.*

Employee Retirement Income Security Act (ERISA). Statute enacted to protect employees, particularly lower-echelon employees, from discrimination with respect to employee benefit plans. Under the ERISA statute, employee benefit plans, such as pension and profit-sharing, may receive tax-qualified status only if they do not discriminate in favor of owner-employees or other highly compensated executives.

Employment-at-will. Refers to a relationship between an employer and an employee in which no contractual relationship exists between the parties with respect to duration of the term of employment. Either party is free to terminate the employment at any time with or without notice.

Environmental impact statement. Report that must be prepared pursuant to the requirements of federal and state environmental protection statutes whenever a proposed major project will have a significant impact on the environment. See also *Negative impact report*.

Equipment lease. Document by which equipment owned by one party is conveyed to another party for the use of that second party for a stipulated time.

Equity. Ownership interest held in property after excluding the value of any liens on the property, such as a mortgage.

ERISA. See *Employee Retirement Income Security Act*.

Essential facilities test. See *Bottleneck test*.

Exclusive dealing. In antitrust law, arrangements whereby two parties agree to work only with each other in the sale and purchase of goods or services. When entities are vertically related, as opposed to horizontally related, an exclusive-dealing arrangement is analyzed under the rule of reason. However, when entities are horizontally related, an exclusive-dealing arrangement may be deemed a concerted refusal to deal, which is a per se violation of antitrust laws. See also *Concerted refusal to deal, Per se rule,* and *Rule of reason*.

Exclusive provider organization (EPO). Form of preferred provider organization (PPO) that obliges the enrollee to select a provider from a defined group of contracting providers rather than allowing the enrollee the option on a case-by-case basis of using a contracting provider or a noncontracting provider.

Experience rating procedure. Rating system used by conventional health care insurers, such as Blue Cross/Blue Shield, in setting their premium rates. The rates charged to a particular group are based on that group's own utilization experience.

Fair employment laws. Federal and state statutes that prohibit discriminatory treatment of certain protected classes of employees, such as racial minorities and women.

Federal Trade Commission (FTC). Department of the federal government that regulates trade in interstate commerce. The FTC, along with the Department of Justice, enforces the federal antitrust laws.

Fee schedule. List of established charges or allowances for specified medical and dental procedures.*

Fee splitting. Paying a part of the fees for medical services received by a licensed medical practitioner to an unlicensed person or entity.

Fiduciary duty. In corporate law, the obligation of officers and directors of a corporation to maximize profits for the shareholders; generally the obligation of anyone in a position of trust to protect the interests of the beneficiaries of that trust.

Financing lease. Lease that is in effect a disguised loan security agreement in which the lessor is the lender and the lessee is the borrower. The lease is really a security agreement under which the "rents" paid by the lessee over the course of the lease term represent an amount sufficient to amortize principal and interest payments on the loan.

First service organization (FSO). In ERISA, an organization whose principal business is the performance of services, such as health care, legal services, and accounting services, as opposed to generating income through the use of capital, such as through inventory, machinery, or equipment.

Foundation. Organization that has been endowed with funds for future use, often for the purpose of engaging in charitable activities. The term is also used to describe an organization that seeks charitable contributions to further the activities of its sponsoring hospital.

Franchise. Right granted by an entity to market that entity's products in a certain defined territory or to use that entity's trademark and marketing techniques to sell defined goods or services in that defined territory.

Fraud and abuse laws. See *Medicare-Medicaid antifraud and abuse statute*.

FTC. See *Federal Trade Commission*.

Full-complement standard. In labor law, a standard used to determine whether an employer is a successor employer to the party from which it acquired a business for collective bargaining purposes. It refers to the time when the employer that has acquired the business enterprise has hired the full work force that it will be using in its operations.

General partnership. Partnership in which all of the partners share the profits and bear the losses, debts, and liabilities from the association according to the percentage of their respective investments. See also *Partnership* and *Limited partnership*.

Good faith and fair dealing. Expression used by courts to state that in contractual relationships, parties are expected to deal with each other justly and honestly and without bad or illegitimate motives.

Ground lease. Lease to the land only, not to any structure located on the land.

Group practice. Combined practice of three or more physicians and/or dentists who share office space, equipment, records, office personnel, expenses, or income.*

HCFA. See *Health Care Financing Administration*.

Health Care Financing Administration (HCFA). Component of the U.S. Department of Health and Human Services that administers the Medicare program and certain aspects of state Medicaid programs.*

Health maintenance organization (HMO). Organization that has management responsibility for providing comprehensive health care services on a prepayment basis to voluntarily enrolled persons within a designated population.*

Health Maintenance Organization Act of 1973 (HMO Act). Federal statute that generally provides for the establishment of federally qualified HMOs, that is, HMOs that are established under and that meet the requirements of the HMO Act.

HHS. See *United States Department of Health & Human Services.*

Home health care. Provision of health care services such as nursing, therapy, and health-related homemaker or social services in the patient's home.*

Horizontally related entities. In antitrust law, two entities who deal with the same product or service in the same market at the same level in the hierarchy of providers of that product or service, such as two hospitals or two durable medical equipment suppliers. See also *Vertically related entities.*

Hospital-affiliated facility. Facility that is associated in some degree with a hospital.

Hospital-affiliated ambulatory surgical center (HAASC). Entity affiliated with or owned by a hospital but is a separately identifiable entity that is physically, administratively, and financially independent and distinct from other hospital operations.

IHCC. See *Integrated health care corporation.*

Implied contract. Contractual relationship that is not created or evidenced by the explicit agreement of the parties, but [is] inferred by the law, as a matter of reason and justice from their acts or conduct, the circumstances surrounding the transaction making it a reasonable, or even a necessary, assumption that a contract existed between them by tacit understanding. [Derived from *Black's Law Dictionary*, 4th revised edition, p. 395.]

Implied-in-fact covenant. Contractual promise that is inferred by the actions or words of the parties rather than from an express written contract.

Indemnification. Reimbursement by one party to another for losses or damage suffered by that other party.

Indenture. Legal document that defines the terms under which a security, such as a debenture or a bond, is issued.

Individual practice association (IPA). Partnership, corporation, association, or legal entity that provides for prepaid health care to subscribers through an arrangement with licensed physicians, dentists, osteopaths, or other health care personnel to provide their services in accordance with a method of compensation established by the entity.*

Integrated health care corporation (IHCC). Joint venture between a hospital and members of its medical staff that plans and carries out a number of specific activities, such as the development of alternative delivery systems.

Internal Revenue Code (I.R.C.). Statute containing the United States tax laws.

Internal Revenue Service (IRS). Department of the federal government whose function is to interpret and enforce the tax laws.

Inure. To accrue to the benefit of. See *Inurement.*

Inurement (or private inurement). Receipt of a significant benefit by private parties without adequate payment for such benefit. In the tax law, inurement generally refers to a situation in which private parties have received benefits because of or through the efforts of tax-exempt organizations.

Investment tax credit (ITC). Credit provided by the tax law to encourage investment in certain types of equipment. Tax reform proposals before Congress in 1986 eliminate the ITC.

IPA. See *Individual practice association.*

IRC. See *Internal Revenue Code.*

IRS. See *Internal Revenue Service*.

ITC. See *Investment tax credit*.

Joint employer. In labor law, two separate and distinct employers, such as a hospital and an employee leasing agency, who are considered to be jointly responsible for the same employees and are therefore both required to honor a collective bargaining agreement that those employees may have with either of the employers.

Joint venture. Creation by two or more legally independent parties of a new enterprise that is jointly owned by such parties, who share the economic risks and rewards of the venture. As used in this book the term *joint venture* specifically refers to joint ventures among health care providers.

Lay. Not of a certain profession. As used in this book, the term *lay* refers to a party or entity that is not licensed as a health care practitioner.

Lease. Agreement under which one party agrees to convey and the other party agrees to accept either real property, such as land, or personal property, such as equipment, for a stipulated period in exchange for money or something else of value.

Lessee. Party to a lease who acquires the use of the property being leased.

Lessor. Owner of property who leases such property to another.

Letter of intent. Letter agreement by which the parties express their intention to participate in a transaction such as a joint venture.

Leverage. To raise capital by borrowing. Persons whose assets are highly leveraged have little or no equity in those assets.

Liability. Obligation by law to pay a debt or to take responsibility for the reimbursement of losses.

Licensure. Formal process by which a government agency grants an individual the legal right to practice an occupation or grants an organization the legal right to engage in an activity, such as the operation of a hospital, and prohibits all other individuals and organizations from legally doing so, to ensure that the public health, safety, and welfare are reasonably well protected.*

Life safety. See *Life Safety Code*.

Life Safety Code. Standard developed and updated regularly by the National Fire Protection Association that specifies construction and operational conditions to minimize fire hazards and provide a system of safety in case of fire.*

Limited liability. Restriction or limitation on a party's obligation to repay debts or reimburse losses. The liability is restricted or limited to a certain amount, usually the amount that the party has invested in a venture. An example is a shareholder's limited liability in a corporation; under normal circumstances, the scope of such liability is limited to the amount of the shareholder's investment.

Limited partnership. Partnership in which some partners are general partners, who are responsible for partnership business operations, and others are limited partners, who have no active role in the enterprise and whose liability for partnership debts and losses is limited to the amount of their investment. See also *Partnership* and *General partnership*.

Lithotripter. Medical equipment that aids in the treatment of kidney stones through the use of sonic waves.

Magnetic resonance imaging (MRI). Service providing diagnosis of disease typically through visualization of cross-sectional images of body tissue, using strong static magnetic and radio-frequency fields to monitor body chemistry noninvasively, unimpeded by bone, and using no ionizing radiation or contrast agents.*

Management contract. Agreement by which one party agrees to render management services to another for a fee.

Master indenture. Legal document that defines the terms under which a security, such as a debenture or bond, is issued to a group of individual borrowers (the *obligated group* under the master indenture), such as a hospital parent company, the hospital, and hospital-affiliated entities.

Master plan. Plan established by local governments in accordance with standards set forth in state statutes that describe the established and proposed future uses of land within the local government's jurisdiction. All zoning ordinances passed by the local governments must be in accordance with this master plan.

Medicaid. Federal program, created by Title XIX—Medical Assistance, a 1965 amendment to the Social Security Act, that provides health care benefits to indigent and medically indigent persons. The Medicaid program is administered by the individual states.*

Medical staff-hospital (MeSH). Type of joint venture formed by a hospital and members of its medical staff to engage in certain specified enterprises beneficial to both groups.

Medicare. Federal program, created by Title XVIII—Health Insurance for the Aged, a 1965 amendment to the Social Security Act, that provides health insurance benefits primarily to persons over the age of 65 and others eligible for Social Security benefits. See also *Medicare, Part A*, and *Medicare, Part B*.*

Medicare, Part A. Hospital Insurance Program, the compulsory portion of Medicare, which automatically enrolls all persons aged 65 and over entitled to benefits under Old Age, Survivors, Disability and Health Insurance Program or railroad retirement, persons under 65 who have been eligible for disability for more than two years, and insured workers (and their dependents) requiring renal dialysis or kidney transplantation.*

Medicare, Part B. Supplementary Medical Insurance Program, the voluntary portion of Medicare, which includes physician's services and in which all persons entitled to Part A, the Hospital Insurance Program, may enroll on a monthly premium basis.*

Medicare-Medicaid antifraud and abuse statute. Section 1877(b) of the Social Security Act, which prohibits the knowing or willful solicitation or receipt of any payment (including any kickback, bribe, or rebate) in return for referring a patient to any provider for an item or service for which payment may be made under Medicare or Medicaid.

Medicare beneficiary. Person who is insured under the Medicare program and therefore entitled to receive benefits from the program.

Merger. Absorption of one corporation into another one or the combination of two or more corporations into one or several different corporations.

MeSH. See *Medical staff-hospital*.

Money purchase pension plan. In ERISA, a pension plan in which employer contributions are predetermined but are not dependent on the employer's profit.

Mortgage. Document conveying one party's property to another party as security for a loan. See also *Deed of trust*.

National Labor Relations Board (NLRB). Administrative agency under the Department of Labor that is responsible for overseeing employee relations under the National

Labor Relations Act and serving as an appeal board for disputes under collective bargaining agreements.

Negative impact report. Statement that a proposed major project has no significant or potentially adverse impact on the environment. See also *Environmental impact statement.*

NLRB. See *National Labor Relations Board.*

No-action letter. Letter granted by the federal Securities and Exchange Commission or state corporate regulatory agencies indicating that they will take no action against the parties of a particularly described transaction for violations of the law provided that the parties proceed as described in their letter of application.

Nonaccredited investor. Investor who does not fall within the limits of the federal securities law definition of an accredited investor but who has experience in financial matters and is capable of evaluating the merits and risks of an investment. See also *Accredited investor.*

Noncorporate lessor rules. In the tax law, certain rules that limit tax benefits in leases when the lessor is not a corporation. See also *Lessor.*

Nonqualified nonrecourse financing. In the tax law, financing that does not qualify for inclusion in the amount that a party paid for an asset for purposes of determining the allowable investment tax credit (ITC) because that financing is nonrecourse financing. See also *Nonrecourse financing.*

Nonrecourse financing. Financing or debt for which the borrower has no personal liability. In the event of a default on the loan, the lender can only take back the item given as security for the loan and cannot go against any other assets of the borrower.

Off balance sheet financing. Means of financing a project so that the expense of the project does not appear as a debit on one party's balance sheets because the other parties to the venture provide the financing.

Offering. Placing a security into the market for sale to investors.

Outpatient care center. See *Ambulatory care center.*

Overinclusiveness. Principle of antitrust law that considers a restraint on competition to be unreasonable if it substantially reduces competitors in the marketplace.

Parent corporation. Corporation that owns or controls another corporation, called the subsidiary corporation. See also *subsidiary corporation.*

Parent-subsidiary control. For ERISA purposes, control by one organization that owns at least 80 percent of one or more organizations.

Partnership. Association of two or more persons who agree to conduct certain business activities together. See also *General partnership* and *Limited partnership.*

Partnership agreement. Contract in which the parties forming a partnership agree to do business together.

Pass-through entity. In the tax law, a type of organization, such as a partnership, that passes its taxes and tax benefits through to its members, who then declare them on their own tax returns.

Passive shareholder. Shareholder who does not have an active role in the affairs of the corporation. See also *Shareholder.*

Per se rule. Antitrust principle that certain types of arrangements are unlawful **as** a matter of law; for example, arrangements such as price fixing have been shown by experience to be inherently anticompetitive and are therefore in themselves illegal. See also *Rule of reason.*

Personal property. Property that is not affixed to the land, such as equipment, vehicles, furniture.

Pension plan. Plan maintained by an employer for the benefit of its employees, according to which a certain monthly sum will be paid to the employee at the time of the employee's retirement. Pension plans usually provide for contributions by both the employer and the employee. For ERISA purposes, a pension plan is qualified if it meets certain requirements set forth in the ERISA statute. See also *Qualified pension plan.*

Potential market entrant doctrine. Antitrust theory under which an arrangement involving competitors who participate in a joint activity in which neither had previously participated may be determined to be a restraint on competition if as a result of the arrangement one participant in the venture who would have entered the market alone but for the venture (a potential market entrant) does not do so because of the venture and therefore only one new competitor is created in the marketplace instead of the two that may otherwise have been created.

PPO. See *Preferred provider organization.*

Preferred provider organization (PPO). Term applied to a variety of direct contractual relationships between hospitals, physicians, insurers, employers, or third-party administrators in which providers negotiate with group purchasers to provide health services for a defined population and which typically share three characteristics: (1) a negotiated system of payment for services that may include discounts from usual charges or ceilings imposed on a charge, per diem, or per discharge basis, (2) financial incentives for individual subscribers (insureds) to use contracting providers, usually in the form of reduced copayments and deductibles, broader coverage of services, or simplified claims processing, and (3) an extensive utilization review program.*

Preferred stock. Stock in a corporation that has some sort of preference over other classes of stock as to dividends and rights to assets at liquidation.

Prevailing charge. Fee for a service or product that is commonly charged by physicians or providers in an area.

Price fixing. Per se violation of antitrust laws in which two or more competitors in a market agree to maintain a minimum or maximum level of prices for the goods or services that they market.

Primary care center. Facility that provides primary care on a scheduled basis and is open approximately eight hours per day, that is staffed by a physician's assistant or a primary care physician, that is supported by basic laboratory and sometimes radiology services, and that provides continuity of care.*

Private letter ruling. In the tax law, an opinion letter from the Internal Revenue Service stating whether adverse tax consequences may result if the parties follow a certain proposed course of action.

Private offering. Means for selling securities that are not listed on an exchange and are exempt from registration with federal or state authorities.

Professional component. Under Medicare, those physician services that are related to identifiable medical services to individual patients and that are paid for on a reasonable-charge basis.*

Professional corporation. Corporation composed of at least one shareholder, and this shareholder must be licensed under the laws of a state to offer professional services, such as medical care or legal services. A professional corporation can have no shareholders who are not licensed professionals.

Professional fee. See *Professional component.*

Professional service corporation. For ERISA purposes, a corporation that is organized to render professional services and that has at least one shareholder who is licensed under state law or is otherwise legally authorized to provide the type of services for which the corporation is organized. A physician's office practice that is organized under state law as a professional corporation is an example of a professional service corporation for ERISA purposes.

Profit-sharing plan. Plan maintained by an employer that offers employees the opportunity to share in the profits of the employer. Under ERISA, a profit-sharing plan is qualified if it complies with the terms and provisions of ERISA statute. See also *Qualified profit-sharing plan.*

Promissory estoppel. Principle under which a court in equity protects a party that does not have an enforceable contract but who has reasonably relied on the representations of another to his or her detriment.

Prospective pricing. Method of third-party payment by which rates of payment to providers for services to patients are established in advance for the coming fiscal year, and providers are paid these rates for services delivered regardless of the costs actually incurred in providing these services.* See also *Reimbursement* and *Diagnosis-related group.*

Prospective pricing system (PPS). System of reimbursement that uses the prospective pricing method. See also *Prospective pricing.*

Public offering. Means by which shares of stock or other securities are publicly traded, that is, sold to a large number of investors by means of brokers.

Punitive damages. Damages imposed by a court, either by statute or on general public policy grounds, to punish a party for particularly serious behavior vis-a-vis another party.

Qualified commercial financing. In the tax law, financing that qualifies for inclusion into the amount paid for an asset on which a party may claim an investment tax credit (ITC), because no related party is involved in the financing, the financing does not exceed 80 percent of the amount that the borrower paid for the property, and the lender is a commercial lender.

Qualified pension plan. Under ERISA, a pension plan for which the contributions by the employer on behalf of an employee are not immediately taxable as income to the employee.

Qualified profit-sharing plan. Under ERISA, a profit-sharing plan for which the contributions by the employer on behalf of an employee are not immediately taxable as income to the employee.

Rate review. Prospective review by a government or private agency of a hospital's budget and financial data. Rate reviews are performed for the purpose of determining the reasonableness of the hospital rates and evaluating proposed rate increases.*

Real property. Property that constitutes land or that which is affixed to the land, such as a building.

Reasonable charges. Physicians' fee limitations that are determined on the basis of the lowest of actual charge, customary charge, or prevailing charge and other profiles added under the Tax Equity and Fiscal Responsibility Act of 1982 (Public Law 97-248) and Medicare provider-based physician regulations.*

Reasonable costs. All necessary and proper costs incurred by providers in rendering service to Medicare beneficiaries, determined on the basis of actual costs according to the methodologies and limits set forth in the Medicare statute and program regulations, and, because of the Medicare prospective pricing system, used as the basis of payment only for noninpatient services and the services of institutions exempt from the prospective pricing system.*

Registration exemptions. For a security, the statutes, rules, or regulations under which a security may be exempted from registering with appropriate securities regulators.

Rehabilitation tax credit. Credit allowed by the tax law against taxes. The rehabilitation tax credit represents a percentage of amounts spent rehabilitating certain historic or old real property.

Reimbursement. Payment by a third-party payer to a health care provider in connection with the provision of services to patients covered by that third-party payer. See also *Cost-based reimbursement*.

Reserve powers. Term used to designate those powers and responsibilities vis-a-vis the board of directors that are reserved to the corporate members in the case of a not-for-profit corporation or to shareholders in the case of a for-profit corporation, Reserve powers are often bifurcated into those that are *statutory* in nature, that is, that are set forth in the corporate statutes of a state, and those that are developed as a matter of policy by the corporation. Examples of statutory reserve powers are the powers reserved by corporate law to corporate members or shareholders to approve amendments to the articles of incorporation or bylaws and to appoint or remove members of the board of directors. Examples of nonstatutory reserve powers are powers reserved to corporate members or shareholders to approve operating and capital budgets and to approve significant expenditures over approved budgets.

Robinson-Patman Act. Antitrust statute that prohibits predatory pricing because of its adverse effect on competition.

Rule of reason. Principle of antitrust law that states that a restraint must be unreasonable to be considered an unlawful restraint on competition. See also *Per se rule*.

Safe harbor. Legal expression indicating that a party can be reassured of complying with the provisions of a statute if that party complies strictly with certain guidelines encompassed within the statute or within regulations interpreting it. Such guidelines create a safe harbor.

Safe-harbor pension plan. Provision in the ERISA statute that allows an employer to exclude leased employees working for it from its own qualified employee benefit plan if the company from which the employer is leasing employees maintains its own qualified pension plan that provides for immediate participation and total vesting of all pension rights and interests.

Sale-leaseback. Transaction in which one party sells property to a second party and then leases that property back from the second party.

SEC. See *Securities and Exchange Commission*.

Security. Instrument of an ownership interest that shows an investment in a common enterprise that is expected to generate profits derived solely from the efforts of others.

Securities and Exchange Commission (SEC). Commission established by the federal government to regulate the sale and purchase of securities and to enforce federal securities laws.

Selective contracting. System in which a third-party payer, such as a state Medicaid agency, enters into contracts with a selected group of health care providers to provide medical services at certain prices established in the contracts to the beneficiaries of that third-party payer.

Service agreement. See *Service contract*.

Service bureau. Company that provides services, such as secretarial, bookkeeping, data processing, word processing, receptionist, and telephone, to others for a fee.

Service contract. Agreement by which one party agrees to render specified services to another for a fee.

Share. See *Stock*.

Shareholder. Party owning stock in a corporation.

Sherman Act. Federal antitrust statute that prohibits all contracts, combinations, and conspiracies in restraint of trade and that prohibits all monopolies or attempts to monopolize.

Single employer. In labor law, two nominally separate entities that are deemed to be one employer for employment law purposes.

Special project joint venture. Health care joint venture in which the participants undertake a certain defined project, such as the acquisition of medical equipment. See also *Joint venture*.

Spill-over collusion. In antitrust cases, refers to the situation in which legitimate restraints that are a necessary part of a joint venture spill over into the venturers' separate competitive businesses.

Statute. Law, either federal or state, that is adopted by the legislature and signed into law by the executive.

Stock. Evidence of ownership interest in a corporation. Stock is usually held as shares of a corporation.

Stockholder. See *Shareholder*.

Subchapter S corporation. In the tax law, a corporation organized and governed by the provisions of Subchapter S of the tax code. A Subchapter S corporation is a close corporation that resembles a partnership in that income of the corporation is not taxed at the corporate level but is passed through to the shareholders.

Subsidiary corporation. Corporation that is owned or controlled by another corporation, termed the parent. See *parent corporation*.

Successor employer. Refers to a situation in which a new employer is bound by a collective bargaining agreement with a group of employees to which a prior employer was a party because that new employer conducts essentially the same business as the former employer and has as a majority of its work force former employees of the previous employer.

Successor organization. In the tax law, an entity that is set up with the assets of another entity to perform the same business as the previous entity.

Take-out loan. Long-term (permanent) loan that is used to pay off construction loans (short-term loans) once a construction project is completed.

Tax credit. Certain sum that may be subtracted from taxes due.

Tax Equity and Fiscal Responsibility Act of 1982 (TEFRA) (Public Law 97-248). Budget law that includes a series of provisions relating to Medicare and Medicaid, extending Section 223 (hospital cost limits) to include the total operating costs of inpatient hospital services, establishing a target rate on the rate of increase, and establishing incentive payments to hospitals for the first time.* This statute also made significant revisions to the ERISA statute to prohibit discrimination in qualified employee benefit plans in favor of officers, shareholders, and highly compensated employees.

Tax exemption. Right granted by the tax code that removes the obligation to pay taxes.

Tax shelter. In the tax law, a device by which income that would ordinarily be taxable is sheltered from taxation, that is, used or invested in such a way as to avoid taxation.

Tax-exempt organization. In the tax law, an entity that, by law, is not obligated to pay taxes.

Tax-exempt use property. In the tax law, property that is used by a tax-exempt party. The tax law provides that tax credits and other benefits may not be claimed by any taxpayer with respect to property that is tax-exempt use property.

Technical component. Under Medicare, or other third-party reimbursement plans, the portion of the charge representing services that are related to the use of the medical facility and that are not professional services.

TEFRA. See *Tax Equity and Fiscal Responsibility Act of 1982.*

Third-party payer. Party to an insurance or prepayment agreement—usually an insurance company, prepayment plan, or government agency—responsible for paying to the provider designated expenses incurred on behalf of the insured.*

Trade. In securities law, the business of buying and selling securities. In tax law, *trade* refers to a party's business.

Trademark. Some symbol or mark used to identify or indicate an association with the business of a party. A trademark is legally reserved by that party for its sole use.

True lease. Lease in which the lessor remains the owner of the property. See also *Financing lease.*

Tying. In antitrust law, an arrangement in which a party having control over the market for a particular service or product provides that service or sells that product to another only on the condition that the other party also purchase a second product or service from the first party. The second product or service is *tied* to the first product or service: one cannot be purchased without the other.

U.C.C. See *Uniform Commercial Code.*

Unbundling. Practice of billing under Medicare part B for nonphysician services that are provided to hospital inpatients and that are furnished to the hospital by an outside supplier or another provider. Under the prospective pricing system [PPS], unbundling is prohibited, and all nonphysician services provided in an inpatient setting are to be paid as hospital services.*

Undercapitalized. Having an insufficient amount of capital with which to conduct normal business operations.

Underinclusiveness. Principle of antitrust law according to which an arrangement is an unreasonable restraint if it excludes a significant number of potential participants from the market, thereby rendering them unable to compete effectively.

Underwriter. Party that underwrites a security issue, that is, agrees to purchase, for a fee, securities or bonds from a corporation or a municipality at a fixed time for a fixed purchase price with a view to redistribution to public investors.

Uniform Commercial Code (U.C.C.). Standardized statute that has been substantially adopted in the majority of states and that contains the laws governing most commercial transactions, that is, transactions between merchants.

United States Department of Health & Human Services (HHS). Branch of the United States government that is responsible for overseeing health-related issues in the country and is reponsible for overseeing the Health Care Financing Administration (HCFA) among other agencies.

Unrelated business income. Income earned by a tax-exempt entity that is nevertheless taxable because it was earned in the regular course of a business that is unrelated to the tax-exempt purposes of the organization.

Urgent care center. Facility that provides primary and urgent care treatment on a less than 24-hour per day basis and that is supported by laboratory and radiology services but does not receive patients transported by ambulance, is not equipped to treat true medical emergencies such as heart or stroke victims, and does not provide continuity of care.*

Variance. In zoning law, permission from the local planning agencies to deviate from the usual zoning requirements.

Venture capital company. Company whose function is to provide capital for new business ventures. A venture capital company guarantees a certain amount of financial support to the business usually in return for a share of the profits should the venture prove to be successful.

Vertically related entities. In antitrust law, refers to two or more entities who are in the same market but at different levels in the hierarchy of providers of a product or service, such as a hospital and a supplier or a hospital and physicians. See also *Horizontally related entities.*

Vest, vesting. To give a party an immediate fixed legal right. Under ERISA, vesting gives an employee a fixed right to benefit from a pension plan. This right cannot be taken away if the employee is terminated or terminates his or her employment before retirement age.

Whistle-blower statutes. Federal and state statutes that protect employees from retaliation by employers for reporting employer violations of statutory safety and environmental standards.

Wrongful discharge. Termination of an employee for an illegitimate cause.

Zoning. Ordinances enacted by a local government that divide the area under its jurisdiction into different sections or classifications and indicate what uses, such as residential, commercial, or light industrial, are permitted in those zones.

Index

The letter (g) following a page number indicates that the term may be found in the glossary.

Accelerated cost recovery system (ACRS), 58, 243(g)
  equipment acquisitions and, 66-67
  real estate leasing and, 67-68
  taxable income and, 65-68
Acceptance of assignment, 118
Accredited investors, 45, 243(g)
Accretion, collective bargaining and, 161-62, 243(g)
Acquisition indebtedness, 65, 243(g)
Adjusted average per capita cost (AAPCC), Medicare and, 124, 243(g)
Adjusted community rate (ACR), Medicare and, 124, 243(g)
Affiliated service groups (ASGs), 80-82, 243(g)
  avoidance of designation of, 89-91
  defined, 78, 82
  management companies and, 85
  multiple, 84-85
  rules for, 85-89
Alter-ego theory, liability and, 17
Alternative health care systems, 3, 5, 244(g). See also Health maintenance organizations (HMOs) and Preferred provider organization (PPO)
  ERISA and, 87-88
  regulation of, 102-3

Ambulatory care, 5, 244(g)
Ambulatory surgical clinic, 244(g)
  ERISA and, 86
  Medicare and, 118-20
  state regulation of, 101
American Medical Association, ethical restrictions of, 144-45
Ancillary restraints, antitrust law and, 180-81, 244(g)
Antidiscrimination rules. See ERISA
Antifraud and abuse statutes, 138-44, 244(g)
Antikickback laws, Medicaid, 137-38
Antitrust law, 173-84, 244(g)
  joint venture operations and, 180-84
  joint venture practices and, 182-84
  joint venture structure and, 174-80
  preferred provider organizations (PPOs) and, 175
A-organization (A-ORG), 82-83
  defined, 78, 244(g)
Articles of incorporation, 31, 244(g)
  for-profit corporations and, 39
  not-for-profit corporations and, 41
ASG. See Affiliated service groups
Assignment
  acceptance of, 118, 245(g)
  of leases, 31
At-risk contract, 123

At-risk limits, 69-70
Attorneys. *See* Legal counsel
Attribution rules, 82

Bad-faith dealings, employment laws and, 165-66
Bargaining. *See* Collective bargaining
Bill of sale, 32
Billing procedures, management and, 33
Blue Sky laws, 46
B-organization (B-ORG), 83-84
  defined, 78, 82, 245(g)
Borrowing capital, joint venture financing and, 26
Bottleneck test, 179, 245(g)
Brother-sister control, 79, 245(g)
  defined, 78
Business. *See also* ERISA
  commonly controlled, 78, 79-80
  defined under ERISA, 79
  qualifying, under tax law, 70
Bylaws, 31, 245(g)
  for-profit corporations and, 39
  not-for-profit corporations and, 41

C corporation, 70
Capital
  corporations and, 17
  hospital need for, 5
  joint venture financing and, 26-27
Captive referrals, 144
Casual sales exception, 61
Certificate-of-need laws, 97-99, 246(g)
  equipment acquisitions and, 102
  HMOs and, 102-3
  hospital-affiliated ambulatory surgical centers (HAASC) and, 120
  laboratories and, 101
  outpatient facilities and, 100-101
Certification under Medicare, 116
Charitable trust doctrine, 18, 41, 246(g)
Clayton Act, 174, 177
Clinical laboratories, Medicare and, 121-22
Close corporation, 18, 246(g)
Closely held corporation, 69, 246(g)
Closing, 32-33, 246(g)
Coinsurance, waiver of, 143-44
Collective bargaining, 151-62, 246(g)
  accretion and, 161-62
  conditions of employment and, 160-61
  employer's duty of, 155-58
  employer's status and, 158-61
  successor employers and, 152-54
Commercial financing, qualified, 70
Commercial symbol, franchise law and, 48
Common stock, 17, 40, 246(g)
Common-law employee, 79, 246(g)
  employee leasing and, 91-92
Common-law employee test, 135
Commonly controlled business, 79-80
  defined, 78
Community of interest, franchise law and, 49, 246(g)
Community rating for HMOs, 102, 246(g)
Compensation, 34
Competition in health care services, 5
  antitrust law and, 176-77. *See also* Antitrust law
Competitive medical plan (CMP), Medicare and, 124-25, 247(g)
Comprehensive outpatient rehabilitation facilities (CORFs), 120-21
Concerted refusal to deal, antitrust law and, 178, 247(g)
Conditions of employment, 160-61
Congress, Medicare and, 113-14
Continuity of corporations, 16, 18
Continuity of the enterprise, 152-53
Continuity of the work force, 153-54
Contracts, 32, 123, 247(g)
  implied, 165, 251(g)
Contractual form of joint venture, 15-16, 247(g)
Convenience rule, 61, 247(g)
Copperweld Corp. v. Independence Tube Co., 177
Corporate law, 39-41
Corporate practice of medicine, 133-36, 247(g)
Corporations
  board of directors of, 40, 41
  characteristics of, 16
  defined, 16, 247(g)
  ERISA and. *See* ERISA
  for-profit, 16-18
    corporate law and, 39-40
    taxation and, 57, 67
  liability and, 17
  not-for-profit, 18-19
    corporate law and, 41
  professional, 40, 82
  subsidiary, 61
Cost contract, 123

Debt-financed rules, 65, 248(g)
Decertification petition, union, 154
Decision bargaining, 155, 248(g)
Deductions. *See also* Taxation
  at-risk limits and, 69
Deed of trust, 31, 248(g)
Delivery systems. *See* Alternative health care systems
Depreciation allowance, tax-exempt status and, 66, 248(g)
Diagnosis-related groups (DRGs), 113-14, 248(g)
Diagnostic radiology centers, Medicare and, 122-23
Disclosure statements
  joint venture formation and, 28-29
  securities law and, 46-47
Discriminatory pricing, antitrust law and, 183-84, 248(g)
Disqualified lease, 67, 248(g)
Documents, legal, 30-32. *See also* name of specific document
Double taxation, 18, 19, 248(g)
Due diligence, 25, 28
Durable medical equipment, Medicare and, 126, 248(g)
Duty to bargain, 155-58

Economic joint venture. *See* Joint venture
Effects bargaining, 155, 248(g)
Eligible organization under Medicare, 123-24
Emergency centers, Medicare and, 117, 249(g)
Employee Retirement Income Security Act. *See* ERISA
Employees, leased
  collective bargaining and, 156-57, 159-61
  ERISA and, 79, 91-92
Employer
  status of, collective bargaining and, 158-61
  ERISA and. *See* ERISA
Employment
  conditions of, 160-61
  state laws pertaining to, 162-66
Employment-at-will, 163, 249(g)
Environmental impact regulations, 103-5
Environmental impact statement, 104, 249(g)
Equipment
  acquisition of, tax-exempt status and, 66-67
  certificate-of-need for, 98, 102

  high-technology, 66
  lease of, 31, 249(g)
    ERISA and, 87, 90
  Medicare and, 126
  noncorporate lessor rules and, 68-69
ERISA (Employee Retirement Income Security Act), 77-92, 249(g)
  affiliated service groups (ASGs) and, 80-82
  avoidance of designation of, 89-91
  rules for, 85-89
  alternative health care system and, 87-88
  ambulatory surgical clinic and, 86
  A-organization and, 82-83. *See also* A-organizations
  B-organization and, 83-84. *See also* B-organizations
  common-law employees and, 91-92
  commonly controlled businesses and, 79-80
  employee leasing and, 91-92
  equipment leasing and, 90
  individual practice association (IPA) and, 88
  magnetic resonance imaging center and, 86
  management companies and, 85
  medical pavilion and, 89
  multiple affiliated service groups and, 84-85
  occupational medicine center and, 87
  reference laboratory and, 88-89
  safe-harbor pension plan and, 91
Essential-facilities test, 179
Estoppel, promissory, 165, 246(g)
Estoppel certificate, 32
Ethics, AMA and, 144-45
Exclusive dealing, antitrust law and, 182-83, 249(g)
Exclusive provider organization (EPO), 103, 249(g)
Exemptions from securities law, 44-46
Experience rating for HMOs, 102, 249(g)

Facilities fee, Medicare and, 115-16
Facilities lease, 31
Fair dealing, good faith and, 164
Federal franchise law, 48
Federal law
  antifraud and abuse, 138-44

antitrust, 173-84
  for certificates-of-need, 97, 98
  for health maintenance organizations (HMOs), 102-3
  for preferred provider organizations (PPOs), 103
  for securities, 43-46
Federal Trade Commission Act, 48
Federal Trade Commission (FTC), 249(g)
  franchise law and, 29, 48
Fee splitting, 135-36, 250(g)
Fiduciary duty, general partners and, 63, 250(g)
Financing joint ventures, 26-27
  documents pertaining to, 31
Financing lease, defined, 27, 250(g)
First service organization (FSO), 80-86
  ASG rules and, 86, 89-91
  defined, 78, 250(g)
For-profit corporations, 16-18
  conversion to, 41
  corporate law and, 39-40
  taxation and, 57, 67
Franchises, 48-49
  defined, 48, 250(g)
  law pertaining to, 47-51
Franchise agreement, 32
Fraud, statutes against. *See* Antifraud and abuse statutes
Freestanding ambulatory surgical center (ASC), 118, 244(g)
FSO. *See* First service organization
Full-complement standard, 153, 250(g)

General partners
  in limited partnership, 43
General partnership agreement, 30
General partnerships, 19-20, 250(g). *See also* Partnerships; Limited partnerships
  law pertaining to, 42
  securities law and, 43-44
Good faith and fair dealing, 164-65, 250(g)
Government approval of joint ventures, 28
Grant deed, 32
Ground lease, 32, 250(g)

Health care delivery systems. *See* Alternative health care systems

Health Maintenance Organization Act of 1973, 102, 250(g)
Health maintenance organizations (HMO), 21, 250(g)
  antitrust law and, 176
  ERISA and, 87-88
  Medicare and, 123-25
  regulation of, 102-3
  tax-exempt status of, 59
High-technology equipment
  Medicare and, 115
  tax-exemption and, 66
HMO. *See* Health maintenance organization
Holding company, certificate-of-need and, 99
Home health care agency, Medicare and, 125-26, 251(g)
Hospice, Medicare and, 121
Hospital-affiliated ambulatory surgical centers (HAASCs), 119-20, 251(g)
Hospital participation agreement, 32
Hospitals
  ambulatory surgical centers affiliated with, 119-20
  capacity of, 5
  capital needs of, 5
  certificate-of-need for, 98, 100-101
  licensure of, 99-100
  medical staff partnership with, 3-4, 23
  Medicare and. *See* Medicare
  outpatient centers of, 100-101, 117-18
  rate review, 100
  tax-exempt status of, 60-61
    loss of, 62

Implied contract, 165, 251(g)
Income tax. *See* Taxation
Incorporation, 39. *See also* Corporations
Indemnity agreement, 32
Indenture, 31, 251(g)
Independent clinical laboratories, Medicare and, 122
Individual practice association (IPA), 251(g)
  ERISA and, 88
  Medicare and, 123
Inducements, inurement problems and, 63-64
Insurance, joint venture formation and, 30
Integrated health care corporation (IHCC), 3-4, 23, 251(g)

Internal Revenue Service (IRS). *See* Taxation
Intrastate offering exemptions, 45-46
Inurement, 251(g). *See* Private inurement
Investment tax credit (ITC), 251(g)
　at-risk limits and, 69
　equipment acquisitions and, 66-67
　joint venture financing and, 26, 27
　noncorporate lessor rules and, 69
　nonrecourse financing and, 70
　partnership and, 57
　pass-through of, 70-71
　taxable income and, 65-67, 69-71
Investors, registration exemptions and, 45
Isolated transactions, 46
ITC. *See* Investment tax credit

Joint-employer status, 158-61
Joint venture
　defined, 3, 252(g)
　formation of, 25-33
　future of, 190-91
　objectives of, 5-6
　operation of, 33-34
　structures of, 15-25
Joint venture agreement, 30

Labor law, 151-66. *See also* Collective bargaining
　state, 162-66
Laboratories
　clinical, Medicare and, 121-22
　regulation of, 101
Land use regulations, 103-5
Law. *See* Antitrust; Corporate; Federal; Franchise; Labor; Partnership; Securities; State
Lawyers. *See* Legal counsel
Lease
　assignment of, 31
　defined, 252(g)
　disqualified, 67
　facilities, 31
　financing, 27
　ground, 32
　true, 27
Leased employees
　collective bargaining and, 156-57, 159-61
　ERISA and, 79, 91-92
Leasing
　documents pertaining to, 31-32
　employee, 79, 91-92
　　collective bargaining and, 156-57, 159-61

equipment, 31
　ERISA and, 87, 90-92
　joint venture financing and, 26-27
　real estate, 67-68
　tax-exempt status and, 66-68
Legal compliance, 34
Legal counsel
　joint venture formation and, 27-28
　tax interpretive rulings and, 29
Legal documents, joint venture formation and, 30
Licensing agreement, 32
　franchise law and, 49-51
Licensure requirements, 99-100, 252(g)
　laboratories and, 101
　outpatient facilities and, 101
　unlicensed entity and, 134
Limited liability, for-profit corporations and, 17, 252(g)
Limited offering registration exemptions, 45
Limited partnership agreement, 30
Limited partnerships, 20-21, 252(g). *See also* General partnerships
　law pertaining to, 42
　taxation and, 58-59

Management, 33
　contracts for, 32, 253(g)
　of corporation, 16
　of limited partnership, 20
Management companies, ERISA and, 85
Marketing plans, franchise law and, 49
Medicaid, 253(g)
　antifraud and abuse statutes and, 138-44
　antikickback laws and, 137-38
　self-referral and, 140-43
Medical ethics, AMA and, 144-45
Medical pavilion, ERISA and, 89
Medical staff-hospital partnership (MeSH), 3-4, 23, 253(g)
Medicare, 113-26, 253(g)
　ambulatory surgical center and, 115, 118-20
　antifraud and abuse statutes and, 138-44, 253(g)
　certification under, 116
　competitive medical plan (CMP) and, 124-25
　comprehensive outpatient rehabilitation facilities (CORFs) and, 120-21

diagnostic radiology centers and, 122-23
durable medical equipment (DME) and, 126
emergency centers and, 117
facilities fee under, 115-16
health maintenance organizations (HMOs)and, 123-25
home health care agency and, 125-26
hospice and, 121
hospital-affiliated ambulatory surgical centers (HAASCs) and, 119-20
hospital outpatient care centers and, 117-18
individual practice association (IPA) and, 123
new technology and, 115
preferred provider organizations (HMOs) and, 123
primary care centers and, 116-17
prospective pricing system (PPS) of, 4, 113-14
reimbursement mechanisms under, 115
self-referrals and, 140-43
urgent care centers and, 116-17
waiver of coinsurance and, 143-44
Mergers, antitrust law and, 174-76, 253(g)
Money purchase pension plan, 91, 253(g)
Mortgage, 31, 253(g)
Multiple affiliated service groups, 84-85

National Labor Relations Board (NLRB), 253(g). See Collective bargaining
Negative impact report, 104, 254(g)
No-action letter, 139, 254(g)
No-cost surgery, Medicare and, 120
Nonaccredited investors, 45, 254(g)
Noncorporate lessor rules, 68-69, 254(g)
Nonqualified nonrecourse financing, 70, 254(g)
Not-for-profit corporations, 18-19
  conversion of, 41
  corporate law and, 41

Occupational medicine center, ERISA and, 87
Off balance sheet financing, 5, 254(g)

Outpatient facilities
  comprehensive rehabilitative, 120-21
  Medicare and, 115-16, 117-18
  regulations on, 100-101
Overinclusiveness, antitrust law and, 174-78, 254(g)
Ownership
  ERISA and, 82
  of property, tax-exempt status and, 66
Ownership interest, 136-37

Parent-subsidiary control, 79, 254(g)
  defined, 78
Partial closing of business, collective bargaining and, 157-58
Partnership, medical staff-hospital (MeSH), 3
Partnership agreement, 42, 254(g)
Partnership law, 42-43
Partnerships, 19-21, 254(g). See also General partnerships; Limited Partnerships
  noncorporate lessor rules and, 68-69
  private inurement and, 62-63
  taxation and, 58
Pass-through of ITC, 70-71, 254(g)
Pension plan, 91, 255(g)
Per se antitrust violations, 173, 254(g)
Physician participation agreement, 32
Physicians
  employment of, corporate practice of medicine and, 135
  ownership of joint venture by, 136-37
  surplus of, 5
Planning joint ventures, 25-26
Potential market entrant doctrine, 177-78, 255(g)
PPO. See Preferred provider organization (PPO)
Preferred provider organization (PPO), 21-23, 255(g)
  antitrust law and, 175, 178, 179, 180
  ERISA and, 87-88
  Medicare and, 123
  regulation of, 103
Preferred stock, 17, 40, 255(g)
Prevailing charge, Medicare and, 117, 255(g)
Pricing, discriminatory, antitrust law and, 183-84

Primary care centers, Medicare and, 116-17, 255(g)
Private inurement, 20
 inducements and, 63-64
 tax-exempt status and, 62-64
Private letter ruling, 20, 255(g)
Professional corporations, 40, 82, 255(g)
Professional service corporation, 80-82, 256(g)
Promissory estoppel, 165, 256(g)
Property, ownership of, tax exemption and, 66-68
Prospective pricing system (PPS), 4, 113-14, 115, 256(g)
Public policy, wrongful discharge and, 164
Purchase and sale agreement, 32
Purpose of the venture, antitrust law and, 179

Qualified C corporation, 70
Qualified commercial financing, 70, 256(g)
Qualifying business, 70

Radiology, diagnostic, Medicare and, 122-23
Rate review, regulations on, 100, 256(g)
Real estate leasing, tax-exempt status and, 67-68
Reasonable cost reimbursement, 113, 114, 115, 257(g)
Reference laboratory, ERISA and, 88-89
Registration requirements
 Blue Sky laws and, 46
 exemptions from, 44-46, 257(g)
 joint venture formation and, 28-29
 securities law and, 44-46
 tax shelters and, 58-59
Regulations concerning joint ventures, 97-105
 antifraud and abuse, 139
 certificate-of-need, 97-99
 environmental impact, 103-5
 health maintenance organizations (HMOs) and, 102-3
 land use, 103-5
 licensure, 99-100
 preferred provider organizations (PPOs) and, 103
 rate review and, 100
 zoning, 104
Reimbursement, 113-27, 257(g)
 Medicare, 113-26. *See also* Medicare
 third-party, 127
Rental income, tax-exempt status and, 65
Reserve powers, not-for-profit corporations and, 41, 257(g)
Restricted offering registration exemptions, 45
Right of control, employment of physicians and, 135
Royalty agreement, 32
 franchise law and, 50-51
Rule of reason, antitrust and, 173, 257(g)

Safe-harbor, 79, 83, 91, 257(g)
Sale-leaseback, 26, 257(g)
Securities and Exchange Commission (SEC), 29, 257(g)
 disclosure requirements and, 46-47
 registration with, 44
 exemptions from, 44-46
Securities laws, 43-47
 disclosure requirements, 46-47
 federal, 43-46
 exemptions from, 44-46
 state, 46
Security, defined, 43, 257(g). *See also* Shares of stock
Security agreement, 31
Security offering, 28-29. *See also* Shares of stock
 laws pertaining to, 43-47
Self-referrals, state laws on, 136-38, 140-43
Service agreement, 67, 258(g)
Service bureau, 258(g)
 collective bargaining and, 156
 hospital acting as, 99
Service contracts, 32, 258(g)
Service receipts percentage (SRP), 83
Shareholders' agreement, 31, 40
Shares of stock, 258(g)
 for-profit corporations and, 16-17, 40
 SEC registration and, 29
Sherman Act, 174
Significant beneficial interests, 136
Single-employer status, 158-61, 258(g)
Special project joint venture, defined, 3, 258(g)

Spillover collusion, antitrust law and, 181-82, 258(g)
Staffing, 34
  management and, 33
State Blue Sky laws, 46
State franchise law, 48
State laws
  for certificates-of-need, 97-99
  on employment, 162-66
  on environmental impact, 103-5
  for franchises, 48
  for health maintenance organizations (HMOs), 102-3
  on land use, 103-5
  for licensure, 99-100, 134
  Medicaid and, 137-39
  for preferred provider organizations (PPOs), 103
  for rates, 100
  for securities, 46
  on self-referrals, 136-38
Statutory warranty deed, 32
Subcontracting, collective bargaining and, 155-57
Subsidiary corporation, 61, 258(g)
  taxability of, 62-63
Successor employers, 152-54, 258(g)
Successor organization, 68, 258(g)

Tax Equity and Fiscal Responsibility Act of 1982 (TEFRA), 91
Tax shelters, limited partnership and, 58, 259(g)
Taxable participants in joint ventures, 60-61, 65-71
  accelerated cost recovery system (ACRS) and, 65-68
  investment tax credit (ITC) and, 65-67, 69-71
Taxation, 57-71. See also Tax-exempt status; ERISA
  corporate structure and, 57
  double, 18, 19
  general partnerships and, 19-20, 58
  interpretive rulings and, 29-30
  joint venture financing and, 26-27, 29
  limited partnerships and, 58-59
  not-for-profit corporations and, 18-19
Tax-exempt status, 259(g). See also Taxation
  accelerated cost recovery system and, 65-68
  casual sales exception and, 61
  convenience rule and, 61
  drawbacks of, 60
  equipment acquisitions and, 66-67
  general partnerships and, 20
  HMOs and, 59
  interpretive rulings and, 20-30
  investment tax credits and, 65-67, 69-71
  joint venture financing and, 26-27
  leasing and, 67-69
  loss of, 62-65
  not-for-profit corporations and, 18, 19, 41
  participants' tax status and, 61-71
  partnerships and, 20, 58
  private inurement and, 62-64
  property ownership and, 66-68
  qualifying for, 59-60
  real estate leasing and, 67-68
  taxable income and, 60-61
  unrelated business income and, 64-65
Tax-exempt use property, 66, 259(g)
TEFRA (Tax Equity and Fiscal Responsibility Act of 1982), 91, 258(g)
Third-party reimbursement, 127
Total receipts percentage (TRP), 83
Trade, defined under ERISA, 79, 259(g). See also ERISA
Transfer documents, 32
True lease, defined, 27, 259(g)
Trust, charitable, 18, 41
Tying arrangements, antitrust law and, 183, 259(g)

Unbundling services, defined, 114, 259(g)
Underinclusiveness, antitrust law and, 178-79, 259(g)
Underwriters, joint venture financing and, 29, 259(g)
Unfair labor practices, 158. See also Collective bargaining
Uniform Commercial Code (U.C.C.) financing statement, 31
Uniform Limited Partnership Act, 42
Union. See Collective bargaining
Union-demand standard, 153
United States v. Greber, 139-40, 140, 141
United States v. Universal Trade and Industries, 141
Unlicensed entity, 134
Unrelated business income, 60, 64-65, 260(g)
Urgent care centers, Medicare and, 116-17, 260(g)

Index

Variance, zoning regulations and, 104-105, 260(g)

Waiver of coinsurance, 143-44
Warranty deed, 32

Whistle-blower statutes, 163, 260(g)
Wrongful discharge cases, 163-65, 260(g)

Zoning, 104, 260(g)